Native Life in South Africa

Solomon Tshekisho Plaatje

Table of Contents

Native Life in South Africa

Solomon Tshekisho Plaatje

Kessinger Publishing reprints thousands of hard–to–find books!

```
Native Life in South Africa, Before and Since
the European War and the Boer Rebellion
```

[South African (ethnic Tswana) Editor, Author, Statesman. 1876?–1932.] First Secretary–General of the South African Native National Congress (forerunner of the ANC), 1912–1917. Author of "Mhudi", generally considered the first novel written by a black South African.

[The two portraits are not available for this ASCII text. They are titled "The Author." and "Mrs. S. T. Plaatje. Without whose loyal co–operation this book would never have been written."]

Foreword (Native Life in South Africa electronic text):

Sol Plaatje began work on `Native Life in South Africa' in 1914, while on his way to Britain to plead with the Imperial Government against the Natives' Land Act of 1913, as part of a deputation of the South African Native National Congress. The book was intended as a means of reaching the British public with the deputation's message.

The method seemed sound enough — it was quite similar in form to the successful deputation which had pleaded to keep Bechuanaland (modern Botswana) under direct Imperial control in 1895. But circumstances were different in 1914 — South Africa had been granted self–government, and the First World War began shortly after the deputation's arrival in England and distracted all parties. This latter event also influenced the final form of the book, as Plaatje played to the patriotic sentiment so strong in Britain at the time. For all his appeals, Plaatje did not succeed: the Act went on to become one of the first steps toward the system of Apartheid. For all that, there is sometimes in defeat the seeds of victory — these troubles united black South Africans like nothing before, and Plaatje's successors, in the form of the ANC, finally succeeded in the early 1990's.

The Natives' Land Act of 1913, which forbade natives to buy or rent land, except in a few small reserves consisting largely of wasteland, was finally overturned in 1991.

Thanks should be given to Neil Parsons, for his advice on this subject, and for being so kind as to research and write the introduction that follows.

Alan R. Light

 July, 1998.

Monroe, North Carolina (USA).

Introduction, by Neil Parsons

"Native Life in South Africa" is one of the most remarkable books on Africa, by one of the continent's most remarkable writers. It was written as a work of impassioned political propaganda, exposing the plight of black South Africans under the whites–only government of newly unified South Africa. It focuses on the effects of the 1913 Natives' Land Act which introduced a uniform system of land segregation between the races. It resulted, as Plaatje shows, in the immediate expulsion of blacks, as "squatters", from their ancestral lands in the Orange Free State now declared "white". But Native Life succeeds in being much more than a work of propaganda. It is a vital social document which captures the spirit of an age and shows the effects of rural segregation on the everyday life of people.

Solomon Tshekeisho Plaatje was born in 1878 in the lands of the Tswana–speaking people, south of Mafeking. His origins were ordinary enough. What was remarkable was the aptitude he showed for education and learning after a few years schooling under the tuition of a remarkable liberal German Lutheran missionary, the Rev. Ludorf. At the age of sixteen Plaatje (using the Dutch nickname of his grandfather as a surname) joined the Post Office as a mail–carrier in Kimberley, the diamond city in the north of Cape Colony. He subsequently passed the highest clerical examination in the colony, beating every white candidate in both Dutch and typing.

From Kimberley the young Plaatje went on to Mafeking, where he was one of the key players in the great siege of 1899–1900. As magistrate's interpreter he was the vital link between the British civil authorities and the African majority beleaguered inside the town's military perimeter. Plaatje's diaries from this period, published long after his death, are a remarkable record both of the siege and of his early prose experimentation — mixing languages and idioms, and full of bright humour.

After the war Plaatje became a journalist, editor first of one Tswana language newspaper at Mafeking and then of another at Kimberley. Like other educated Africans he came out of the war optimistic that the British would enfranchise all educated and propertied males in the defeated Boer colonies (Transvaal and Orange Free State) without regard to race. But in this he, and the others, were soon sorely disappointed. The British gave a whites–only franchise to the defeated Boers and thus conceded power to a Boer or white Afrikaner parliamentary majority in the 1910 Union of South Africa which brought together the two Boer colonies with Cape Colony and Natal. Clinging to the old but diminished "colour blind" franchise of the Cape, Plaatje remained one of the few Africans in South Africa with a parliamentary vote.

Plaatje's aggravation with the British government can be seen in an unpublished manuscript of 1908–09 titled "Sekgoma — the Black Dreyfus". In this booklet he castigated the British for denying legal rights (specifically habeas corpus) to their African subjects outside the Cape Colony.

Plaatje became politically active in the "native congress" movement which represented the interests of educated and propertied Africans all over South Africa. He was the first secretary–general of the "South African Native National Congress", founded in 1912 (which renamed itself as the African National Congress or ANC ten years later).

The first piece of major legislation presented to the whites–only parliament of South Africa was the Natives' Land Act, eventually passed in 1913, which was designed to entrench white power and property rights in the countryside — as well as to solve the "native problem" of African peasant farmers working for themselves and denying their labour power to white employers.

The main battle ground for the implementation of the new legislation was the Orange Free State. White farmers took the cue from the Land Act to begin expelling black peasants from their land as

Native Life in South Africa

"squatters", while the police began to rigorously enforce the pass-laws which registered the employment of Africans and prescribed their residence and movement rights.

The Free State became the cockpit of resistance by the newly formed SANNC. Its womens' league demonstrated against pass law enforcement in Free State towns. Its national executive sent a delegation to England, icluding Plaatje, who set sail in mid-1914. The British crown retained ultimate rights of sovereignty over the parliament and government of South Africa, with an as yet unexercised power of veto over South African legislation in the area of "native affairs".

The delegation received short shrift from the government in London which was, after all, more than preoccupied with the coming of the Great War — in which it feared for the loyalty of the recently defeated Afrikaners and wished in no way to offend them. But, rather than return empty-handed like the rest of the SANNC delegation, Plaatje decided to stay in England to carry on the fight. He was determined to recuit, through writing and lecturing, the liberal and humanitarian establishment to his side — so that it in turn might pressure the British government.

Thus it was that Plaatje resumed work on a manuscript he had begun on the ship to England. "Native Life in South Africa". The book was published in 1916 by P. S. King in London. It was dedicated to Harriette Colenso, doughty woman camnpaigner who had inherited from her father, Bishop Colenso, the mantle of advocate to the British establishment of the rights of the Zulu nation in South Africa.

While in England Plaatje pursued his interests in language and linguistics by collaborating with Professor Daniel Jones of the University of London — inventor of the International Phonetic Alphabet (IPA) and prototype for Professor Higgins in Shaw's "Pygmalion" and thus the musical "My Fair Lady". In the same year as Native Life was published, 1916, Plaatje published two other shorter books which brought together the European languages (English, Dutch and German) he loved with the Tswana language. "Sechuana Proverbs" was a listing of Tswana proverbs with their European equivalents. "A Sechuana Reader" was co-authored with Jones, using the IPA for Tswana orthography.

Plaatje returned to South Africa but went once again to England after the war's end, to lead a second SANNC delegation keen to make its mark on the peace negotiations in 1919. This time Plaatje managed to get as far as the prime minister, Lloyd George, "the Welsh wizard". Lloyd George was duly impressed with Plaatje and undertook to present his case to General Jan Smuts in the South African government, a supposedly liberal fellow-traveller. But Smuts, whose notions of liberalism were patronizingly segregationist, fobbed off Lloyd George with an ingenuous reply.

Disillusioned with the flabby friendship of British liberals, Plaatje was increasingly drawn to the pan-Africanism of W. E. B. Du Bois, president of the NAACP in the United States. In 1921 Plaatje sailed for the United States on a lecture tour that took him through half the country. He paid his own way by publishing and selling 18,000 copies of a booklet titled "The Mote and the Beam: an Epic on Sex-Relationship 'twixt Black and White in British South Africa" at 25 cents each. In the following year, after Plaatje had left, this new edition of "Native Life in South Africa" was published, by the NAACP newspaper "The Crisis" edited by Du Bois.

Plaatje returned home to Kimberley to find the SANNC a spent force, despite its name change to ANC, overtaken by more radical forces. At a time when white power was pushing ahead with an ever more intense segregationist programme, based on anti–black legislation, Plaatje became a lone voice for old black liberalism. He turned from politics and devoted the rest of his life to literature. His passion for Shakespeare resulted in mellifluous Tswana translations of five plays from "Comedy of Errors" to "Merchant of Venice" and "Julius Caesar". His passion for the history of his people, and of his family in particular, resulted in a historical novel, "Mhudi (An Epic of South African Native Life a Hundred Years Ago)", dedicated to his daughter Olive who had died in the influenza epidemic while Plaatje was overseas — described in the dedication as "one of the many victims of a settled system".

"Mhudi" was published by the missionary press at Lovedale in 1930, in a somewhat bowdlerized version. It has since been republished in more pristine form and is today considered not just the first but one of the very best novels published by a black South African writer in English.

Plaatje lived an extraordinary life but died a largely disappointed man. His feats of political journalism had been largely forgotten and his creative talents had hardly yet been recognised — except in the confined world of Tswana language readership. But today Plaatje is regarded as a South African literary pioneer, as a not insignificant political actor in his time, and as a cogent commentator on his times. He was an explorer in a fascinating world of cultural and linguistic interaction, who was in retrospect truly a "renaissance man".

Related Reading:

Sol T. Plaatje (ed. John Comaroff with Brian Willan Andrew Reed), "Mafeking Diary: a Black Man's View of a White Man's War", Athens, Ohio: Ohio University Press Cambridge Meridor Press, 1990. (1st edn. London: Macmillan, 1973, publ. as The Boer War Diary of Sol T. Plaatje).

Sol. T. Plaatje (ed. Tim Couzens), "Mhudi", Cape Town: Francolin, 1996; definitive edition.

Brian Willan, "Sol Plaatje: South African Nationalist, 1876–1932", London: Heinemann, 1984.

Brian Willan (ed. comp.), "Sol Plaatje: Selected Writings", Athens, Ohio: Ohio University Press, 1996.

Neil Parsons is a Professor of History at the University of Botswana. He is author of "King Khama, Emperor Joe, and the Great White Queen", which details the journey of the Batswana delegation to England of 1895, and other books relating to the history of the region.

To

Miss Harriette E. Colenso,

```
"Nkosazana Matotoba ka So-Bantu",
Daughter of the late Rt. Rev. J. W. Colenso
(In his life-time Bishop of Natal and "Father of the Zulus").



In recognition of her unswerving loyalty to
the policy of her late distinguished father
and unselfish interest in the welfare of


    the South African Natives,



    This Book is Dedicated.
```

(A) Who is the Author?

After wondering for some time how best to answer this question, we decided to reply to it by using one of several personal references in our possession. The next puzzle was: "Which one?" We carefully examined each, but could not strike a happy decision until some one who entered the room happened to make use of the familiar phrase: "The long and the short of it". That phrase solved the difficulty for us, and we at once made up our mind to use two of these references, namely, the shortest and the longest. The first one is from His Royal Highness the Duke of Connaught, and the second takes the form of a leading article in the `Pretoria News'.

==

        Central South African Railways,
        High Commissioner's Train.

On February 1, 1906, Mr. Sol Plaatje acted as Interpreter when I visited the Barolong Native Stadt at Mafeking, and performed his duty to my entire satisfaction.

        (Signed) Arthur. Mafeking,
February 1, 1906. ==

We commence to-day an experiment which will prove a success if only we can persuade the more rabid negrophobes to adopt a moderate and sensible attitude. We publish the first of a series of letters from a native correspondent of considerable education and ability, his name is Solomon Tshekisho Plaatje. Mr. Plaatje was born in the district of Boshof, his parents being Barolongs, coming originally from Thaba Ncho, and trekking eventually to Mafeking. He attended the Lutheran Mission School at the Pniel Mission Station, near Barkly West, as a boy, under the Rev. G. E. Westphal; and at thirteen years he passed the fourth standard, which was as far as the school could take him. For the next three years he acted as pupil-teacher, receiving private lessons from the Rev. and Mrs. Westphal. At the age of sixteen he joined the Cape Government service as letter-carrier in the Kimberley Post Office.

There he studied languages in his spare time, and passed the Cape Civil Service examination in typewriting, Dutch and native languages, heading the list of successful candidates in each subject. Shortly before the war he was transferred to Mafeking as interpreter, and during the siege was appointed Dutch interpreter to the Court of Summary Jurisdiction, presided over by Lord Edward Cecil. The Magistrate's clerks having taken up arms, Mr. Plaatje became confidential clerk to Mr. C. G. H. Bell, who administered Native affairs during the siege. Mr. Plaatje drew up weekly reports on the Native situation, which were greatly valued by the military authorities, and in a letter written to a friend asserted with some sense of humour that "this arrangement was so satisfactory that Mr. Bell was created a C.M.G. at the end of the siege."

Had it not been for the colour bar, Mr. Plaatje, in all probability, would have been holding an important position in the Department of Native Affairs; as it was, he entered the ranks of journalism as Editor, in the first place, of `Koranta ea Becoana', a weekly paper in English and Sechuana, which was financed by the Chief Silas Molema and existed for seven years very successfully. At the present moment Mr. Plaatje is Editor of the `Tsala ea Batho' (The People's Friend) at Kimberley, which is owned by a native syndicate, having its headquarters in the Free State. Mr. Plaatje has acted as interpreter for many distinguished visitors to South Africa, and holds autograph letters from the Duke of Connaught, Mr. Chamberlain, and other notabilities. He visited Mr. Abraham Fischer quite lately and obtained from him a promise to introduce a Bill into Parliament ameliorating the position of the Natives of the Orange River Colony, who are debarred by law from receiving titles to landed property. Mr. Plaatje's articles on native affairs have been marked by the robust common sense and moderation so characteristic of Mr. Booker Washington. He realizes the great debt which the Natives owe to the men who brought civilization to South Africa. He is no agitator or firebrand, no stirrer-up of bad feeling between black and white. He accepts the position which the Natives occupy to-day in the body politic as the natural result of their lack of education and civilization. He is devoted to his own people, and notes with ever-increasing regret the lack of understanding and knowledge of those people, which is so palpable in the vast majority of the letters and leading articles written on the native question. As an educated Native with liberal ideas he rather resents the power and authority of the uneducated native chiefs who govern by virtue of their birth alone, and he writes and speaks for an entirely new school of native thought. The opinion of such a man ought to carry weight when native affairs are being discussed. We have fallen into the habit of discussing and legislating for the Native without ever stopping for one moment to consider what the Native himself thinks. No one but a fool will deny the importance of knowing what the Native thinks before we legislate for him. It is in the hope of enlightening an otherwise barren controversy that we shall publish from time to time Mr. Plaatje's letters, commending them always to the more thoughtful and practical of our readers. — `Pretoria News', September, 1910.

(The writer of this appreciation, the Editor of the Pretoria evening paper, was Reuter's war correspondent in the siege of Mafeking.)

(B) Prologue

We have often read books, written by well-known scholars, who disavow, on behalf of their works, any claim to literary perfection. How much more necessary, then, that a South African native workingman, who has never received any secondary training, should in attempting authorship disclaim, on behalf of his work, any title to literary merit. Mine is but a sincere narrative of a melancholy situation, in which, with all its shortcomings, I have endeavoured to describe the difficulties of the South African Natives under a very strange law, so as most readily to be understood by the sympathetic reader.

The information contained in the following chapters is the result of personal observations made by the author in certain districts of the Transvaal, Orange "Free" State and the Province of the Cape of Good Hope. In pursuance of this private inquiry, I reached Lady Brand early in September, 1913, when, my financial resources being exhausted, I decided to drop the inquiry and return home. But my friend, Mr. W. Z. Fenyang, of the farm Rietfontein, in the "Free" State, offered to convey me to the South of Moroka district, where I saw much of the trouble, and further, he paid my railway fare from Thaba Ncho back to Kimberley.

In the following November, it was felt that as Mr. Saul Msane, the organizer for the South African Native National Congress, was touring the eastern districts of the Transvaal, and Mr. Dube, the President, was touring the northern districts and Natal, and as the finances of the Congress did not permit an additional traveller, no information would be forthcoming in regard to the operation of the mischievous Act in the Cape Province. So Mr. J. M. Nyokong, of the farm Maseru, offered to bear part of the expenses if I would undertake a visit to the Cape. I must add that beyond spending six weeks on the tour to the Cape, the visit did not cost me much, for Mr. W. D. Soga, of King Williamstown, very generously supplemented Mr. Nyokong's offer and accompanied me on a part of the journey.

Besides the information received and the hospitality enjoyed from these and other friends, the author is indebted, for further information, to Mr. Attorney Msimang, of Johannesburg. Mr. Msimang toured some of the Districts, compiled a list of some of the sufferers from the Natives' Land Act, and learnt the circumstances of their eviction. His list, however, is not full, its compilation having been undertaken in May, 1914, when the main exodus of the evicted tenants to the cities and Protectorates had already taken place, and when eyewitnesses of the evils of the Act had already fled the country. But it is useful in showing that the persecution is still continuing, for, according to this list, a good many families were evicted a year after the Act was enforced, and many more were at that time under notice to quit. Mr. Msimang, modestly states in an explanatory note, that his pamphlet contains "comparatively few instances of actual cases of hardship under the Natives' Land Act, 1913, to vindicate the leaders of the South African Native National Congress from the gross imputation, by the Native Affairs Department, that they make general allegations of hardships without producing any specific cases that can bear examination." Mr. Msimang, who took a number of sworn statements from the sufferers, adds that "in Natal, for example, all of these instances have been reported to the Magistrates and the Chief Native Commissioner. Every time they are told to find themselves other places, or remain where they are under labour conditions. At Peters and Colworth, seventy–nine and a hundred families respectively are being ejected by the Government itself without providing land for them."

Some readers may perhaps think that I have taken the Colonial Parliament rather severely to task. But to any reader who holds with Bacon, that "the pencil hath laboured more in describing the afflictions of Job than the felicities of Solomon," I would say: "Do, if we dare make the request, and place yourself in our shoes." If, after a proper declaration of war, you found your kinsmen driven from pillar to post in the manner that the South African Natives have been harried and scurried by Act No. 27 of 1913, you would, though aware that it is part of the fortunes of war, find it difficult to suppress your hatred of the enemy. Similarly, if you see your countrymen and countrywomen driven from home, their homes broken up, with no hopes of redress, on the mandate of a Government to which they had loyally paid taxation without representation — driven from their homes, because they do not want to become servants; and when you know that half of these homeless ones have perforce submitted to the conditions and accepted service on terms that are unprofitable to themselves; if you remember that more would have submitted but for the fact that no master has any use for a servant with forty head of cattle, or a hundred or more sheep; and if you further bear in mind that many landowners are anxious to live at peace with, and to keep your people as tenants, but that they are debarred from doing so by your Government which threatens them with a fine of 100 Pounds or six months' imprisonment, you would, I think, likewise find it very difficult to maintain a level head or wield a temperate pen.

For instance, let us say, the London County Council decrees that no man shall rent a room, or hire a house, in the City of London unless he be a servant in the employ of the landlord, adding that there shall be a fine of one hundred pounds on any one who attempts to sell a house to a non-householder; imagine such a thing and its effects, then you have some approach to an accurate picture of the operation of the South African Natives' Land Act of 1913. In conclusion, let me ask the reader's support in our campaign for the repeal of such a law, and in making this request I pray that none of my readers may live to find themselves in a position so intolerable.

When the narrative of this book up to Chapter XVIII was completed, it was felt that an account of life in South Africa, without a reference to the war or the rebellion would be but a story half told, and so Chapters XIX–XXV were added. It will be observed that Chapters XX–XXIV, unlike the rest of the book, are not the result of the writer's own observations. The writer is indebted for much of the information in these five chapters to the Native Press and some Dutch newspapers which his devoted wife posted to him with every mail. These papers have been a source of useful information. Of the Dutch newspapers special thanks are due to `Het Westen' of Potchefstroom, which has since March 1915 changed its name to `Het Volksblad'. Most of the Dutch journals, especially in the northern Provinces, take up the views of English-speaking Dutch townsmen (solicitors and Bank clerks), and publish them as the opinion of the South African Dutch. `Het Westen' (now `Het Volksblad'), on the other hand, interprets the Dutch view, sound, bad or indifferent, exactly as we ourselves have heard it expressed by Dutchmen at their own farms.

Translations of the Tipperary Chorus into some of the languages which are spoken by the white and black inhabitants of South Africa have been used here and there as mottoes; and as this book is a plea in the main for help against the "South African war of extermination", it is hoped that admirers of Tommy Atkins will sympathize with the coloured sufferers, who also sing Tommy Atkins' war songs.

This appeal is not on behalf of the naked hordes of cannibals who are represented in fantastic pictures displayed in the shop-windows in Europe, most of them imaginary; but it is on behalf of five million loyal British subjects who shoulder "the black man's burden" every day, doing so without looking forward to any decoration or thanks. "The black man's burden" includes the faithful performance of all the unskilled and least paying labour in South Africa, the payment of direct taxation to the various Municipalities, at the rate of from 1s. to 5s. per mensum per capita (to develop and beautify the white quarters of the towns while the black quarters remain unattended) besides taxes to the Provincial and Central Government, varying from 12s. to 3 Pounds 12s. per annum, for the maintenance of Government Schools from which native children are excluded. In addition to these native duties and taxes, it is also part of "the black man's burden" to pay all duties levied from the favoured race. With the increasing difficulty of finding openings to earn the money for paying these multifarious taxes, the dumb pack-ox, being inarticulate in the Councils of State, has no means of making known to its "keeper" that the burden is straining its back to breaking point.

When Sir John French appealed to the British people for more shells during Easter week, the Governor-General of South Africa addressing a fashionable crowd at the City Hall, Johannesburg, most of whom had never seen the mouth of a mine, congratulated them on the fact that "under the strain of war and rebellion the gold industry had been maintained at full pitch," and he added that "every ounce of gold was worth many shells to the Allies." But His Excellency had not a word of encouragement for the 200,000 subterranean heroes who by day and by night, for a mere pittance, lay down their limbs and their lives to the familiar "fall of rock" and who, at deep levels ranging from 1,000 feet to 1,000 yards in the bowels of the earth, sacrifice their lungs to the rock dust which develops miners' phthisis and pneumonia — poor reward, but a sacrifice that enables the world's richest gold mines, in the Johannesburg area alone, to maintain the credit of the Empire with a weekly output of 750,000 Pounds worth of raw gold. Surely the appeal of chattels who render service of such great value deserves the attention of the British people.

Finally, I would say as Professor Du Bois says in his book `The Souls of Black Folk', on the relations between the sons of master and man, "I have not glossed over matters for policy's sake, for I fear we have already gone too far in that sort of thing. On the other hand I have sincerely sought to let no unfair exaggerations creep in. I do not doubt that in some communities conditions are better than those I have indicated; while I am no less certain that in other communities they are far worse."

Chapter I A Retrospect

I am Black, but comely, O ye daughters of Jerusalem, as the tents of Kedar,
   as the curtains of Solomon.
Look not upon me because I am black, because the sun hath looked upon me:
   my mother's children were angry with me; they made me
the keeper of the vineyards; but mine own vineyard have I not kept.
         The Song of Songs.

Awaking on Friday morning, June 20, 1913, the South African Native found himself, not actually a slave, but a pariah in the land of his birth.

The 4,500,000 black South Africans are domiciled as follows: One and three-quarter millions in Locations and Reserves, over half a million within municipalities or in urban areas, and nearly a million as squatters on farms owned by Europeans. The remainder are employed either on the public roads or railway lines, or as servants by European farmers, qualifying, that is, by hard work and saving to start farming on their own account.

A squatter in South Africa is a native who owns some livestock and, having no land of his own, hires a farm or grazing and ploughing rights from a landowner, to raise grain for his own use and feed his stock. Hence, these squatters are hit very hard by an Act which passed both Houses of Parliament during the session of 1913, received the signature of the Governor–General on June 16, was gazetted on June 19, and forthwith came into operation. It may be here mentioned that on that day Lord Gladstone signed no fewer than sixteen new Acts of Parliament — some of them being rather voluminous — while three days earlier, His Excellency signed another batch of eight, of which the bulk was beyond the capability of any mortal to read and digest in four days.

But the great revolutionary change thus wrought by a single stroke of the pen, in the condition of the Native, was not realized by him until about the end of June. As a rule many farm tenancies expire at the end of the half–year, so that in June, 1913, not knowing that it was impracticable to make fresh contracts, some Natives unwittingly went to search for new places of abode, which some farmers, ignorant of the law, quite as unwittingly accorded them. It was only when they went to register the new tenancies that the law officers of the Crown laid bare the cruel fact that to provide a landless Native with accommodation was forbidden under a penalty of 100 Pounds, or six months' imprisonment. Then only was the situation realized.

Other Natives who had taken up fresh places on European farms under verbal contracts, which needed no registration, actually founded new homes in spite of the law, neither the white farmer nor the native tenant being aware of the serious penalties they were exposed to by their verbal contracts.

In justice to the Government, it must be stated that no police officers scoured the country in search of lawbreakers, to prosecute them under this law. Had this been done, many 100 Pound cheques would have passed into the Government coffers during that black July, the first month after Lord Gladstone affixed his signature to the Natives' Land Act, No. 27 of 1913.

The complication of this cruel law is made manifest by the fact that it was found necessary for a high officer of the Government to tour the Provinces soon after the Act came into force, with the object of "teaching" Magistrates how to administer it. A Congress of Magistrates — a most unusual thing — was also called in Pretoria to find a way for carrying out the King's writ in the face of the difficulties arising from this tangle of the Act. We may add that nearly all white lawyers in South Africa, to whom we spoke about this measure, had either not seen the Act at all, or had not read it carefully, so that in both cases they could not tell exactly for whose benefit it had been passed. The study of this law required a much longer time than the lawyers, unless specially briefed, could devote to it, so that they hardly knew what all the trouble was about. It was the Native in the four Provinces who knew all about it, for he had not read it in books but had himself been through its mill, which like an automatic machine ground him relentlessly since the end of the month of June. Not the least but one of the cruellest and most ironical phases — and nearly every clause of this Act teems with irony — is the Schedule or appendix giving the so–called Scheduled Native Areas; and what are these "Scheduled Native Areas"?

They are the Native Locations which were reserved for the exclusive use of certain native clans. They are inalienable and cannot be bought or sold, yet the Act says that in these "Scheduled Native Areas" Natives only may buy land. The areas being inalienable, not even members of the clans, for whose benefit the locations are held in trust, can buy land therein. The areas could only be sold if the whole clan rebelled; in that case the location would be confiscated. But as long as the clans of the location remain loyal to the Government, nobody can buy any land within these areas. Under the respective charters of these areas, not even a member of the clan can get a separate title as owner in an area — let alone a native outsider who had grown up among white people and done all his farming on white man's land.

If we exclude the arid tracts of Bechuanaland, these Locations appear to have been granted on such a small scale that each of them got so overcrowded that much of the population had to go out and settle on the farms of white farmers through lack of space in the Locations. Yet a majority of the legislators, although well aware of all these limitations, and without remedying any of them, legislate, shall we say, "with its tongue in its cheek" that only Natives may buy land in Native Locations.

Again, the Locations form but one–eighteenth of the total area of the Union. Theoretically, then, the 4,500,000 Natives may "buy" land in only one–eighteenth part of the Union, leaving the remaining seventeen parts for the one million whites. It is moreover true that, numerically, the Act was passed by the consent of a majority of both Houses of Parliament, but it is equally true that it was steam–rolled into the statute book against the bitterest opposition of the best brains of both Houses. A most curious aspect of this singular law is that even the Minister, since deceased, who introduced it, subsequently declared himself against it, adding that he only forced it through in order to stave off something worse. Indeed, it is correct to say that Mr. Sauer, who introduced the Bill, spoke against it repeatedly in the House; he deleted the milder provisions, inserted more drastic amendments, spoke repeatedly against his own amendments, then in conclusion he would combat his own arguments by calling the ministerial steam–roller to support the Government and vote for the drastic amendments. The only explanation of the puzzle constituted as such by these "hot–and–cold" methods is that Mr. Sauer was legislating for an electorate, at the expense of another section of the population which was without direct representation in Parliament. None of the non–European races in the Provinces of Natal, Transvaal and the "Free" State can exercise the franchise. They have no say in the selection of members for the Union Parliament. That right is only limited to white men, so that a large number of the members of Parliament who voted for this measure have no responsibility towards the black races.

Before reproducing this tyrannical enactment it would perhaps be well to recapitulate briefly the influences that led up to it. When the Union of the South African Colonies became an accomplished fact, a dread was expressed by ex–Republicans that the liberal native policy of the Cape would supersede the repressive policy of the old Republics, and they lost no time in taking definite steps to force down the throats of the Union Legislature, as it were, laws which the Dutch Presidents of pre–war days, with the British suzerainty over their heads, did not dare enforce against the Native people then under them. With the formation of the Union, the Imperial Government, for reasons which have never been satisfactorily explained, unreservedly handed over the Natives to the colonists, and these colonists, as a rule, are dominated by the Dutch Republican spirit. Thus the suzerainty of Great Britain, which under the reign of Her late Majesty Victoria, of blessed memory, was the Natives' only bulwark, has now apparently been withdrawn or relaxed, and the Republicans, like a lot of bloodhounds long held in the leash, use the free hand given by the Imperial Government not only to guard against a possible supersession of Cape ideals of toleration, but to effectively extend throughout the Union the drastic native policy pursued by the Province which is misnamed "Free" State, and enforce it with the utmost rigour.

During the first year of the Union, it would seem that General Botha made an honest attempt to live up to his London promises, that are mentioned by Mr. Merriman in his speech (reproduced elsewhere) on the second reading of the Bill in Parliament. It would seem that General Botha endeavoured to allay British apprehensions and concern for the welfare of the Native population. In pursuance of this policy General Botha won the approbation of all Natives by appointing Hon. H. Burton, a Cape Minister, to the portfolio of Native Affairs. That the appointment was a happy one, from the native point of view, became manifest when Mr. Burton signalized the ushering in of Union, by releasing Chief Dinizulu–ka–Cetywayo, who at that time was undergoing a sentence of imprisonment imposed by the Natal Supreme Court, and by the restoration to Dinizulu of his pension of 500 Pounds a year. Also, in deference to the wishes of the Native Congress, Mr. Burton abrogated two particularly obnoxious Natal measures, one legalizing the "Sibalo" system of forced labour, the other prohibiting public meetings by Natives without the consent of the Government. These abrogations placed the Natives of Natal in almost the same position as the Cape Natives though without giving them the franchise. So, too, when a drastic Squatters' Bill was gazetted early in 1912, and the recently formed Native National Congress sent a deputation to interview Mr. Burton in Capetown; after hearing the deputation, he graciously consented to withdraw the proposed measure, pending the allotment of new Locations in which Natives evicted by such a measure could find an asylum. In further deference to the representations of the Native Congress, in which they were supported by Senators the Hon. W. P. Schreiner, Colonel Stanford, and Mr. Krogh, the Union Government gazetted another Bill in January, 1911, to amend an anomaly which, at that time, was peculiar to the "Free" State: an anomaly under which a Native can neither purchase nor lease land, and native landowners in the "Free" State could only sell their land to the white people.

The gazetted Bill proposed to legalize only in one district of the Orange "Free" State the sale of landed property by a Native to another Native as well as to a white man, but it did not propose to enable Natives to buy land from white men. The object of the Bill was to remove a hardship, mentioned elsewhere in this sketch, by which a "Free" State Native was by law debarred from inheriting landed property left to him under his uncle's will. But against such small attempts at reform, proposed or carried out by the Union Government in the interest of the Natives, granted in small instalments of a teaspoonful at a time — reforms dictated solely by feelings of justice and equity — ex–Republicans were furious.

From platform, Press, and pulpit it was suggested that General Botha's administration was too pro–English and needed overhauling. The Dutch peasants along the countryside were inflamed by hearing that their gallant leader desired to Anglicize the country. Nothing was more repellent to the ideas of the backveld Dutch, and so at small meetings in the country districts resolutions were passed stating that the Botha administration had outlived its usefulness. These resolutions reaching the Press from day to day had the effect of stirring up the Dutch voters against the Ministry, and particularly against the head. At this time General Botha's sound policy began to weaken. He transferred Hon. H. Burton, first Minister of Natives, to the portfolio of Railways and Harbours, and appointed General Hertzog, of all people in the world, to the portfolio of Native Affairs.

The good-humoured indulgence of some Dutch and English farmers towards their native squatters, and the affectionate loyalty of some of these native squatters in return, will cause a keen observer, arriving at a South African farm, to be lost in admiration for this mutual good feeling. He will wonder as to the meaning of the fabled bugbear anent the alleged struggle between white and black, which in reality appears to exist only in the fertile brain of the politician. Thus let the new arrival go to one of the farms in the Bethlehem or Harrismith Districts for example, and see how willingly the Native toils in the fields; see him gathering in his crops and handing over the white farmer's share of the crop to the owner of the land; watch the farmer receiving his tribute from the native tenants, and see him deliver the first prize to the native tenant who raised the largest crop during that season; let him also see both the Natives and the landowning white farmers following to perfection the give-and-take policy of "live and let live", and he will conclude that it would be gross sacrilege to attempt to disturb such harmonious relations between these people of different races and colours. But with a ruthless hand the Natives' Land Act has succeeded in remorselessly destroying those happy relations.

First of all, General Hertzog, the new Minister of Native Affairs, travelled up and down the country lecturing farmers on their folly in letting ground to the Natives; the racial extremists of his party hailed him as the right man for the post, for, as his conduct showed them, he would soon "fix up" the Natives. At one or two places he was actually welcomed as the future Prime Minister of the Union. On the other hand, General Botha, who at that time seemed to have become visibly timid, endeavoured to ingratiate himself with his discontented supporters by joining his lieutenant in travelling to and fro, denouncing the Dutch farmers for not expelling the Natives from their farms and replacing them with poor whites. This became a regular Ministerial campaign against the Natives, so that it seemed clear that if any Native could still find a place in the land, it was not due to the action of the Government. In his campaign the Premier said other unhappy things which were diametrically opposed to his London speeches of two years before; and while the Dutch colonists railed at him for trying to Anglicize the country, English speakers and writers justly accused him of speaking with two voices; cartoonists, too, caricatured him as having two heads — one, they said, for London, and the second one for South Africa.

The uncertain tenure by which Englishmen in the public service held their posts became the subject of debates in the Union Parliament, and the employment of Government servants of colour was decidedly precarious. They were swept out of the Railway and Postal Service with a strong racial broom, in order to make room for poor whites, mainly of Dutch descent. Concession after concession was wrung from the Government by fanatical Dutch postulants for office, for Government doles and other favours, who, like the daughters of the horse-leech in the Proverbs of Solomon, continually cried, "Give, give." By these events we had clearly turned the corner and were pacing backwards to pre-Union days, going back, back, and still further backward, to the conditions which prevailed in the old Republics, and (if a check is not applied) we shall steadily drift back to the days of the old Dutch East Indian administration.

The Bill which proposed to ameliorate the "Free" State cruelty, to which reference has been made above, was dropped like a hot potato. Ministers made some wild and undignified speeches, of which the following spicy extract, from a speech by the Rt. Hon. Abraham Fischer to his constituents at Bethlehem, is a typical sample —

"What is it you want?" he asked. "We have passed all the coolie* laws and we have passed all the Kafir laws. The `Free' State has been safeguarded and all her colour laws have been adopted by Parliament. What more can the Government do for you?" And so the Union ship in this reactionary sea sailed on and on and on, until she struck an iceberg — the sudden dismissal of General Hertzog.

— * A contemptuous South African term for British Indians. —

To the bitter sorrow of his admirers, General Hertzog, who is the fearless exponent of Dutch ideals, was relieved of his portfolios of Justice and Native Affairs — it was whispered as a result of a suggestion from London; and then the Dutch extremists, in consequence of their favourite's dismissal, gave vent to their anger in the most disagreeable manner. One could infer from their platform speeches that, from their point of view, scarcely any one else had any rights in South Africa, and least of all the man with a black skin.

In the face of this, the Government's timidity was almost unendurable. They played up to the desires of the racial extremists, with the result that a deadlock overtook the administration. Violent laws like the Immigration Law (against British Indians and alien Asiatics) and the Natives' Land were indecently hurried through Parliament to allay the susceptibilities of "Free" State Republicans. No Minister found time to undertake such useful legislation as the Coloured People's Occupation Bill, the Native Disputes Bill, the Marriage Bill, the University Bill, etc., etc. An apology was demanded from the High Commissioner in London for delivering himself of sentiments which were felt to be too British for the palates of his Dutch employers in South Africa, and the Prime Minister had almost to apologize for having at times so far forgotten himself as to act more like a Crown Minister than a simple Africander. "Free" State demands became so persistent that Ministers seemed to have forgotten the assurances they gave His Majesty's Government in London regarding the safety of His Majesty's coloured subjects within the Union. They trampled under foot their own election pledges, made during the first Union General Election, guaranteeing justice and fair treatment to the law−abiding Natives.

The campaign, to compass the elimination of the blacks from the farms, was not at all popular with landowners, who made huge profits out of the renting of their farms to Natives. Platform speakers and newspaper writers coined an opprobrious phrase which designated this letting of farms to Natives as "Kafir−farming", and attempted to prove that it was almost as immoral as "baby−farming". But landowners pocketed the annual rents, and showed no inclination to substitute the less industrious "poor whites" for the more industrious Natives. Old Baas M——, a typical Dutch landowner of the "Free" State, having collected his share of the crop of 1912, addressing a few words of encouragement to his native tenants, on the subject of expelling the blacks from the farms, said in the Taal: "How dare any number of men, wearing tall hats and frock coats, living in Capetown hotels at the expense of other men, order me to evict my Natives? This is my ground; it cost my money, not Parliament's, and I will see them banged (barst) before I do it."

It then became evident that the authority of Parliament would have to be sought to compel the obstinate landowners to get rid of their Natives. And the compliance of Parliament with this demand was the greatest Ministerial surrender to the Republican malcontents, resulting in the introduction and passage of the Natives' Land Act of 1913, inasmuch as the Act decreed, in the name of His Majesty the King, that pending the adoption of a report to be made by a commission, somewhere in the dim and unknown future, it shall be unlawful for Natives to buy or lease land, except in scheduled native areas. And under severe pains and penalties they were to be deprived of the bare human rights of living on the land, except as servants in the employ of the whites — rights which were never seriously challenged under the Republican regime, no matter how politicians raved against the Natives.

Chapter II The Grim Struggle between Right and Wrong, and the Latter Carries the Day

Woe unto them that decree unrighteous decrees, and that write grievousness
  which they have prescribed;
To turn aside the needy from judgment, and to take away the fruit
  from the poor of my people, that widows may be their prey,
  and that they may rob the fatherless.
        Isaiah.

On February 18, 1913, General L. Lemmer, member for Marico, Transvaal, asked the Minister of Lands: — (a) How many farms or portions of farms in the Transvaal Province have during the last three years been registered in the names of Natives; (b) what is the extent of the land so registered; and (c) how much was paid for it?

The Minister of Lands replied: (a) 78 farms; (b) 144,416 morgen; and (c) 94,907 Pounds.

Some very disturbing elements suggest themselves in this question and in its prompt answer. A question of the kind should have taken some time to reach Pretoria from the seat of Parliament; more time to search for and compile the necessary information, and further time to get the answer to the Table of the House of Assembly in Capetown. For instance, on March 11 Mr. T. L. Schreiner called for an explanation in connexion with the same return. He had to ask again on April 1, the answer in each instance being that the required "information had been telegraphed for and would be laid on the table when it is available" (vide Union Hansard, pp. 777 and 1,175). It was only on May 13 — two months and two days after — that an answer to Mr. Schreiner's question of March 11 could be furnished.

Again, on May 20 Mr. Schreiner called for a similar return, embracing the four Provinces of the Union.* If it were so easy for General Lemmer to get a reply in regard to the Transvaal, where most of the registration took place, it should have been relatively more easy to add the information from the Cape and Natal, since no registration could have taken place in the Orange "Free" State, where Natives cannot buy land. But strange to say, all that Mr. Schreiner could get out of the Minister was a promise to furnish a reply when it is available, and it does not appear to be on record that it was ever furnished during that session. Therefore, a Native cannot be blamed for suspecting that when General Lemmer asked his question, the return was "cut and dried" and available to be laid on the table as soon as it was called for.

— * It does not appear to have occurred to any one to call for a return showing transfers of land from blacks to whites. —

Another significant point is that the questioner did not want to know the extent of land bought by Natives, but of the land "registered in their names" during the period; and Mr. Schreiner was able to show later in the session by an analysis of the return that it mainly comprised land awarded to Native tribes by the Republican Government, some of it when they conquered the country. They include farms bought or awarded to Natives as long ago as the early 60's and 70's, but the owners were not able to obtain titles as the late Republican Government did not allow Natives to register land in their own names. They had been held in trust for them by European friends or missionaries, and it was only during the last three years that the owners claimed direct titles, which right was restored to them since the British occupation.

But the Lemmer Return did its fell work. It scared every white man in the country. They got alarmed to hear that Natives had during the past three (!) years "bought" land to the extent of 50,000 morgen per annum.

Thanks to Mr. Schreiner's questions, however, the misleading features of the statistical scarecrow were revealed — but, unfortunately too late.

Origin of the Trouble

On February 28, 1913, Mr. J. G. Keyter (a "Free" State member) moved: That the Government be requested to submit to the House DURING THE PRESENT SESSION a general Pass and Squatters Bill to prohibit coloured people (1) from WANDERING ABOUT WITHOUT A PROPER PASS; (2) from SQUATTING ON FARMS; and (3) from SOWING ON THE SHARE SYSTEM.

Mr. T. P. Brain,* another "Free" Stater, seconded the motion.

— * This gentleman died during 1913. —

Mr. P. G. W. Grobler,* a Transvaaler, moved (as an amendment) to add at the end of the motion: "and further TO TAKE EFFECTIVE MEASURES TO RESTRICT THE PURCHASE AND LEASE OF LAND BY NATIVES."

— * Mr. Grobler forfeited his seat when he was convicted of complicity in the recent rebellion. —

Mr. Schreiner strongly protested against both the motion and the amendment.

The Minister for Native Affairs* spoke somewhat against Mr. Keyter's motion but promised to comply with Mr. Grobler's amendment, which promise he redeemed by introducing a Natives' Land Bill.

— * Hon. J. W. Sauer, Minister of Native Affairs, died a month after the Bill became law. —

Before the Bill was introduced, the Minister made the unprecedented announcement that the Governor–General had given his assurance that the Royal Assent would not be withheld from the Natives' Land Bill. Section 65 of the South African Constitution provides that the King may disallow an Act of Parliament within twelve months after the Governor–General signed it. And the abrogation of the Constitution, as far as this Bill is concerned, literally gave licence to the political libertines of South Africa; as, being thus freed from all legislative restraint, they wasted no further time listening to such trifles as reason and argument.

The following are extracts from the debates on the Natives' Land Bill as reported in the Union Hansard of 1913.

The adjourned debate on the motion for the second reading of the Natives Land Bill was resumed by

MR. J. X. MERRIMAN (Victoria West). It was with very great reluctance (the right hon. gentleman said) that he rose to speak on this measure. It would have been more convenient to have given a silent vote, but he felt, and he was afraid, that after many years of devoted attention to this question of the native policy of South Africa, he would not be doing his duty if he did not give this House — for what it was worth — the result of his experience through these years.

He should like to emphasize a brighter side of the question, and that was to point out that the Natives, if they were well managed, were an invaluable asset to the people of this country. (Hear, hear.) Let them take our trade figures and compare them with the trade figures of the other large British Dominions. Our figures were surprising when measured by the white population, but if they took the richest Dominion that there was under the British Crown outside South Africa, and took the trade value of those figures per head of the white population, and multiply those figures by our European population, then they might very well apply any balance they had to our native population, and then they would see, strangely enough, that upon that basis it worked out that the actual trade of three Natives was worth about that of one white man. That, of course, was a very imperfect way of looking at the value of these people, because the trade value of some of these Natives was far greater than the trade value of some of our white people. He had merely indicated these trade figures to show what an enormous asset we had in the Natives in that respect. Let them think what the industry of the Natives had done for us. Who had built our railways, who had dug our mines, and developed this country as far as it was developed? Who had been the actual manual worker who had done that? The Native: the coloured races of this country. We must never forget that we owed them a debt in that respect — a debt not often acknowledged by what we did for them. Proceeding, he said that they ought to think what they owed to the docility of the Natives, and the wonderfully easy way in which they had been governed when treated properly. He also paid a tribute to the honesty of the Natives.

What must strike any one was the fact that though this Bill was really, to a certain extent, a beginning, or was thought to be in certain quarters, of a revolution in their dealing with the native races, it was not even mentioned in the speech of the Governor–General. It fell upon them like a bolt from the blue. He remembered the afternoon. They had heard a very impassioned and very heated speech from the hon. member for Ficksburg on the enormous danger of squatting in the Free State, and that was the occasion for introducing a general statement of the policy of the Government towards the Natives and the introduction of this Bill. He did not think that that was the way they liked to see a thing of this magnitude approached. They often heard demands for what was called a general declaration of policy with regard to native affairs — a policy which should be applied to the highest civilized Native, the owner of a farm, and the naked barbarian. They could not do it. People who demanded a general declaration of that kind had not had the experience which some of them had had. The hon. member who spoke before him said that he was in favour of the underlying principle of the Bill. What was the underlying principle? The underlying principle was what one read into the Bill. One hon. member read into it that it was the separation of the two races. That might have been done when the two races first came in contact at the Fish River, but it could not be done now. Since then they had been developing the country with the labour of these people. They had been advancing by our aid. They had mixed themselves up with these people in an inextricable fashion and then some said "Haul your native policy out of the drawer and begin with a policy of separation." He was sure that the hon. member who had brought in the Bill had no idea of that sort in his mind. Another person had the idea that they were going to set up a sort of pale — a sort of kraal in which they were going to drive these people. Then another gentleman sneered at the policy hitherto adopted, and he said that one side said that the policy towards the Natives should be firm and just, while the other side said that it should be just and firm.

It seemed to him that they had not got sufficient information. Beyond the bald statistics which were given by the Minister in the course of his interesting and moderate speech, they had nothing. They were going into a thing that would stir South Africa from end to end, and which affected hundreds of thousands of both races. They had no information as to what were the ideas of the Natives. It was unfortunate that, owing to this lack of information, wrong ideas had got about with regard to this Bill. It was difficult to find out what the Native thought about these things; he doubted whether anybody could say that he had got at the mind of the Native. The only way, and he must say that he did not take it as a real indication, was what they wrote in their newspapers. He was alarmed, but not surprised, at some of the articles in their newspapers, because they took their views from the heated speeches and writings in party newspapers all over the country, and they were very much alarmed. He thought that before a Bill of this sort was passed, there should be some attempt made to get their views. As far as one section was concerned, the Bill was going to set up a sort of pale — that there was going to be a sort of kraal in which all the Natives were to be driven, and they were to be left to develop on their own lines. To allow them to go on their own lines was merely to drive them back into barbarism; their own lines meant barbarous lines; their own lines were cruel lines. All along they had been bringing them away from their own lines. It reminded him of what an English writer said about a similar policy in Ireland, because when the English went to Ireland they regarded the Native Irish in the way some extreme people here regarded the Natives of South Africa. They thought they would root them out. They treated them as dogs, and thought that they were dogs. They set up a pale. They set the Irish within that pale, to develop upon their own lines, but there were always Englishmen living in that pale, just as in the same way they found Europeans living among Natives. Sir George Davis in describing this policy wrote that it was the intention of the Government to set up a separation between English and Irish, intending in time that the English should root out the Irish. If they changed the Irish for Natives they would see how the illustration would apply. A policy more foredoomed to failure in South Africa could not be initiated. It was a policy that would keep South Africa back, perhaps for ever. (Hear, hear.) What would be the effect of driving these civilized Natives back into reserves? At the present time, every civilized man — if they treated him properly — every civilized man was becoming an owner of land outside native reserve, and therefore he was an asset of strength to the country. He was a loyalist. He was not going to risk losing his property. He was on the side of the European. If they drove these people back into reserve they became our bitterest enemies. Therefore, he viewed anything that tended that way with the gravest suspicion. Again, in this Bill there was not sufficient distinction between those Natives who tried to educate themselves and the ordinary raw barbarian. They were all classed under the word "Native".

He came now to what was the main object of the Bill, and that was: to do away with the squatting evil. Why was there a squatting evil? Was it the fault of the Native? (An hon. member: No.) Was it the fault of the law? (No.) They had got the most stringent laws concerning Natives of all the laws in the whole country, in the Province of which his hon. friend (Mr. Keyter) was a member. He did not think anything was more surprising than when they came to look at the increases in the native population in the Orange Free State. They had a huge native population in the Cape, and the increase during the census periods from 1904 to 1911 — he wanted hon. members to pay some attention to this, because it showed the value of legislation — the increase in the Cape Province during that period was 8.33 per cent. In Natal, which had a huge — in fact, an overwhelming — native population, curiously enough, the increase was the same, even to the actual decimal figure, viz., 8.33 per cent.: but some allowance must be made, because a large number of Natives were out at work in the mines. Now, in the Transvaal — and in taking the Transvaal figures these did not apply as regarded squatting, because the increase was mainly due to the number of Natives employed in the mines. In the Transvaal the Natives increased by 30.1 per cent. Now, when they came to his friend's little State, where the most stringent laws were made to keep out the Natives, how much did they suppose the Natives increased in the Free State? By no less than 44 per cent. (Opposition cheers.) Was that the fault of the Natives? No, it was because — having the most stringent laws — the people found it best to evade those laws. (Hear, hear.) He hoped his hon. friend would be a little tolerant. Do let him pick the mote out of his own eye before he tried to pick the beam out of other people's. (Hear, hear.) In the Free State these laws were very severe; for instance, punishments — amazing punishments — were given, and yet the result was the increase in five years by 44 per cent. of their native population. This was something that they should take a warning by. They were going to do away with the squatter in appearance, but he would still survive as a labour tenant. They might do away with the labour tenant, and he would still be surviving as a labour servant. How was the Government to distinguish between these? They had in the Cape a law which stated how many labour tenants a man should have upon his farm.

What they wanted in this country was administration and not more legislation, and if they were to put the laws which they had into force in the Free State at the present time he had no doubt that there would be a rebellion. (Hear, hear.) They would have platforms swarming with people who would say that they could not grow one bag of mealies without the Natives. But they had the laws to do it. Now they went and tried in this Bill to make a uniform law. Turning towards the Minister, Mr. Merriman said: "My poor friend! that after all the years we had laboured together he of all people should be the author of a uniform law on native matters! (Laughter.) I say this more in sorrow than in anger — (laughter) — because the conditions were totally different in the four Provinces."

In the Free State, proceeded Mr. Merriman, the people had most excellent laws from their point of view for keeping out the Natives — stringent, Draconian, and violent laws, but they were not carried out, and the Natives had flooded the country. All they wanted to do was to turn the Native from a tenant to a labour tenant, and then salvation would be at hand. He could not see very much difference between the two, except that one was a contented advancing man and the other a discontented man approaching very closely to the Russian serf — he was a soul. Shortly we should hear of a farm being up for sale with so many souls.

In the Transvaal the problem had been complicated by the decisions of the Court and the curious way in which some ground had been given out in the Zoutpansberg district, where, he was told, farms had been given out on which the Natives had been living for years, and these farms — with the Natives on them — had come into the possession of companies and individuals, and now it was proposed to turn the Natives off. That would not be an agreeable thing, but he would not offer an opinion now as to the justice of it.

He would like to revert to the state of things which had grown up under the Draconian laws of the Free State. According to a very interesting Blue–book containing reports of magistrates, one magistrate had reported that "the pernicious system of squatting was detrimental to the working farmer, the Native reaping the whole of the benefit." The man who worked generally reaped the whole benefit in the long run. In the Harrismith district there were some 40,000 Natives against some 8,000 Europeans. How did they get there? Having been a Free State burgher he knew that the Natives had not forced their way in. These Natives ploughed on the half–shares, and he would like to know whether they were labour tenants or squatters. If they were squatters it would require very little dexterous management to convert them into labour tenants. The Magistrate of Hoopstad, went on Mr. Merriman, had referred to the pernicious system of native squatters. But why did not the Free State magistrates do something and put the law in force? That was the principal reason why the House was forced to pass that Bill without information, and without giving any opportunity to people who had the deepest interest in this matter to have their views heard, or to let them know what the House was going to do because the magistrates in the Free State would not enforce the law. He did think that was rather hard. In conclusion Mr. Merriman said: I dare say I may have said a great many things which may be distasteful to my hon. friends, but I do claim their attention because at a time when they were not in such a dominant position as they are now, I pleaded for right and justice for them. Therefore, they should not take it amiss from me, because now they are in a dominant position, I plead also for justice, toleration, moderation, and delay in this matter.

MR. H. MENTZ (Zoutpansberg) said the right hon. gentleman had earned their gratitude for the high tone in which he had carried the debate. The speech which he had delivered was a most instructive one, and although the speaker was not in entire agreement with him on all points, he was in agreement on the point that the matter was one to be handled with prudence, but it was to be regretted that under the Bill a Commission was to be appointed. The Minister should not listen to the request for a postponement of the question, by referring it to a Select Committee. If they were to refer the Bill to a Select Committee, it would never be passed this year.

MR. G. L. STEYTLER (Rouxville) expressed his thanks to the Government for bringing forward the Bill. He said he felt that it was not a complete solution of the whole question, but it was certainly a step in the right direction.

MR. A. FAWCUS (Umlazi) said that as the representative of 70,000 Natives in Natal, not one of whom so far as he knew had a vote, he should like, on their behalf, to thank the right hon. member for Victoria West for the manner in which he had handled this question. In the course of his speech the right hon. gentleman asked, what did the Natives think about this Bill before the House? His (Mr. Fawcus') opinion was that the Natives did not think anything at all about it. He should not think there was one Native in a thousand in South Africa who was aware that this matter, so vitally affecting their future, was at present at issue. The hon. member for Middelburg had referred to the Natives as "schepsels".* He believed the day was rapidly passing away when we should refer to Natives as "schepsels". They were an easy-going folk, and they thought little about title deeds and land laws. So great was the Native's attachment to the land on which he lived, in many instances, that they could not rackrent him off it. These were the people that the Bill wished to dispossess and drive off the land. The figures placed before them showed that THE LAND HELD BY EUROPEANS PER HEAD WAS FIFTY TIMES THE AMOUNT HELD PER HEAD BY THE NATIVES. Surely there was no need at the present time for legislation which would prevent Natives getting a little more land than they now had. He did not think it could be put down to the fault of the Native if he was willing to buy and live on land rather than pay rent. The figures given in this connexion were very instructive. EIGHT ACRES PER HEAD WERE HELD BY THE NATIVES IN THE CAPE, SIX ACRES IN NATAL, ABOUT 1 1/2 ACRES in the Transvaal, and about one-third of an acre in the Free State. He thought this Bill was perhaps coming on a little before there was any necessity for it.

— * Creatures. —

MR. C. G. FICHARDT (Ladybrand) said he felt very much that the Bill that was before the House did not carry out all that should be carried out, and that was equality of justice. IF THEY WERE TO DEAL FAIRLY WITH THE NATIVES OF THIS COUNTRY, THEN ACCORDING TO POPULATION THEY SHOULD GIVE THEM FOUR-FIFTHS OF THE COUNTRY, OR AT LEAST A HALF. How were they going to do that? As he said in the earlier part of his remarks, he was prepared to accept the Bill as something to go on with, but he hoped that in the future it would not constitute a stumbling-block. He would much rather have seen that the matter had been gone into more fully, and that some scheme had been laid before them so that they might have more readily been able to judge how the Bill would work. It was because of all these difficulties that he felt that they could only accept the Bill if it laid down that there was no intention of taking the country from the white people and handing it over to the blacks.

MR. J. G. KEYTER (Ficksburg) said he wished to openly denounce, and most emphatically so, that the people or the Government of the Orange Free State had treated the coloured people unreasonably or unjustly, or in any way oppressively. On the contrary, the O.F.S. had always treated the coloured people with the greatest consideration and the utmost justice. The O.F.S. had made what Mr. Merriman called stringent laws. He (Mr. Keyter) called them just laws. They TOLD THE COLOURED PEOPLE PLAINLY THAT THE O.F.S. WAS A WHITE MAN'S COUNTRY, AND THAT THEY INTENDED TO KEEP IT SO. (Hear, hear.) THEY TOLD THE COLOURED PEOPLE THAT THEY WERE NOT TO BE ALLOWED TO BUY OR HIRE LAND, and that they were not going to tolerate an equality of whites and blacks; and he said that they were not going to tolerate that in the future, and if an attempt were made to force that on them, they would resist it at any cost to the last,* for if they did tolerate it, they would very soon find that they would be a bastard nation. His experience was that the Native should be treated firmly, kept in his place and treated honestly. They should not give him a gun one day and fight him for it the next day. They should tell him, as the Free State told him, that IT WAS A WHITE MAN'S COUNTRY, THAT HE WAS NOT GOING TO BE ALLOWED TO BUY LAND THERE OR TO HIRE LAND THERE, AND THAT IF HE WANTED TO BE THERE HE MUST BE IN SERVICE.

— * By passing the Bill, the Government conceded all the extravagant demands
   of the "Free" Staters; yet, a year later they took up arms
   against the Government. —

MR. J. A. P. VAN DER MERWE (Vredefort) deprecated sending the Bill to a Select Committee, arguing that the House itself should decide it. He referred to the difficulties experienced by farmers in the Free State. If a farmer refused to allow a Native to farm on the share system he simply refused to work. There were thousands of Natives on the farms there who hired ground and did little work. The farmers had to keep their children at home to do the work. Some of the Natives hired ground, did some sowing, then went to work in Johannesburg, and paid the owner of the farm half what he reaped from the harvest. That was not satisfactory. He was pleased to see the provisions the Minister proposed to make in this regard, and expressed the hope that the Native would only be tolerated among the whites as a labourer. The Bill would meet what he considered a great want, and, as it was an urgent matter, he hoped the proposal for a Select Committee would not be agreed to.

Third Reading Debate.

SIR LIONEL PHILLIPS (Yeoville): But why should a Bill of this sort be brought before them now? The Government in the past had not been bashful in the appointing of Commissions, and one question he would ask was why, in this important matter, the Government had not appointed a Commission to take all the evidence and then come to the House with a measure which the House would have to approve of. Instead of that, they were cancelling the rights the Natives had in South Africa, and creating a very awkward hiatus between the time the Commission would be appointed and the time the Commission could define the areas which would be regarded as white areas and the areas which would be regarded as native areas. That was the one serious blot upon this measure.

He could see no justification, except that the hon. Minister, yielding to pressure from a certain section on that side of the House, had hastily brought on this measure. He thought from the speeches made in the House it was the consensus of opinion that Natives should not have farms in areas that were essentially white, just as it was desirable that white men should not be found in areas essentially native. And especially when they told the native population that they were taking away from them a right they had to–day, and they were going to substitute that right by appointing a Commission, they were giving them very little justification for being satisfied with this measure. He did not think they were going to gain anything by putting the cart before the horse. He did not know if Mr. Schreiner was accurate, but he told them that, roughly, in the Transvaal, where the matter was most acute, the Native population had bought something like 12,000 or 15,000 morgen of land in twelve years. That, he thought, showed there was no extreme urgency for the measure. To that extent he agreed entirely with the hon. member, and he believed the Minister would be well advised to send the Bill to a Select Committee, so that many of the details, which were extremely complicated and difficult, might be thrashed out in that atmosphere, rather than on the floor of the House. (Opposition cheers.)

MR. E. N. GROBLER (Edenburg) said: The present was one of the best measures that the Government had so far brought forward, and it appeared clear that they had a Government which truly represented the wishes of the public. It was impossible to delay the solution of the Native problem, and legislation on the subject had for a long time past been asked for.* At the same time, he did not entirely agree with the methods, proposed to be applied, and he did not like the system of allocating reserves for Natives. When once those reserves had been allocated, would it not result in injury to agriculture and cattle breeding? The farmers would suffer from lack of labour, and that deficiency would be a growing one. Neither could he agree to the principle of expropriation of land belonging to whites in order to increase the size of the native reserves. He considered the Bill was a complicated one. The matter should be settled by way of taxation, in the following way. All Natives who were in the service of whites should be exempted from taxation, and treated as well as possible, and other Natives should be encouraged to take similar service. There were enormous reserves where the Natives could go and live,** and if they refused to go there they should be required to pay a stiff tax. Then they would go and work for white people. The hon. member for Tembuland had offered many objections to the Bill. They should make that hon. member king of Tembuland. In a country of the blind a man with one eye would be king.

— * By a "solution of the Native problem", "Free" State farmers generally mean
  the re−establishment of slavery. ** It will be observed that these and similar mythological disquisitions
    subsequently formed General Botha's assurances to Mr. Harcourt.
    See Chapter XVI. But some light is thrown on the subject
    of these visionary Native Reserves by Mr. Fawcus' speech
    based on official statistics (page 36 [above — last Fawcus quote]). —

MR. P. DUNCAN (Fordsburg) said he hoped the Minister would not take the view of the last speaker. Under the Bill it would be possible for farmers to accumulate on their land as many Natives as they could get, so long as they could use them as servants. (Labour cheers.) So far as he could see, even if it were carried out to the extent that it was proposed to go, it would not very much reduce the social contact which at present existed between whites and natives.

SIR W. B. BERRY (Queenstown) said he would like to know why the Minister had run away from the Bill that had passed the second reading, and now tabled another Bill in the shape of many amendments. One would naturally complain that, seeing that they had in that House a Native Affairs Committee, a non−party committee, specially chosen to consider all matters relating to native affairs, that Bill, which was a most important matter and dealt with native affairs from A to Z, should have been referred to that committee. The same thing happened last session in reference to a Bill the Minister of Native Affairs kept on the paper until nearly the end of the session, and the House had to take the very unusual step almost on the last day of moving that committee proceedings on that Bill be taken that day six months. He (Sir W. B. Berry) proposed to move a similar amendment to the motion now before the House. In the remarks he addressed when the Bill came up for second reading he had ventured to say that there was no call for a bill of that nature at all; there was no need for a Bill revolutionizing the attitude of the Union with respect to the natives generally. The only clue they could get to the reason why the Bill was introduced was that a few die–hards on the other side of the House had given the Minister to understand that unless he brought in a Bill of that kind, or of a similarly drastic nature, the position of the Government was in danger. He hoped some of these die–hards would come forward that evening and tell them plainly and bluntly why they wanted that Bill, why they were going to thrust it on the country without any notice, and why they were calling on the House to revolutionize the whole tenour and the whole order of things in regard to land matters as far as the Natives were concerned. Proceeding, the hon. member said the only justification that had been offered for this Bill was that a large amount of land had been transferred from Europeans to Natives. An analysis of the return, however, showed that only sixteen farms in the Transvaal had been so transferred during the last three years. Surely that was not any justification why the European people of the Union should get into a panic and why the administration of the day were seeking to place on the Statute Book this most drastic legislation. Another reason why he objected to this Bill was that it purported to appoint a Commission to investigate to what extent and in what parts and in what time land should be selected by the Commission for the purpose of being reserved as additional native areas within the Union. They were not given any guarantee that the Commission was going to be appointed nor any guarantee that it would ever report, but at the same time whilst these indefinite assurances were attempted to be given to the House there was no getting over this fact, that there was no time limit in the Bill by which the real enacting clause in the Bill was to have any cessation. When he spoke on this Bill before he supported it only on the understanding that a time limit was to be put in, or that it should be an annual Bill. He said unhesitatingly that the whole tendency of the Bill, as it stood at the second reading, and more especially as it stood with the amendments by the Minister on the notice paper, was to drive the Native peasant off the land. The only refuge that that Native had was the town.

The country had not been prepared in any way for a Bill of this kind. A cry had been heard throughout the land against the iniquities proposed in the Bill. If it had been found absolutely necessary that legislation of this kind should be introduced, the least that could be expected was that ample time should be given to the Natives to thoroughly acquire a knowledge of the contents of the measure. That opportunity had not been given them, and in this respect there was a very serious grievance. For the good order and peace of the Union there was a very great danger ahead. He had understood from those well versed in native affairs that one of the greatest dangers that could threaten us was to give the Natives anything in the shape of a common grievance. Divide and rule had been a wise precaution in the government of the Natives. When a common grievance was found by four or five million people one could understand how great that grievance must be. One amendment the Minister had put on the paper must give serious pause. The late Minister of Native Affairs issued to members last session a Squatters Bill. The greatest objection to that measure, and one which he thought led to its withdrawal, was that it proposed to remove thousands upon thousands of natives from land which they had been in the occupation of for scores of years. It was in consequence of the disturbance which that Bill caused throughout the Union that it was withdrawn. In one of the amendments on the paper the present Minister of Native Affairs brought back in a somewhat clandestine manner the most objectionable feature of the Bill that was withdrawn.

Mr. Speaker: The amendment is not yet before the House.

SIR W. B. BERRY: What Bill is it then that is to go into Committee? (Hear, hear.) Is it the Bill which was read a second time or the Bill comprised in the Minister's amendments? He moved that the House go into committee on the Bill this day six months.

MR. T. L. SCHREINER (Tembuland), in seconding the amendment, said that sufficient notice had not been given of the provisions of the Bill, although the Natives, thanks to the time which had elapsed since the second reading, were better acquainted with the measure than they were a little while ago.

Mr. Schreiner proceeded to quote opinions from native newspapers on the Bill. The `Tsala ea Batho', of Kimberley, said: "We are standing on the brink of the precipice. We appealed to certain members of Parliament against the suspension clause in Mr. Sauer's Land Bill, and the result of our appeal has been an agreement between Sir Thomas Smartt and the Minister to the effect that the first part of the Bill only be proceeded with. The effect of this agreement is infinitely worse than the whole Bill. In its entirety, there were certain saving clauses, one of them practically excluding the Cape Province from the operation of the Bill. Under the present agreement, all these clauses are dropped, and section 1 of the Bill, which prohibits the sale of land between Europeans and Natives (pending the report of a future Commission) is applicable to all parts of the Union, including the Cape Province. Now, then, if this suspension clause becomes law, what is going to happen? It is simply this: That the whole land policy of the Union of South Africa is the land policy of the Orange Free State, and it will be as difficult to abrogate that suspension as it is difficult to recall a bullet, once fired through some one's head, and resuscitate the victim. Our object then should be to prevent the pistol being fired off, as prevention is infinitely better than cure." One paper that he was quoting from was (Mr. Schreiner went on to say) pleased, because it believed that this Bill was going to Select Committee. There was another native paper, published in Natal, which acknowledged the efforts which the missionaries had made on behalf of the Natives in regard to this Bill. There was a native paper, published at Dundee, which said that, if the Bill were in the interests of the Natives, and the Government were actuated by a sincere regard for them, they would not have hesitated to publish it broadcast, instead of being in such haste to push the matter through the House.*

— * All efforts to induce the South African Government to circulate
translations of the Natives' Land Act among the Natives of the Union
have proved fruitless. — Author. —

Mr. Schreiner (continuing) referred to the resolution passed by the Natal Missionary Conference, and the views expressed by the Chairman of the Transvaal Missionary Conference in opposition to the Bill. He mentioned that it had been decided in Johannesburg to call a meeting of missionary societies throughout the Union, to determine what action could be taken in case clause 1 was proceeded with. He had also received a telegram from the Witwatersrand Church Council, stating that a telegram had been sent to the Minister strongly protesting against section 1 being enacted before the proposed Commission had thoroughly investigated the whole question of alternative areas. Mr. Schreiner urged that, if they proceeded with this Bill, and passed clause 1 of the old Bill, and appointed a Commission, these restrictions with regard to purchase and sale, which the Natives had feared, and which the missionaries, on behalf of the Natives, feared and protested against, would become a fact. For that reason, he said they should rather put off the Bill.

Every one was feeling the pressure of their legislative duties. Was this the time, therefore, for passing a measure of such a far-reaching character, and where every clause demanded the most careful consideration and scrutiny? Was it the right thing because he had a majority at his back for the Minister to say that they must get this Bill through this session? He held that this was not right. It was not fair to those who had the solution of the question at heart. (Cheers.)

SIR E. H. WALTON (Port Elizabeth, Central) said he entirely supported the amendment of the hon. member for Queen's Town. He had a telegram from a mass meeting of Natives held in Port Elizabeth, in which they hoped that the House would postpone decision on this question until the Commission had sat and reported. That seemed to him an entirely reasonable request, and it seemed all the more necessary that this should be done on account of the very large alterations that it had been found necessary to make in the Bill.

They had native protests from all parts of South Africa against this measure, and when one saw what was proposed in this Act, they could not wonder at these protests. (Hear, hear.) Therefore he put it that these protests should receive fair consideration from members on all sides of the House. Legislation of this kind was unfortunate from the point of view of the Natives. The more intelligent of the Natives in this country were asking for time. They said: "You are putting this thing upon us, give us time to consider it. Allow this Commission to get to work, allow this Commission to put before us the provisions you are going to make for us, and when this is done we will submit to anything that is fair." No man, and the Native was just a man like the rest of us, liked the old arrangements to be disturbed, because it upset him, and the Native might oppose it, because he was frightened. They must admit that they had not given the native leaders and chiefs an opportunity to come down to Cape Town and give their views. It was unfortunate that this measure had been more or less rushed. There was no mention of it in the Governor-General's speech, and therefore the Natives were not prepared for the consideration of the question.

MR. M. ALEXANDER (Cape Town, Castle) said he was still of opinion that a very dangerous principle was introduced in the Bill, especially so far as the Cape was concerned. In the speech delivered by the Governor-General at the opening of the session there was not the slightest reference to the present measure, which apparently had been brought in as an afterthought, and something must have occurred after the Governor-General's speech was delivered, otherwise one could not conceive of such an important Bill being omitted from the speech. As it was the Bill would simply hang things up until the Commission reported, and now the House would be legislating in the dark. The vast majority of Natives had declared themselves to be against the Bill. He had had no desire whatever that party capital should be made out of the measure — (hear, hear) — but he desired to see a measure which would bear the mark of statesmanship, and not of panic and hurry. Their Commission could report before next session, and then in the early stages of the session a Bill could be introduced and be adopted on its merits. In the interests of South Africa, in the interests of the Natives, and in the interests of just legislation let the Government withdraw the Bill, and appoint a Commission, and then justice and not injustice would be done. (Hear, hear.)

DR. A. H. WATKINS (Barkly) said that there was a tacit understanding that the Minister would refer this Bill, if he were not prepared to accept a purely temporary measure, to a Select Committee. During the three years of the Union Parliament every matter practically dealing with Natives had been brought before the Select Committee on Native Affairs and their opinion had been asked. For some reason, which it was difficult for him to understand, the Minister had not seen fit to carry out that course. Sixteen days had elapsed since the second reading of this Bill was taken on which the Select Committee could have sat morning after morning and dealt with the Bill.

The necessity of passing only a temporary measure instead of appearing to pass a measure which would permanently deal with this question, was more evident to-night than when they took the second reading.

MR. H. M. MEYLER (Weenen) said that he would support the motion of Sir Bisset Berry. He thought it would be a great injustice to the Natives, and especially the Natives of Natal, who really knew nothing of this measure, to force it through now. Since the second reading, his attention had been drawn to certain provisions in this Bill, which made it more dangerous still to hurry legislation, because he found that, although there was an exemption in the Bill as regarded agreements lawfully entered into, the vast majority of the agreements at present in force amongst the Natives of Natal were not strictly lawful, according to their Statute law. As they had no less than 380,000 Natives squatting on private lands in Natal, according to the Minister's own figures, it would be a fatal mistake to do anything to upset these people, until they had something ready to provide for them instead. The difficulty was that under the Natal law no oral contract was binding for more than twelve months, and many of those squatters had not got oral contracts, but were more or less on sufferance on the farms. It would be a great danger to pass legislation which would lead to the moving of a large portion of these people before they got an inch of land provided for their use. He objected to legislation being brought forward too hurriedly, and when they had got 4 1/2 millions of Natives, only an infinitesimal portion of whom could possibly know the nature of the Bill, and seeing that it affected them as well as the white population, they had a perfect right to have it explained to them by the Government officials and let their members of Parliament for the divisions in which they lived give their opinions on the question. That would take months, and it was impossible to get a proper opinion of the Natives until hon. members had been away from the House for some time. The Right Hon. the Prime Minister admitted they should stand as the guardians of the Natives, and admitted that they should go slowly, and he hoped the hon. Minister would be willing to reconsider the Bill and allow it to be put off, and let them have an interim report, at any rate, from the Commission, before they were asked to pass legislation in that matter.

The Bill was contested at every stage and numerous divisions were challenged. In each instance, the Speaker would put the Question, and the "steam-roller" would go to work with the inevitable result. The division lists ranged from 17 against 71 to 32 against 60, the majority in each case being in favour of repression. It would be just as well to give at least one of these division lists. The English names in the majority are those of some Natal members (Ministerialists) or representatives of purely Dutch constituencies: —

DIVISION

Dr. A. H. Watkins (Barkly) called for a division, which was taken with the following result.

AYES — 32.

Andrews, William Henry Baxter, William Duncan Berry, William Bisset Blaine, George Boydell, Thomas Brown, Daniel Maclaren Creswell, Frederic Hugh Page Duncan, Patrick Fawcus, Alfred Fitzpatrick, James Percy Henderson, James Henwood, Charlie Hunter, David Jagger, John William King, John Gavin Long, Basil Kellett Macaulay, Donald Madeley, Walter Bayley Meyler, Hugh Mowbray Nathan, Emile Oliver, Henry Alfred Quinn, John William Rockey, Willie Runciman, William Sampson, Henry William Schreiner, Theophilus Lyndall Searle, James Smartt, Thomas William Walton, Edgar Harris Watkins, Arnold Hirst

Morris Alexander and J. Hewat tellers.

NOES — 57.

Alberts, Johannes Joachim Becker, Heinrich Christian Bosman, Hendrik Johannes Botha, Louis Brain, Thomas Phillip Burton, Henry Clayton, Walter Frederick Cronje, Frederik Reinhardt Currey, Henry Latham De Beer, Michiel Johannes De Jager, Andries Lourens De Waal, Hendrik Du Toit, Gert Johan Wilhelm Geldenhuys, Lourens Graaff, David Pieter de Villiers Griffin, William Henry Grobler, Evert Nicolaas Grobler, Pieter Gert Wessel Joubert, Christiaan Johannes Jacobus Joubert, Jozua Adriaan Keyter, Jan Garhard Kuhn, Pieter Gysbert Lemmer, Lodewyk Arnoldus Slabbert Maasdorp, Gysbert Henry Malan, Francois Stephanus Marais, Johannes Henoch Marais, Pieter Gerhardus Merriman, John Xavier Meyer, Izaak Johannes Myburgh, Marthinus Wilhelmus Neethling, Andrew Murray Neser, Johannes Adriaan Nicholson, Richard Granville Oothuisen, Ockert Almero Orr, Thomas Rademeyer, Jacobus Michael Sauer, Jacobus Wilhelmus Serfontein, Hendrik Philippus Smuts, Jan Christiaan Smuts, Tobias Steyl, Johannes Petrus Gerhardus Steytler, George Louis Theron, Hendrik Schalk Theron, Petrus Jacobus George Van der Merwe, Johannes Adolph P. Van der Walt, Jacobus Van Eeden, Jacobus Willem Van Heerden, Hercules Christian Venter, Jan Abraham Vermaas, Hendrik Cornelius Wilhelmus Vintcent, Alwyn Ignatius Vosloo, Johannes Arnoldus Watt, Thomas Wilcocks, Carl Theodorus Muller Wiltshire, Henry

H. Mentz and G. A. Louw, tellers.

Chapter III The Natives' Land Act

I blush to think that His Majesty's representative signed a law like this,
  and signed it in such circumstances.
        Rev. Amos Burnet
        (Chairman and General Superintendent of
        the Transvaal and Swazieland District,
        Wesleyan Methodist Church).

Up to now we have dealt with the history of the Land Act from its commencement, and all the speeches and official documents we have mentioned hitherto say nothing about restricting Europeans in their ownership of land. And no matter what other principles one might read into the Act, it would be found that the principles underlying it were those of extending the "Free" State land laws throughout the Union — an extension by which Natives would be prohibited from investing their earnings in land whereon they could end their days in peace.

There seems to be good reason for believing that the Government were advised, by the legal advisers of the Crown, that the Natives' Land Bill would be class legislation of a kind that would never be allowed by His Majesty's Government. The originators of the Bill, however, were determined so to circumvent the constitutional quibble raised by the legal advisers as to seal our doom; and by adroitly manipulating its legal phrases, it seems that it was recast in such a manner as to give it a semblance of a paper restriction on European encroachment on native rights. But class legislation the Act is, for whereas in his travels about South Africa, since the passing of this Act, the author has met many a native family with their stock, turned out by the Act upon the roads, he never met one white man so hounded by the same Act, and debarred from living where he pleased.

The squatters form a particular section of the community specifically affected by the Land Act; and there is no such person in South Africa as a white squatter. Although it is insistently affirmed that the law applies both to Europeans and Natives, the conclusion cannot be avoided that it is directed exclusively against the Native. This is the naked truth that turns all other explanations of the fact into mere shuffling and juggling. And the reader will find that in Section 11, at the end of the statute which is here reproduced (whether the omission of Europeans was a mistake of the Parliamentary draftsmen, or the printers, we know not), it is expressly stated that "this Act may be cited for all purposes as the NATIVES' Land Act, 1913." Who, then, will continue to argue that it was intended for Europeans as well?

No. 27, 1913.]

ACT
TO Make further provision as to the purchase and leasing of Land
by Natives and other Persons in the several parts of the Union and for
other purposes in connection with the ownership and occupation of Land
by Natives and other Persons.

Be it enacted by the King's Most Excellent Majesty, the Senate and the House of Assembly of the Union of South Africa, as follows: —

1. (1) From and after the commencement of this Act, land outside the scheduled native areas shall, until Parliament, acting upon the report of the commission appointed under this Act, shall have made other provision, be subjected to the following provisions, that is to say: —

Except with the approval of the Governor–General —

   (a) a native shall not enter into any agreement or transaction
      for the purchase, hire, or other acquisition from a person
      other than a native, of any such land or of any right thereto,
      interest therein, or servitude thereover; and

   (b) a person other than a native shall not enter into
      any agreement or transaction for the purchase, hire,
      or other acquisition from a native of any such land

or of any right thereto, interest therein, or servitude thereover.

(2) From and after the commencement of this Act, no person other than a native shall purchase, hire or in any other manner whatever acquire any land in a scheduled native area or enter into any agreement or transaction for the purchase, hire or other acquisition, direct or indirect, of any such land or of any right thereto or interest therein or servitude thereover, except with the approval of the Governor–General.

(3) A statement showing the number of approvals granted by the Governor–General under sub–sections (1) and (2) of this section and giving the names and addresses of the persons to whom such approvals were granted, the reasons for granting the same, and the situation of the lands in respect of which they were granted, shall, within six weeks after the commencement of each ordinary session of Parliament, be laid upon the Tables of both Houses of Parliament.

(4) Every agreement or any other transaction whatever entered into in contravention of this section shall be null and void ab initio.

2. (1) As soon as may be after the commencement of this Act the Governor–General shall appoint a commission whose functions shall be to inquire and report —

   (a) what areas should be set apart as areas within which natives
       shall not be permitted to acquire or hire land or interests in land;

   (b) what areas should be set apart as areas within which
       persons other than natives shall not be permitted to acquire or hire
       land or interests in land.

The commission shall submit with any such report —

   (i) descriptions of the boundaries of any area which it proposes
       should be so set apart; and

   (ii) a map or maps showing every such area.

(2) The commission shall proceed with and complete its inquiry and present its reports and recommendations to the Minister within two years after the commencement of this Act, and may present INTERIM reports and recommendations: Provided that Parliament may by resolution extend (if necessary) the time for the completion of the commission's inquiry. All such reports and recommendations shall be laid by the Minister, as soon as possible after the receipt thereof, upon the Tables of both Houses of Parliament.

3. (1) The commission shall consist of not less than five persons, and if any member of the commission die or resign or, owing to absence or any other reason, is unable to act, his place shall be filled by the Governor–General.

(2) The commission may delegate to any of its members the carrying out of any part of an inquiry which under this Act it is appointed to hold and may appoint persons to assist it or to act as assessors thereto or with any members thereof delegated as aforesaid, and may regulate its own procedure.

(3) The reports and recommendations of the majority of the commission shall be deemed to be the reports and recommendations of the commission: Provided that any recommendations of any member who dissents from the majority of the commission shall, if signed by him, be included in any such report aforesaid.

(4) The commission or any member thereof or any person acting as assistant, or assessor, or secretary thereto may enter upon any land for the purposes of its inquiries and obtain thereon the information necessary to prosecute the inquiries. The commission shall without fee or other charge have access to the records and registers relating to land in any public office or in the office of any divisional council or other local authority.

4. (1) For the purposes of establishing any such area as is described in section TWO, the Governor–General may, out of moneys which Parliament may vote for the purpose, acquire any land or interest in land.

(2) In default of agreement with the owners of the land or the holders of interests therein the provisions of the law in force in the Province in which such land or interest in land is situate relating to the expropriation of land for public purposes shall apply and, if in any Province there be no such law, the provisions of Proclamation No. 5 of 1902 of the Transvaal and any amendment thereof shall mutatis mutandis apply.

5. (1) Any person who is a party to any attempted purchase, sale, hire or lease, or to any agreement or transaction which is in contravention of this Act or any regulation made thereunder shall be guilty of an offence and liable on conviction to a fine not exceeding one hundred pounds or, in default of payment, to imprisonment with or without hard labour for a period not exceeding six months, and if the act constituting the offence be a continuing one, the offender shall be liable to a further fine not exceeding five pounds for every day which that act continues.

(2) In the event of such an offence being committed by a company, corporation, or other body of persons (not being a firm or partnership), every director, secretary, or manager of such company, corporation, or body who is within the Union shall be liable to prosecution and punishment and, in the event of any such offence being committed by a firm or partnership, every member of the firm or partnership who is within the Union shall be liable to prosecution and punishment.

6. In so far as the occupation by natives of land outside the scheduled native areas may be affected by this Act, the provisions thereof shall be construed as being in addition to and not in substitution for any law in force at the commencement thereof relating to such occupation; but in the event of a conflict between the provisions of this Act and the provisions of any such law, the provisions of this Act shall, save as is specially provided therein, prevail:

Provided that —

(a) nothing in any such law or in this Act shall be construed
   as restricting the number of natives who, as farm labourers,
   may reside on any farm in the Transvaal;

(b) in any proceedings for a contravention of this Act
   the burden of proving that a native is a farm labourer
   shall be upon the accused;

(c) until Parliament, acting upon the report of the said commission,
   has made other provision, no native resident on any farm
   in the Transvaal or Natal shall be liable to penalties
   or to be removed from such farm under any law,
   if at the commencement of this Act he or the head of his family
   is registered for taxation or other purposes
   in the department of Native Affairs as being resident on such farm,
   nor shall the owner of any such farm be liable to the penalties
   imposed by section FIVE in respect of the occupation of the land
   by such native; but nothing herein contained shall affect any right
   possessed by law by an owner or lessee of a farm to remove
   any native therefrom.

7. (1) Chapter XXXIV of the Orange Free State Law Book and Law No. 4 of 1895 of the Orange Free State shall remain of full force and effect, subject to the modifications and interpretations in this section provided, and sub–section (1) (a) of the next succeeding section shall not apply to the Orange Free State.

(2) Those heads of families, with their families, who are described in article TWENTY of Law No. 4 of 1895 of the Orange Free State shall in the circumstances described in that article be deemed to fall under the provisions of Ordinance No. 7 of 1904 of that Province or of any other law hereafter enacted amending or substituted for that Ordinance.

(3) Whenever in Chapter XXXIV of the Orange Free State Law Book the expressions "lease" and "leasing" are used, those expressions shall be construed as including or referring to an agreement or arrangement whereby a person, in consideration of his being permitted to occupy land, renders or promises to render to any person a share of the produce thereof, or any valuable consideration of any kind whatever other than his own labour or services or the labour or services of any of his family.

8. (1) Nothing in this Act contained shall be construed as, —

(a) preventing the continuation or renewal (until Parliament
   acting upon the report of the said commission has made
   other provision) of any agreement or arrangement lawfully
   entered into and in existence at the commencement of this Act
   which is a hiring or leasing of land as defined in this Act; or

(b) invalidating or affecting in any manner whatever
   any agreement or any other transaction for the purchase of land
   lawfully entered into prior to the commencement of this Act,
   or as prohibiting any person from purchasing at any sale
   held by order of a competent court any land which was hypothecated
   by a mortgage bond passed before the commencement of this Act; or

(c) prohibiting the acquisition at any time of land or interests in land
   by devolution or succession on death, whether under
   a will or on intestacy; or

(d) preventing the due registration in the proper deeds office
   (whenever registration is necessary) of documents giving effect
   to any such agreement, transaction, devolution or succession
   as is in this section mentioned; or

(e) prohibiting any person from claiming, acquiring,
   or holding any such servitude as under Chapter VII,
   of the Irrigation and Conservation of Waters Act, 1912,
   he is specially entitled to claim, acquire, or hold; or

(f) in any way altering the law in force at the commencement of this Act
   relating to the acquisition of rights to minerals,
   precious or base metals or precious stones; or

(g) applying to land within the limits in which a municipal council,
   town council, town board, village management board,
   or health committee or other local authority
   exercises jurisdiction; or

(h) applying to land held at the commencement of the Act by any society
   carrying on, with the approval of the Governor–General,
   educational or missionary work amongst natives; or

(i) prohibiting the acquisition by natives from any person whatever
   of land or interests in land in any township lawfully established
   prior to the commencement of this Act, provided it is
   a condition of the acquisition that no land or interest in land
   in such township has at any time been or shall in future be,
   transferred except to a native or coloured person; or

(j) permitting the alienation of land or its diversion from
   the purposes for which it was set apart if, under section
   ONE HUNDRED AND FORTY–SEVEN of the South African Act, 1909,
   or any other law, such land could not be alienated or so diverted

except under the authority of an Act of Parliament; or

(k) in any way modifying the provisions of any law whereby
   mortgages of or charges over land may be created
   to secure advances out of public moneys for specific purposes
   mentioned in such law and the interest of such advances,
   or whereunder the mortgagee or person having the charge
   may enter and take possession of the land so mortgaged or charged
   except that in any sale of such land in accordance with such law
   the provisions of this Act shall be observed.

(2) Nothing in this Act contained which imposes restrictions upon the acquisition by any person of land or right thereto, interests therein, or servitudes thereover, shall be in force in the Province of the Cape of Good Hope, if and for so long as such person would, by such restrictions, be prevented from acquiring or holding a qualification whereunder he is or may become entitled to be registered as a voter at parliamentary elections in any electoral division in the said Province.

9. The Governor–General may make regulations for preventing the overcrowding of huts and other dwellings in the stadts, native villages and settlements and other places in which natives are congregated in areas not under the jurisdiction of any local authority, the sanitation of such places and for the maintenance of the health of the inhabitants thereof.

10. In this Act, unless inconsistent with the context, —

"scheduled native area" shall mean any area described in the Schedule to this Act;

"native" shall mean any person, male or female, who is a member of an aboriginal race or tribe of Africa; and shall further include any company or other body of persons, corporate or unincorporate, if the persons who have a controlling interest therein are natives;

"interest in land" shall include, in addition to other interest in land, the interest which a mortgagee of, or person having charge over, land acquires under a mortgage bond or charge;

"Minister" shall mean the Minister of Native Affairs;

"farm labourer" shall mean a native who resides on a farm and is bona fide, but not necessarily continuously employed by the owner or lessee thereof in domestic service or in farming operations:

Provided that —

(a) if such native reside on one farm and is employed
   on another farm of the same owner or lessee he shall be deemed
   to have resided, and to have been employed, on one and the same farm;

(b) such native shall not be deemed to be bona fide employed

unless he renders ninety days' service at least
in one calendar year on the farm occupied by the owner or lessee
or on another farm of the owner or lessee and no rent is paid
or valuable consideration of any kind, other than service,
is given by him to the owner or lessee in respect of residence
on such farm or farms.

A person shall be deemed for the purposes of this Act to hire land if, in consideration of his being permitted to occupy that land or any portion thereof —

(a) he pays or promises to pay to any person a rent in money; or

(b) he renders or promises to render to any person a share of the produce
of that land, or any valuable consideration of any kind whatever
other than his own labour or services or the labour or services
of his family.

11. This Act may be cited for all purposes as the Natives' Land Act, 1913.

The foregoing result of a legislative jumble is "the law", and this law, like Alexander the coppersmith, "hath done us much harm". Mr. Sauer carried his Bill less by reason than by sheer force of numbers, and partly by promises which he afterwards broke. Among these broken promises was the definite assurance he gave Parliament that the Bill would be referred to the Select Committee on Native Affairs, so that the Natives, who are not represented in Parliament, their European friends and the Missionary bodies on behalf of the Natives, could be able at the proper time to appear before this committee and state any objection which they might have to the Bill. But when that time came, the Minister flatly refused to refer it to the committee. This change of front is easily explained, because the weight of evidence which could have been given before any Parliamentary committee would have imperilled the passage of the Bill.

As might have been expected, the debate on the Bill created the greatest alarm amongst the native population, for they had followed its course with the keenest interest. Nothing short of a declaration of war against them could have created a similar excitement, although the hope was entertained in some quarters, that a body of men like the Ministerialists in Parliament (a majority of whom are never happier than when attesting the Christian character of their race) would in course of days attend the Holy Communion, remember the 11th Commandment, and do unto others as they would that men should do unto them. Our people, in fact a number of them, said amongst themselves that even Dutchmen sing Psalms — all the Psalms, including the 24th; and, believing as they did that Dutchmen could have no other religion besides the one recommended in the New Testament and preached by the predikants of the Dutch Reformed Church, were prepared to commend their safety to the influence of that sweet and peaceable religion. However, some other Natives, remembering what took place before the South African war, took a different view of these religious incidents. Those Natives, especially of the old Republics, knew that the only dividing fence between the Transvaal Natives and complete slavery was the London Convention; they, therefore, now that the London Convention in fact had ceased to exist, had evil forebodings regarding the average Republican's treatment of the Natives, which was seldom influenced by religious scruples, and they did not hesitate to express their fears.

Personally we must say that if any one had told us at the beginning of 1913, that a majority of members of the Union Parliament were capable of passing a law like the Natives' Land Act, whose object is to prevent the Natives from ever rising above the position of servants to the whites, we would have regarded that person as a fit subject for the lunatic asylum. But the passing of that Act and its operation have rudely forced the fact upon us that the Union Parliament is capable of producing any measure that is subversive of native interests; and that the complete arrest of native progress is the object aimed at in their efforts to include the Protectorates in their Union. Thus we think that their sole reason for seeking to incorporate Basutoland, Swaziland and Bechuanaland is that, when they have definitely eliminated the Imperial factor from South Africa, as they are unmistakably trying to do, they may have a million more slaves than if the Protectorates were excluded.

In this connexion, the realization of the prophecy of an old Basuto became increasingly believable to us. It was to this effect, namely: "That the Imperial Government, after conquering the Boers, handed back to them their old Republics, and a nice little present in the shape of the Cape Colony and Natal — the two English Colonies. That the Boers are now ousting the Englishmen from the public service, and when they have finished with them, they will make a law declaring it a crime for a Native to live in South Africa, unless he is a servant in the employ of a Boer, and that from this it will be just one step to complete slavery." This is being realized, for to-day we have, extended throughout the Union of South Africa, a "Free" State law which makes it illegal for Natives to live on farms except as servants in the employ of Europeans. There is another "Free" State law, under which no Native may live in a municipal area or own property in urban localities. He can only live in town as a servant in the employ of a European. And if the followers of General Hertzog are permitted to dragoon the Union Government into enforcing "Free" State ideals against the Natives of the Union, as they have successfully done under the Natives' Land Act, it will only be a matter of time before we have a Natives' Urban Act enforced throughout South Africa. Then we will have the banner of slavery fully unfurled (of course, under another name) throughout the length and breadth of the land.

When the Natives' Land Bill was before Parliament, meetings were held in many villages and locations in protest against the Ministerial surrender to the Republicans, of which the Bill was the outcome. At the end of March, 1913, the Native National Congress met in Johannesburg, and there a deputation was appointed to go to Capetown and point out to the Government some, at least, of the harm that would follow legislation of the character mapped out in Parliament on February 28 when the Land Act was first announced. They were to urge that such a measure would be exploitation of the cruelest kind, that it would not only interfere with the economic independence of the Natives, but would reduce them for ever to a state of serfdom, and degrade them as nothing has done since slavery was abolished at the Cape. Missionaries also, and European friends of the Natives, did not sit still. Resolution after resolution, telegraphic and other representations, were made to Mr. Sauer, from meetings in various parts of the country, counselling prudence. Even such societies as the Transvaal Landowners, who had long been crying for a measure to separate whites from blacks, and vice versa, urged that the Bill should not be passed during the same session in which it was introduced, that the country should be given an opportunity to digest it, in order, if necessary, to suggest amendments.

The Missionary bodies, too, represent a following of Natives numbering hundreds of thousands of souls, on whose behalf they pleaded for justice. These bodies urged that before passing a law, prohibiting the sale and lease of land to Natives, and expelling squatters from their homes, the Government should provide locations to which the evicted Natives could go. But all these representations made no impression upon the Government, who, instead, preferred to act upon the recommendation of thirteen diminutive petitions (signed in all by 304 Dutchmen in favour of the Bill)* than to be guided by the overwhelming weight of public opinion that was against its passage. Thus it became clear that the Native's position in his own country was not an enviable one, for once a law was made prohibiting the sale of landed property to Natives, it would be almost impossible to get a South African Parliament to amend it.

— * One of these thirteen petitions had only four signatures,
  which was but one better than that of the Tooley Street tailors. —

The Government, which at the beginning assured Parliament of their humane intentions, proceeded to delete the mildest clauses of the measure and to insert some very harsh ones; and almost each time that the Bill came before the House, one or two fresh drastic clauses were added. But it is comforting to note that even Parliament was not entirely satisfied with this, its heroic piece of legislation. Thus Mr. Meyler of Natal did, as only a lawyer could with a view to recasting the Bill, some very useful work in pointing out the possible harm with which the Bill was fraught. We wish that his clever speeches and observations (much of which have come true), might yet be sifted out of the big Parliamentary Reports, and published in a concise little pamphlet.

Sir David Hunter, another member of Natal, expressed himself as follows: —

While every one seemed animated with a desire to do what was right and just to the Natives, there was a feeling that certain of the details of the measure required amendment. He was more than pleased when the Minister closed the debate by a speech in which he seemed to be willing to meet the wishes of those in the House who thought that amendment was required. He could not have imagined that the Bill would develop into the shape into which it had developed, and had he known that so great an alteration would take place in the general effect of the measure from what was foreshadowed by the hon. Minister when he had made that interesting speech on the second reading he (the speaker) could not have conscientiously voted for the second reading. He would have been better pleased had a resolution been taken not to bring in a Bill until the Commission had reported. That was the position he had taken up all through and he would much rather now that the matter should be dealt with in that way. If, however, the Bill was to be pressed through there should be guarantees in it which should allay all suspicion. Anything affecting the native people required to be done gradually and should be placed before them a long time before the change took place. He hoped there would yet be some steps taken to give them a greater sense of security. To give some idea of the feeling in the minds of the Natives he read a letter from a gentleman in Natal, largely interested in the Natives, which had expressed the opinion that the Natives stood uncompromisingly against any change in their present status until the Commission had reported. He hoped the hon. Minister would even yet endeavour to do something to meet their views.

Mr. C. H. Haggar (Roodepoort) said that from the point of those who had worked successfully in turning the uncivilized man into the civilized man the Bill was bound to be a failure. It was necessary not only to have legislation theoretically just, but also practically right and good. But there were many who felt that so far from the effect of that Bill being good it would be disastrous to a very large extent. The great sin which they had been committing was that they had always been legislating ahead of the people, and there had not been sufficient preparation for the changes which were proposed in that Bill; the Natives were not ready for it. The hon. member for Victoria West had said that there was a disposition in certain directions to repress the Natives. He (the speaker) believed that there was a feeling that white men had some divine right to the labour of the black, that the black people were to be hewers of wood and drawers of water, and he wanted to say that while men were obsessed with that feeling they would never be able to legislate fairly. They had no more divine right to the labour of the black people than they had to the labour of the white. To his mind the great point was, should their policy be one of repression or a policy of inspiration? They had inspired the Natives to a certain extent, but no sooner had they created an appetite than they had told the Natives they should go no further. Their policy was the policy of Tantalus. That Bill would create a feeling of insecurity in the minds of the Natives. There were those who said that if the Natives would not submit to dictation they should be wiped out. But that should not be their policy. They must cease the policy of repression and let it be one of wide inspiration.

But alas! these and similar pleadings had about as much effect upon the Ministerial steam-roller as the proverbial water on a duck's back. With a rush the Natives' Land Bill was dispatched from the Lower House to the Senate, adopted hurriedly by the Senate, returned to the Lower House, and went at the same pace to Government House, and there receiving the Governor-General's signature, it immediately became law. As regards the Governor-General's signature, His Excellency, if Ministers are to be believed, was ready to sign the Bill (or rather signified his intention of doing so) long before it was introduced into Parliament. This excited haste suggests grave misgivings as to the character of the Bill. Why all the hurry and scurry, and why the Governor-General's approval in advance? Other Bills are passed and approved by the Governor, yet they do not come into operation until some given day — the beginning of the next calendar year, or of the next financial year. But the Natives' Land Act became law and was operating as soon as it could be promulgated.

After desperately protesting, with individual members of Parliament and with Cabinet Ministers, and getting nothing for their pains, the delegates from the Native Congress wrote Lord Gladstone, from an office about two hundred yards distant from Government House, requesting His Excellency to withhold his assent to the Natives' Land Bill until the people mostly concerned (i.e. the Natives) had had a chance of making known to His Majesty the King their objection to the measure. His Excellency replied that such a course "was not within his constitutional functions." Thereby the die was cast, and the mandate went forth that the land laws of the Orange "Free" State, which is commonly known as "the Only Slave State", shall be the laws of the whole Union of South Africa. The worst feature in the case is the fact that, even with the Governments of the late Republics, the Presidents always had the power to exempt some Natives from the operation of those laws, and that prerogative had been liberally used by successive Presidents. Now, however, without a President, and with the prerogative of the King (by the exercise of which the evils of such a law could have been averted) disowned by the King's own Ministers on the spot, God in the heavens alone knows what will become of the hapless, because voteless, Natives, who are without a President, "without a King", and with a Governor-General without constitutional functions, under task-masters whose national traditions are to enslave the dark races.

Chapter IV One Night with the Fugitives

Es ist unkoeniglich zu weinen — ach,
Und hier nicht weinen ist unvaeterlich.
    Schiller.

"Pray that your flight be not in winter," said Jesus Christ; but it was only during the winter of 1913 that the full significance of this New Testament passage was revealed to us. We left Kimberley by the early morning train during the first week in July, on a tour of observation regarding the operation of the Natives' Land Act; and we arrived at Bloemhof, in Transvaal, at about noon. On the River Diggings there were no actual cases representing the effects of the Act, but traces of these effects were everywhere manifest. Some fugitives of the Natives' Land Act had crossed the river in full flight. The fact that they reached the diggings a fortnight before our visit would seem to show that while the debates were proceeding in Parliament some farmers already viewed with eager eyes the impending opportunity for at once making slaves of their tenants and appropriating their stock; for, acting on the powers conferred on them by an Act signed by Lord Gladstone, so lately as June 16, they had during that very week (probably a couple of days after, and in some cases, it would seem, a couple of days before the actual signing of the Bill) approached their tenants with stories about a new Act which makes it criminal for any one to have black tenants and lawful to have black servants. Few of these Natives, of course, would object to be servants, especially if the white man is worth working for, but this is where the shoe pinches: one of the conditions is that the black man's (that is the servant's) cattle shall henceforth work for the landlord free of charge. Then the Natives would decide to leave the farm rather than make the landlord a present of all their life's savings, and some of them had passed through the diggings in search of a place in the Transvaal. But the higher up they went the more gloomy was their prospect as the news about the new law was now penetrating every part of the country.

One farmer met a wandering native family in the town of Bloemhof a week before our visit. He was willing to employ the Native and many more homeless families as follows: A monthly wage of 2 Pounds 10s. for each such family, the husband working in the fields, the wife in the house, with an additional 10s. a month for each son, and 5s. for each daughter, but on condition that the Native's cattle were also handed over to work for him. It must be clearly understood, we are told that the Dutchman added, that occasionally the Native would have to leave his family at work on the farm, and go out with his wagon and his oxen to earn money whenever and wherever he was told to go, in order that the master may be enabled to pay the stipulated wage. The Natives were at first inclined to laugh at the idea of working for a master with their families and goods and chattels, and then to have the additional pleasure of paying their own small wages, besides bringing money to pay the "Baas" for employing them. But the Dutchman's serious demeanour told them that his suggestion was "no joke". He himself had for some time been in need of a native cattle owner, to assist him as transport rider between Bloemhof, Mooifontein, London, and other diggings, in return for the occupation and cultivation of some of his waste lands in the district, but that was now illegal. He could only "employ" them; but, as he had no money to pay wages, their cattle would have to go out and earn it for him. Had they not heard of the law before? he inquired. Of course they had; in fact that is why they left the other place, but as they thought that it was but a "Free" State law, they took the anomalous situation for one of the multifarious aspects of the freedom of the "Free" State whence they came; they had scarcely thought that the Transvaal was similarly afflicted.

Needless to say the Natives did not see their way to agree with such a one–sided bargain. They moved up country, but only to find the next farmer offering the same terms, however, with a good many more disturbing details — and the next farmer and the next — so that after this native farmer had wandered from farm to farm, occasionally getting into trouble for travelling with unknown stock, "across my ground without my permission", and at times escaping arrest for he knew not what, and further, being abused for the crimes of having a black skin and no master, he sold some of his stock along the way, beside losing many which died of cold and starvation; and after thus having lost much of his substance, he eventually worked his way back to Bloemhof with the remainder, sold them for anything they could fetch, and went to work for a digger.

The experience of another native sufferer was similar to the above, except that instead of working for a digger he sold his stock for a mere bagatelle, and left with his family by the Johannesburg night train for an unknown destination. More native families crossed the river and went inland during the previous week, and as nothing had since been heard of them, it would seem that they were still wandering somewhere, and incidentally becoming well versed in the law that was responsible for their compulsory unsettlement.

Well, we knew that this law was as harsh as its instigators were callous, and we knew that it would, if passed, render many poor people homeless, but it must be confessed that we were scarcely prepared for such a rapid and widespread crash as it caused in the lives of the Natives in this neighbourhood. We left our luggage the next morning with the local Mission School teacher, and crossed the river to find out some more about this wonderful law of extermination. It was about 10 a.m. when we landed on the south bank of the Vaal River — the picturesque Vaal River, upon whose banks a hundred miles farther west we spent the best and happiest days of our boyhood. It was interesting to walk on one portion of the banks of that beautiful river — a portion which we had never traversed except as an infant in mother's arms more than thirty years before. How the subsequent happy days at Barkly West, so long past, came crowding upon our memory! — days when there were no railways, no bridges, and no system of irrigation. In rainy seasons, which at that time were far more regular and certain, the river used to overflow its high banks and flood the surrounding valleys to such an extent, that no punt could carry the wagons across. Thereby the transport service used to be hung up, and numbers of wagons would congregate for weeks on both sides of the river until the floods subsided. At such times the price of fresh milk used to mount up to 1s. per pint. There being next to no competition, we boys had a monopoly over the milk trade. We recalled the number of haversacks full of bottles of milk we youngsters often carried to those wagons, how we returned with empty bottles and with just that number of shillings. Mother and our elder brothers had leather bags full of gold and did not care for the "boy's money"; and unlike the boys of the neighbouring village, having no sisters of our own, we gave away some of our money to fair cousins, and jingled the rest in our pockets. We had been told from boyhood that sweets were injurious to the teeth, and so spurning these delights we had hardly any use for money, for all we wanted to eat, drink and wear was at hand in plenty. We could then get six or eight shillings every morning from the pastime of washing that number of bottles, filling them with fresh milk and carrying them down to the wagons; there was always such an abundance of the liquid that our shepherd's hunting dog could not possibly miss what we took, for while the flocks were feeding on the luscious buds of the haak–doorns and the orange–coloured blossoms of the rich mimosa and other wild vegetation that abounded on the banks of the Vaal River, the cows, similarly engaged, were gathering more and more milk.

The gods are cruel, and one of their cruellest acts of omission was that of giving us no hint that in very much less than a quarter of a century all those hundreds of heads of cattle, and sheep and horses belonging to the family would vanish like a morning mist, and that we ourselves would live to pay 30s. per month for a daily supply of this same precious fluid, and in very limited quantities. They might have warned us that Englishmen would agree with Dutchmen to make it unlawful for black men to keep milch cows of their own on the banks of that river, and gradually have prepared us for the shock.

Crossing the river from the Transvaal side brings one into the Province of the Orange "Free" State, in which, in the adjoining division of Boshof, we were born thirty–six years back. We remember the name of the farm, but not having been in this neighbourhood since infancy, we could not tell its whereabouts, nor could we say whether the present owner was a Dutchman, his lawyer, or a Hebrew merchant; one thing we do know, however: it is that even if we had the money and the owner was willing to sell the spot upon which we first saw the light of day and breathed the pure air of heaven, the sale would be followed with a fine of one hundred pounds. The law of the country forbids the sale of land to a Native. Russia is one of the most abused countries in the world, but it is extremely doubtful if the statute book of that Empire contains a law debarring the peasant from purchasing the land whereon he was born, or from building a home wherein he might end his days.

At this time we felt something rising from our heels along our back, gripping us in a spasm, as we were cycling along; a needlelike pang, too, pierced our heart with a sharp thrill. What was it? We remembered feeling something nearly like it when our father died eighteen years ago; but at that time our physical organs were fresh and grief was easily thrown off in tears, but then we lived in a happy South Africa that was full of pleasant anticipations, and now — what changes for the worse have we undergone! For to crown all our calamities, South Africa has by law ceased to be the home of any of her native children whose skins are dyed with a pigment that does not conform with the regulation hue.

We are told to forgive our enemies and not to let the sun go down upon our wrath, so we breathe the prayer that peace may be to the white races, and that they, including our present persecutors of the Union Parliament, may never live to find themselves deprived of all occupation and property rights in their native country as is now the case with the Native. History does not tell us of any other continent where the Bantu lived besides Africa, and if this systematic ill–treatment of the Natives by the colonists is to be the guiding principle of Europe's scramble for Africa, slavery is our only alternative; for now it is only as serfs that the Natives are legally entitled to live here. Is it to be thought that God is using the South African Parliament to hound us out of our ancestral homes in order to quicken our pace heavenward? But go from where to heaven? In the beginning, we are told, God created heaven and earth, and peopled the earth, for people do not shoot up to heaven from nowhere. They must have had an earthly home. Enoch, Melchizedek, Elijah, and other saints, came to heaven from earth. God did not say to the Israelites in their bondage: "Cheer up, boys; bear it all in good part for I have bright mansions on high awaiting you all." But he said: "I have surely seen the affliction of my people which are in Egypt, and have heard their cry by reason of their taskmasters; for I know their sorrows, and I am come down to bring them out of the hands of the Egyptians, and to bring them up out of that land unto a good land and a large, unto a land flowing with milk and honey." And He used Moses to carry out the promise He made to their ancestor Abraham in Canaan, that "unto thy seed will I give this land." It is to be hoped that in the Boer churches, entrance to which is barred against coloured people during divine service, they also read the Pentateuch.

It is doubtful if we ever thought so much on a single bicycle ride as we did on this journey; however, the sight of a policeman ahead of us disturbed these meditations and gave place to thoughts of quite another kind, for — we had no pass. Dutchmen, Englishmen, Jews, Germans, and other foreigners may roam the "Free" State without permission — but not Natives. To us it would mean a fine and imprisonment to be without a pass. The "pass" law was first instituted to check the movement of livestock over sparsely populated areas. In a sense it was a wise provision, in that it served to identify the livestock which one happened to be driving along the high road, to prove the bona fides of the driver and his title to the stock. Although white men still steal large droves of horses in Basutoland and sell them in Natal or in East Griqualand, they, of course, are not required to carry any passes. These white horse–thieves, to escape the clutches of the police, employ Natives to go and sell the stolen stock and write the passes for these Natives, forging the names of Magistrates and Justices of the Peace. Such native thieves in some instances ceasing to be hirelings in the criminal business, trade on their own, but it is not clear what purpose it is intended to serve by subjecting native pedestrians to the degrading requirement of carrying passes when they are not in charge of any stock.

In a few moments the policeman was before us and we alighted in presence of the representative of the law, with our feet on the accursed soil of the district in which we were born. The policeman stopped. By his looks and his familiar "Dag jong" we noticed that the policeman was Dutch, and the embodiment of affability. He spoke and we were glad to notice that he had no intention of dragging an innocent man to prison. We were many miles from the nearest police station, and in such a case one is generally able to gather the real views of the man on patrol, as distinct from the written code of his office, but our friend was becoming very companionable. Naturally we asked him about the operation of the plague law. He was a Transvaaler, he said, and he knew that Kafirs were inferior beings, but they had rights, and were always left in undisturbed possession of their property when Paul Kruger was alive. "The poor devils must be sorry now," he said, "that they ever sang `God save the Queen' when the British troops came into the Transvaal, for I have seen, in the course of my duties, that a Kafir's life nowadays was not worth a ——, and I believe that no man regretted the change of flags now more than the Kafirs of Transvaal." This information was superfluous, for personal contact with the Natives of Transvaal had convinced us of the fact. They say it is only the criminal who has any reason to rejoice over the presence of the Union Jack, because in his case the cat–o'–nine–tails, except for very serious crimes, has been abolished.

"Some of the poor creatures," continued the policeman, "I knew to be fairly comfortable, if not rich, and they enjoyed the possession of their stock, living in many instances just like Dutchmen. Many of these are now being forced to leave their homes. Cycling along this road you will meet several of them in search of new homes, and if ever there was a fool's errand, it is that of a Kafir trying to find a new home for his stock and family just now."

43

"And what do you think, Baas Officer, must eventually be the lot of a people under such unfortunate circumstances?" we asked.

"I think," said the policeman, "that it must serve them right. They had no business to hanker after British rule, to cheat and plot with the enemies of their Republic for the overthrow of their Government. Why did they not assist the forces of their Republic during the war instead of supplying the English with scouts and intelligence? Oom Paul would not have died of a broken heart and he would still be there to protect them. Serve them right, I say."

So saying he spurred his horse, which showed a clean pair of hoofs. He left us rather abruptly, for we were about to ask why we, too, of Natal and the Cape were suffering, for we, being originally British subjects, never "cheated and plotted with the enemies of our Colonies", but he was gone and left us still cogitating by the roadside.

Proceeding on our journey we next came upon a native trek and heard the same old story of prosperity on a Dutch farm: they had raised an average 800 bags of grain each season, which, with the increase of stock and sale of wool, gave a steady income of about 150 Pounds per year after the farmer had taken his share. There were gossipy rumours about somebody having met some one who said that some one else had overheard a conversation between the Baas and somebody else, to the effect that the Kafirs were getting too rich on his property. This much involved tale incidentally conveys the idea that the Baas was himself getting too rich on his farm. For the Native provides his own seed, his own cattle, his own labour for the ploughing, the weeding and the reaping, and after bagging his grain he calls in the landlord to receive his share, which is fifty per cent of the entire crop.

All had gone well till the previous week when the Baas came to the native tenants with the story that a new law had been passed under which "all my oxen and cows must belong to him, and my family to work for 2 Pounds a month, failing which he gave me four days to leave the farm."

We passed several farm–houses along the road, where all appeared pretty tranquil as we went along, until the evening which we spent in the open country, somewhere near the boundaries of the Hoopstad and Boshof districts; here a regular circus had gathered. By a "circus" we mean the meeting of groups of families, moving to every point of the compass, and all bivouacked at this point in the open country where we were passing. It was heartrending to listen to the tales of their cruel experiences derived from the rigour of the Natives' Land Act. Some of their cattle had perished on the journey, from poverty and lack of fodder, and the native owners ran a serious risk of imprisonment for travelling with dying stock. The experience of one of these evicted tenants is typical of the rest, and illustrates the cases of several we met in other parts of the country.

Kgobadi, for instance, had received a message describing the eviction of his father–in–law in the Transvaal Province, without notice, because he had refused to place his stock, his family, and his person at the disposal of his former landlord, who now refuses to let him remain on his farm except on these conditions. The father–in–law asked that Kgobadi should try and secure a place for him in the much dreaded "Free" State as the Transvaal had suddenly become uninhabitable to Natives who cannot become servants; but "greedy folk hae lang airms", and Kgobadi himself was proceeding with his family and his belongings in a wagon, to inform his people–in–law of his own eviction, without notice, in the "Free" State, for a similar reason to that which sent his father–in–law adrift. The Baas had exacted from him the services of himself, his wife and his oxen, for wages of 30s. a month, whereas Kgobadi had been making over 100 Pounds a year, besides retaining the services of his wife and of his cattle for himself. When he refused the extortionate terms the Baas retaliated with a Dutch note, dated the 30th day of June, 1913, which ordered him to "betake himself from the farm of the undersigned, by sunset of the same day, failing which his stock would be seized and impounded, and himself handed over to the authorities for trespassing on the farm."

A drowning man catches at every straw, and so we were again and again appealed to for advice by these sorely afflicted people. To those who were not yet evicted we counselled patience and submission to the absurd terms, pending an appeal to a higher authority than the South African Parliament and finally to His Majesty the King who, we believed, would certainly disapprove of all that we saw on that day had it been brought to his notice. As for those who were already evicted, as a Bechuana we could not help thanking God that Bechuanaland (on the western boundary of this quasi–British Republic) was still entirely British. In the early days it was the base of David Livingstone's activities and peaceful mission against the Portuguese and Arab slave trade. We suggested that they might negotiate the numerous restrictions against the transfer of cattle from the Western Transvaal and seek an asylum in Bechuanaland. We wondered what consolation we could give to these roving wanderers if the whole of Bechuanaland were under the jurisdiction of the relentless Union Parliament.

It was cold that afternoon as we cycled into the "Free" State from Transvaal, and towards evening the southern winds rose. A cutting blizzard raged during the night, and native mothers evicted from their homes shivered with their babies by their sides. When we saw on that night the teeth of the little children clattering through the cold, we thought of our own little ones in their Kimberley home of an evening after gambolling in their winter frocks with their schoolmates, and we wondered what these little mites had done that a home should suddenly become to them a thing of the past.

Kgobadi's goats had been to kid when he trekked from his farm; but the kids, which in halcyon times represented the interest on his capital, were now one by one dying as fast as they were born and left by the roadside for the jackals and vultures to feast upon.

This visitation was not confined to Kgobadi's stock, Mrs. Kgobadi carried a sick baby when the eviction took place, and she had to transfer her darling from the cottage to the jolting ox–wagon in which they left the farm. Two days out the little one began to sink as the result of privation and exposure on the road, and the night before we met them its little soul was released from its earthly bonds. The death of the child added a fresh perplexity to the stricken parents. They had no right or title to the farm lands through which they trekked: they must keep to the public roads — the only places in the country open to the outcasts if they are possessed of a travelling permit. The deceased child had to be buried, but where, when, and how?

This young wandering family decided to dig a grave under cover of the darkness of that night, when no one was looking, and in that crude manner the dead child was interred — and interred amid fear and trembling, as well as the throbs of a torturing anguish, in a stolen grave, lest the proprietor of the spot, or any of his servants, should surprise them in the act. Even criminals dropping straight from the gallows have an undisputed claim to six feet of ground on which to rest their criminal remains, but under the cruel operation of the Natives' Land Act little children, whose only crime is that God did not make them white, are sometimes denied that right in their ancestral home.

Numerous details narrated by these victims of an Act of Parliament kept us awake all that night, and by next morning we were glad enough to hear no more of the sickening procedure of extermination voluntarily instituted by the South African Parliament. We had spent a hideous night under a bitterly cold sky, conditions to which hundreds of our unfortunate countrymen and countrywomen in various parts of the country are condemned by the provisions of this Parliamentary land plague. At five o'clock in the morning the cold seemed to redouble its energies; and never before did we so fully appreciate the Master's saying: "But pray ye that your flight be not in the winter."

Chapter V Another Night with the Sufferers

Heureux ceux qui sont morts dans le calme des soirs,
Avant ces jours affreux de carnage et de haine!
Ils se sont endormis, le coeur rempli d'espoirs,
Dans un reve d'amour et de concorde humaine!

Ils n'ont pas entendu la sinistre remeur
Qui monte des hameaux consumes par la flamme,
Ni les cris des enfants et des vierges en pleurs,
Ni le gemissement des vieillards et des femmes!
      Heureux les morts!
        Maurice Kufferath.

We parted sadly from these unfortunate nomads of an ungrateful and inhospitable country, after advising them to trek from the Union into the arid deserts of Bechuanaland. In our advice we laid special stress upon the costliness of such an expedition as theirs and upon the many and varying regulations to be complied with, on such a trek, through the Western Transvaal. But, cost whatever it may, they, like ourselves, understood that as the law stood they would be better off and safer beyond the boundaries of the Union.

From here we worked our way into the Hoopstad district. There we saw some Natives who were, as it were, on pins and needles, their landlords having given them a few days in which to consider the advisability of either accepting the new conditions or leaving their houses. Our advice to these tenants was to accept, for the time being, any terms offered by their landlords, pending an appeal to His Majesty the King; we also passed through a few farms where the white farmers were visibly sympathetic towards the harried Natives. Some of the white farmers were accepting Natives as tenants on their farms in defiance of the law. We naturally thanked these for their humanity and went our way, promising never to disclose their magnanimity to the Government officials. "What has suddenly happened?" one of these landlords asked. "We were living so nicely with your people, and why should the law unsettle them in this manner?"

We may here mention that a fortnight later we were in General Botha's constituency in the Transvaal. A few days before we arrived there a meeting of white farmers was held at one of the Dutch farm–houses at which it was resolved to take the fullest advantage of the new law, which had placed the entire native population in the hands of the farmers. It was further resolved that a Kafir who refused to become a servant should at once be consigned to the road.

A similar resolution was passed at another meeting of landlords at another place. Part of the proceedings of this meeting was reported in some, though not all, of the Dutch newspapers. Without breaking our promise not to disclose any names of landlords who felt it a duty to resist injustice, even though it bears the garb of law, we will mention Mr. X., a Boer farmer, of the farm ——, near Thingamejig, between the town of —— and the river ——. He protested at the meeting, stating that the Transvaalers were not compelled to turn the Natives out, and that they were only debarred from taking any new native tenants; that it was wicked to expel a Kafir from the farm for no reason whatever, and so make him homeless, since he could not, if evicted, go either to another farm or back to his old place. For expressing his views so frankly Mr. X. was threatened by his compatriots with physical violence! His opponents also said that, if he continued to harbour Kafirs on his farm as tenants, they would hold him responsible for any stock that they might lose. The incidents of the meeting were related to the Natives by Mr. X. himself. He told the Natives, further, that he would go to the expense of fencing his farm with the Natives inside, so that they may be out of the reach of his infuriated neighbours.

We spent the next night in some native huts on a farm in the district of Hoopstad. On that occasion we met a man who had had a month's notice to leave his farm, and was going from farm to farm in search of a new place. He had heard alarming stories about evictions wherever he went. During that evening we were treated to some more pitiful stories concerning the atrocities of the wretched land Act. Many native wanderers had actually passed that farm during the preceding few days, trudging aimlessly from place to place in search of some farmer who might give them a shelter. At first they thought the stories about a new law were inventions or exaggerations, but their own desperate straits and the prevailing native dislocation soon taught them otherwise.

The similarity in the experiences of the sufferers would make monotonous reading if given individually, but there are instances here and there which give variety to the painful record, and these should yield the utmost satisfaction to the promoters of the Act, in proving to them the fell measure of their achievement. One example of these experiences was that of a white farmer who had induced a thrifty Native in another district to come and farm on his estate. The contract was duly executed about the end of May, 1913. It was agreed that the Native should move over to the new place after gathering his crops and sharing them with his old landlord, which he did in the third week in June. On his arrival, however, the new landlord's attitude towards him aroused his suspicions; his suspicions were confirmed when, after some hesitation, the landlord told him that their contract was illegal. Having already left his old place the legal embargo was also against his return there, and so his only course was to leave that place and wander about with his stock and family. They went in the direction of Kroonstad, and they have not been heard of since.

The next example is that of the oldest man in the "Free" State. He had been evicted (so we were told during that evening on the farm) along with his aged wife, his grey–headed children, the children's children and grandchildren. We may here add that we read a confirmation of this case in the English weekly newspaper of Harrismith. The paper's reference to this case will also illustrate the easy manner in which these outrageous evictions are reported in white newspapers. There is no reference to the sinister undercurrent and hardships attending these evictions. The paper in question, the `Harrismith Chronicle', simply says: —

==

AN ANCIENT COUPLE

A venerable Native whose age is no less than 119 years, accompanied by his wife, aged 98, and a son who is approaching 80, left Harrismith on Tuesday by train for Volksrust. The old man acquired some property in the Transvaal, and is leaving this district to start a new home with as much interest in the venture as if he were a stripling of twenty. The old lady had to be carried to the train, but the old man walked fairly firmly. The aged couple were the centre of much kindly attraction, and were made as comfortable as possible for their journey by the railway officials. It is difficult to realize in these days of rapid change that in the departure from the "Free" State of this venerable party we are losing from our midst a man who was born in 1794, and has lived in no less than three centuries of time. Good luck to them both; may they still live long and prosper!

Now, as a matter of fact, this "ancient couple" had not left the "Free" State of their own free will. Their stock had been expelled from their grazing areas, and they were told that they could only continue to graze if the centenarian tenant agreed to supply a certain number of labourers to work on the landowner's farm and with his sons ceased to do any ploughing as tenants. This system of sharing the crops has been followed ever since the Boers planted themselves in the "Free" State, and the family had had no other means of support. Happily the aid of Providence in the case of this "ancient couple" was speedy, as the old people quickly found an asylum on the farm of Mr. P. ka I. Seme, a native solicitor in the Transvaal.

At the same place on the same evening we were told of a conversation between a well–known Dutchman and a Native. "The object of this law," said the Burgher, "is to goad the Natives into rebellion, so that the Government may legally confiscate what little ground was left to them, and hand over the dispossessed Kafirs and their families to work for the farmers, just for their food." The policy of goading the Natives into rebellion is not wholly foreign to Colonial policy; but the horrible cruelty to which live stock is exposed under the new Act is altogether a new departure. King Solomon says, "The righteous man regardeth the life of his beast, but the tender mercies of the wicked are cruel"; but there is a Government of professed Bible readers who, in defiance of all Scriptural precepts, pass a law which penalizes a section of the community along with their oxen, sheep, goats, horses and donkeys on account of the colour of their owners. The penalty clause (Section 5) imposes a fine of 100 Pounds on a landowner who accommodates a Native on his farm; and if after the fine is paid the Native leaves his stock on the farm to go and look for a fresh place, there will be an additional fine of 5 Pounds for every day that the Native's cattle remain on that farm. They must take the road immediately and be kept moving day and night until they die of starvation, or until the owner (who is debarred, by Section 1, from purchasing a pasturage for his cattle) disposes of them to a white man.

Such cruelty to dumb animals is as unwarranted as it is unprecedented. It reads cruel enough on paper, but we wish that the reader had accompanied us on one journey, say, during the cold snap in the first week in August, when we travelled from Potchefstroom to Vereeniging, and seen the flocks of those evicted Natives that we met. We frequently met those roving pariahs, with their hungry cattle, and wondered if the animals were not more deserving of pity than their owners. It may be the cattle's misfortune that they have a black owner, but it is certainly not their fault, for sheep have no choice in the selection of a colour for their owners, and no cows or goats are ever asked to decide if the black boy who milks them shall be their owner, or but a herd in the employ of a white man; so why should they be starved on account of the colour of their owners? We knew of a law to prevent cruelty to animals, but had never thought that we should live to meet in one day so many dumb creatures making silent appeals to Heaven for protection against the law. "What man has nerve to do, man has not nerve to see", and oh! if those gifted Parliamentarians could have been mustered here to witness the wretched results of one of their fine days' work for a fine day's pay! But "they bind heavy burdens and grievous to be borne", then draw their Parliamentary emoluments and retire to the quiet of their comfortable homes, to enjoy more rest than is due to toilers who have served both God and humanity.

During this same night in Hoopstad district we were also told of the visit of a Dutch farmer in the middle of June, 1913, to his native tenants. One of the Natives — named Kgabale — was rather old. His two sons are delving in the gold mines of Johannesburg, and return home each spring time to help the old man and their two young sisters to do the ploughing. The daughters tend the fields and Kgabale looks after the stock. By this means they have been enabled to lead a respectable life and to pay the landowner fifty per cent. of the produce every year, besides the taxes levied by the Government on Natives. Three weeks before our visit, the farmer came to cancel Kgabale's verbal contract with him and to turn the family into unpaid servants, in return for the privilege of squatting on his farm. As Kgabale himself was too old to work, the farmer demanded of him that his two sons should return immediately from Johannesburg to render manual service on his farm, failing which, the old man should forthwith betake himself from the place. He gave Kgabale seven days to deliver his two sons.

Naturally this decision came upon Kgabale and his daughters like a bolt from the blue. The poor old man wandered from place to place, trying to find some one — and it took him two days to do so — who could write, so as to dictate a letter to his sons in Johannesburg, informing them of what had happened. The week expired before he could get a reply from Johannesburg. The landlord, in a very abusive mood, again demanded the instant arrival of his two sons from Johannesburg, to commence work at the farm–house the very next morning. Kgabale spent the whole night praying that at least one of his sons might come. By daybreak next morning no answer had arrived, and the Dutchman came and set fire to the old man's houses, and ordered him then and there to quit the farm. It was a sad sight to see the feeble old man, his aged wife and his daughters driven in this way from a place which they had regarded as their home. In the ordinary course, such a calamity could have been made more tolerable by moving to the next farm and there await the arrival and advice of his sons; but now, under the Natives' Land Act, no sympathetic landowner would be permitted to shelter them for a single day. So Kgabale was said to have gone in the direction of Klerksdorp.

One of the sons arrived a week after the catastrophe. He found his old home in ruins, and that his aged parents and their children had become victims of the turpitude of an Act of Parliament. The son went in search of his relatives across the Vaal, but it was not known if they succeeded in finding the refuge which the law had made unlawful.

Among the squatters on the same farm as Kgabale was a widow named Maria. Her husband in his lifetime had lived as a tenant on the farm, ploughing in shares until his death. After his death Maria kept on the contract and made a fair living. Her son and daughter, aged fourteen and sixteen respectively, took turns at herding her cattle and assisting the mother in other ways. During the ploughing season, they hired assistance to till the fields, but they themselves tended and reaped the harvest and delivered 50 per cent of the produce to the landowner. Such were the conditions on which she was allowed to live on the farm. Maria, being a widow, and her son being but a youth, it was hoped that the landlord would propose reasonable terms for her; but instead, his proposal was that she should dispose of her stock and indenture her children to him. This sinister proposal makes it evident that farmers not only expect Natives to render them free labour, but they actually wish the Natives to breed slaves for them. Maria found it difficult to comply with her landlord's demand, and as she had no husband, from whom labour could be exacted, the Dutchman ordered her to "clear out, and," he added with an oath, "you must get another man before you reach your next place of abode, as the law will not permit you to stay there till you have a man to work for the Baas." Having given this counsel the landlord is said to have set fire to Maria's thatched cottage, and as the chilly south–easter blew the smoke of her burning home towards the north–west, Maria, with her bedclothes on her head, and on the heads of her son and daughter, and carrying her three–year–old boy tied to her back, walked off from the farm, driving her cows before her. In parting from the endeared associations of their late home, for one blank and unknown, the children were weeping bitterly. Nor has any news of the fate of this family been received since they were forced out on this perilous adventure.

Chapter VI Our Indebtedness to White Women

O woman! in our hours of ease
Uncertain, coy, and hard to please,
 And variable as the shade
By the light quivering aspen made;
When pain and anguish wring the brow,
 A ministering angel thou.
          Scott.

Some farmers (unfortunately too few) who had at first intended to change the status of their native tenants, had been obliged to abandon the idea owing to the determined opposition of their wives. One such case was particularly interesting. Thus, at Dashfontein, the wife of a Dutch farmer, a Mr. V., on whose property some native families were squatting, got up, one morning, and found the kitchen–maid very disagreeable. The morning coffee had been made right enough, but the maid's "Morre, Nooi" (Good morning, ma'am) was rather sullen and almost bordering on insolence. She did her scullery work as usual, but did not seem to care, that morning, about wasting time inquiring how baby slept, and if Nonnie had got rid of her neuralgia, and so on. She spoke only when spoken to and answered mainly in monosyllables. Mrs. V. was perplexed.

"What is the matter, Anna?" she asked.

"Nothing, Nooi," replied Anna curtly.

Mrs. V. tried some of her witty jokes, but they seemed to be wasted on Anna. After jesting with the servant had failed, scolding was next tried, but nothing seemed to bring back the girl's usual cheerfulness. "Oh, Anna," said the mistress at length, "you make me think of the olden days, when such disagreeable whims on the part of frowning maids used to be cured by ——"

Anna was evidently not listening, and, if she had heard the mistress, she did not care two straws (or one straw for that matter) what cures Mrs. V.'s great–grandmother had prescribed for sullen servant girls. In fact, Anna had become a wild Kafir, for though she went about her work in silence, her face bore an expression which seemed to speak louder than her mouth could have done. She was clearly engaged in serious thought. The mistress tried to dismiss from her mind the inexplicable attitude of her servant, but the frowning look on Anna's face made the attempts unsuccessful. The fact that when Anna went home, the previous night, she was happiness personified, did not decrease Mrs. V.'s perplexity.

"There must be something wrong," Mrs. V. concluded, after vainly trying ruse after ruse to get a smile out of her servant girl. "Something is amiss. I wonder if one of those well–dressed Kafirs from Potchefstroom had been prowling about the farm and instilling in Anna's simple mind all kinds of silly notions, about town flirts and black dandies, silk dresses in Potchefstroom and similar vuilgoed (rubbish). And if a town Kafir is going to marry Anna, where on earth am I going to get a reliable servant to whom I could securely entrust my home when I have occasion to go to town or to the seaside on a shorter or longer vacation? Who could cook and attend to my husband's and children's peculiar wants, if Anna is going to leave us? It seems certain that Anna's heart is not on the farm," she said to herself. "It was there right enough when she went home last night, but it is clear that some one has stolen it during the night. Anna is helplessly lovesick. I must find out who it is. The swain must be found and induced to come and join, or supervise, our squatters. We cannot let him take her away, for what will the homestead be without Anna? I was looking forward to her marrying on the farm and giving her a superior cottage so that other Kafir girls may see how profitable it is to be good. Anna leaving the farm, O, nee wat! (Oh, no). We must find out who it is; but wait, there is old Gert (her father) coming, with old Jan (her uncle). I must find out from them who had been intruding into the company of their daughters last night. I should warn them to be on the alert lest Anna elopes to Potchefstroom with somebody, probably to take the train and go farther — to Johannesburg or Kimberley, as did Klein Mietje, whom I had hoped to train as our housemaid ——"

"Good morning, Auta Gert, how is Mietje and the kleintjes (little ones)?"

Auta Gert's demeanour was a greater puzzle to Mrs. V. than his daughter's when he replied, "So, so."

Mrs. V. (between horns of the same dilemma): "And you, Auta Jan?"

"Ja, Missus," replied Jan.

Mrs. V.'s perplexity was intense, for it became evident that the two Natives were there as a deputation, charged with some grave mission. Before she uttered another word the two Natives asked for an interview.

"Not to waste much time, Missus," began old Gert, "a thunderbolt has burst on the native settlement on the farm, and Dashfontein is no longer a home to us ——"

"No longer a home!" exclaimed Mrs. V. "I hope you idiotic Kafirs are not going to be so foolhardy as to leave me, leave the Baas, and leave the farm upon which your fathers and mothers lie buried. Do not you know that during this very week numbers of Natives have been calling on the Baas, asking him for places of abode, complaining that they have been turned adrift, with their little ones and their hungry animals, for refusing to become servants to farmers on whose property they had been ploughing on shares? White men have suddenly become brutes and have expelled Natives with whom they have lived from childhood — Natives whose labour made the white man wealthy are turned away by people who should treat them with gratitude. And are you going to leave your old home just when the Devil appears to have possessed himself of the hearts of most farmers? In your own interest, apart from my own and the Baas's, Auta Gert, you should have left us long ago when you could find a place elsewhere. Are you so deaf and blind as not to hear and see the change which has come over the country of late? White men formerly punished a Kafir who had done some wrong, now they worry him from sheer cussedness. You must be mad, Auta Gert, to try and leave us. What is going to become of your family and your beautiful cattle. No wonder that Anna is so upset. I have been thinking that some rondlooper (vagabond) from the towns had been trying to take her away."

As Mrs. V. spoke she was agreeably surprised to find the sobering effect which her rebuke seemed to have upon her husband's native tenants. She knew her influence over them, especially over the old native families, but in all her dealings and close association with them she could not remember an impromptu speech of hers that produced such immediate results. The faces of the two Natives brightened up, and they kept looking at one another as she spoke. At length she turned round towards the stoep and there was Anna, for the first time that morning, interested in and delighted by what she said. Usually it would have been a serious breach of the rules of the house for Anna to listen when the Missus was speaking about something that did not immediately concern her scullery duties; but Mrs. V.'s satisfaction was unbounded on seeing the bright look on her servant's face, which she had hitherto vainly sought.

"Now, you see," said Anna to her father, "I told you it would never happen if the Missus can help it."

At this, the men could scarcely suppress a laugh. The Missus looked round again, and said:

"Anna, have you Kafirs plotted to fool me this morning? Because I take such a deep interest in your welfare, you have so far forgotten yourselves that you connived with your parents to come over to my house and fool me on my own farm? What is the meaning of all this?"

Auta Gert unfolded his story. The Baas was at the native settlement the previous day. He called a meeting of the native peasants and told them of the new law, under which no Kafir can buy a farm or hire a farm. He added that, according to this law, their former relations of landlord and tenants have been made a criminal offence, for which they could be fined a hundred pounds, and he gave them ten days to decide whether they would become his servants or leave the farm.

"Go away, Auta Gert; you were dreaming, my husband would never talk such nonsense. You have been with him from childhood, long before I ever knew him, and yet you do not know that my husband is incapable of uttering anything half so wicked?"

"He said it was the law, the new law."

"Of course you need some stringent measures against the useless, sneaking and prowling loafers, but there is no fear that such laws could apply to Natives like you and Mietje and your children."

"But, Nooi, the Baas told us to leave the farm as the law did not permit him to ——"

"Get you gone, Auta Gert, he was joking. You must know that the law did not buy this farm. The old Baas purchased it from Baas Philander. I personally helped to add up the number of morgen and to calculate the money, and there was not a penny piece from any Government. Go home, Auta Gert, and leave everything to me, and do not let me hear you saying Dashfontein is no longer your home."

"Well, Nooi," assented the Natives with some relief, "if you say it is all right, then it must be so, and we will go back and reap our mealies in peace, and if a policeman comes round demanding a hundred pounds we will tell him to arrest us and take us to the Nooi of the farm. Good–bye, Nooi."

"Good–bye, Auta Gert; good–bye, Auta Jan —— Poor Anna, my dear little maid, why did you not tell Nooi this morning that you were worried over this matter. Really, Anna, I was thinking that you were lovesick. How did poor old Mietje take it? Sadly, did she. Well, I will speak to the Baas about it. He had no business to attempt to bring bad luck over us by disturbing our peaceful Natives with such godless tidings. Tell your mother that Nooi says it will be all right."

A few days later, Hendrik Prins, the farm manager in the employ of Mr. V., was due at the native settlement to see the steam sheller at work and also to receive the landowner's share of the produce. Instead of Prins, Mr. V. attended in person. Each Native regarded this unusual occurrence as the signal for their impending eviction and thought that day would see their last transaction with their old master and landlord.

Mr. V. counted the separate bags filled with mealies and Kafir corn placed in groups around the sheller. He counted no fewer than 12,300 bags, and knew that his share would total 6,150, representing about 3,000 Pounds gross. Could he ever succeed in getting so much, with so little trouble, if poor whites tilled his lands instead of these Natives? he thought. After all, his dear Johanna was right. This law is blind and must be resisted. It gives more consideration to the so–called poor whites (a respectable term for lazy whites), than to the owners of the ground. He, there and then, resolved to resist it and take the consequences.

The grain was all threshed; a number of native girls were busy sewing up the bags, and the engine–driver ordered his men to yoke his oxen and pull the machine away. Mr. V. ordered Auta Gert to call all the `volk' together as he had something to tell them. Auta Gert, knowing the determination of his mistress, did so in confidence that they were about to receive some glad tidings. But the other folks came forward with a grievous sense of wrong. The fact that some Natives on the adjoining property had been turned away three days before and sent homeless about the country, their places being taken by others, who, tired of roaming about and losing nearly everything, had come in as serfs did not allay their fears. Auta Hans was already conjuring up visions of a Johannesburg speculator literally "taking" his Cape shorthorns for a mere bagatelle, as they did to William Ranco, another evicted squatter from Hoopstad.

Mr. V., the farmer, mounted a handy wagon hard by and commenced to address the crowd of blacks who gathered around the wagon at the call of Gert.

"Attention! Listen," he said. "You will remember that I was here last month and explained to you the new law. Well, I understand that that explanation created the greatest amount of unrest amongst the Natives in the huts on my farm. Personally, I am very sorry that it ever came to that, but let me tell you that your Nooi, my wife, says it is not right that the terms under which we have lived in the past should be disturbed. I agree with her that it is unjust, and that the good Lord, who has always blessed us, will turn His face from us if people are unsettled and sent away from the farm in a discontented mood." (Loud and continued applause, during which Mr. V. took out his pouch of Magaliesburg tobacco and lit his pipe.) "The Nooi," he continued after a few puffs, "says we must not obey this law: she even says, if it comes to physical ejectment, or if they take me to prison, she is prepared to go to Pretoria in person and interview General Botha." (More cheers, during which the Natives dispersed to cart away their mealies amidst general satisfaction.)

* * * * *

The writer visited Dashfontein in July, 1913, when the above narrative was given him word for word by old Gert.

As old Gert narrated the story, Aunt Mietje, his wife, who had had timely notice of the impending visit of the morulaganyi (editor) from her husband (who slaughtered a sheep in honour of the occasion), superintended with interesting expectations over frizzling items in the frying–pan on her fireplace. Her bright eyes, beaming from under her headkerchief, suggested how she must have been the undisputed belle of her day. The rough wooden table was covered with the best linen in the native settlement, and on it were laid some clean plates, and the old yet shining cutlery reserved for special occasions, besides other signs of an approaching evening meal. Having learnt the art from an experienced housewife on whose farm her people were squatting, and improved upon her teaching, she was famous in the neighbourhood for the excellence of her cooking. Her only worry in that department was her seeming lack of success in training her daughters up to her elevation. She is usually sent for when important visitors come to Dashfontein, and would then don her best costume of coloured German print, and carry down with her the spotless apron which Mrs. V. gave her the preceding New Year; and in spite of her advancing years, she would cause Anna, and every other upstart at the homestead, instinctively to play second fiddle to her. And when we suggested that our wife could measure swords (or, shall we say, forks) with her as a cook, she giggled and remembered some white man's proverb about the proof of the pudding being in the eating.

After the harrowing experience of the previous week, during which we were forced to see our fellow–beings hounded out of their homes, and the homes broken up; their lifelong earnings frittered away by a law of the land, their only crime being the atrocious one of having the same colour of skin as our own, and finding ourselves suddenly landed on an oasis, the farm of a kind Dutchman and his noble wife, on whose property, and by whose leave, little black piccaninnies still played about in spite of the law, it can be readily understood with what comfort we sat down and did justice to the good things provided by Aunt Mietje. In the course of her preparation every step of hers suggested that she entertained no sort of misprised opinion about her superiority over her compeers; and nothing pleased her better than when she dazzled her husband and family connexions with deeds which proved her superiority over her contemporaries, in everything that tends to make the virtuous and industrious house–wife. She gave a dramatic ending to her husband's narrative when she said —

"Who would have thought that Hannetje, naughty little Hannetje, who was so troublesome when my sister used to nurse her — who would have thought that she would ever prove to be the salvation of our people? Who ever anticipated that all the strong Boers, on whom we had relied, would desert us when the fate of our whole tribe hung in the balance? Natives have been moving from north to south, and from south to north, all searching at the same time for homes and grazing for their cattle. During the last few weeks the roads were hidden in clouds of dust, sent up by hundreds of hoofs of hundreds of cattle, their owners with them, vainly seeking places of refuge; but in the case of Dashfontein, we reclined on a veritable Mount Ararat, by grace of naughty little Hannetje, whom God in His mysterious foresight had raised up to be Mrs. van V., proprietress of Dashfontein. If my prayers are of any value, God will appoint in heaven a special place for her when she gets there, though, for the sake of our people, I hope that time is very far distant. However, I hope to be somewhere near: in truth, I should like to accompany her, when Elijah's chariot comes for her soul, so as to render her what little aid I can on board, when she soars through unknown tracts of space to the spirit world on high, so that if there be any uncomfortable questions about her maiden vagaries, I may be there to attest that she has since atoned a hundred fold for each, and thus accelerate her promotion. No no, Hannetje is not a Boer vrouw, she is an angel."

Chapter VII Persecution of Coloured Women in the Orange Free State

Ripe persecution, like the plant
Whose nascence Mocha boasted,
Some bitter fruit produced, whose worth
Was never known till roasted.

When the Free State ex–Republicans made use of the South African Constitution — a Constitution which Lord Gladstone says is one after the Boer sentiment — to ruin the coloured population, they should at least have confined their persecution to the male portion of the blacks (as is done in a milder manner in the other three Provinces), and have left the women and children alone. According to this class legislation, no native woman in the Province of the Orange "Free" State can reside within a municipality (whether with or without her parents, or her husband) unless she can produce a permit showing that she is a servant in the employ of a white person, this permit being signed by the Town Clerk. All repressive measures under the old Republic (which, in matters of this kind, always showed a regard for the suzerainty of Great Britain) were mildly applied. Now, under the Union, the Republicans are told by the Imperial authorities that since they are self–governing they have the utmost freedom of action, including freedom to do wrong, without any fear of Imperial interference. Of this licence the white inhabitants of the Union are making the fullest use. Like a mastiff long held in the leash they are urging the application of all the former stringent measures enacted against the blacks, and the authorities, in obedience to their electoral supporters, are enforcing these measures with the utmost rigour against the blacks because they have no votes.

Hence, whereas the pass regulations were formerly never enforced by the Boers against clergymen's wives or against the families of respectable native inhabitants, now a minister's wife has not only to produce a pass on demand, but, like every woman of colour, she has to pay a shilling for a fresh pass at the end of the month, so that a family consisting of, say, a mother and five daughters pay the municipality 6s. every month, whether as a penalty for the colour of their skins or a penalty for their sex it is not clear which.

There is some unexplained anomaly in this woman's pass business. If the writer were to go and live in the "Free" State, he could apply for and obtain letters of exemption from the ordinary pass laws; but if his wife, who has had a better schooling and enjoyed an older civilization than he, were to go and reside in the "Free" State with her daughters, all of them would be forced to carry passes on their persons, and be called upon to ransack their skirt pockets at any time in the public streets at the behest of male policemen in quest of their passes. Several white men are at present undergoing long terms of imprisonment inflicted by the Orange "Free" State Circuit Courts for criminally outraging coloured women whom the pass laws had placed in the hollow of the hands of these ruffians. Still many more mothers are smothering evidence of similar outrages upon innocent daughters — cases that could never have happened under ordinary circumstances.

The Natives of the "Free" State have made all possible constitutional appeals against these outrages. In reply to their petitions the Provincial Government blames the municipalities. The latter blame the law and the Union Parliament, and there the matter ends. We have read the "Free" State law which empowers the municipalities to frame regulations for the control of Natives, etc., but it must be confessed that our limited intelligence could discern nothing in it which could be construed as imposing any dire penalties on municipalities which emancipate their coloured women from the burden of the insidious pass law and tax. Hon. Mr. H. Burton, as already stated, was Minister for Native Affairs before the Union Government surrendered to the "Free" State reactionaries. A deputation consisting of Mrs. A. S. Gabashane, Mrs. Kotsi and Mrs. Louw, women from Bloemfontein — the first-named being a clergyman's wife — waited on him in Capetown on the subject of these grievances, and he assured them that in response to representations made by the Native Congress, he had already written to Dr. Ramsbottom, the Provincial Administrator, asking him to persuade the "Free" State municipalities to relieve the native women from this burden. And if to relieve native women in the "Free" State from a burden which obtains nowhere else in the Union were unlawful, as the municipalities aver, Mr. Burton — a K.C. — would have been the last person to ask them to break the law.

Subsequently the women petitioned Lady Gladstone for her intercession. But we wonder if the petition was ever handed to Lady Gladstone by the responsible authority who, in this instance, would have been the Department of Native Affairs. Notwithstanding all these efforts, native women in the "Free" State are still forced to buy passes every month or go to prison, and they are still exposed to the indecent provision of the law authorizing male constables to insult them by day and by night, without distinction.

After exhausting all these constitutional means on behalf of their women, and witnessing the spread of the trouble to the women and children of the country districts under the Natives' Land Act, the male Natives of the municipalities of the Province of the Orange "Free" State saw their women folk throwing off their shawls and taking the "law" into their own hands. A crowd of 600 women, in July, 1913, marched to the Municipal Offices at Bloemfontein and asked to see the Mayor. He was not in, so they called for the Town Clerk. The Deputy–Mayor came out, and they deposited before him a bag containing their passes of the previous month and politely signified their intention not to buy any more passes. Then there occurred what `John Bull' would call, "——l with the lid off".

At Jagersfontein there was a similar demonstration, led by a jet–black Mozambique lady. She and a number of others were arrested and sentenced to various terms of imprisonment. The sentences ranged from about three weeks to three months, and the fines from 10s. to 3 Pounds. They all refused to pay the fines, and said their little ones could be entrusted to the care of Providence till their mothers and sisters have broken the shackles of oppression by means of passive resistance. As the prison authorities were scarcely prepared for such a sudden influx of prisoners there was not sufficient accommodation for fifty–two women, who were conveyed on donkey carts to the adjoining village of Fauresmith.

When this happened, Winburg, the old capital of the "Free" State, also had a similar trouble. Eight hundred women marched from the native location to the Town Hall, singing hymns, and addressed the authorities. They were tired of making friendly appeals which bore no fruit from year's end to year's end, so they had resolved, they said, to carry no more passes, much less to pay a shilling each per month, PER CAPITA, for passes. A procession of so many women would attract attention even in Piccadilly, but in a "Free" State dorp it was a stupendous event, and it made a striking impression. The result was that many of the women were arrested and sent to prison, but they all resolutely refused to pay their fines, and there was a rumour that the Central Government had been appealed to for funds and for material to fit out a new jail to cope with the difficulty.

This movement served to exasperate the authorities, who rigorously enforced the law and sent them to jail. The first batch of prisoners from Bloemfontein were conveyed south to Edenburg; and as further batches came down from Bloemfontein they had to be retransferred north to Kroonstad. In the course of our tour in connexion with the Natives' Land Act in August, 1913, we spent a week–end with the Rev. A. P. Pitso, of the last–named town. Thirty–four of the women passive resisters were still incarcerated there, doing hard labour. Mrs. Pitso and Mrs. Michael Petrus went with us on the Sunday morning to visit the prisoners at the jail.

A severe shock burst upon us, inside the prison walls, when the matron withdrew the barriers and the emaciated figures of ladies and young girls of our acquaintance filed out and greeted us. It was an exceptionally cold week, and our hearts bled to see young women of Bloemfontein, who had spent all their lives in the capital and never knew what it was to walk without socks, walking the chilly cemented floors and the cold and sharp pebbles without boots. Their own boots and shoes had been taken off, they told us, and they were, throughout the winter, forced to perform hard labour barefooted.

Was ever inhumanity more cold–blooded?

Do these "Free" Staters consider their brutality less brutal because it happens to be sanctioned by law?

Is Heaven so entirely unmindful of our case that it looks on with indifference when indignity upon indignity is heaped, not only upon our innocent men, but even upon our inoffensive women?

Tears rolled down our cheeks as we saw the cracks on their bare feet, the swellings and chronic chilblains, which made them look like sheep suffering from foot–and–mouth disease. It was torture to us to learn the kind of punishment to which they were subjected and the nature of the work they were called upon to perform; these facts were stated to us in the presence of the prison officials, and they were communicated by us to the Native Affairs Department merely as a matter of course. But what must be the effect of this brutal punishment upon girls who knew only city life? To our surprise, however, they vowed never to buy passes, even if they had to come back.

A month later, when we visited Bloemfontein, a majority of those who were at the Kroonstad jail had already returned to their homes, and the family doctors were doing a roaring trade. Their practice, too, was most likely to continue to boom as the sufferers were still determined to buy no more women's passes.

This determination caused a white man to suggest that "instead of being sent to prison with hard labour, these madcaps should be flogged" — and this because the women refuse to be outraged by law.

Our visit to Kroonstad took place just after the Circuit Court had convicted the white superintendent of the Kroonstad Native Location for an outrage upon a coloured woman. He arrested her in the location ostensibly because she could not produce her residential pass, and in the field between the location and the town through which he had to escort her to prison he perpetrated the atrocity. In sentencing him to four years' hard labour, the Chief Justice said for a similar crime upon a white woman a black man would be liable to the death penalty.

When General Botha assumed the portfolio of Native Affairs at the time of this trouble, the writer, as General Secretary of the Congress, telegraphed to him the greetings of the South African Native Congress, and pointed out to him that over two hundred coloured women were at that time languishing in jail for resenting a crime committed upon them, a crime which would have been considered serious in any other place outside the "Free" State. The chivalrous General replied in a Dutch telegram containing this very courteous reply: "It shall be my endeavour, as hitherto, to safeguard the just interests of the inhabitants of this land irrespective of colour."

General Botha's assurances are so sweet, especially when they are made to persons who are not in a position to influence his electoral support. The Natives, who know the "sweets" of these assurances cannot be blamed if they analyse the Premier's assurances in the light of their past experience, especially the phrase "as hitherto". To them it conveys but one idea, namely, "If the future policy of the South African Government found it convenient to send coloured women to prison in order to please the ruling whites, they will, AS HITHERTO, not hesitate to do so."

While on the subject of native women, it is deeply to be regretted that during this year, while the Empire is waging a terrible war for the cause of liberty, His Excellency the Governor–General in South Africa should have seen his way to issue a Basutoland Proclamation — No. 3 of 1915. This law decrees that under certain penalties, no native woman will be permitted to leave Basutoland "without the permission of her husband or guardian". The Proclamation on the face of it may look comparatively harmless, but its operation will have wide and painful ramifications amounting to no less than an entrenchment of the evils embraced in polygamy; and in carrying out this decree civilization will have to join hands with barbarism to perpetuate the bondage, and accentuate the degradation, of Basuto women.

It is a fact that no respectable Mosuto woman wants to leave her husband or guardian; but the economic conditions of to–day press very heavily on polygamous wives. Their lord and master finding himself no longer able to provide for half a dozen houses at a time, bestows on them the burden and anxieties of wifehood without its joys, namely, a husband's undivided care and the comforts due to wives in monogamous marriages.

Some of these polygamous wives have from time to time sought relief in emigrating to European centres where they could earn their own living and send food and raiment to their little ones. A woman cannot always be blamed for having entered into a polygamous marriage. More often than not, she did so in obedience to the wishes of her aged parents. The old people, in many instances, have judged present day economics from the standard of their own happy days when there was plenty of land and rainfalls were more regular; when the several wives and children of a rich cattle–owner could always have enough grain, eat meat, drink milk and live happily. But times are altered and even a monogamist finds the requirements of one wife quite a stupendous handful. The country is so congested that the little arable land left them yields hardly any produce. I have seen it suggested in official documents that sheep–breeding should be limited in Basutoland as there is not enough grazing for the flocks. And under this economic stress these surplus wives are sometimes driven to accept the overtures of unscrupulous men who gradually induce them to wallow in sin; hence too, they give birth to an inferior type of Basuto.

That such a law should be adopted during the reign of Chief Griffith, their first Christian Chief and the first monogamist who ever ruled the Basuto, is disappointing. And while we resent the policy of the British authorities in the Union, who promote the interests of the whites by repressing the blacks, we shall likewise object to an attempt on the part of the same authorities in the native territories to protect the comfort of black men by degrading black women. God knows that the lot of the black woman in South Africa is bad as it is. One has but to read the report of the Commission recently appointed by the Union Government to inquire into cases of assault on women to find that their condition is getting worse. Presumably the evidence was too bad for publication, but the report would seem to show that in South Africa, a country where prostitution was formerly unknown, coloured women are gradually perverted and demoralized into a cesspool for the impurities of the family lives of all the nationalities in the sub–continent.

In her primitive state, the native girl was protected against seduction and moral ruin by drastic penalties against the seducer, which safeguards have since the introduction of civilized rule been done away with. With tribes just groping their way from barbarism towards civilization natural hygienic and moral laws have been trampled upon, and for this state of affairs the white man's rule is not wholly free from blame. It should be a crime to defile a potential mother and a woman should continue to be regarded as the cradle of the race and her person remain sacred and inviolate under the law, as was the case in former times.

The only charge that could be brought up against primitive native socialism was that by tolerating polygamy it had incidentally legalized concubinage; but taking all circumstances into consideration, it is doubtful if the systematic prostitution of to-day is a happy substitution for the polygamy of the past.

There were no mothers of unwanted babies; no orphanages, because there were no stray children; the absence of extreme wealth and dire poverty prevented destitution, and the Natives had little or no insanity; they had no cancer or syphilis, and no venereal diseases because they had no prostitutes.

Have we not a right to expect a better state of affairs under civilized European rule?

It is apparently in revolt of similar horrible conditions that when the war broke out, British and Continental women were fighting for the vote with a view to liberating their sex and race from kindred impurities, for the soul rises up in "divine discontent" against a state of affairs which no nation should tolerate — evils to which the coloured women of South Africa are now a prey.

To this kind of degeneracy may also be traced the undoing of the finer elements of the native social system, the undermining of their health and of the erstwhile splendid physique of the African race and the increasing loss of the stamina of our proverbially magnificent men and women. The effect of these evils and of the abuses inherent to the liquor traffic is manifest in several of the tribes who are to-day but shadows of their former selves.

The safeguarding of our maidens and women folk from the evils of drink, greed and outrages resulting from indefensible pass laws and the elimination of bad habits among men by a rightful policy will restore that efficiency, loyalty, and contentment which aforetime were the boast of pioneer administrators in British South Africa, and which if fostered will render them a magnificent asset to the Empire for all time.

But as often as the coloured woman has been attacked she has humbly presented "the other cheek". Evidence of her characteristic humility is to be found in the action of the coloured women of the "Free" State, whose persecution by the South African Government, at the instance of certain "Free" State Municipalities, prompted the writing of this chapter. After the war broke out (the Bloemfontein `Friend' tells us) the native women of that city forgot their own difficulties, joined sewing classes, and helped to send clothing to the afflicted Belgians in Europe. Surely such useful members of the community deserve the sympathy of every right-minded person who has a voice in the conduct of British Colonial administration; so let us hope that this humble appeal on their behalf will not be in vain.

Chapter VIII At Thaba Ncho: A Secretarial Fiasco

Man's inhumanity to man makes countless thousands mourn.
    Burns.

The beginning of September, 1913, found us in the Lady Brand district. Besides numerous other sufferers of the land plague, the writer was here informed of one case that was particularly distressing, of a native couple evicted from a farm in the adjoining district. After making a fruitless search for a new place of abode, they took out a travelling pass to go to Basutoland with their stock. But they never, so the story went, reached their destination. We were told that they were ambushed by some Dutchmen, who shot them down and appropriated their stock. To a stranger the news would have been incredible, but, being a Free Stater born, it sounded to us uncommonly like the occurrences that our parents said they used to witness in the early days of that precious dependency. We were further told that one of the Dutch murderers had been arrested and was awaiting his trial at the next criminal sessions. As both the native man and woman were shot, it seemed difficult to conceive how the prosecution could find the necessary evidence to sustain a charge of murder.

The trial duly came off at Bloemfontein a month or two later, and the evidence in court seemed more direct and less circumstantial than we had expected. For, not only were the stolen cattle found in the possession of the prisoner, but the bullet picked up near the bodies of the dead refugees (according to the evidence given in court) fitted the prisoner's pistol. General Hertzog personally attended the court at Bloemfontein and conducted the defence; and, presumably more by his eloquence than anything else, he convinced a white jury of the guiltlessness of the accused, who was acquitted and acclaimed outside the court by his friends as a hero. In justice to the police it must be added that they re–arrested this man and charged him with the theft, or with being in possession of the deceased Natives' cattle. On this charge the prisoner was convicted before the Circuit Court a few months later, and in sentencing him to three years, with hard labour, the presiding judge is said to have made some references to the previous trial and the manner in which the prisoner had escaped the capital sentence.

From Lady Brand we travelled south towards Wepener, not far from the Basuto frontier. Evictions around here were numerous, but beyond the inevitable hardships of families suddenly driven from home, they had not suffered any great amount of damage. Being near to the Basuto border, a Native in these parts, when ejected, can quickly take his stock across the boundary, and leaving them in friendly pastures, under sympathetic laws, go away to look for a new place. But it became abundantly clear that the influx of outsiders into Basutoland could not continue at the rate it was then proceeding without seriously complicating the land question in Basutoland, where chieftains are constantly quarrelling over small patches of arable land.

A pitiable spectacle, however, was the sight of those who had been evicted from the centre of the Orange "Free" State. It was heartrending to hear them relate the circumstances of their expulsions, and how they had spent the winter months roaming from farm to farm with their famishing stock, applying in vain for a resting place. Some farmers were apparently sympathetic, but debarred from entertaining such applications by the sword of Damocles — the 100 Pound fine in Section 5 of the Natives' Land Act — they had perforce to refuse the applicants. The farms hereabout are owned by Boers and English settlers, but many are owned by Germans, Jews, Russians, and other Continentals.

Some of the proprietors do not reside on the farms at all; they are either Hebrew merchants or lawyers, living in the towns and villages away from the farms. Many have no wish to part with the Natives, who seem invariably to have treated their landlords well, but they are forced to do so by the law.

It seems a curious commentary on the irony of things that South Africa, which so tyrannically chases her own Natives from the country, receives at this very time with open arms Polish, Finnish, Russian and German Jews, who themselves are said to have fled from the tyranny of their own Governments in Europe. With a vengeance, it looks like "robbing Peter to pay Paul".

Standing by the side of a kopje, very early on that September morning, it was a relief to see the majestic tops of the mountains of Basutoland, silhouetted against the rising sun, beyond the Caledon River, which separates the "Free" State from Basutoland.

A number of fugitives were at that time driving little lots of stock across the broad and level flats which extend in the direction of the Basutoland Protectorate. How comforting to know that once they crossed the river, these exiles could rest their tired limbs and water their animals without breaking any law. Really until we saw those emaciated animals, it had never so forcibly occurred to us that it is as bad to be a black man's animal as it is to be a black man in South Africa.

To think that this "Free" State land from which these people are now expelled was at one time, and should still be, part and parcel of Basutoland; and to remember that the fathers of these Natives, who are now fleeing from the "Free" State laws, were allies of the Boers, whom they assisted to drive the Basutos from this habitable and arable part of their land; that with their own rations, their own horses, their own rifles, and often their own ammunition, they helped the Boers to force the Basutos back into their present mountain recesses, and compelled them to build fresh homes in all but uninhabitable mountain fastnesses, in many instances inaccessible to vehicles of any kind, in order (as was said at the time) to give themselves "more elbow−room"; to see them to−day fleeing from the laws of their perfidious Dutch allies, expelled from the country for which they bled and for which their fathers died; and to find that, at the risk of intensifying their own domestic problems in their now diminutive and overcrowded Mountain State, the Basutos are nobly offering an asylum to those who had helped to deprive them of their country; and to remember that this mean breach of faith, on the part of ex−Republicans towards their native allies, is facilitated by the protection of the Union Jack, sheds, in regard to the Basutos, a glorious ray of light upon black human nature.

Look at these exiles swarming towards the Basuto border, some of them with their belongings on their heads, driving their emaciated flocks attenuated by starvation and the cold. The faces of some of the children, too, are livid from the cold. It looks as if these people were so many fugitives escaping from a war, with the enemy pressing hard at their heels.

It was a distressing sight. We had never seen the likes of it since the outbreak of the Boer War, near the Transvaal border, immediately before the siege of Mafeking. Even that flight of 1899 had a buoyancy of its own, for the Boer War, unlike the present stealthy war of extermination (the law which caused this flight), was preceded by an ultimatum. But the sight of a people who had loyally paid taxation put to flight in these halcyon times, by a Parliament the huge salaries of whose members these very exiles, although unrepresented in its body, have meekly helped to pay, turned one's weeping eyes to Heaven, for, as Jean Paul says, "There above is everything he can wish for here below." But if the Native of other days has been sold by the perfidy of his Dutch allies of the day, the British soldiers and British taxpayer of the present day have been deceived by "we don't know who". They fought and died and paid to unfurl the banner of freedom in this part of the globe, and the spectacle before us is the result. This must be what A. H. Keene referred to when he said, "The British public were also dumb, and with that infinite capacity for being gulled which is so remarkable in a people proud of their common sense, acquiesced in everything."

Visiting the farms, we found some native tenants under notice to leave. We informed them that Mr. Edward Dower, the Secretary for Native Affairs, would be in Thaba Ncho the following week, and advised them to proceed to the town and lay their difficulties before this high representative of the Union Government, with a request for the use of his good offices to procure for them the Governor–General's permission to live on farms, a course provided in Section 1 of the Natives' Land Act. We made no promises, as previous requests for such permission had been invariably ignored. But we hoped that the Government Secretary's meeting with the sufferers and speaking with them face to face would soften the implacable red–tape and official circumlocution, and perhaps even open the way towards a modification of the administration of this legislative atrocity; but we were mistaken.

The meeting duly took place on Friday, September 12, 1913. A thousand Natives gathered at the racecourse on the wide level country between the railway station and Thaba Ncho town. A few historical facts relative to Thaba Ncho might not be out of place.

Thaba Ncho (Mount Black) takes its name from the hill below which the town is situated. Formerly this part of Africa was peopled by Bushmen and subsequently by Basutos. The Barolong, a section of the Bechuana, came here from Motlhanapitse, a place in the Western "Free" State, to which place they had been driven by Mzilikasi's hordes from over the Vaal in the early 'twenties. The Barolongs settled in Thaba Ncho during the early 'thirties under an agreement with Chief Mosheshe. The Seleka branch of the Barolong nation, under Chief Moroka, after settling here, befriended the immigrant Boers who were on their way to the north country from the south and from Natal during the 'thirties. A party of immigrant Boers had an encounter with Mzilikasi's forces of Matabele. Up in Bechuanaland the powerful Matabele had scattered the other Barolong tribes and forced them to move south and join their brethren under Moroka. Thus during the 'thirties circumstances had formed a bond of sympathy between the Boers and Barolongs in their mutual regard of the terrible Matabele as a common foe.

But the story of the relations between the Boers and the Barolong needs no comment: it is consistent with the general policy of the Boers, which, as far as Natives are concerned, draws no distinction between friend and foe. It was thus that Hendrik Potgieter's Voortrekkers forsook the more equitable laws of Cape Colony, particularly that relating to the emancipation of the slaves, and journeyed north to establish a social condition in the interior under which they might enslave the Natives without British interference. The fact that Great Britain gave monetary compensation for the liberated slaves did not apparently assuage their strong feelings on the subject of slavery; hence they were anxious to get beyond the hateful reach of British sway. They were sweeping through the country with their wagons, their families, their cattle, and their other belongings, when in the course of their march, Potgieter met the Matabele far away in the Northern Free State near a place called Vecht–kop. The trekkers made use of their firearms, but this did not prevent them from being severely punished by the Matabeles, who marched off with their horses and live stock and left the Boers in a hopeless condition, with their families still exposed to further attacks. Potgieter sent back word to Chief Moroka asking for assistance, and it was immediately granted.

Chief Moroka made a general collection of draught oxen from amongst his tribe, and these with a party of Barolong warriors were sent to the relief of the defeated Boers, and to bring them back to a place of safety behind Thaba Ncho Hill, a regular refugee camp, which the Boers named "Moroka's Hoek". But the wayfarers were now threatened with starvation; and as they were guests of honour amongst his people, the Chief Moroka made a second collection of cattle, and the Barolong responded with unheard–of liberality. Enough milch cows, and sheep, and goats were thus obtained for a liberal distribution among the Boer families, who, compared with the large numbers of their hospitable hosts, were relatively few. Hides and skins were also collected from the tribesmen, and their tanners were set to work to assist in making veldschoens (shoes), velbroeks (skin trousers), and karosses (sheepskin rugs) for the tattered and footsore Boers and their children. The oxen which they received at Vechtkop they were allowed to keep, and these came in very handy for ploughing and transport purposes. No doubt the Rev. Mr. Archbell, the Wesleyan Methodist missionary and apostle to the Barolong, played an active part on the Barolong Relief Committee, and, at that time, there were no more grateful people on earth than Hendrik Potgieter and his party of stricken voortrekkers.

After a rest of many moons and communicating with friends at Cape Colony and Natal, the Dutch leader held a council of war with the Barolong chiefs. He asked them to reinforce his punitive expedition against the Matabele. Of course they were to use their own materials and munitions and, as a reward, they were to retain whatever stock they might capture from the Matabele; but the Barolongs did not quite like the terms. Tauana especially told Potgieter that he himself was a refugee in the land of his brother Moroka. His country was Bechuanaland, and he could only accompany the expedition on condition that the Matabele stronghold at Coenyane (now Western Transvaal) be smashed up, Mzilikasi driven from the neighbourhood and the Barolong returned to their homes in the land of the Bechuana, the Boers themselves retaining the country to the east and the south (now the "Free" State and the Transvaal). That this could be done Tauana had no doubt, for since they came to Thaba Ncho, the Barolong had acquired the use of firearms — long–range weapons — which were still unknown to the Matabele, who only used hand spears. This was agreed to, and a vow was made accordingly. To make assurance doubly sure, Tauana sent his son Motshegare to enlist the co–operation of a Griqua by the name of Pieter Dout, who also had a bone to pick with the Matabele.

Pieter Dout consented, and joined the expedition with a number of mounted men, and for the time being the Boer–Barolong–Griqua combination proved a happy one. The expedition was successful beyond the most sanguine expectations of its promoters. The Matabele were routed, and King Mzilikasi was driven north, where he founded the kingdom of Matabeleland — now Southern Rhodesia — having left the allies to share his old haunts in the south.

This successful expedition was the immediate outcome of the friendly alliance between the Boers in the "Free" State and Moroka's Barolong at Thaba Ncho. But Boers make bad neighbours in Africa, and, on that account, the Government of the "Free" State thereafter proved a continual menace to the Basuto, their neighbours to the east. Pretexts were readily found and hostile inroads constantly engineered against the Basuto for purposes of aggression, and the friendliness of the Barolong was frequently exploited by the Boers in their raids, undertaken to drive the Basuto further back into the mountains. This, however, must be said to the honour of the mid–nineteenth century "Free" Staters, in contrast to the "Free" Staters of later date: that the earlier "Free" Staters rewarded the loyalty of their Barolong allies by recognizing and respecting Thaba Ncho as a friendly native State; but it must also be stated that the bargain was all in the favour of one side; thereby all the land captured from the Basuto was annexed to the "Free" State, while the dusky warriors of Moroka, who bore the brunt of the battles, got nothing for their pains. So much was this the case that Thaba Ncho, which formerly lay between the "Free" State and Basutoland, was subsequently entirely surrounded by "Free" State territory.

Eventually Chief Moroka died, and a dispute ensued between his sons concerning the chieftainship. Some Boers took sides in this dispute and accentuated the differences. In 1884, Chief Tsipinare, Moroka's successor, was murdered after a night attack by followers of his brother Samuel, assisted by a party of "Free" State Boers. It is definitely stated that the unfortunate chief valiantly defended himself. He kept his assailants at bay for the best part of the day by shooting at them through the windows of his house, which they had surrounded; and it was only by setting fire to the house that they managed to get the chief out, and shoot him. As a matter of fact the house was set on fire by the advice of one of the Boers, and it is said that it was a bullet from the rifle of one of these Boers that killed Chief Tsipinare.

President Brand, the faithful ally of the dead chieftain, called out the burghers who reached Thaba Ncho after the strife was over. He annexed Thaba Ncho to the "Free" State, and banished the rival chief from "Free" State territory, with all his followers. The Dutch members of the party which assassinated the chief were put upon a kind of trial, and discharged by a white jury at Bloemfontein.

Of course, Boers could not be expected to participate in any adventure which did not immediately lead to land grabbing. But, fortunately for some Barolongs, the dead chief had in his lifetime surveyed some farms and granted freehold title to some of the tribesmen. In fact, his death took place while he was engaged in that democratic undertaking. The Boer Government, which annexed the territory, confiscated all the land not yet surveyed, and passed a law to the effect that those Barolongs who held individual title to land could only sell their farms to white people. It must, however, be added that successive Boer Presidents have always granted written exemptions from this drastic measure. So that any Native who wanted to buy a farm could always do so by applying for the President's permission, while, of course, no permission was necessary to sell to a white man; several Natives, to the author's knowledge, have thus bought farms from Natives, and also from white men, by permission of the State President, and the severity of the prohibition was never felt. But after the British occupation in 1900, the Natives keenly felt this measure, as the Governor, when appealed to by a Native for permission to buy a farm, always replied that he had no power to break the law. Thus, under the Union Jack, sales have gone on from black to white, but none from white to black, or even from black to black. In the crowd which met Mr. Dower that morning were two Barolong young men who had lately inherited a farm each under the will of their deceased uncle, and the law will not permit the Registrar of Deeds to give them title to their inheritance; their numerous representations to the Union authorities have only met with promises, while lawyers have taken advantage of the hitch to mulct them in more money than the land is worth. The best legal advice they have received is that they should sell their inheritances to white men. Now the Natives' Land Act, as applied to the whole Union of South Africa, is modelled on these highly unsatisfactory conditions relating to land in the "Free" State. The six months' imprisonment, the 100 Pounds fine, and other penalties for infringement of the Land Act, are borrowed from Chapter XXXIV of the "Free" State laws, to which reference is made in Section 7 of the Natives' Land Act. Section 8 of the Natives' Land Act is a re–enactment of some of the reprehensible "Free" State land laws which had been repealed by the Crown Colony Government after the British occupation in 1900. When the Natives' Land Bill was before Parliament the Opposition moved that the remaining native farms be scheduled as a native area, where Natives might purchase farms, of course from other Natives. The passage of such an amendment was more than could be expected as the real object of the Natives' Land Bill was to block every possible means whereby a Native may acquire land from a Native, or from any one else; but when the motion was rejected the Natives of Thaba Ncho were exceedingly alarmed. They telegraphed their fears to Mr. Sauer, who promised to visit them when Parliament rose, but his purpose was frustrated by his death, immediately after the passage of the Act.

To return to Mr. Dower's meeting, the Native Affairs Secretary received a warm welcome from the Natives, who hoped that his coming would show them a way out of their dilemma. As already stated, a thousand Natives came from the surrounding farms, some on horseback, others on bicycles, and other conveyances such as carts, wagons, etc.; they included evicted wanderers and native tenants under notice to leave their farms, with letters of eviction and other evidence in their pockets; they included some refugees, who had likewise been evicted from other districts — refugees who, as one of them put it, were "constantly on the move, and hurried hither to plead for shelter for our homeless families, now living in wagons."

The morning was showery. Thaba Ncho Hill in the background, always visible for scores of miles in every direction, towered high above the surrounding landscape. Its stony slopes covered with a light mist from peak to base, it stood like a silent witness to the outraged treaty between the Barolong and the Boers.

Mr. Dower, who was accompanied by his secretary (Mr. Apthorpe) and the Thaba Ncho Magistrate (Major Robertson) and the Location Superintendent, addressed the Natives for half an hour. The speeches were correctly interpreted by Mr. Jeremiah Makgothi, a native farmer, and formerly a local school teacher, who collaborated with Canon Crisp in the translation of the Scriptures into Serolong for the world–renowned S.P.C.K. The Rev. P. K. Motiyane, the local Wesleyan minister, also assisted in the task of interpretation.

Mr. Dower made some pathetic references to the life and work of the late Hon. J. W. Sauer, the great Cape politician who had just passed away; then he proceeded to refer at length to sundry inconsequential topics of minor local significance; and, having repeated his great pleasure at seeing them, without making a single reference to the momentous measure that was ravaging the Natives of the country, the Government Secretary resumed his seat amidst looks of astonishment and consternation from the assembled Natives.

The Rev. J. D. Goronyane, a gentleman who, as secretary to the late chiefs, played a leading part in the Boer–Barolong relations of the nineteenth century, was the next speaker. He thanked the Secretary for coming. No people, he said, regretted Mr. Sauer's death more than the Barolong; they had looked forward to meeting him in connexion with the new cloud now looming over the country in the shape of the Land Act, and they were sorry that his coming had been frustrated by a Higher Power. Turning to Mr. Dower, he said: "All the people you see before you are frightened by the new law. They have come here for nothing else but to hear how they are expected to live under it."

Other speakers followed, but when the actual sufferers began to narrate their experiences there were so many who wished to come forward that the leaders decided that, their cases being more or less similar, they should wait and hear how the representative of the Government would deal with the cases of those who had already spoken.

==

MR. DOWER'S REPLY

He regretted that, as one speaker had said, some people read the Act through the spectacles coloured by their desires. Others seemed to be glad at the uncertainty and endeavoured to keep on turning the wheel of discontent. It was true that some people were imposing on the Natives, but, on the whole, there was a reasonable desire to comply with the Act, although it was not always properly understood. Few individuals had been evicted, though many had received notice. Some of the notices given under a misapprehension, and with a desire not to contravene the Act, had, since the Magistrates' explanations, actually been withdrawn. "So your best course is to explain the facts to your Magistrates, if possible, in the presence of the master." (A Voice: "Who'll bring him there?") After explaining that the principle of the Act was a first step towards territorial segregation, Mr. Dower said it gave protection to some parts of the country which formerly were not so protected. He mentioned as an instance that more than one–half of the farms formerly owned by Natives in that district were no longer in their possession. In other Provinces THE ACT WAS RESTRICTIVE, while IN THE FREE STATE IT WAS PROHIBITIVE. The old practice of "sowing on the halves" might continue so long as the lawfully executed contracts lasted; but at the expiration of those contracts the practice should cease, as Parliament had decided on its abolition. It amounted to a partnership between a white man and a black man. With a civilized Native the system might have been good, but a raw Native always got the worst of the partnership. He would advise them to make the best temporary arrangements within the four corners of the law. It might be by adopting one of three alternatives: (1) Become servants (in which case it would be legal for a master to give them pieces of land to plough and graze a number of stock); or (2) move into the reserve — (voices: "Where is the reserve?"); or (3) dispose of the stock for cash. (Sensation.) The arrangement would only be temporary until Parliament took further steps in terms of the Commission's report. It would be better than trekking from pillar to post, till all the cattle had died out, and eventually returning penniless. Farmers always had the right to evict their native tenants. (A voice: "But we could go elsewhere.") Because some old laws which had been repealed had now been re–enacted, let them not think that there was a desire to oppress. "They may have been unjust, as you say, but understand that this law is not the last thing said by Parliament. A final settlement must depend on the recommendations of the Commission, and such action will be taken as will be to the lasting interests of white and black. The Lands Commission has already held its first sitting, and you will be serving your best interests by bringing all your information to the Magistrate, so that it be laid before the Commission. Show by your wise action that you are inspired by the justice of your case. The course of agitation will not help you. Remove suspicions and mistrust from your minds, and bring cases of real hardships to the Magistrate, who will see that this Act is administered as smoothly as possible. But THE ACT DOES NOT PROVIDE FOR ANY SPECIAL CASES IN THE FREE STATE being submitted to the Governor–General under the first section of the Act."

The concluding statement settled the minds of those who had expected from the Government any protection against the law, and the disappointment under which the meeting broke up was indescribable. This law is full of rude shocks, and this day this spokesman of the Government told the Natives that in the other three Provinces the Governor–General will only exercise his right in exceptional cases, while in the "Free" State the law did not permit him to exercise it even in such cases, so that the Government alone knows why that provision was inserted.

Chapter IX The Fateful 13

He hath disgraced me and laughed at my losses, mocked at my gains,
  scorned my nation, thwarted my bargains, cooled my friends,
  heated mine enemies; and what is his reason? I am a Kafir.
Hath not a Kafir eyes? hath not a Kafir hands, organs, dimensions,
  senses, affections, passions? Is he not fed with the same food,
  hurt with the same weapons, subject to the same diseases,
  healed by the same means, warmed and cooled by the same summer and winter
  as a white Afrikander?
If you prick us, do we not bleed? If you tickle us, do we not laugh?
  If you poison us, do we not die? And if you wrong us,
  shall we not revenge? If we are like you in the rest,
  we will resemble you in that.
        Merchant of Venice.

The Natives of South Africa, generally speaking, are intensely superstitious. The fact that they are more impressionable than tractable causes them, it seems, to take naturally to religion, and seems a flat contradiction of Junius's assertion that "there are proselytes from atheism, but none from superstition." With some South African tribes it is unlucky to include goats amongst the animals paid by a young man's parents as the dowry for his bride; it was equally bad to pay dowry in odd numbers of cattle. The payment must be made in an even number of oxen, sheep, or other animals or articles, such as two, four, six, eight, ten, and so on. The man who could not afford more than one sheep to seal the marriage contract would have to exchange his goat for a sheep to make up a presentable pair. If he were too poor to do that, a needle or any other article was admissible to make up the dowry to an even number, and so avoid giving one or three, or more odd numbers of articles. Conscious as they were of the existence of some Supreme Being, but worshipping no God, true or false, the white man's religion which makes such a worship obligatory through a mediator found easy access among so susceptible a people; and with equal ease they likewise adopted the civilization of the white man. But the Natives received not only the white man's civilization and his religion, but have even gullibly imbibed his superstitions. Thus is their dread of the figure 13 accounted for. The Native witch-doctors in the early days took advantage of their credulity, whilst civilized people traded on their susceptibilities, and the semi-civilized Natives also traded upon the fears of their more impressionable brethren.

To give a concrete case or two, we might say that when the main reservoir of the Kimberley waterworks was built, one of the labourers one week-end lost the whole of his weekly pay. He inquired, and searched everywhere he could think of, but nobody had seen his missing purse. But on Monday morning he conceived a plan for the recovery of his lost purse. In pursuance of this plan, on the Monday he asked for and obtained a day off; then he declared to the gang of labourers that he was going to the nearest location to consult a bone-thrower. Instead of going to the location, however, he went to the open country, gathered some plants, returned to the dormitories while the others were at work, boiled the herbs in a pot of water and put it aside to cool. When the workmen returned for their midday meal he announced an imaginary consultation he had had with the bone-thrower, and that that functionary had divined the whereabouts of the purse; it was to the effect that the purse had been stolen and was in the possession of a fellow-worker. "The doctor," he said, "gave me some herbs. I have cooked them, and by his direction each of you is invited to immerse his hands in the decoction which is now cool. If you are not the thief, nothing would happen to you, but to the one who has stolen my money," he added with emphasis, "the doctor said that the medicine will snap the thief's fingers clean off and leave him only with the palm."

One by one the men dipped their hands in the "medicine", and as they took turns at the pot, one young fellow at length became visibly disturbed, and believing that the concoction was true, he confessed to the theft and undertook to refund the money, rather than lose his fingers.

Another case was this. "A Transkeian missionary once heard of the serious indisposition of a Native. It was not a natural sickness, it was believed, but was the effect of sorcery, and news in that sense was noised abroad. Such cases primitive Natives believe to be beyond the skill of a medical man. White doctors, they would say, know next to nothing at all about such things. They do not believe in witchcraft and how could they be expected to be able to smell it out of a patient. Only a witch-doctor — if he is more skilful — can smell out and subdue the charm directed by another witch-doctor into the body of the bewitched.

Having heard this piece of native philosophy on witchcraft, the missionary startled the Natives by telling them in their own tongue that he could cure the disease. And he did cure it. He captured a baby lizard from the rocks which abound in the craggy undulations of most parts of the Transkei. He hid it in the inside pocket of his coat and proceeded to the sick-bed with some real medicines in his hand. "When a man who is not sick imagines himself sick," says Dr. Kellogg, "he must be sick indeed," and truly, in accordance with this saying, the Native was dangerously ill. A bone-thrower, who had in the presence and hearing of the sick man divined his malady, pronounced that he was not only bewitched by a snake, but also that the reptile was within him and was eating him to death. In these circumstances the missionary administered an emetic to the reluctant patient, in the presence of some incredulous spectators, who had never known a white man to extract a reptile from the person of a bewitched Native. Further, by some agility of the hand, the missionary produced from his pocket unobserved, just as the emetic was acting, the baby lizard he had taken from the rocks. So smartly was this done that everybody, including the patient, believed the reptile to have been extracted from his body by the power of the medicine administered by the missionary. The sick man at once stood up and walked, and the missionary was known, by all who witnessed the marvel, as the greatest witch–doctor of the neighbourhood.

In like manner, when some civilized Christians made remarks on New Year's Day about the figure 13, there was much gossiping among the more superstitious Natives as to the form of trouble which the year 1913 had in store for the Natives, although none knew that a revolutionary law of Draconian severity would be launched in their midst during this eventful year.

The powerful African potentate, Menelik of Abyssinia (whose death had been falsely circulated no fewer than seven times during the past dozen years), really died in 1913.

Letsie II, paramount chief of the semi–independent Basuto nation, departed this life during this same year.

Dinizulu (son of the great Cetewayo, whose impis slew the Prince Imperial in 1879), who was born to inherit the throne of his fathers, and who lived to be one of the most disappointed men of his day, spent many years in prison and in exile, and was known in his lifetime as the Black Napoleon; was released from prison by the Union Government, and given back his pension of 500 Pounds per annum. Sharing the hopes of his people that in accordance with the Government's erstwhile good intentions now tottering before a growing Republicanism, Zululand would be restored to the Zulus, and he established as their ruler under the Crown. He, too, died in the year 1913.

An unusually large number of good and noble men of greater or lesser renown were gathered to their fathers during this year.

It is perhaps not generally known that few British statesmen did so much for the South African Natives, in so short a term of service at the Colonial Office, as the Hon. A. Lyttleton. And he, too, left us rather suddenly during this troublous year of 1913. In this year, too, South Africa was visited by a drought which for severity was pronounced to be unprecedented in the knowledge of all the old inhabitants. Remarks — some pithy, some ugly — were made upon the drought by Dutchmen. They all remembered how the God of their fathers used to send them nice soaking rains regularly each spring–time, and that it usually continued to nourish the plants and other of the country's vegetation throughout the summer, and they concluded that there must be some reason why He does not do it now. The majority of Dutchmen whom the writer thus overheard attributed the visitation to the sins of the foreigners, who are fast buying up the country, and cursing it by settling godless people upon it. One or two saw in it the vengeance of the Supreme Being for the unnecessary persecution of His black creatures, but they were afraid to say this aloud. "See," said one, "is the drought not worse in the `Free' State where Kafirs seem to be very hard hit by this new law?" This was true. Dutchmen's cattle were dying of poverty in the "Free" State, and the land was so parched in some parts that it seemed difficult to believe that grass could ever grow in these places again, supposing the long–looked–for rain came at last.

On our birthday, October 9, 1913, they hanged four murderers who had been condemned to death at the preceding criminal sessions. The selection of the morning of our birthday for the execution of four prisoners at our home was curious as executions in Kimberley take place only about once or twice in ten years. The event, of course, was purely accidental; but middle–aged Natives seemed to have an aptitude for remembering catastrophes which, in the lives of their fathers and their fathers' fathers, followed such coincidences. Whilst the executions were taking place, on the morning of our birthday, an ugly ocean tragedy was taking place away out on the Atlantic. The `Vulturno' was ablaze with a number of passengers on board. Innocent white men and women were being roasted alive, because the sea was too rough to permit their transfer from the burning ship to the rescuing liners; and so they perished, literally, "between the devil and the deep sea" — within full view of relief.

Dutchmen as a rule are like Natives in that they live as long as they can, and die only when they must; but in the Transvaal a Dutch farmer all but exterminated his family on this day with a revolver, which he had previously secured for the purpose. On this day also the mind of an English miner at Randfontein having suddenly become unhinged, he shot his wife, his baby, and his aunt, then coolly pocketing the pistol, he cycled down to the school, called out his two children, shot them down in cold blood, and retired to a quiet place where he put an end to his own life. During that fateful week in which disaster followed disaster in rapid succession, there occurred the following, namely, the colliery disaster at Cardiff, which left a thousand dependents without breadwinners, to say nothing of the damage to property, which is estimated at over 100,000 Pounds. There were also railway accidents and aviation disasters, causing damage to life and property. There were commercial troubles due to the Johannesburg strike in July, and this effect of the strike indicates the influence exercised by the "golden city" over South African commerce. In that sad upheaval in the labour world many innocent people lost their lives and property, and unfortunately, as is always the case, besides adding largely to the taxpayers' burdens, seriously affected people who had nothing to do with the strike. Yet when some of our friends expressed thankfulness that the year did not have thirteen months, we were obstinate enough to refuse to waste valuable time in considering the subject.

Individuals, like communities, suffered heavily from one cause or another in the year 1913. Thus the writer's little family also had its baptism of sorrow. On New Year's Day of that year 1913, his little boy, a robust child of three months, was prattling in the house. He first saw the light in the last quarter of 1912, on the very day we opened and christened our printing office, so we named him after the great inventor of printing type: he was christened Johann Gutenberg. Somehow or other he could never keep well after the New Year, for though he tried to look pleasant, it was visibly under serious difficulties. It had been our fortune, during a married life of fifteen years, to keep our children in remarkably good health; but the health of this little fellow showed unmistakable evidence that this immunity was reaching its end. Vehement attacks of whooping cough now overtook the little ones. The others got rid of it during the winter months, but with Gutenberg the disease developed into inflammation of this organ, and of that; and taking the whole year from January to December, it would not be too much to say that the little boy scarcely enjoyed three full months of good health. And by the end of the year it was clear that he was going the way of half a dozen cousins who were gathered into eternity all during one month — December, 1913. Before the New Year was a week old, the doctor, who had then become a regular member of the family, gave us the final warning.

For a month past loving aunts had tenderly relieved the child's inexperienced parents of the daily ministrations and of the more exacting night watches. After the doctor's warning there came "the calm before the storm". It only lasted for one day; the deceptive strength which had temporarily buoyed the

71

little patient up was now passing away and the inevitable reaction was setting in. Oh, if he were only a year older so that he could have communicated to us by speech his feelings and his wants! His little body, which stood the long sickness with such fortitude, got frail. His bright eyes, high forehead and round cheeks remained, however, to defy the waste of the disease. The parson came and uttered words of encouragement. "Symptoms of death," he said, pointing to the sick-bed (and he was no novice in such matters) "were very far from there," but the surroundings of the sick-bed seemed to us to ring out the command with a force as strong as six peals of thunder, saying "Suffer little children to come unto Me," and such Divine orders, comprehensible only to those to whom they are issued, took precedence of any words of encouragement that may be uttered by a mortal minister of religion. That these good men of God know the ways of their Master is patent in that they always couple the encouragement to the sick, or to the friends of the sick, with the advice to surrender to the Divine injunction. The grandmother of the child was composed. "When the Lord's will is to be done," she said, "no mortal can stay it," but his aunts were restless. "Go, call the doctor at once," they demanded. He came, gave a solemn look and stood silent. After feeling the pulse he said: "The child has collapsed. I have done all I could and can do no more." Next came the anxious looks of the other attendants, the footfalls of inquiring neighbours, messages to nearer and further relatives about the pronounced "collapse".

This was at noon, and each one expected that he could hold out for two hours at the most; but he breathed throughout the afternoon with a gallantry that was wonderful in its way. His large round eyes turned upward as though they had become blind to their immediate surroundings. It seemed that those eyes could no longer see the objects in the room and its anxious inmates; truly they could no longer see the sun or the moon and stars that night. Kimberley was no longer a home to the little chap whose short lease of life was clearly drawing to an end. A new outlook seemed to have dawned over his now brightening face. His eyes were riveted on the New Jerusalem, the City of God, and he seemed to be in full communion with the dear little cousins who preceded him thither during the previous month. Evidently they were beckoning him to leave this wicked South Africa and everything in it, and come to eternal glory. In this condition we left him early in the afternoon to answer the call of our daily and nightly drudgery — it would be gross extravagance to call it "duty" — an occupation which has no reverence for mournful occasions. At 9.15 p.m., just about the time of his birth sixteen months before, the little soul was relieved of its earthly bonds.

There he lay robed in a simple white gown, his motionless form being an eloquent testimony of the indelible gap left in our domestic circle as a visitation of 1913. But the celestial expression of his face, his deep-brown colour, and his closed eyelids, seemed to say to us: "Be at ease, I have conquered."

Still, it must be confessed that to us this wrench was a most painful experience, and that the doctrine of "Thy will be done" was found to be a great deal more than a mere profession of faith. The sympathies of relatives, friends, and other mourners, their deeds and words of condolence, followed by a solemn religious service, took the sting out of the affliction, although it must again be confessed that so deep was our sorrow for the dead child's mother that for some time we could not bear to look her in the face.

Painful and unusual solemnities and formulae were gone through during the next day, and these again were lightened by the kind and sympathetic assistance of genuine friends, like Messrs. Joseph Twayi, H. S. Poho, and others, some of them delegates to a Temperance Conference then sitting in Kimberley.

In the absence of the pastors of St. Paul's Mission, who were both attending the annual synod at Pniel, two Wesleyan ministers — Rev. Jonathan Motshumi of Kimberley, and Rev. Shadrach Ramailane of Fauresmith — took charge of the funeral service, and a row of carriages followed the hearse to the West End Cemetery.

As the procession turned round Cooper's corner into Green Street, Kimberley, something caused us to look out of the carriage window; we then caught sight of one of the carriages that formed the procession in which some little girl friends and relatives of the deceased were driving, their plain white dresses relieved only by a scrap of black ribbon here and there. Their silent sympathy, expressed with girlish shyness, was evident, though their snow–white dresses were in striking contrast to the colour of their carriage and of the horses, and the sombre black of the rest of the funeral party. As we saw the solemn procession and heard the clank of the horses' hoofs, we were suddenly reminded of that journey in July, 1913, when we met that poor wandering young family of fugitives from the Natives' Land Act. A sharp pang went through us, and caused our heart to bleed as we recalled the scene of their night funeral, forced on them by the necessity of having to steal a grave on the moonless night, when detection would be less easy. Every man in this country, we thought, be he a Russian, Jew, Peruvian, or of any other nationality, has a claim to at least six feet of South African soil as a resting place after death, but those native outcasts, who in the country of their birth, as a penalty for the colour of their skin, are made by the Union Parliament to lead lives like that awarded to Cain for his crime of fratricide, they might, as in the case of that wandering family, be even denied a sepulchre for their little ones.

The solemnity of the funeral procession, of which we formed the mainmast, almost entirely disappeared from our mind, to be succeeded by the spirit of revolt against this impious persecution as these things came before us. What have our people done to these colonists, we asked, that is so utterly unforgivable, that this law should be passed as an unavoidable reprisal? Have we not delved in their mines, and are not a quarter of a million of us still labouring for them in the depths of the earth in such circumstances for the most niggardly pittance? Are not thousands of us still offering up our lives and our limbs in order that South Africa should satisfy the white man's greed, delivering 50,000,000 Pounds worth of minerals every year? Have we not quarried the stones, mixed, moulded and carried the mortar which built the cities of South Africa? Have we not likewise prepared the material for building the railways? Have we not obsequiously and regularly paid taxation every year, and have we not supplied the Treasury with money to provide free education for Dutch children in the "Free" State and Transvaal, while we had to find additional money to pay the school fees of our own children? Are not many of us toiling in the grain fields and fruit farms, with their wives and their children, for the white man's benefit? Did not our people take care of the white women — all the white women, including Boer fraus — whose husbands, brothers and fathers were away at the front — in many cases actively engaged in shattering our own liberty? But see their appreciation and gratitude! Oh, for something to —

Strike flat the thick rotundity o' the world!

Crack Nature's moulds, all germins spill at once!
  That make ungrateful man!

When one is distressed in mind there is no greater comforter than an appropriate Scriptural quotation. Our bleeding heart was nowhere in the present procession, which apparently could take care of itself, for we had returned in thought to the July funeral of the veld and its horrid characteristics; and a pleasant reaction set in when we recalled a verse of Matthew which says: "The foxes have holes, and the birds of the air have nests, but the Son of Man hath not where to lay His head." How very Christlike was that funeral of the veld. It resembled the Messiah's in that it had no carriages, no horses, no ordained ministers, nor a trained choir singing the remains into their final resting place. The veld funeral party, like the funeral party of the Son of Man, was in mortal fear of the representatives of the law; it, like that party, had not the light of the sun, nor the light of a candle, which charitable friends in our day would usually provide for the poorest of the poor under ordinary circumstances. Still, it was not cold at Golgotha, or should not be to-day as it was on the first Good Friday; but even the Madonna and the disciples must have had some house in which to gather to discuss the situation.

One of the most astounding things in connexion with the unjust treatment of the Natives by the Whites of South Africa is the profound silence of the Dutch Reformed Church, which practically is now the State Church of South Africa. This Christian body does not only exclude coloured worshippers from participating in its services, but would arraign them before the law, or otherwise violently assault them should they visit its places of worship at other times.

When it is remembered that the predikants of the Dutch Reformed Church in the old Republics dare not pronounce the benediction on a coloured congregation, we think it will not be considered unfair to say that the calculatingly outrageous treatment of the coloured races of South Africa by the Boer section of that community is mainly due from the sanction it receives from the Dutch Reformed Church. If the predikants of the Dutch Reformed Church would but tell their congregations that it was gross libel on the Christian faith, which they profess, to treat human beings as they treat those with loathsome disease — except when it is desired to exploit the benefits, such as their taxes and their labour which these outraged human beings confer upon the Dutch: we say that if the predikants would but instruct their congregations so, then this stain, which so greatly disfigures the Christian character of the Boers would be removed.

The Dutch almost worship their religious teachers; and they will continue these cruelties upon the Natives as long as they believe that they have the approval of the Church. Let the predikants then tell their people that tyranny is tyrannical even though the victims are of a different race, and the South African Dutch will speedily abandon that course.

Just two instances by way of illustration. Ten years ago we attended an election meeting at Burghersdorp, a typical Dutch constituency at the Cape. The present Minister of Railways and Harbours was wooing the constituency, and he appeared to be the favourite candidate among three others. Dutchmen from the surrounding farms flocked to attend the meeting. The speeches were all in the Taal. No hall in the town was large enough to hold the number that came, so the four candidates addressed the gathering in the Market Square. This was how Mr. Burton asked the Dutch electors for their votes: "Whenever you speak of making South Africa comfortable to Afrikanders, do not forget that the blacks are the original Afrikanders. We found them in this country, and no policy can possibly succeed which aims at the promotion of the interests of one section of the Afrikander race to the neglect of another section."

There were a few native listeners in the throng, and we blacks at once thought that the speaker had held out the red−rag to the bull, and that every word of this candid statement would cost him at least fifty Dutch votes. But we were agreeably surprised, for the open air rang with the loud cheers and "Hoor, hoors"* from hundreds of leather−lunged Boers. One old farmer turned round to Tommy — the blackest Native in the crowd — held him by the shoulders, and shouted as brusquely as his tongue could bend to the vernacular: "Utloa, utloa, utloa!"**

— * "Hear, hear", in Dutch. ** "Hear, hear", in Sesuto. —

Mr. Burton was returned at the head of the poll.

A more recent instance: In 1913, the South African Asiatic laws operated so harshly against British Indians that Westminster and Bombay demanded instant reform. In deference to this outside intervention the Union Government appointed the Solomon Commission to inquire into the matter. While the investigations were in progress, emphatic protests were constantly uttered against this "outside interference". Some of the South Africans went as far as to assert that "if Imperialism meant a `coolie'* domination in South Africa, then it was about time that South Africa severed her Imperial bonds." The clamourers who designated the inquiry as a concession to outsiders seemed almost to dictate to the Commission not to recommend anything that "savours of a surrender to the coolies".*

— * A contemptuous South African term for British Indians. —

But when General Smuts, in terms of the Commission's report and as a concession to Anglo−Indian feeling, tabled a Bill in 1914, to amend the hardships before they had been a year in operation, the clamour at once died down; and we have not heard that any one in South Africa was a penny the poorer as a result of this "outside interference", and its consequent "surrender to the coolies".

Dutchmen only follow their leaders. Hence, let the leaders direct them into cruel ways as they are seemingly doing at the present time, then if Mr. Burton's assertions be right (and we think no one will deny that he is right when he says the one−sided policy can never succeed), these leaders, instead of producing a South Africa which is rich and contented, will only succeed in producing a South Africa which is poor and discontented. Those, too, who wish well for South Africa and are at the same time sympathizers of the present Government, let them also strive to induce the Ministry to cease its policy of dilly−dallying and of equivocation at the expense of the coloured tax−payers. So that the Dutch throughout South Africa, as did the Dutch of Cape Colony, under the able leadership of Jan Hendrik Hofmeyr, may pursue a fresh course — the course of political righteousness. When the Labour Party discover that white votes alone will not give it the reins of Government, its leaders will most probably advocate a native franchise in the Northern Colonies similar to the native franchise of the Cape. And we can assure them that the first man who would successfully tackle such a problem will not only secure for his party the votes thus created, but that sheer gratitude will in future place at his disposal the coloured vote of the Cape as well.

It is also our belief, in regard to the Dutch, that if a trusted leader from among them were to propose a native franchise for the Northern Provinces, the proposal would ultimately be accepted.

The predikants of the Dutch Reformed Church, who largely influence the leadership of the South African Dutch, ought to know that the English colonist can be just as devilish as the Boers on questions of colour; and that some of them, with their superior means and education have almost out-Boered the Boer in this matter; but that even they have been held in check by the restraint imposed upon them by the English Churches in the country. Thus, knowing the Dutchman's obedience to the commands of his pastor, we are afraid that if ever there come a day of reckoning for the multifarious accumulation of wrongs done to the Natives, the Dutch Reformed Church, owing to its silent consent to all these wrongs, will have a lot to answer for.

Chapter X Dr. Abdurahman, President of the A.P.O. / Dr. A. Abdurahman, M.P.C.

(Native of the Cape, and M.B.C. of Edinburgh)

President of the African Political Organization
on the South African Colour Trouble

The following presidential address was delivered by Dr. Abdurahman at Kimberley on September 29, 1913, at the opening of the tenth annual Conference of the A.P.O. His Worship Councillor E. Oppenheimer, Mayor of Kimberley, presided: —

Nearly two years have elapsed since we last met in Conference — two years crowded with events that have an important bearing on the future of South Africa, and especially on the Coloured races. Thanks, however, to the A.P.O. newspaper, every intelligent Coloured man is acquainted with those events, and there is no need for me to dwell in detail on any one of them. Nevertheless, a cursory enumeration will be desirable in order to answer certain questions I propose to submit to you: it will be further necessary to make a retrospect of the conditions that prevailed at the time when White South Africa, amid exuberant exultations, and a chorus of hosannahs, wildly welcomed the Act of Union as a beacon light, that would blaze down through ages of history, indicating the commencement of peace and prosperity for the land, and the birth of a new nation — the foundation of a new nationalism.

Ushered in by its authors with the blare of trumpets, and with an incense of self-adulation for their vaunted achievement, it surely cannot have belied their sanguine hopes, and proved to have been nothing more than a dream of Alnaschar. Whether Europeans are wholly satisfied with the results of Union is their business; but I think we are warranted in looking for some indication of the fruits of that Act from our point of view. But, before doing so, let us take a cursory glance at the condition of the Coloured races in pre-Union days, and then, after a rapid review of the legislation since that memorable date, we will ask ourselves: How have those events impressed the minds of the Coloured races, and what is our duty to ourselves and to our country?

Such are the questions that I propose to put myself to-night, and I shall endeavour to answer them in the most candid and straightforward manner possible. Justice and equity are our demands — are inherent rights of every man, especially a free-born British subject, even in South Africa. Heedless, therefore, as to whether some of our views please or displease the privileged section of this country's population, we are in duty bound to speak out our honest convictions boldly and fearlessly. I shall endeavour to state my opinions, therefore, without any heat, but with a cold, passionless calmness that is possible only to those who, despite bitter experiences, base their remarks on stern facts and undeniable realities.

Of late, it has become the fashion in the Press of the Union to dub any one who has to utter unpleasant truths an emotionalist. That is, of course, not argument. The silent suffering of years that must have been undergone by the Coloured man in South Africa is not likely to have left much of the emotional side of humanity in his composition. However, unpalatable as the facts may be that I have to present for your consideration to-night, I trust that my critics will be honest enough on this occasion to face them boldly. They may question their accuracy, if they will, or dispute the validity of my deductions from these facts. That is the honest course for them to adopt. Furthermore, I trust that White South Africa, especially those who boast loudest of British traditions, will remember that it is an inalienable right of a British subject, no matter in what part of the Empire he may be, to address his fellow-subjects on the momentous question of Government. "If," declared an English lawyer, "no man could have awakened the public mind to the errors and the abuses in our English Government, how could it have passed on from stage to stage, through reformation and revolution, so as to have arrived from barbarism to such a pitch of happiness and perfection?" Such an inquiry as I now propose will not be without its lessons. If South Africa is worthily fulfilling her mission; if she has been faithful to her trust; if she is promoting the cause of civilization, and if her actions are based upon humanitarianism, then she may strenuously and conscientiously proceed on the course she has been following. But if it can be shown that there is no ethical basis to her policy of dealing with Coloured races, that humanitarianism as a dominating factor is invariably wanting, and that underlying her present policy is the principle of class aggrandizement, then we may urge her to halt ere it is too late, and pursue another course.

Cape Colony

Now although there never was a time when the white and the black races stood on a footing of practical equality — civilly and politically — it is a fact that, under the old Cape constitution, theoretical equality was ensured to all, irrespective of race or creed. The Coloured races were, in this Colony, treated with much consideration, if not with absolute equality. The advancement made by them under that regime was always held up to the world's admiration. It was regarded as convincing proof that a policy based upon justice was the right one to be followed in governing subject races. The peaceful habits of the Coloured races since the granting of the old Cape Constitution is a complete vindication of the broad liberalism entertained by English statesmen sixty years ago. "It is the earnest desire of Her Majesty's Government that all her subjects at the Cape, without distinction of class or colour, should be united by one bond of loyalty, and we believe that the exercise of political rights enjoyed by all alike will prove one of the best methods of attaining this object." Thus reads the dispatch of the Duke of Newcastle to Governor Cathcart, when transmitting "to the Colony of the Cape of Good Hope Ordinances which confer one of the most liberal constitutions enjoyed by any of the British possessions."

But even in the Cape, prior to Union, signs were not wanting that some slight reactions had set in. By degrees the doctrine of equal rights, which formed the basis of the Cape Constitution, despite its resuscitation by the famous declaration of the great Rhodes, was losing its force. However, in the face of minor infractions of the principle of equal rights, and some invasions of the necessary corollary to that principle, the right to equal opportunity — in the industrial as well as in the political world — we were not wholly dissatisfied with the White man's rule in the Cape.

The Northern Colonies

Now let us consider the position in the Northern Colonies, especially in the misnamed Free State. There a very different picture is presented. From the days that the voortrekkers endeavoured to escape English rule, from the day that they sought the hospitality of Chief Moroka, the history of the treatment of the blacks north of the Orange River is one long and uninterrupted record of rapine and greed, without a solitary virtue to redeem the horrors which were committed in the name of civilization. Such is the opinion any impartial student must arrive at from a study even of the meagre records available. If all were told, it would indeed be a blood-curdling tale, and it is probably well that the world was not acquainted with all that happened. However, the treatment of the Coloured races, even in the Northern Colonies, is just what one might expect from their history. The restraints of civilization were flung aside, and the essentials of Christian precepts ignored. The northward march of the voortrekkers was a gigantic plundering raid. They swept like a desolating pestilence through the land, blasting everything in their path, and pitilessly laughing at the ravages from which the native races have not yet recovered. Their governments were founded on the principle that is subversive of all Christian ethics, that the Coloured man was entitled to no recognition either in Church or State. Cruelty and oppression amounting to serfdom were, and still are, the outstanding features of the Free State. And he would be a bold man who would assert that the native races have progressed at all as a result of contact with the white man in the Free State. Progress could not be looked for under such circumstances, for nowhere are there any signs that the Free State was ever inspired by altruistic motives.

Such was the condition of things at the time of Union. Injustice, repression, and inhumanity characterized the treatment of the Coloured races in the north: justice, benevolence, and equality of opportunity in the south. Now, it is said that "where slavery is prohibited, there civil liberty must exist; where civil liberty is denied, there slavery follows." These maxims, every student of history will admit, have been abundantly verified in the history of South Africa. Take, for instance, a comparison of the condition of the Coloured people of this town and that of Bloemfontein, the capital of the Orange Free State. Your member of Parliament has stated that in Kimberley our people are a credit to the district, and the most advanced and progressive Coloured people in South Africa. This is no doubt due to the excellent educational facilities with which you have been provided for some considerable time, to the liberty and freedom you enjoy, and to the kindly treatment you have received at the hands of the Europeans. In Bloemfontein, on the other hand, there are practically no educational facilities for children, who, as soon as they reach the age of fifteen, must enter the service of a white man, or be cast into prison. There is no freedom, no liberty, and the result is that the Coloured people of the capital of that British Slave State are uneducated, poor, and degraded.

Here, then, one can easily see the results produced by the two different systems of governing Coloured races — the benevolent and the despotic. In the north the denial of civil rights produced a state of virtual slavery, and the recent denial of the complete enfranchisement of the Coloured people in the Union has similarly resulted in the passing of an Act — the Natives' Land Act, which means nothing less than the partial enslavement of the races throughout the Union. With two such divergent policies in force in South Africa, it is not surprising that the Coloured races viewed with the gravest apprehension the Union of the Colonies upon a basis which would give the Northern Colonies sufficient power and influence to shape the legislation of the Union. And I have no hesitation in declaring that when Union was accomplished, and the Coloured people were partially disfranchised, the death–knell of political equality for the Coloured races was sounded, and the triumph of the north over the south was heralded.

Sincere regrets were expressed by our friends at the abridgement of our rights and the curtailment of our privileges that were effected by the South Africa Act. Fervent hopes were entertained by Cape politicians that not only would we not suffer any injustice, but the position of the Coloured races in the north would be improved, and their rights eventually be admitted. They fondly believed that the leavening influence of the Cape ideas would mitigate the barbarity of those of the northerner. We had no reason to doubt the sincerity of our friends' beliefs, but we had no faith in the northerners — men whose public professions and practice were void of a vestige of justice or honour in their dealings with the Coloured races.

In November, 1904, when the question of Union was under discussion, I expressed myself thus: "In a central Parliament there would be the danger of the policies of the north slowly creeping into our Colony, and undermining our Constitution. The men of the north have already told us what they would do if they got into power; and European friends, numerous and influential as they might be, would not be able to safeguard the interests of the Coloured people." How far that prediction has been verified is well known to every Coloured man.

The position of the Coloured man at the time of the Union was such as I have described.

Since Union

Scarcely had the blessing of the Almighty been invoked on the proceedings of the Union Parliament at the opening of its first session when, to its eternal shame and infamy, it placed upon its statute book a law that would debar Christ Himself from membership of the Dutch Reformed Church. A Parliament capable of such blasphemy is capable of any iniquity.

Then followed the Marriage Bill and the Squatters' Bill, both abortive measures, but, nevertheless, showing clearly the attitude of mind of the white rulers towards the Coloured races. In order to find employment for poor whites, Coloured railway employees who had served the country faithfully and well were dismissed. A white South Africa has been declared in the Union Parliament and from every platform. The white race must preserve its dominance. To this end a rigorous policy of repression was adopted; and the enthusiastic hopes of an extension of franchise rights to our northern fellow–men, that was entertained by Cape politicians and the Imperial Parliament, is now as far distant as the Greek Kalends. I shall not recount the long catalogue of other persecutions and injustices. We have all felt some of them in one phase of life or other.

So serious had matters become in 1911 that in my warning to the Coloured races against the dangers that such a policy must entail, I was bold enough to declare at our Johannesburg Conference that when Europeans were ready they would enter upon a war of extermination. I was severely taken to task for imputing such inhuman motives to Europeans. I was denounced in even worse language than has been used towards the labour leaders in the recent strike. No vituperative epithet was strong enough to fling at my head. My statement met with almost universal condemnation at the hands of the editors of the white Press; but it was condemned not on account of any falsity in it, but simply because it was unwise and inexpedient to make such remarks. Barely eighteen months have elapsed from the time when I made that prediction ere we find the Union Parliament pass the Natives' Land Act, which creates conditions, if not amounting to extermination, yet designed to enslave the Natives of this country. That tyrannical mandate is scattering multitudes of Natives from their homes. Mother earth is to them now only a step–dame. They may enter either into perpetual bondage on the farm, or spend "a sunless life in the unwholesome mine".

To–day there is also a revival of persecution in the Free State. The old laws of the dark days are being enforced with relentless rigour. The sanctity of homes is violated. Wives are compelled to carry passes. Mothers driven to abandon their offspring of tender years and seek employment. Daughters are wrenched from parental care and control, and forced into the service of some white scoundrel. Husbands are not allowed to work at their trades for themselves without paying 5s. per month for the privilege. Such is the condition of things in the slave State. And all this is done behind the power of the British flag which floats over that Province, and yet these acts were impossible while the Free State lacked the power to face British public opinion. Moreover, in the Cape Colony the Free State laws are gradually being introduced. The Curfew Laws are enforced. A distinct colour line is being drawn in every phase of life, more distinctly since General Smuts declared that colour and colour only is to be the dividing line.

Such a long list of tyrannical acts of persecutions as I could make out — persecutions of the Coloured people as a class as well as individually — can point to but one conclusion, and that is that the whites are determined at all hazards to repress all aspirations of the Coloured people for a higher life, to deny all opportunities of betterment, to keep them politically, civilly and industrially as slaves, and even to force those who have risen back into a state worse than slavery. South Africa is fast becoming

A land of tyrants, and a den of slaves,
Where wretches seek dishonourable graves.

Duty of Europeans

What is the duty of Europeans towards the Coloured races of the country? Take the oft–repeated assertions of Europeans themselves. Their leaders are fond of talking of their responsibilities to us. They have everlastingly had, or used to have until quite recently, on their lips these nice–sounding phrases about "our duties and our responsibilities to our Coloured brothers". But are such phrases not hollow and meaningless? If Europeans have duties towards the Coloured people, what else is implied than the need for humane dealings, and endeavours to ameliorate their lot, and uplift them in the scale of civilization. If that is what their duties mean, let us ask how far they have fulfilled them.

Instead of kindly, humane treatment, we find barbarous cruelty and inhumanity. Instead of ameliorating our lot they endeavour to accentuate its bitterness. Instead of aiming at our upliftment they seek to degrade us. Instead of lending a helping hand to those struggling to improve themselves they thrust them back remorselessly and rigorously. Instead of making it possible for them to enjoy the blessings of an enlightened Christianity and a noble civilization, they refuse them the right to live, unless they are content to slave for farmers or descend into the bowels of the earth to delve the gold which enslaves the world, and before whose charms all freedom flies. In short, the object of the white man's rule to–day is not to develop the faculties of the Coloured races so that they may live a full life, but to keep them for ever in a servile position. The spirit that underlies this view of governing Coloured races spread into this Colony with the Union, and is now universal throughout South Africa.

The Coloured people resent this, and one cannot be astonished at the feeling of violent hostility that has sprung up. It is a natural result. And, in the words of Carlyle, it may be said that "to whatever other griefs the Coloured people labour under, this bitterest grief — injustice — super–adds itself: the unendurable conviction that they are unfairly dealt with, that their lot in this world is not founded on right, nor even on necessity and might, is neither what it should be, nor what it shall be." The Coloured peoples are sentient beings. Their souls smart under the stigma of injustice. They are nursing a sullen revengeful humour of revolt against the white rule. They have lost respect for the white man, and are refusing to give their best to the country.

The duty of Europeans is plain. Show the Coloured people that the Government is for the good of all, not for the privileged class. Prove that the first aim is not to keep us as hewers of wood and drawers of water to men who have the power. Engage the Coloured races by their affection. Grant them equal opportunities. If you do so, then the happy harmonization of the whole community will be achieved, and you may be sure of receiving the grateful return of the affection and respect of the Coloured races.

The treatment we might reasonably expect from the dominant race is just what they themselves would expect were they in our position. We have as much right to the land of South Africa as they. We have as much right as they to be governed on the same basis of humanity. In the language of one of England's greatest statesmen, Europeans themselves would have been shut out from all the blessings they enjoy, of peace, of happiness, and of liberty if there had been any truth in these principles which some gentlemen have not hesitated to lay down as applicable to the case of Africa. "Had those principles been true, we ourselves," said William Pitt, "had languished to this hour in that miserable state of ignorance, brutality, and degradation, in which history proves our ancestors to have been immersed. Had other nations adopted those principles in their conduct towards us; had other nations applied to Great Britain the reasoning which some of the Senators of this very Island now apply to Africa, ages might have passed without our emerging from barbarism; and we, who are enjoying the blessings of British civilization, of British laws, and British liberty, might at this hour have been little superior either in morals, in knowledge, or refinement, to the rude inhabitants of the coast of Guinea."

Such were the words of Pitt in a speech he delivered in 1792 in the course of a debate on the Slave Trade. His opinions were vastly different from those of our South African Premier, who only refrains from using the sjambok, so he has told us, on no other ground than that it might also hurt himself, and who is determined to allow no native representative in the Union Parliament as long as the Almighty spares him to be overlord. He does not look forward as Pitt did to the day when "We (British) might behold the beams of science and philosophy breaking in upon Africa, which, at some happy period, may blaze with full lustre." But this policy of repression cannot last much longer. If a handful of Indians in a matter of conscience can so firmly resist what they consider injustice, what could the Coloured races not do if they were to adopt this practice of passive resistance? We must all admire what these British Indians have shown, and are showing, in their determination to maintain what they deem to be their rights. The inhumanity of the Free State has driven our women to resist the law. Numbers of them went to jail rather than carry passes. The Coloured races applaud the noble actions of those brave daughters of Africa. I am convinced that if our people as a whole were prepared to suffer likewise we could gain redress of our most serious grievances while General Botha is still alive. Are we to be driven to that course? Europeans should ask themselves that question, and ask it promptly. For example, if the 200,000 Natives on the mines were, in the language of the white Labour Party, to "down" tools, and prefer to bask in the sun than to go down the mines; if the farm labourer at harvesting time refused to work for one shilling and sixpence a day, the economic foundation of South Africa would suddenly shake and tremble with such violence that the beautiful white South Africa superstructure which has been built on it would come down with a crash, entailing financial ruin such as the world has never witnessed before. If Europeans wish to prevent such a calamity in this country, they must pursue the right course and encourage the Coloured people of South Africa to improve their position and become more useful citizens than they have ever been. They will themselves participate in the blessings that spring from our improvement and prosperity, and they will receive "ample recompense for their tardy kindness (if kindness it can be called) in no longer hindering" our progress.

We also should urge Europeans to go back to the path of justice, to retrace their steps along the route they appear to have been travelling of late. They can influence the Legislature. Whatever Parliament does is done in the name of the white people, and whites should, if they wish to see South Africa a happy, prosperous and peaceful country, check the Parliament in its mad career. It is worse than insensate folly to pursue that path any further. Many people have revolted at less oppression than we have had to suffer. At present we have no other course than to endure in silence the persecution of our tyrants, and conform to the servitude imposed on us. We may well exclaim that this is a country where

The wanton whites new penal statutes draw
Whites grind the blacks, and white men rule the law.

Nevertheless, it is not too late to mend. The estrangement between the two races is not irreconcilable. Europeans could, with advantage to the country, if they would only be men, show the Coloured people that the white man's rule is for the good of all, not for the privileged class only. If they grant the Coloured races equal opportunities, and do not penalize them on account of race or colour, they may see a happy realization of the dreams of the wisest statesmen that all classes should be contented, and should work together for the good of all.

Dr. Abdurahman's address provided material for leading articles in the South African papers during that and the following week, the criticisms, with very few exceptions, being more or less hostile. Not

82

one of them, however, accused him of telling untruths; but they vehemently resented the tone of his speech, which they characterized as inflammatory. One daily paper showed some inconsistency in the matter. It upbraided the doctor for his attack upon oppressive legislation, and two days later, presumably after second thoughts, came out with a leading article urging Europeans to check their oppression of the blacks, and in their own interests deal justly by the native and coloured sections of the population. By the Natives it was said that under the present circumstances the speech could have been better for a little moderation; but they nevertheless pronounced it the clearest and most accurate representation of their condition under the Union Administration that was ever uttered on a South African platform.

It should be remembered that Dr. Abdurahman delivered his address at a time when the operation of the Land Act was raging like a plague in the Northern Provinces, and its victims included an old man of 119 years, respected by his white neighbours, with his nonogenarian wife, and his sons aged seventy and eighty.

From the point of view of the Native, it is satisfactory to note that such sincere white students of the native question as Dr. J. E. Mackenzie of Kimberley, and Rev. Chas. Phillips of Johannesburg, when asked to dissociate themselves from Dr. Abdurahman's charges of "cruelty, inhumanity," etc., refused to do so until it could be pointed out that he had spoken untruths; that, however, could more easily be done by a shrug of the shoulders than by adducing substantial facts.

Again, it is doubtful if any South African journalist possesses the experience of Mr. Vere Stent, the editor of the `Pretoria News'. Mr. Stent as a Kimberley youth spent many years in the de Beers mining compounds, working with Natives of nearly all African tribes. He was war correspondent in Ashanti and other parts of Africa, and also with the Republican troops under General Joubert in the Northern Transvaal in the 'eighties, and saw the Boers (whose primitive artillery could not dislodge a native tribe that was impregnably entrenched inside a cave) closing up the mouth of the cave and sealing up the masonry, then leaving the Natives, men, women and children, to smother to death with their belongings inside the cave. Further, Mr. Stent accompanied Cecil Rhodes to the Mattopo hills, where the late Colossus went unarmed to hold with the Matabele chiefs the pourparler which brought about the peace of Southern Rhodesia. In the siege of Mafeking, Mr. Stent was Reuter's war correspondent, and all things considered, it must be conceded that he is better qualified to write on a subject of this kind than all the critics of Dr. Abdurahman.

Commenting on Dr. Abdurahman's address, in the course of a leading article Mr. Stent said:

Here is no paid agitator, but a professional man and a scholar, who is addressing the Coloured workers of South Africa from the lowest Aborigine to the Bantu, from the Bantu to the Coloured tradesman, from the Coloured tradesman to the professional man, of whom there are a few like himself, a great mass of unenfranchised human beings that suffer under disabilities and actual and obvious injustice.

This vast proletariat is slowly cohering. Tribal feuds are being forgotten. The anti−colour laws of South Africa, and particularly of the north — which makes no difference between the savage Zulu fresh from his kraal and the stately Malay, between the Mashaangan and a man like Dr. Abdurahman himself — are welding together this vast human mass, in the flux of a single grievance, and that grievance, the disability put upon colour qua colour by the law.

What if some day, and sooner than we think, that great mass becomes mobile, learns to co-operate, and moves irresistibly together?

What, again, which is more likely, if its molecules realize the power of their inertia, if they simply decide quite constitutionally and without violence to do nothing, pending a remedy of their grievances?

It will, of course, be said that Dr. Abdurahman is a picturesque extremist; that his position is an abnormal one; that he does not speak for the Coloured people and the Natives as a whole. Do not let us be too certain on the last point.

As to the first, there runs through the speech, holding it together and making it difficult to attack, a single plain statement in it — a steel strong thread of truth.

He throws quite a new light upon the Voortrekkers when he says: —

"The northward march of the Voortrekkers was a gigantic plundering raid. They swept like a desolating pestilence through the land, blasting everything in their path, and pitilessly laughing at the ravages from which the native races have not yet recovered." But from the point of view of the native races, the description is a true one.

To say of the Natives' Land Act, "That tyrannical mandate is scattering multitudes of Natives from their homes" is extravagant. Only a few so far have been disturbed, but many must be disturbed for the Natives' Land Act is tyrannical. In fact, though couched in the flowing language of an orator, the speech on the whole is not an unfair summing up of the grievances of the coloured people, and there is a very solemn warning in it. The European labour agitators may well envy Dr. Abdurahman: his logic, his doctrine and his power of invective. He has so much to complain of, he asks for so very little. Just equality of opportunity. He does not propose to set up any Trades' Hall government within a government; he does not talk about or attempt to incite to riot or revolution; he does not speak for a few skilled artisans who are living in comfort, and sometimes luxury, upon the sweat of the black man's brow; he speaks for the dark, submerged 5,000,000 South Africans upon whom light is very slowly breaking.

It should also be recorded that long before Dr. Abdurahman became President of the Coloured Organization, white men have been delivering speeches, some of them rather indignant, on the treatment of His Majesty's coloured and native subjects in South Africa. We will refer to just a few for example:

"I will leave out of account altogether," said His Excellency, "the unwise and hard things said by reckless and unthinking white men about Natives; I will only ask white men to consider whether they have ever calculated the cumulative effect on the Natives of what I may call the policy of pin-pricks? In some places a Native, however personally clean, or however hard he may have striven to civilize himself, is not allowed to walk on the pavement of the public streets; in others he is not allowed to go into a public park or to pay for the privilege of watching a game of cricket; in others he is not allowed to ride on the top of a tram–car, even in specified seats set apart for him; in others he is not allowed to ride in a railway carriage except in a sort of dog–kennel; in others he is unfeelingly and ungraciously treated by white officials; in others he may not stir without a pass, and if, for instance, he comes, as thousands of Natives do, from the farm on which he resides to work in a labour district — (an act which is highly beneficial to the State and commendable in the eyes of all white men) — he does not meet with facilities, but with elaborate impediments. In the course of his absence from home he may have to take out at least eight different passes, for several of which he has the additional pleasure of paying, though he would be much happier without them; and it is possible that, in an extreme case, he may have to conform to no fewer than twenty different pass regulations. Now, let a white man put himself in the position of a black man, and see how he would like it, and let him ask whether such regulations and laws really make his task easier?" — Lord Selborne, before the Congregation of the University of the Cape of Good Hope, February 27, 1909.

The Hon. Dewdney W. Drew, M.A., who was member of the Legislative Council under the Crown Colony Government in the Orange River Colony, now misnamed the Orange "Free" State, is one of the leading South African journalists. In his pamphlet on the Native Question, about four years ago, Mr. Drew made the following remarks:

Most Europeans adopt towards the Natives the privilege of the aristocrat — not always with the manners of an aristocrat. Many whites expect as a matter of course obeisance and service from all Natives, and think it perfectly natural to cuff and correct them when they make mistakes. Any resentment is apt to draw down severe punishment. In the law courts the Natives do not get the same justice as the whites. A Native convicted of an offence gets, in the first place, the punishment which a white man would get and something extra for the colour of his skin — often lashes. The bias of white juries in trying Natives charged with offences against whites is such as to have brought the jury system into disrepute, and become a chief argument among lawyers for its entire abolition. The Natives suffer various restrictions on their liberty; they may not use the side–walks, nor visit a friend's house after a certain hour at night, nor move abroad, or even exist anywhere in this "white man's country" without a pass. All the police, if not all Europeans, have the right to arrest and search them, and the exercise of this right is made sometimes a means of shamefully molesting their women. In one Colony the Natives are not allowed to own land, and in another they can only do so under virtually prohibitive conditions. If the tenant families residing upon a farm grow beyond a certain limited number — three or five — the surplus are liable to be driven off by the police. As a rule only the worse–paid forms of work are permitted to the Natives, and even these are grudged them. A legislator rises in one Colony to move that all native messengers and other native servants in the Government offices be immediately discharged and replaced by poor whites. In another Colony, the papers and the public chorus with joy to hear that the C.S.A.R. has been able to reduce its native staff, and hopes ultimately to get rid of them all. There are municipalities in which Natives, if they drive a cab, have to pay a higher licence than a white man, and in which they are not permitted to make bricks unless they do so for a white employer. In these municipalities they are not allowed to educate their children above the age of sixteen, nor may they keep their daughters at home under their own protection after that age, except the girls find positions in service, in which case they may sleep under the roof of their parents if the distance is not too great. And, of course, the Natives pay relatively a higher taxation than the whites. Articles which they use, but which are little bought by the whites, are marked for special customs duties. For instance, the white farmers' machinery is duty free, but in several Colonies the native hoes pay an ad valorem tax of 25 per cent. So of shawls; the Customs officer is content to take 12 1/2 per cent on the kind used by Europeans, but when he comes to the native shawl, the duty is again 25 per cent. In addition to these stiff indirect taxes, the Native pays direct taxes amounting to one–sixth part of their average annual wage. Not only they, but even the most respectable coloured people, are in some places not allowed to ride in trams or walk in the parks, or attend public sports, or evening concerts, or even follow a deceased white, though he should be their own father, to his last resting place in the European cemetery. As to the laws, they realize, in all the Colonies but one, Wellington's great ideal for the people, by having nothing to do with them except obey them. In addition to this treatment, varying from mere pin–pricks to oppression, they are mostly referred to in the Press, in public speeches, and private conversation, with words of opprobrium and contempt as "niggers" and "black brutes". The occasional outbreaks of a few, usually maddened with drink which Europeans have sold to them, are put to the discredit of the whole race. Those who, when they hear of a case of rape, talk about the black peril, forget apparently that it is largely the result of a bad environment. In their own country the Natives are by no means lacking in respect to white womanhood. A European lady travelling in Basutoland without escort would probably be safer there than in England under the like condition. The Hon. H. Burton, Attorney–General of the Cape Colony, reports, after visiting the Transkei, that in that great reserve, where ten thousand Europeans are surrounded by a million Natives, the molestation of white women is a thing unheard of. . . . Obviously the treatment which the Natives get is not on the whole such as he can be expected to like, and the drift of things appears to be towards greater harshness, especially towards severer pass laws and the stricter denial of property rights. In one of our Parliaments a Commission has just reported in favour of breaking up the reserves and bringing the Natives under a system resembling slavery.

Chapter XI The Natives' Land Act in Cape Colony

It must not be lost sight of that all land held by Europeans
　in Africa has been acquired by conquest or diplomacy,
　and that the aboriginal Natives have been ousted by the white man:
　that being so, I cannot see any reason why the Native
　should not be allowed to buy back what he has lost; in my opinion
　he should be encouraged to do so. . . .
He is a better citizen than the thriftless European who lives
　from hand to mouth and makes no effort to better his circumstances. . . .
Legislation should be carefully watched lest endeavours be made
　to deprive deserving Natives of the privilege of acquiring title to land.
　In the Transvaal strong efforts are being made to restrict
　the acquisition of land by Natives; but I can see
　neither justice nor reason in such a measure. If the Native
　by his education, honesty, thrift and industry has got the means
　to buy land, even in the Transvaal, why should he not be allowed
　to do so? . . .
The Natives are already pretty tightly "squeezed" in the matter of land

in South Africa, and it is time this "squeezing" process came to an end.
They must have somewhere to live. What would we do in this country
without them?

Mr. J. Hemming, a Cape Magistrate.

During the month of October, 1913, the fell work of the iniquitous provisions of the Natives' Land Act was done so remorselessly that the British blood of certain editors of Natal dailies rose superior to their Colonial prejudices and they lashed out against such wicked and wholesale injustice on the part of the legislation against the peaceful native population. It has already been pointed out that when the Secretary for Native Affairs started to tour the districts, to teach Magistrates how to enforce the new Plague Act, some people thought that the tour was part of a scheme to alleviate the distress that followed the enforcement of the Natives' Land Act, but the Natives and those of their sympathizers who followed Mr. Dower's itinerary very soon discovered that the authorities were waging a war of extermination against the blacks; and that they were bent upon reducing the independent black peasantry to a state of thraldom. Commenting on Mr. Dower's visit to the "Free" State, the `Natal Advertiser' of October 4, 1913, said: —

The explanation of the Natives' Land Act, given to the Barolongs of Thaba Nchu by Mr. Dower, is so illuminative of the wretched unsatisfactoriness of the Act that the occasion certainly merits notice. It would be difficult to conceive a more thoroughgoing and drastic condemnation of the Act than this attempt at faint praise of it, delivered by the Secretary of the Native Affairs Department. All he can say to these unfortunate Natives is, that it would be better to engage as labourers or sell up than to trek from pillar to post, till all their cattle had died. As to saying that farmers always had power to evict, the interrupting Native hit the nail on the head by his ejaculation: "But we could go elsewhere."

On October 5, the daily papers published the following telegram from Johannesburg:

As the result of the passing of the Natives' Land Act, groups of Natives are to be seen in the different Provinces seeking for new land. They have crossed over from the Free State into Natal, from Natal into the Transvaal, and from the Transvaal into British Bechuanaland. . . .

Yesterday a native arrived in Johannesburg from the Umvoti district, Natal, and reported that a chief, together with his tribe, had been evicted from a farm in the Greytown district, Natal, and that feeling in the matter had become acute.

In the Western Transvaal hundreds of natives are crossing over into the Bechuanaland Protectorate, and in the Eastern Transvaal they are concentrating on three farms in the Wakkerstroom district that have been bought by a native land company.

At present the attention of those working for the repeal of the law is being concentrated on the collection of funds for the purpose of sending a deputation to England. They hope to arouse public opinion there by lectures and other means.

The `Natal Mercury' said:

We pointed out at the time that the Act was passed that it was being rushed through the House without any proper inquiry and without much regard for native opinion or native feeling in a matter that affected their most vital interests. It was replied that the administration of the Act would be carried out on sympathetic lines, and that Mr. Sauer would make himself personally responsible for the administration being carried out in a manner which would inflict the least possible hardships on the Natives affected. The industrial crisis was followed by the untimely end of Mr. Sauer which made his tour impossible, and the Act now seems to be put in force on the most approved red-tape lines, with the result that the Natives are in a state of great alarm and agitation. At the recent Missionary Conference at Maritzburg on July 8, the question was the subject of considerable discussion, and a series of resolutions were passed.

What is happening is that in many places the Natives are being driven off land where they have been from time immemorial, so to speak. They consider the Act as an attempt to drive them into slavery, and numbers of them are being placed in the position of having no place to which to go.

It must not be supposed, however, that all English colonial journalists regretted the operation of this atrocious law. The `Cape Times', for instance, vied with the Hertzog press in congratulating the minister on having successfully passed it, and in belittling the hardships of the victims of the Act. One English farmer wrote to the `Farmer's Weekly' that the evictions were effective, but at the same time he regretted that "as long as the Native kept to the public road he still had a resting place for the hollow of his foot." The Native had been successfully legislated off the land, and apparently this farmer wanted him to be legislated off the roads as well. Another English journalist wrote to the `Sunday Post' that the hardships are exaggerated, as he had himself seen only twelve families evicted in one day and on one farm. The question which this statement suggests is: How many families must be ejected from one farm in one day to constitute a hardship; and whether this journalist would view with the same coolness a law which forcibly turned twelve white families off a farm, against the wishes of themselves and the landowner?

Again, it cannot be said that South African politicians as a whole were indifferent to the suffering of the luckless victims of the Land Act, but they eased their consciences with the palliative thought that the sufferers were not so many. However this blissful though erroneous self-satisfaction was nailed to the counter by the Rev. A. Burnet of Transvaal, when he said: "I have yet to learn that a harsh law becomes less harsh, and an act of injustice less unjust, because only a few people are affected by it."

The section of the law debarring Natives from hiring land is particularly harsh. It has been explained that its major portion is intended to reduce the Natives to serfs; but it should also be noted that the portion of the Act that is against Natives acquiring any interest whatsoever in land aims directly at dispossessing the Natives of their live stock. Section 5 provides for a fine of 100 Pounds, or six months' imprisonment, to a farmer convicted of accommodating a Native on his farm. And if after the fine is paid, the Native leaves the stock on the farm, for a number of days, while he goes to search for another place, there will be a fine of 5 Pounds per diem for each day the cattle remain on the farm. The cattle should be consigned to the road immediately the order is given for the ejection, and they should remain without food till their owner sells them, or finds employment under a farmer as a wage-earner. Thus it would seem that the aim of Section 5 is not only to prohibit native occupation of land, but, in addition to it, makes it impossible for him to be a cattle owner.

When this harsh provision of the law was brought to the notice of Cape politicians, they shrugged their shoulders and remarked that they were happy that things in the Cape were not so bad. But this is no excuse at all, for in accordance with the wording of the Act, as substantiated by its results upon the Cape Natives, the condition of these Natives is worse in many instances than it is among the Natives of Natal, or of the Transvaal. In these two Provinces a European who has no intention of evicting his Natives may retain their services under certain restrictions (see Sub-sect. 6 (c)); but in the Cape and the Orange "Free" State, the Native, according to Section 1, may retain no interest whatever in land, including the "ploughing on shares".

Well-to-do Natives, from Grahamstown to the Transkeian boundaries, mainly derived their wealth from this form of occupation. It enabled them to lead respectable lives and to educate their children. The new prohibitions tended to drive these Natives back into overcrowded locations, with the logical result that sundry acute domestic problems, such as disordered sanitation caused by the smallness of the location, loss of numerous heads of cattle owing to the too limited pasturage in the locations, are likely to arise. These herds of cattle have been the Natives' only capital, or the Natives' "bank", as they truthfully call them, so that, deprived of this occupation, the down-grade of a people, under an unsympathetic quasi-Republican Government like the present Union Administration, must be very rapid.

The fact that the traditional liberal policy of Cape Colony has broken down through this law can no longer be disputed: indeed, the only comfort that had been held out to the Natives was that Mr. Sauer would make the Natives' Land Act a dead letter. This statesman having since died, we were anxious to see how the Cape Natives were faring under the Act, so we left Kimberley on November 1, 1913, on a tour of observation in the eastern districts of the Cape Province. Our programme included visits to two alleged defenders of the Act, in the persons of Rev. James Henderson of Lovedale, and Mr. Tengo Jabavu of King Williamstown, editor of the Xosa Ministerial newspaper. Our object in visiting these gentlemen was to acquaint ourselves with their point of view, and if possible to arrive at an agreement with them.

We reached Alice in the forenoon and walked through the town to the famous Native Institution. We made our first acquaintance with Lovedale, and we hardly remember having seen so many native boys housed in any one place before. But it pained us to think what must be the future lot of this great gathering of young fellows, who are now debarred by law from rights of ownership of the soil of South Africa, their own homeland.

During our three hours' stay at Lovedale we had an interview with Mr. Henderson, the Principal, about things in general, and the Native College Scheme in particular, and lastly, but not least, about the Native Land Act. Unfortunately we could learn nothing from the eminent educator, for we found that his conclusions were based on second-hand information. He had never met any member of the Government, or their representatives, in fact it was news to the Principal that in going to Lovedale, that morning, we had met men on their way from the Magistrate's office in Alice, not far away, who had been definitely warned by the Magistrate against re-ploughing their old lands on the farms. Of course Mr. Henderson was moved with sympathy for a people so ruthlessly treated by a Government they had loyally served. And it would seem that the Principal of Lovedale had since made independent inquiries, for we have read in the Lovedale paper other evidence of the operation of this drastic law that had not come under our own observation. Thus in supporting the case of the Native Deputation in the Imperial Parliament on July 28, 1914, Sir Albert Spicer effectively read passages from the `Christian Express', the organ of Lovedale.

One of the instructors at Lovedale very kindly lent us a horse, and Mr. Moikangoa accompanied us to an all-night meeting at Sheshegu, a famous political "rendezvous" which has acquired this distinction because it is the centre of numerous little locations, within easy reach of four surrounding Magistracies. At the all-night meeting at Sheshegu there were chiefs, headmen, and other Natives from the Peddie, Fort Beaufort and Alice districts. There were a number of school teachers also from these districts, and two or three native storekeepers. The disclosures made by the several speakers concerning the operation of the Land Act among the Natives made one's heart bleed. The chieftain Kapok Mgijima, who entertained many of the visitors to the meeting, had his own peculiar experience under the Act. Not only had he been debarred from re-ploughing his own lands, but he had also been ordered to move his oxen from a farm owned by a European, where for fourteen years he had grazed his oxen. Another Native, who had been ploughing in the direction of King Williamstown, was warned by the authorities not to resume his ploughing in 1913. He could only do so as a servant in the employ of a white landowner. He was further warned that if he connived with the white man to cheat the law, by representing themselves as master and servant, they would, when found out to be still carrying on their old relation of landlord and tenant, be dealt with very severely.

The landlord was furious. "Why," he asked, "did you tell them of your intention? You should have done your business quietly; now that you have apprised them they will watch us, you fool."

"But," said the Native, "owing to the existence of East Coast fever in Transkei, no animals can be taken from one plantation to another without a magisterial permit disclosing the object of the removal. I had to tell what I wanted to come here for. I was asked at the Magistrate's office if I did not know the law. I said that I was aware of such a new law, which had created a lot of disturbance in the Northern Provinces, but I had never heard that it was applicable to the Cape. To this the Magistrate's clerk replied that it was not a Provincial law, it was a law of the Union, of which the Cape formed part. There were certain exemptions, the clerk added, but they did not exempt the Cape Natives from the prohibition of ploughing on white men's farms and grazing their cattle on those farms."

Other speakers narrated their experiences under the Act, and these experiences showed that the Plague Act was raging with particular fury in the old Cape Districts of Fort Beaufort, Grahamstown, King Williamstown, and East London. At this meeting it was resolved to support a movement to send an appeal to His Majesty the King, against this law.

Our visit to these places took place just after the glorious showers of the early summer. On the wider tracts of land owned by Europeans the grass looked invitingly green. The maiden soil, looking beautiful and soft after the soaking rains, cried silently for cultivation. The people who had hitherto depended on such cultivation for their subsistence were now prohibited by reason of their colour from earning their usual livelihood, as directed by Almighty God, "In the sweat of thy brow shalt thou eat bread."

This prohibition seems particularly contemptible when it is remembered that the majority of the

Natives of these locations are Fingoes, and that their fathers in the early days joined the British in fighting most of the Kafir wars, side by side with British troops. They shared in all the massacres and devastating raids committed upon the British settlers by unfriendly native tribes. As a mark of recognition of their loyalty to the Government, and of their co–operation with the British forces in the field of battle, this country was given, in the name of Her late Majesty Victoria, to their chiefs by a British Governor. But in spite of this treaty, the people have been gradually dispossessed of the land during the past three–quarters of a century. Hence the occupation, now crystallized into ownership, passed bit by bit into white hands. Hitherto the right to live on, and to cultivate, lands which thus formerly belonged to them was never challenged, but all that is now changed. Naturally the ingratitude meted out to these people by the authorities in return for services consistently rendered by three successive generations of them will be a blow, not only to the economic independence of a loyal and patriotic people, but to the belief in British sense of justice.

Chapter XII The Passing of Cape Ideals

Naboth was right to hold on to his home. There were garnered memories
  that all the wealth of Ahab could not buy.
    Ward Beecher.

From the great meeting place — Sheshegu — we went through the Alice district. In this district we met several men who would get no crops — their annual income — the next year, as the law had placed an embargo on their ordinary avocation. King Williamstown was also visited, and there at a meeting held in the Baptist Church, which was kindly lent for the purpose by the Rev. Mr. Pierce, it was unanimously resolved to appeal to His Majesty the King against the Natives' Land Act. Mr. W. Sebe presided over this meeting of representative Natives, and Mr. Bassie translated the Act.

At Queenstown a similar resolution was passed by practically the whole meeting. Beyond answering questions at each of these meetings, the writer said little else besides reading the Act, which told its own tale. Many Natives who had never seen a copy of the Act before, but who had heard its praises sung by interested parties and had believed the false teachers, attended the meetings to oppose any undue interference with "the law". But these men were appalled when the law was read to them, sentence by sentence, and translated by their own teachers in their own tongue. Then a discussion would follow, invariably ending with the query: "Can a Parliament capable of passing such a law still be trusted by the community concerned?"

The Queenstown meeting, which was held in the Native Baptist School kindly lent by Messrs. Damane and Koti, was more interesting than the others because it is the only one of the many native meetings we attended where there was any dissent. There were four dissentients at Queenstown, and we take this opportunity of congratulating all genuine enemies of native welfare on the fact that they had four staunch protagonists of colour, who showed more manliness than Mr. Tengo–Jabavu because they attended the meeting. Still, if the courage of these opponents was admirable, we confess we did not like the gross callousness, and what seemed to us an indecent disregard of native suffering that was manifest in their conduct: when the story of the hardships of unfortunate victims of the Land Act was narrated they laughed, and repeated the newspaper excuse that the evictions were not directly due to the Act.

We agree with them that evictions have always taken place, since the first human couple was sent out of the Garden of Eden, yet they must admit that until the Union Parliament passed the Natives' Land Act there never was a law saying to the native population of South Africa, "You must not settle anywhere, under a penalty of 100 Pounds, unless you are a servant." These unsympathetic Natives made no effort to defend the Act itself, but attempted to bluff the meeting with the supposed danger of "reprisals by spiteful Boers, who, they said, will be more vindictive if Natives dared to appeal to the King, over the heads of the Boer Government." But the meeting would not be bluffed. One speaker especially remarked that the Act embodied the very worst form of vindictiveness, and the sooner the whole world understood the Union Parliament's attitude towards the blacks the better it would be. The meeting agreed that no slavery could be worse than to be outlawed in your own homes, and the motion was carried against the said four dissentients.

We interviewed a number of the Natives passing through Queenstown, and the result showed that many and varied were the vicissitudes of the Natives in the eastern districts of the Cape Province.

From Queenstown we touched some of the north—eastern districts of the Cape Province. In one of these districts a fairly prosperous Native was farming as a tenant on a farm. By sheer industry he had earned and enjoyed the respect of all who knew him. His landlord, a white man, was particularly proud of him. This Native went into town one morning and as he passed the Magistrate's Court on his way to the stores, a messenger hailed him inside. Having entered the office, the Assistant Magistrate served him with a notice to leave his hired farm, on which he had been a tenant since his youth, and which was as much a home to him as to the proprietor. The landlord, on hearing of this, naturally resented this usurpation on the part of the authorities, who, he said, had unduly interfered with his private affairs. Next day the Baas drove into the town to interview the Magistrate, and to remonstrate with him on what he thought to be the unauthorized interference of the Assistant Magistrate.

He and the Magistrate read and re—read the Natives' Land Act, and both came to the conclusion that it was a law that was as complicated as it was unnecessary; but the Magistrate, being a representative of the law, decided that, rightly or wrongly, it must be obeyed.

This visit of the Baas to the Magistrate had made our native friend hopeful that it would result in averting the calamity that threatened him and his family, but, to his utter dismay, the landlord on returning soon undeceived him and gave his own opinion of "the most peculiar and wicked law" that he had ever heard of. Although Dutchmen had known and had heard of some strange laws, yet this Dutchman was so full of indignation at the strangeness of this law that his description of it was made up of largely untranslatable Dutch adjectives. These adjectives, however, could not relieve the suffering of his native tenant from the wound inflicted by the law in his sudden expulsion from his home. It seems clear that no South African Native, on leaving a Dutch farm, had ever received a more respectable send—off than our friend did on leaving his farm in compliance with the Natives' Land Act. The white landlord accompanied him right up to the boundary of the farm which for seventeen years had been his home, and which he was so cruelly forced to leave. For the first time in his life, as the Dutchman said, he shook hands with a Kafir. And, as he did so, he called down the direst curses upon the persons responsible for the impasse — curses, by the way, which seem to be liberally answered.

It would, perhaps, be interesting to add what has happened since. Our native friend took his family to the town, because the Act is not enforceable in municipal areas. Leaving his family there, he started roaming about the districts, looking for a place where he could graze his cattle. In the course of the wandering his stock thinned down, owing to death from starvation and other causes. At home his old master found he could not get on without him, so learning of the whereabouts of the Native and also of his sad plight, the master sent out to him and advised him to return home, graze his stock there, and "hang the legal consequences." May they never be found out.

It has now amounted to this that white men who wish to deal humanely with their native friends must resort to clandestine methods, to enable a Native and his stock to drink the fresh water and breathe the pure air in the wide tracts of South Africa, for by law Natives have now less rights than the snakes and scorpions abounding in that country. Can a law be justified which forces the people to live only by means of chicanery; and which, in order to progress, compels one to cheat the law officers of the Crown? This case is but one of many that came under our own observation, and there may be many more of which we know nothing.

The `Cape Times', the leading Bothaite daily newspaper of the Cape, has defended every action of the Union, including the dismissal of English Civil servants. It justifies this last act by alleging that the dismissed officials did not know Dutch. Consequently it could not be expected that this journal could have any qualms about a law enacted specifically to repress black men. It supported every harsh clause of the Natives' Land Bill, including Clause 1. However, when the native deputation to England gave proofs of the ravages of the "plague law" in Cape Colony, the `Cape Times', instead of defending its pet law, said: "The complaint to which they give precedence is particularly instructive," and so, quoting from the deputation's appeal which says: "In the Cape Colony, where we are repeatedly told that the Act is not in force, the Magistrates of East London, King Williamstown and Alice prohibited native tenants from reploughing their old hired lands last October, and also ordered them to remove their stock from grazing farms," this ministerial daily adds: "It is unnecessary to consider the justice or otherwise of this complaint for it is perfectly clear that if a Magistrate oversteps the bounds of the law, it is a matter to be dealt with by the Union Government."

It will be observed that this is an insinuation that the Magistrates who administer the Land Act at the Cape are exceeding their authority and should be "dealt with by the Union Government". Now, what are the facts? It is well known that all Magistrates, including those at the Cape, are paid to administer every legislative instrument, whether sensible or absurd, passed by the partly literate Parliament of the Union of South Africa. Hence, these Magistrates, in ordering Natives off their farms, and turning native cattle off the grazing areas, are only carrying out Section 1 of the Natives' Land Act. One Cape Magistrate who ruled that to plough on a farm was no breach of the law, WAS "dealt with by the Union Government", for a peremptory order came from Pretoria declaring such a decision to be illegal.

Therefore, so far from the Cape Magistrate "overstepping the bounds of the law" in expelling Natives from the farms and native cattle from their pastures, these Magistrates could legally have done worse, inasmuch as they could, under Section 5, have sent these Natives to prison for contravening Section 1. In justification, then, of its own and of its party's share in this legislative achievement, the `Cape Times' should have sought a more worthy excuse than thus attempting to make scapegoats of a band of fair–minded men who presumably, prior to the Union, never thought it would be part of their duty to administer from the Cape bench an Act which inflicted such gross cruelty.

Who, in the days of the Murrays, Mr. F. Y. St. Leger, and subsequently of Mr. F. E. Garrett, could have thought that the `Cape Times' would in this manner have destroyed its great traditions, built up during the nineteenth century, by sanctioning a law under which Cape Magistrates would be forced to render homeless the Natives of the Cape in their own Cape of Good Hope? The one Colony whose administration, under its wise statesmen of the Victorian era, created for it that tremendous prestige that was felt throughout the dark continent, and that rested largely upon the fact that among its citizens, before its incorporation with the northern states, it knew no distinction of colour, for all were free to qualify for the exercise of electoral rights. The old Cape Colony of our boyhood days, whose administration, despite occasional lapses, managed during a hundred years to steer clear of the familiar massacres and bloodshed of punitive expeditions against primitive tribes, massacres and bloodshed so common in other parts of the same continent; the old Cape Colony whose peaceful methods of civilization acted as an incentive to the Bechuana tribes to draw the sword and resist every attempt at annexation by Europeans other than the British: a resistance so determined that it thwarted the efforts to link German South West Africa with the Transvaal Republic, and so kept open the trade route to Rhodesia for the British. All this done without any effort on the part of the British themselves, and done by the Natives out of regard for Cape Colony ideals. But alas! these Natives are now debarred from tilling the soil of the Cape, except as Republican serfs. What would Sir George Grey, or Bishop Gray, or Saul Solomon, say of this? What would these Empire builders say if they came back here and found that the hills and valleys of their old Cape Colony have ceased to be a home to many of their million brawny blacks, whose muscles helped the conqueror to secure his present hold of the country? What would these champions of justice say if they saw how, with her entrance into the Union, Cape Colony had bartered her shining ideals for the sombre history of the northern states, a history defiled with innocent blood, and a territory soaked with native tears and scandalized by burying Natives alive; and that with one stroke of the pen the so–called federation has demolished the Rhodes's formula of "equal rights for all civilized men, irrespective of colour"? How are the mighty fallen!

But while we sing the funeral dirge of Cape ideals, the Republicans sing songs of gladness. Thus, when Mr. Sauer, a noted disciple of the late Mr. Saul Solomon, died, the `Bloemfontein Friend', the leading Ministerial daily of the "Free" State, said:

He stood uncompromisingly for Rhodes's ideal of complete equality, and it was an open secret that Mr. Sauer, who piloted the Natives' Land Act through Parliament last session, would, had circumstances been different, have been its strongest opponent. It was the irony of fate that made him Minister of Native Affairs when a law had to be passed which appeared to be in entire conflict with his cherished lifelong convictions. The Act he passed embodied the hated northern principles which he had consistently opposed during the whole of his political career, and, as in the case of the Act of Union, it was only Mr. Sauer's influence that allayed the feelings of the intransigent section of the native population.

Mr. Sauer was a convinced disciple of the teachings of Saul Solomon, who founded and preached the gospel of the Cape native policy. In our view that was a mistaken policy. Its principal modern exponent has now been taken away, and if God, and not man, shapes the destinies of nations, we may be pardoned the belief that Mr. Sauer's death at this juncture means something more than the mere passing from the finite into the infinite of one human being.

If this is a brutal utterance, it is at any rate more frank, and therefore more manly, than the vacillating policy of the `Cape Times', the Ministerial organ of the Cape Colony. It is said that "politics make strange bed–fellows", but not even the shrewdest of our political seers could have predicted that in 1913 the `Cape Times' would be found in the same camp as its Republican contemporaries which sing glees over the demolished structure of Cape traditions, and over the passing away of Victorian statesmen and the principles they stood for — Victorian principles, which the `Cape Times' of other days helped to build up in another political camp! How are the mighty fallen!

Dear lovely bowers of innocence and ease,
Seats of my youth when every sport could please,
How often have I loitered o'er thy green,
Where humble happiness endeared each scene!

How often have I paused on every charm:
The shelter'd cot, the cultivated farm,
The never failing brook, the busy mill,
The decent church that topt the neighbouring hill,

The hawthorn bush with seats beneath the shade
For talking age and whisp'ring lovers made!
How often have I blest the coming day,
When toil remitting lent its turn to play!

And all the village train, from labour free,
Led up their sports beneath the spreading tree;
With bashful virgins' sidelong looks of love,
The matron's glance that would these looks reprove.

These were thy charms, sweet Province, sports like these,
With sweet succession, taught e'en toil to please;
These round thy bowers their cheerful influence shed,
These were thy charms — but all these charms are fled.

Sweet smiling village, loveliest of the lawn,
Thy sports are fled and all thy charms withdrawn;
Amidst thy bowers the tyrant's hand is seen
And desolation saddens all thy green:

And trembling, shrinking from the spoiler's hand,
Far, far away, thy children leave the land.
Ill fares the land, to hastening ills a prey,

Where wealth accumulates and men decay.

The Cape Native can thoroughly endorse these sentiments of Oliver Goldsmith, which, however, compared with his own present lot, are mild in the extreme; for it could not have been amid scenes of this description, and with an outlook half as bad as ours, that the same author further sings:

A time there was e'er England's grief began,
When every rood of ground maintain'd its man;
But times are alter'd: Trade's unfeeling train
Usurp the land and dispossess the swain.

Those gentle hours that plenty bade to bloom,
Those calm desires that ask'd but little room,
Those graceful sports that grac'd the peaceful scene,
Liv'd in each look and brighten'd all the green,
These far departing seek a kinder shore,
And rural mirth and manners are no more.

In all my wand'rings round this world of care,
In all my griefs — and God has giv'n my share —
I still had hopes my latest hours to crown,
Amidst these humble bowers to lay me down.

Chapter XIII Mr. Tengo–Jabavu, the Pioneer Native Pressman

Egotists cannot converse; they talk to themselves only.
        Alcott.

There is issued in King Williamstown (Cape) `Imvo', the second oldest newspaper published in any one of the South African native languages. This paper formerly had a kind of monopoly in the field of native journalism, and it deserved a wide reputation. In later years the `Izwi', another native journal, appeared on the scene; and then the King Williamstown pioneer could hardly hold its ground against the new rival. The `Izwi', though somewhat too pronounced against the traditional policy of the Dutch, appealed to a large section mainly by reason of its Imperial sentiment. The result was that Mr. Tengo–Jabavu's paper began to sink into difficulties and had to cast about for a financial rescuer. Prominent supporters of the present Ministry came to the rescue; three out of the ten members of the first Union Cabinet became shareholders in the sinking `Imvo', so that the editor, in a sense, cannot very well be blamed because his paper is native only in language. However, we do not think that he does full justice to his ministerial employers.

God forbid that we should ever find that our mind had become the property of some one other than ourselves; but should such a misfortune ever overtake us, we should at least strive to serve our new proprietor diligently, and whenever our people are unanimously opposed to a policy, we should consider it a part of our duty to tell him so; but that is not Mr. Jabavu's way of serving a master. Throughout the course of a general election, we have known him to feed his masters (the S.A. party), upon flapdoodle, fabricating the mess out of imaginary native votes of confidence for his masters' delectation, and leaving them to discover the real ingredients of the dish, at the bottom of the poll, when the result has been declared.

He did the same thing in the case of the Natives' Land Bill. Thus when he found that the trouble was organizing the Natives on an unprecedented scale, and that the Native Press and the Native Congress were unanimous in denouncing the Grobler–Sauer Bill, a Reuter's telegram appeared in the newspapers purporting to give the proceedings of a meeting of the Natives of King Williamstown, who, it was alleged, approved of the Bill. When the author reached King Williamstown, during this visit, he found the King Williamstown Natives disgusted with what they said was Reuter's speculation upon their feelings. But Reuter's agent on the spot, whose office we also visited, knew nothing about the meeting. The only meeting ever held in the place, we were told, was one of nineteen persons presided over by Mr. Tengo–Jabavu, and when Mr. Jabavu asked the other eighteen Natives present in the meeting besides him to signify their approval of the legislation, Mr. W. D. Soga (a well–known native politician) asked the chairman to place a motion before the meeting, as he was ready to move an amendment. The temper of the meeting having already shown itself unfavourably to the chairman's suggestion, the latter, instead of challenging a positive defeat, suggested an adjournment. This was agreed to for the simple reason that nineteen persons were too few to express the wishes of the 100,000 Natives of King Williamstown. But, the next morning, the message "from Reuter's agent at King Williamstown" appeared in all the daily papers, except that of King Williamstown, conveying the Natives' approval of the Bill, and Mr. Sauer, in Parliament, made capital out of the "mess"–age. But Mr. Tengo–Jabavu lived to rue his action in this matter before very long. His authority, or rather his leadership, of the Natives, was put to the test in March, 1914, when he contested the Tembuland seat against Dr. W. B. Rubusana. Dr. Rubusana had always been supposed to occupy the second place, and Mr. Jabavu the first place, in the estimation of the Natives of the Cape Province: yet, to the surprise of everybody, Mr. Jabavu, although assisted by the Dutch vote, polled only 294 votes, while Dr. Rubusana, who relied entirely on the coloured vote, polled 852.

We mentioned, in a previous chapter, the names of Principal Henderson and Mr. Tengo–Jabavu, as those whom we especially desired to interview during our trip. Having stated the fulfilment of this desire in regard to Mr. Henderson, we now proceed to state it in regard to Mr. Jabavu.

There was to be a meeting of the Natives of King Williamstown, in the Baptist Chapel, on November 3, 1913, to discuss the Natives' Land Act. To this meeting we had been invited by telegram; and in going to King Williamstown we made up our mind to invite Mr. Jabavu to this meeting of Natives of his town, and in fact, to treat him with the same respect as we had shown the Principal of Lovedale with such happy results; but, to our horror, we found that Mr. Jabavu was not only preaching the Backvelders' dangerous politics, that were ruinous to native interests, but that, besides their dangerous politics, he had imbibed their baser quality of ingratitude. For this man had not only enjoyed our free hospitality on three occasions, when he visited up–country, and the hospitality of our relatives at various times in other parts, but when he was about to leave for Europe, on a holiday jaunt, and wanted some one to take charge of his work, we left our own affairs and went to King Williamstown, at our own expense, to fill that post, and we filled it without a fee; but, see his retaliation.

We reached King Williamstown on Saturday evening and called at Mr. Jabavu's house on Sunday afternoon. Mrs. Jabavu said her husband had gone to Stutterheim, and would be back by a late train. On Monday morning we called at Mr. Jabavu's office, and his son whom we saw said his father would be there in the afternoon. We called in the afternoon and was told that he was inside and would see us later. We waited from 2.30 till nearly 4 p.m., chatting with his son, while Mr. Jabavu was closeted in the next room, evidently unwilling to see us. As his son had to leave, we also went away, but returned to his office at 6 p.m., just an hour before the opening of the public meeting to which we wished to invite him. Mr. Jabavu sent a verbal message, with the young lady who had taken in our card to him, to the effect that he was not prepared to see us. That in brief was our reception by the man who edits "a native paper".

We went to the meeting at the Baptist Chapel, which was a huge success. Mr. W. Sebe presided. The editor of the King Williamstown daily paper, an Englishman, attended the meeting in person and took notes for his paper, while no reporter represented the soi–disant native paper of King Williamstown.

When the proceedings of the meeting appeared in the King Williamstown English paper, Mr. Jabavu attempted to discount the report by writing in his own paper that "the `Cape Mercury' evidently does not know that there are Natives and Natives, as well as King Williamstown and King Williamstown, there being town and country," etc. This being a veiled insinuation that the rural native view was opposed to the urban native view at King Williamstown, we could not leave the matter unchallenged, so we posted the following challenge to Mr. Tengo–Jabavu, which he evidently found it impossible to accept: —

Dear Sir, —

`Imvo' comments disparagingly on Monday's meeting, and adds that the Natives who composed the meeting were a handful drawn by curiosity. Now, I challenge `Imvo', or Mr. Tengo–Jabavu, to call a series of three public meetings, anywhere in the district of King Williamstown. Let us both address these meetings immediately after the Natives' Land Act has been read and interpreted to each. We could address the meetings from the same platform, or separately, but on the same day and at the same place. For every vote carried at each of these meetings in favour of his views on the Act I undertake to hand over 15 Pounds to the Grey Hospital (King Williamstown), and 15 Pounds to the Victoria Hospital (Lovedale), on condition that for every vote I carry at any of the meetings, he hand over 15 Pounds to the Victoria Hospital (Mafeking), and 15 Pounds to the Carnarvon Hospital (Kimberley).

That is 30 Pounds for charity, if he will accept.

I will not place difficulties in his way by inviting him to meetings up here, but leave him to call meetings among his own people (if he has any) in his own district, and I will attend at my own expense.

      Yours, etc.
      (Sgd.) Sol. T. Plaatje,
  Editor of `Tsala ea Batho', and Secretary S.A. Native National Congress. 14, Shannon Street, Kimberley.

==

"IMVO'S" REPLY

Dear Sir, — I am instructed by the Editor of "Imvo" to acknowledge the receipt of your letter, and to inform you that as he has not been reading and following your writings, etc., he cannot understand what you mean by it. In short, to let you know that he takes no interest in the matter.

I am, Sir,
Yours truly,
(Sgd.) A. M. Jabavu. "Imvo" Office, King Williamstown,
November 24, 1913.

Poor fellow! He had not met a single member of the Government since the plague law was so rudely sprung upon an unsuspecting country, and since it sent unprotected widows and innocent children adrift, to wander about with their belongings on their heads. Mr. Jabavu had not met any member of Parliament and discussed the measure with him or with a responsible Government official; so he found it awkward to accept a challenge to substantiate his arguments, in the presence of one who had not only discussed the measure with members of Parliament, with Cabinet Ministers and their representatives, but who had also witnessed the ravages of the Act amongst the Natives in the country.

The general complaint of the Natives of King Williamstown, his fellow–townsmen, is that he refuses to attend their meetings and relies on the white daily papers for information about the Natives at large.

But Mr. Jabavu is nothing if he is not selfish. We are informed, and have every reason to believe, that, three months after the Act was passed, he wanted to raise a loan of 200 Pounds on landed security, but was debarred by the Natives' Land Act. The next issue of his paper praised the Act for the sixtieth time and noted the following exception: "There is only one flaw in this otherwise useful Act, which is occasioning a manifest hardship through harsh administration, and that is the provision relating to lending money."

Now, from our point of view, this seems to be the only defensible provision, as it would tend to discourage usury, a common evil in money transactions between Europeans and Natives; but because it interfered with Mr. Jabavu's personal aims, that is the only flaw. The cold–blooded evictions and the Draconian principle against living anywhere, except as serfs, are inconsequential because they have not yet touched Mr. Jabavu's person.

Chapter XIV The Native Congress and the Union Government

Pity and need make all flesh kin. There is no caste in blood
  which runneth of one hue; nor caste in tears, which trickle salt with all.
    Sir Edwin Arnold.

A native meeting was called to meet at Johannesburg on July 25, 1913, under the auspices of the South African Native Congress.

The Congress was attended by Natives from as far south as East London and King Williamstown, and from as far north as the Zoutpansbergen in Northern Transvaal, and also from Natal, Zululand, and from Bechuanaland; in fact from nearer and distant centres in all parts of the country they had gathered to discuss the situation arising from the serious conditions created by the Natives' Land Act. Thus the proceedings of the meeting were conducted under a grave sense of responsibility. There was little of the customary loquaciousness which characterizes native gatherings; and there was much less free translation of the speeches for the benefit of the European visitors. Translations, as a rule, take up a great deal of valuable time, and it was their curtailment on this occasion, apparently, which caused the `Transvaal Leader' — a morning paper of the Rand — to complain that Natives had become unusually secretive and had ceased to be as communicative as at previous meetings. The `Rand Daily Mail', on the other hand, referred to the closing session in a very few lines. It said: "Last evening, a number of Native women attended the Native Congress, attired as befitting the solemnity and importance of the occasion. The orderly behaviour of the 200 or more delegates was attributable to the presence on the platform of Mr. Dube, an able chairman, supported by two native solicitors who passed their B.A. in London."

Mr. R. W. Msimang is a solicitor who was articled to a firm of solicitors in England; but the reference to the second "native solicitor" and "London B.A." is about the most undeserved compliment ever paid to the author, who, until 1914 (a year after the Congress reported by the `Mail'), had never been on board a ship, nor inside a London college.

At the annual Congress, March, 1913, a deputation had been appointed to proceed to Capetown and to present to the Government the native objections against the proposed embargo on the purchase and lease of land. The deputation consisted of Mr. J. L. Dube, Dr. W. B. Rubusana, Mr. Advocate Mangena, Rev. L. Dlepu, Messrs. W. Z. Fenyang, S. Msane, L. T. Mvabaza, D. Le Tanka, and S. T. Plaatje; the writer, however, was not able to proceed to Capetown at the time. The July Congress was specially called to receive the report of the delegates to Capetown, and further to consider what other steps it might be necessary to take.

Dr. Rubusana gave a report on the deputation to Capetown. They had four interviews with the Minister of Native Affairs, and several interviews with members of Parliament, urging the setting aside of some Government farms, to which evicted native tenants might go, as the effect of the Bill, then under discussion, would inevitably be to make numbers of them homeless. The Minister, he said, never denied the possible hardship that would follow the enforcement of such a law, but he seemed to be driven by a mysterious force in the face of which the native interest did not count. What that force was, he said, could only be surmised. General Hertzog, who had always advocated some such measure (though he had never been able to carry it out), had just been excluded from the Botha Cabinet; to placate his supporters, who were very angry over his dismissal, the Government carried out this alleged policy of his, so that while General Hertzog in office was not able to bring about the enslavement of the blacks, General Hertzog out of office succeeded in getting the Government to sacrifice their principles of right and justice and to force the Act through Parliament, in order to retain the support of the "Free" State malcontents.

When every effort with the Ministry failed, the delegates asked for a postponement of the Bill pending the report of the Commission. This also was refused by the Government. Finally he wrote a letter to Lord Gladstone, asking him to withhold his assent to the Bill until he had heard the native view. To this His Excellency replied that such a course was "not within his constitutional functions". All this took place in May, 1913.

In July, Mr. Dube, the president of the Congress, wrote to Lord Gladstone asking for an interview to lay before him the nature of the damage that the Act was causing among the native population. Again His Excellency replied that it was "not within his constitutional functions".

The Natives' Land Act, which was then law, was read to the assembled Natives, most of whom narrated their experiences and the result of their observations of the effect of the Act during the six weeks that it had been in force. Congress considered these, and as a result of their deliberations it was resolved to appeal to His Majesty's Government; and also to take steps to apprise the British public of the mode of government carried on in British South Africa under the Union Jack, and to invoke their assistance to abrogate the obnoxious law that had brought the Congress together.

The Congress considered at length how His Majesty the King and the British public could best help the Natives in these matters; and it was concluded that if South Africa were really British, then any suffering taking place in that country must be of concern to His Majesty the King and the British public. The next point for inquiry by the Congress was the journey of a deputation to be chosen to proceed on this mission, a journey consisting of six thousand miles by sea and a thousand miles by rail. When the Europeans of South Africa went to England to ask the Imperial Government for a Constitution, their delegates were easily sent, because the native taxpayers, although with hardly any hope of benefiting by the gift — which amounted to a curtailment of their rights — were compelled to contribute to the travelling and other expenses of these envoys; but in the Natives' own case no such funds are at his disposal, even though he goes to the Imperial Government to point out that his taxes had been used by a Parliament in which he is unrepresented as a rod for his back. In order to meet this necessary demand for ways and means, Mr. Msane was deputed to tour the country and ask for funds from the Natives. A Johannesburg committee was appointed to superintend this effort and take charge of the funds which he might raise. The members of the said committee were: Messrs. W. F. Jemsana (chairman), Elka M. Cele (treasurer), D. S. Letanka, R. W. Msimang, H. D. Mkize, B. G. Phooko, D. D. Tywakadi, D. Moeletsi, M. D. Ndabezita, H. Selby Msimang (hon. sec.), S. Msane (organizer). Finally a deputation was appointed to proceed to Pretoria to lay before the Union Government three resolutions that the Congress passed. The first, condoling with the Government on the death of Hon. J. W. Sauer, late Minister of Justice and Native Affairs, who died just as the Congress was about to meet; the second resolution, that the Natives dissociated themselves entirely from the industrial struggles on the Witwatersrand and elsewhere, and preferred to seek redress for their grievances through constitutional rather than by violent means.

The third resolution, that humble representations to the authorities against the eviction of Natives from farms, having proved unavailing, the Natives had now decided to raise funds for the purpose and convey their appeal to His Majesty the King and to the British public. That Mr. Msane had been appointed organizer of the appeal fund and that a safe conduct was requested for him to tour the native villages. The following deputation was appointed to present these resolutions to the Union

Government at Pretoria: Chief Karl Kekana and Mr. S. M. Makgatho of the Transvaal, Mr. E. Mamba of the Transkei (Cape), Mr. Saul Msane and Rev. R. Twala (Natal), Mr. S. T. Plaatje (Kimberley), and Mr. J. M. Nyokong of the Orange "Free" State.

Mr. S. F. Malan, the Minister for Native Affairs pro tem. received the deputation in the Government Buildings, which were the Transvaal Houses of Parliament before Union. With the Minister of Native Affairs were Messrs. E. Barrett, Assistant Secretary for Native Affairs, Mr. Pritchard, the Johannesburg Commissioner, and Mr. Cross, a Rand Magistrate. The Minister readily received the resolutions and confessed to a feeling of relief at the moderation of their tone. Further, he listened to the story of hardships already suffered by the Natives, as a result of the enforcement of the Land Act, specific instances of which were given, some being of Natives not far from Pretoria, who, after being evicted from their old homes and having found new homes, were told by the Commissioner that they could not settle therein.

The delegates submitted to the Minister that their complaint was not a sentimental grievance, but real physical suffering. The Minister having listened to these statements, pointed out that this Act was the law of the land, which must be obeyed. He was not so sure, he said, that the Natives could achieve anything by means of a deputation to England as the law had already been signed by His Majesty's representative on the spot without hesitation. He could not see why the Natives should be interfered with when holding meetings and organizing a deputation to go to the King, as long as they kept within the four corners of the law. But it seemed to him that they should have waited until a commission had been appointed under Sections 2 and 3 of the Act. An appeal to the Sovereign, he added, was the inherent right of every British subject; but he expressed the desire that the appeal to England should be dropped until the commission had first made its report. The delegates explained that as the law had in six weeks done so much harm, it was alarming to think what it might do in six months, while there was nothing definite to hope for from the report of a commission not yet appointed, and whose report might conceivably take six years.

The deputation made it clear that the appeal to the King would be dropped if the Government undertook to amend the law pending the report of the commission.

THE NATIVES' LAND ACT IN NATAL

In the following months both the Minister in charge of Native Affairs and the Chief Native Commissioner of Natal asked Rev. John L. Dube, President of the S.A. Native National Congress, to furnish them with information and particulars of Natives in misery as a result of the Natives' Land Act. Mr. Dube had been collecting some concrete cases of hardship, including Chief Sandanazwe of Evansdale, Waschbank, who stated that he and fifty members of his tribe "are given notice to remove, and that he has made representations to the authorities in Maritzburg asking for land without success."

Mr. Dube sent the following letter to the Secretary for Native Affairs, with a list of evicted farm tenants, on September 12, 1913.

Sir, —

The Chief Native Commissioner for Natal approached me shortly after the publication in the Press of my open letter* with a request similar to that made by you, viz., that I should furnish him with particulars and information. From time to time I did so furnish those names to the Chief Commissioner, and I send you herewith a list of those names and also additional names which have come to my knowledge since my correspondence with the Chief Native Commissioner.

— * Mr. Dube was here referring to an open letter which he sent
  to the `Natal Press', explaining the hard lot of the Native victims
  of the Act, and appealing to the colonists to intercede
  with the South African Government on behalf of the sufferers. —

In regard to the concluding paragraph of your letter to the effect that the only result of the Chief Native Commissioner's request was the submission of the case of a Native in the Weenen County who received notice from his landlord over a year ago, you must be misinformed. As you will see from the list, scores of names were furnished to the Native Commissioner, and furthermore, some of the individuals themselves who were suffering hardship were sent by me to the Chief Commissioner and were interviewed by him. The trouble has been that the Chief Commissioner, instead of dealing with these individual cases himself, has, I am informed, in many instances, sent the individuals on to the Magistrates, and my letters also have been forwarded to the Magistrates, with the request that Magistrates would go into the matter. However anxious the Magistrates may be to help in this matter they are but human, and in many cases, I am informed, they are overweighed with other work and have been unable to give the attention to these matters that they required. Moreover the Magistrate acts purely as an official, and the Native who is wandering about the country helpless does not get the immediate sympathy and attention which his case deserves and demands. In many cases the individuals I sent on are under the impression, rightly or wrongly, that nothing is being done for their relief.

If I might make a suggestion, it would be that some independent gentleman should be appointed to investigate these cases — some gentleman who would have sufficient time to devote to the investigation of the various instances of hardship that would come before him, and who would be empowered to do what was necessary to relieve the deserving.

I may say further that since the introduction of the Squatters Bill during the 1912 session of Parliament eviction by farmers has been much increased, possibly in view of the impression that prevailed generally among the farming community that the Squatters Bill or some similar measure was to be re—introduced by the Government, the result being that those Natives who had been evicted by farmers now the Natives' Land Bill has become law, are prevented from entering into agreements with land owners as rent—paying tenants, and only under servile conditions, with the result that in many cases they become wandering and helpless vagrants.

Another form of hardship which prevails very generally as the result of the Natives' Land Act is this: The younger Natives do not receive the wage from farmers as can be easily earned, say, on the Rand mines, with the result that the younger men leave their homes and their fathers and proceed to the mines; the father is unable to supply the labour demanded by the landlord owing to the absence of his sons, and as a result he is evicted — many cases of this sort can be cited.

I may here cite two cases within my personal knowledge: (1) Bhulose was living on Mr. R. Miller's farm, "Dalmeny", near Phoenix. He was evicted with his wife and family in June last. He is seeking a place now to reside on, but cannot obtain one. (2) A native woman Vatplank, a widow with a family, was evicted from the property of a farmer, Mr. Adendorff, near Newcastle; this woman with all her household goods and her family had to camp out on the veld. She was barred by the Act from going to neighbouring farmers for a residence.

I have done my utmost to give you concrete examples and names of persons suffering hardship. If I can supplement the information contained in this letter and in the accompanying list I shall only be too happy to do so.

Might I suggest further that you should ask the Chief Native Commissioner to forward to you all my correspondence with him on this matter? This will show you and the Government that the statements contained in my open letter are not mere fabrications, but are based upon solid facts.

       John L. Dube.

Mr. Dube's list includes evictions from the districts of Greytown, New Hanover, Ekukanyeni, Homeless (a very appropriate name in the circumstances), Howick, Estcourt, and Mid–Illovu.

Here is a specimen of notice: —

I hereby give you Mandwasi notice to leave my farm Blinkwater by the end of July, 1913.

       (Sgd.)
July 20, 1913. Freestone Ridge.

"The wheels of administration moved slowly" (to borrow an official phrase) between the Native Affairs Department and the other departments of State. Thus, while the authorities were temporizing with this and similar representations, the Natives' Land Act was scattering the Natives about the country, creating alarm and panic in different places. The high officials of State, instead of relieving the distress thus caused, were interviewing Natives and urging them not to send a deputation to Europe. The Natives received this advice hopefully. They believed it was an indication that the Government was about to amend the law, in which case, of course, the deputation would be unnecessary; but, besides this advice, the officials in each instance promised no relief.

The Natal Native Commissioner held a similar meeting with a number of Zulus. The meeting asked for some relief for the evicted tenants who were roaming about the country, but the official significantly evaded the point. The disappointment of the meeting, created by his evasive replies, having overcome the proverbial native timidity when in the presence of authority, resulted in one petty chief saying to the Commissioner: "Local authorities levy a tax every year on each of our dogs. We don't know what they do with the money. You have never complained against that waste, so why should you complain if our money is spent in sending a deputation to the King?" The answer, if there was one, is not reported.

General Botha, until then, never met native tax—payers to discuss their grievances with them. But in the latter part of 1913, he actually met some Natives in the Eastern Transvaal, who desired to inform him of the ravages of the Act. But instead of holding out any hope that an asylum would be found for the wanderers, he proceeded to advise them against sending a deputation to England. The Natives having given specific instances of the plight of certain evicted tenants in the neighbourhood, asked for an abode for them, but on that point the Premier would not be drawn. The Government's indifference to native sufferings being thus revealed, the Natives of Vryheid became more eager to help to organize the proposed deputation.

General Botha's efforts against the deputation, without offering any homes to the evicted Natives, was probably the best stimulus towards the deputation fund. The Premier visited a northern tribe some time after and was said to have warned the chief and his people against the pretensions of the Native Congress. When Mr. Dube called there a few days later, they handed him 200 Pounds towards the deputation fund, which they had collected since General Botha's visit. Mr. Saul Msane similarly raised 360 Pounds for the fund in the Eastern Transvaal where the Premier first warned the Natives against the deputation without offering them any relief.

Those Natives who were not immediately affected by the Act were rather lukewarm regarding the proposed deputation. But when the officials warned them against wasting their money on a deputation and told them in the next breath that it was a breach of the law to find an abode for the evicted wanderers, these Natives, perceiving the hollowness of the Government's advice, determined that as a last resort a deputation should be sent to England.

Chapter XV The Kimberley Congress / The Kimberley Conference

Sorrow like this draws parted lives in one, and knits anew the rents
which time has made.
        Lewis Morris.

When everything was ready another special Congress was called to meet at Johannesburg in February, to carry out the deputation's scheme and appoint the delegates to proceed to England. In view of the dissatisfaction of the Government after the July Congress, the author considered it his duty to inform the Government that a meeting was about to take place. This information called forth a peremptory intimation from the Government that because of the recent strike of white men (from which the Natives had publicly disassociated themselves) the Native Congress could not be held. But at the time that this telegraphic prohibition reached us General Smuts, Minister of Defence, was announcing in Parliament that the embargo on public meetings, in areas where, owing to the recent strike (of January, 1914), martial law was proclaimed, had been removed. Logically then General Botha's decision made the previous day in regard to the Congress meeting fell to the ground; and so we telegraphed to Senator Schreiner and Dr. Watkins, members of Parliament, to ascertain if this was so. Both these gentlemen answered that in spite of the removal of the prohibition of public meetings of whites, the Prime Minister directs that the one in regard to the "Native Congress" must stand. Thereupon the writer, after consulting a few native residents in Kimberley, intimated to the executive of the Congress that:

Kimberley, my home, is not yet a Republic in its sentiments. There we have not reached the stage where some one's permission must be asked before a meeting can be held. So we invite the Congress to hospitable and British Kimberley, where public meetings close with singing the British National Anthem and not with singing the "Volkslied" or the "Red Flag", as is the case in meetings at some other South African centres.

After the notices were out the Government sent an intimation to the effect that the Congress was not actually prohibited. That it was only deemed undesirable to allow it to be held at Johannesburg, where a strike had taken place; and that even there the Government no longer objected, provided it be held indoors. But this belated reconsideration was unnecessary as the Kimberley preparations were far advanced and some of the delegates were already on their way to Kimberley.

The Congress was opened in St. John's Hall at 10 a.m. on Friday morning, February 27, 1914, by the Rt. Rev. W. Gore-Browne, Bishop of Kimberley and Kuruman. His lordship was accompanied by Archdeacon de Rougemont and Rev. I. I. Hlangwana of St. Paul's Mission, who gave out the native hymns. In the absence of the president, who reached Kimberley in the afternoon of that day, the Bishop was received by Mr. Makgatho, vice-president of the Congress. After the religious exercise had ended, the Bishop counselled the Congress not to ask for a repeal of the whole Act, but only for relief from the oppressive clauses, and then to wait for the Commission's report in regard to the remainder of the Act. "There may be something good in it," added the Bishop, "as the glittering diamonds of Kimberley are found in blue clay."

Mr. Makgatho, in thanking the Bishop for opening the Congress, thanked him for the allegory, but added, however, that he had never heard of a father who said to his child, "You are hungry, my son, and I am going to prepare some dinner for you, but meanwhile you had better wait outside in the rain." After the Bishop gave the Congress his benediction, Prince Malunge-Ka-Mban-deni of Swaziland was introduced to him, as were the Chiefs Molotlegi and Mamogale of Transvaal, Moiloa of the Bahurutshe, and Messrs. Elka M. Cele of Natal, Meshach Pelem from the Cape, J. M. Nyokong, S. Litheko of the O.F.S., and other native leaders.

In the evening a large public reception was held in the City Hall in honour of the delegates. Kimberley joined wholeheartedly in the function. De Beers Company, which had hitherto shown the greatest hospitality only to European assemblies and not to native conferences and organizations, acted otherwise in the case of this Congress and its requirements. Presumably Mr. Pickering, the secretary of De Beers, had had information that even the mining labourers in the enclosed mining compounds were heart and soul with their countrymen outside; and so the Company's hospitality was extended to the native delegates.

Bioscope films were projected by Mr. I. Joshua, the chairman of the A.P.O., Messrs. Lakey and September, other A.P.O. committee men, acting as masters of ceremonies. The coloured people attended in their hundreds, and cheered the musicians of their native brethren who entertained the people who thronged the City Hall till many were refused admission. The Coloured People's Organization sent a speaker, Mr. H. Van Rooyen, to welcome the delegates on behalf of the African Political Organization. The president of their Ladies' Guild, Mrs. Van der Riet, a school teacher and musician of long standing, attended and played the accompaniment for the Greenport Choir on the pianoforte; Miss M. Ntsiko, who had borne the brunt of the evening's accompaniment, was thus relieved.

Mr. Joseph Kokozela, on behalf of the Kimberley and Beaconsfield branches of the Congress, welcomed the Congress to Kimberley, and presented Mr. Dube, the president, with an address, which was beautifully illuminated by the Sisters of St. Joseph Convent, of Mafeking. Mr. H. Van Rooyen associated his people with the Natives in their present struggle for existence, and Dr. J. E. Mackenzie, who spoke on behalf of the Europeans, made a fine speech. He said that nobility was not confined to any particular race or colour; that men with black skins have been known to be just as noble as men with white skins. Amongst other questions he asked, "What could be more noble than the Bedford boy leader who subsequently became the St. Augustine of Central Africa, or what could be more noble than the action of the two servants of Dr. Livingstone, who carried his body, for hundreds of miles, through difficult forests, to the coast, and thus ensured his burial in Westminster Abbey?"

Dr. Mackenzie's speech was afterwards referred to by several native delegates to the Congress. They said that before they came to Kimberley they felt certain that English ideas were utterly obliterated in the Union of South Africa, and that English sentiments were things of the past; but that Dr. Mackenzie's speech had given them fresh hope, as it was like cold water to a traveller in the desert. It was, they said further, like a dream to hear a white man talk like that in a mixed audience.

The Congress received sympathetic telegrams from such old residents of Kimberley as Sir David Harris and Dr. Watkins. Both these gentlemen telegraphed their felicitations from Parliament.

Mr. H. A. Oliver, member for Kimberley, a great Wesleyan and Sunday School leader, who was at Capetown for the Parliamentary session, instructed his manager at Kimberley to book seats on his account for the senior classes of the Newton Wesleyan Sunday School to attend the Congress entertainment.

The Resident Magistrate of Kimberley telephoned to us on this same day that he had received the following telegram from the Secretary for Native Affairs: —

"LEAVING TO–NIGHT FOR KIMBERLEY TO ATTEND THE NATIVE CONGRESS. INFORM PLAATJE."

It had never previously happened that a representative of the Government attended a coloured political assembly, and it was felt that wiser councils had prevailed with the Government, and that as a result it had decided to meet the Natives, at least half–way. If gambling was one of the indulgences of the Natives, some at least of the delegates would have wagered that Mr. Dower was conveying a concession to the Native Congress, by which it would be unnecessary for the latter to send a deputation to England. So thoroughly was the idea of a concession associated in the mind of the Congress with the approaching visit of Mr. Dower that it postponed the election of delegates for the mission to England. This anticipation was a reasonable one as the Union's recent legislation was in the melting–pot.

The law against British Indians, passed at the same time as the Natives' Land Act, was just then recommended for modification, under pressure brought to bear upon the Imperial Government by the Government of India and other agencies. Again, the Labour members were creating difficulties both at Capetown and Westminster over General Smuts's Deportation Bill, which compelled the Government to amend its conditional banishment clause — a hardship that was not as vital or as absolute as the banishment clauses against black tenants in the Natives' Land Act. Consequently, the native delegates to Congress, representing as they did an overwhelming majority of the inhabitants of South Africa — a section that had received nothing but violent legislation from the South African Parliament since the inauguration of Union — had every reason to expect that, for the first time, a Government emissary was carrying an olive branch to the Natives; but, alas! unlike the industrial strikers, the Natives had no votes to create a constitutional difficulty; unlike the British Indians, they have no Indian Government at their back; therefore, their vital interests, being negligible, could comfortably be relegated to the regions of oblivion, and this hope, like all its predecessors, was falsified.

Mr. Dower attended the Congress on Saturday, February 28, and again on Monday, March 2, and made speeches.

He was profuse in expressions of the gratitude of the Government to the Natives, their leaders and their chiefs, for the loyal co-operation they have always rendered the authorities, and he came to ask them, he said, to perpetuate that loyal co-operation and to refrain from appealing to Great Britain on the Natives' Land Act. To appeal would be to put back the clock of the Native Affairs Department for many years. Of course, it did not matter about the putting back of the Natives' own clock, since its only use is that of an index for the registration of Government taxes, municipal pass fees at one shilling or more per month per Native, and similar phases of the black man's burden. Thus, in answer to questions put by the members of the Congress, Mr. Dower was not able to say that one iota of the provisions of that Draconian law would be modified before the Commission made its report, nor could he give a pledge in the name of the Government that if the Commission reported favourably to the Natives, Parliament would carry into effect the Commission's report, even though the pledge sought took no account of the possibility of the Commission's report being hostile to the interests of the Natives. This then was the character of the visit which the Government Secretary paid to the Native Congress. It was entirely barren of results, and as such it left the Congress as it found it, in bewilderment and gloom.

Fresh fears took hold of the Congress. When the commissioners' names were gazetted, they were not received with any great amount of enthusiasm by the native population, for the best that could be thought of the Natives' Land Commissioners was that they were not associated with any political party. With such a view, it can be understood what were the feelings of the Congress when it thereafter learnt that four of the five commissioners were present, as delegates, at the conference of the Ministerial party held at Capetown two months before (the conference at which Generals Hertzog and De Wet definitely severed their connexion with General Botha), nor was there anything to show that the fifth commissioner was not there also. Therefore, the situation amounted to this, that this Land Commission, which should be composed of impartial members, or, if made up of party politicians, it should at any rate represent the three political parties as well as the Natives, was in reality but a branch of the Ministerial party which foisted this very Land Act upon the country.

It was finally resolved to appoint a deputation of five to accompany the president, Mr. Dube, to England if further efforts failed. The Congress nominated nine names, and the election of five delegates from these was entrusted to a committee of fourteen members of the Congress, who balloted for five and reported the result to the full Congress as follows: —

S. T. Plaatje 13
S. M. Makgatho 9
Saul Msane 6
W. Z. Fenyang 3
T. M. Mapikela 3
Dr. W. B. Rubusana 2
A. K. Soga 2
M. Pellem 2
Chief Mamogale 1

The first—named five were therefore declared elected. Mr. Fenyang subsequently stood down in favour of Dr. Rubusana; Mr. Makgatho was not able to reach Capetown in time for the steamer's departure, so the deputation that eventually accompanied the president to England were: —

1. Dr. Rubusana.
2. S. T. Plaatje.
3. Saul Msane.
4. T. M. Mapikela.

Their instructions were first to approach the Prime Minister and ask him to undertake on behalf of his parliamentary majority to repeal the Natives' Land Act, failing that, to endeavour at least to get the clause rescinded which prevents evicted native tenants from finding settlements anywhere except as servants, and that if the Prime Minister should refuse to grant this request, they were forthwith to appeal to the Imperial Parliament and the British public.

It may be added that the Congress, before it rose, received telegraphic advices from Mr. Gibson of the Cape Church Council, and also from the Hon. W. P. Schreiner, not to appeal to England. These communications encouraged the delegates to believe that intermediate relief was being arranged for, to ameliorate the condition of the wandering evicted Natives, in which case there would, of course, be no occasion to appeal to England. But it subsequently transpired that the Natives were advised against making an appeal to England without the offer of any relief.

Before Congress rose votes of thanks were passed in favour of the Bishop of Kimberley and Kuruman, the De Beers Company, the `Diamond Fields Advertiser' for its liberal reports of the proceedings, Mr. Dower for entertaining the delegates to a dinner on Monday, and also to the residents of Kimberley.

The special thanks of the Congress were voiced by Mr. Makgatho to the various committees, whose strenuous efforts for the comfort of the delegates left nothing to be desired. These were: —

COMMITTEES OF LOCAL BRANCHES

KIMBERLEY. — Messrs. Thos. Leeuw (chairman), S. Marogo (treasurer), Bill Tshabalala, H. Ndlovu, Z. Jumane, A. R. Mashoko, T. Diniso (secretary).

BEACONSFIELD. — Messrs. J. Smith (chairman), W. January, S. Pehla (treasurer), Jas. Ngcezula, Ntshenge, B. Mradu, J. S. Kokozela (secretary).

LOCAL ACCOMMODATION AND REFRESHMENTS COMMITTEE: Mesdames J. Smith, S. Sidziya, M. Mahuma, S. Kawa, Mildred Kokozela and L. Skota; Messrs. J. Chologi, J. Matsebe, S. Pehla, Soga, J. Ngcezula and A. Ntshoko.

CITY HALL RECEPTION COMMITTEE: Mesdames J. J. van der Riet and M. Ntsiko; Messrs. Isaac P. Joshua, Sidney Motlhabi, P. W. Mama, T. Diniso, Tony Msengana and J. G. Motlhabi.

An honorarium of 10 Pounds was voted in favour of the honorary secretary, Mr. S. T. Plaatje.

After the deputation reached Capetown on May 13, 1914, we wrote Lord Gladstone informing him that we were bearers of a petition from the native population to His Majesty the King, which we would ask His Excellency to graciously convey. Of course we expected a short note from His Excellency to the effect that "it was not within his constitutional functions" to meet us, but to our surprise this time His Excellency wrote appointing a meeting with us at noon on May 15 at Government House. But, in the interview, the reason why that particular appointment came within the pale of His Excellency's constitutional functions became apparent: for the Governor–General only made it the opportunity to urge the deputation not to go to England.

The deputation replied that, even in native politics there was always an appeal from the action of an induna to the native chief and from the latter to the ruler; that it was straining the loyalty of the black millions of South Africa to tell them that there was no appeal to His Majesty the King against the oppressive laws of a Parliament in which they had no representatives.

It must be added that although the Governor–General did not say so, yet the barbarous cruelties of this relentless law appeared to have produced a sympathy that was visible in his facial expression. Astonishment and pity were amongst the sensations which seemed to be depicted on Lord Gladstone's face. Still, he held out no hope that his good offices would be used to secure an amelioration of the conditions complained of. All His Excellency advised us to do was to abandon the appeal to England.

"But, your excellency, what about these cruelties that are now in progress?" we asked.

"Oh, well," said Lord Gladstone, "the Natives are not the only sufferers, even in England people have suffered hardships from time to time, till they were compelled to emigrate to America and other places."

"That is true, your lordship, but it is to avert such a contingency, if possible, that the Natives appointed a deputation to lay their case before His Majesty the King, as they have no means to emigrate to America, or any other country."

"Oh, no," he answered, "don't misunderstand me; I only use that as an instance, not that Natives must emigrate."

The Governor–General then repeated the advice not to appeal to the Crown, but he held out no hope of an amendment in the Act, and so the deputation sailed for England.

Previous to this interview, no less a personage than General Botha himself — Premier and Minister for Native Affairs — condescended to meet the deputation. Prior to this meeting, the deputation entertained strong hopes that the Premier would come to it with an offer of, say, at least allowing the hiring of land by Natives, pending the report of the Commission, even though the prohibition to buy land remained in force. But instead of such a minimum, the only hope that General Botha held out was that he had not evicted the Natives on his own farm, and that he had further told some farmers not to evict their Natives. These personal acts of the Premier on his own farm, and with regard to some other farmers, had not helped the entire native population of the Union since the Act was promulgated. Nor would they assist those native wanderers who are now without a home on earth, as General Botha himself could not allow any of them to settle on his farm without breaking the law. Again, it did not seem quite clear how General Botha's efforts in this direction could make any impression on private landowners when his own officials were carrying out wholesale evictions of native tenants, on the Government farms at Standerton and elsewhere, and sending them adrift about the country. The only remedy, and that a partial one, would be to legalize the settlement of tenants who have been evicted. But to this General Botha said, "If I went to Parliament now with a Bill to amend this law they will think I'm mad."

That statement confirmed the decision of the deputation to proceed to England, and accordingly they at once made arrangements for sailing.

One painful fact which these interviews revealed was the ignorance of the Government in matters relating to the Natives. The 5,000,000 blacks of the Union are taxed to maintain what is called the most expensive Civil Service in the world. The officials of the Native Affairs Department, in return for their huge salaries, paid out of the proceeds of taxes levied from relatively the most poorly paid manual labourers in the world, namely, the Native taxpayers, are called "the guardians of the Natives"; but General Botha, the Minister of Native Affairs, "Father of the Natives" and supreme head of the Civil Service, seemed (or pretended) to know absolutely nothing of the manner in which his official underlings play battledore and shuttlecock with the interests of the Native population. To mention but one instance: at one stage of the interview we attempted to enlist his sympathy on behalf of the "Free" State Natives in particular, who, in spite of prohibitive laws in the Boer statute books, had not to our knowledge been debarred by the Boer Government from buying or leasing land. General Botha not only denied that his was the first Boer administration which definitely enforced these prohibitions but he also asserted, with all the dignity of his office, that no living Native had ever bought a farm in the "Free" State from a white man — in short he accused us of telling lies. Fortunately Mr. E. Dower, who remembered that some Native landowners in both the Hoopstad and Thaba Ncho districts of the "Free" State had acquired their properties from white people under the Republican regime, was present at the interview and he then bore out our statement: thus on May 15,

1914, the Prime Minister and Minister of Native Affairs heard for the first time in his life that there were some Natives actually living in the "Free" State who pay him quit-rent on farms which they had bought from white people under Republican rule.

The assertion that "Free" State Natives lost nothing by the enforcement of the Natives' Land Act is but one phase of the maze of ignorance through which the Union Government is groping in a hopeless attempt to discharge their trust to the native taxpayers.

The co-operation of intelligent and responsible native taxpayers, which could sweep away these administrative cobwebs of ignorance, is always at the disposal of the Government if they deigned to avail themselves of it; but they prefer, at enormous cost to the taxpayers (including native taxpayers), to purchase from the non-native section of the community arm-chair views based largely on hearsay evidence, which is often tainted by colour prejudice. Hence the shroud of ignorance which surrounds the native policy of the Union of South Africa.

Chapter XVI The Appeal for Imperial Protection

Of all the characters of cruelty, I consider that as the most odious
 which assumes the garb of mercy.
          Fox.

On arrival in London the native delegates were received by several friends, including Dr. Chas. Garnett, M.A., of the Brotherhood League; Rev. Amos Burnet, of Transvaal, introduced them to the Wesleyan Missionary Committee in session at Bishopsgate; the Anti-Slavery and Aborigines Protection Society communicated with the Colonial Office regarding an interview. The Colonial Secretary agreed to see the deputation on condition that they were accompanied by no one from the Society.

When the native deputation reached England there were a number of South African missionaries on furlough in England who had taken part in Church meetings in Africa, of protest against the Act. Some of these gentlemen had witnessed the cruel operations of the Act; but the decision to receive the native delegates by themselves meant that no such eyewitnesses as these could testify to what they had seen of the working of the Act.

In accordance with the time fixed for the interview, the deputation duly waited upon the Secretary of State, whose reply was more fully given in Parliament. At the interview he took notes on nothing, and asked no questions. On every point he had "the assurance of General Botha" to the contrary.

No headway having been made with the Government, it was resolved upon that the delegates should appeal to the British Parliament and thence to the British public in terms of the native mandate.

Later on Messrs. T. Buxton and J. H. Harris, the secretaries of the A.S. and A.P.S., arranged a meeting for the delegates to meet certain members of Parliament. The meeting took place in No. 11 Committee Room of the House of Commons. The British peerage was represented by Lords Emmott and H. Cavendish Bentinck. After hearing the delegates and asking them questions, the members of

Parliament intimated that their decision would be arrived at later in the absence of visitors. It must be mentioned here that besides the above secretaries of the A.S. and A.P.S. there were also present at this meeting a few sympathizers who were not members of Parliament. They included Miss S. Colenso of Amersham, and the Rev. Dr. Howie of Stirling, and Mrs. Howie, etc.

By the kindness of Mr. and Mrs. Buxton, Mr. and Mrs. Cobden Unwin (in conjunction with Mrs. Saul Solomon), Lady Scott of Westminster, Mrs. S. J. Colenso of Amersham, and Mr. H. E. Wood, J.P., of Camberwell (the latter being a prelude to a successful meeting of the delegates with the Baptist Council of England), Sir Albert Spicer, M.P., and Lady Spicer, and Mr. and Mrs. Harris of Dulwich, receptions — some of them attended by English and Colonial guests — held at the residences of the friends named, were given in honour of the delegates.

==

IN THE HOUSE OF COMMONS

Mr. P. ALDEN: I wish to bring to the notice of the right hon. Gentleman the question of the native lands in South Africa. I happen to have been responsible for a Resolution passed unanimously in this House previous to the passing of the Act of Union, and in the discussion which took place on that occasion the Under–Secretary of State to the Colonies laid it down as one of the duties of the Imperial Parliament to protect in every possible way the interests of the Natives in their land, and protect their rights and liberties in that respect. If we take away the land from the Native we take away his liberty. In reference to the Natives Land Act of 1913, I want to put two or three points before the right hon. Gentleman. In the Union of South Africa, blacks own about 4,500,000 morgen of land, and the whites own fourteen times as much land as the blacks, though, of course, they are very much smaller in number. The inequality is very noticeable in the Transvaal, where there are 300,000 whites holding 31,000,000 morgen of land, and the 1,000,000 Natives only have 500,000 morgen of land which they can call their own.

It has been said over and over again in South Africa that this law applies equally to Europeans and whites as well as to the Natives. There is, they say, no injustice. The European is estopped from this purchase of land, just as the Native is estopped. All I can say in answer to that is that the fallacy is shown the moment you begin to ask what land the Natives have to sell. The native areas are already overcrowded, and they positively have no land which they could sell. When once a Native leaves his farm or is evicted, or has to quit for any reason whatever, the Act does not allow him to purchase, hire or to lease anywhere else for farming purposes except from Natives, who have not the land to lease or to sell. He therefore must become a servant on the farm. There is absolutely nothing else for him to do but to become a servant. This Act has already produced very great hardships. It has produced hardships to the people who were under notice to quit at the time the Act was passed, to the people who have actually since then been evicted from their farms, to the Natives who were in search of land and who are wandering about with their families and stock and have nowhere to settle, and to the Natives who have had to leave their crops unreaped. There are many hundreds of such cases of hardship which have been inflicted under the Act which is being enforced on all sides. I do not wish to go into this question at very great length, because the right hon. Gentleman knows more about it than anybody in the House in all probability, and he knows the difficulties of the situation.

I want to put before him just one point with regard to what can be done. WE CALL OURSELVES THE PROTECTORS OF THE RIGHTS OF THE NATIVES, and we claim that we have always, in season and out of season, insisted that those rights should not be infringed, and that no action should be taken against their liberties. The Imperial Government cannot, of course, intervene in the sense of asking the Government of South Africa either to rescind an Act of Parliament or to amend an Act of Parliament, unless it is their own wish, but I must point out that Clauses 1, 4, and 5 do operate most harshly against the Native, and it might be possible, on the representation of the right hon. Gentleman, for the Prime Minister of South Africa to mitigate the hardships.

Mr. CAVE: The subject to which the hon. Member has referred is no doubt of importance, and no one can quarrel with the tone of the speech in which he has introduced it.

Sir ALBERT SPICER: I quite realize that in South Africa we have a self-governing country, and, therefore, one would be desirous to be very careful in what he said with regard to its administration and legislation. But this, at any rate, is the right place to express the views that are held by very large numbers of people in this country, who have devoted a good deal of time and money in doing what they can to educate and uplift the native races of South Africa. Those of us who know South Africa, are perfectly well aware that whilst it is now a country owned by the white races, it can only be properly and fully developed with the help of the native races, and the better educated they are, the better work they will be able to do for South Africa. This Native Lands Act was passed very hurriedly. Of course, we cannot blame South Africa for passing legislation hastily, seeing that we are accustomed sometimes to do the same thing in the Mother of Parliaments. Again, the appointment of the Commission, which is now inquiring into the subject and is taking evidence, is helping, I think, to produce injustice in some cases, so far as the Natives are concerned, because the introduction of the Lands Act has led farmers to take action to enforce their rights. They have terminated the rent-paying agreements of former tenants, and, knowing that these are precluded from making new agreements for the hire of land, they have either ejected them or have demanded from them three months' unpaid service per annum, which has had the indirect effect of reducing a free people to a condition of service. I could give instances of that from well authenticated sources. I will refer to one only. It is the case of a chief and his people living on land which they and their fathers have dwelt upon for eight generations. The farm was recently purchased by a farmer resident in another province. He decided to terminate the rent-paying conditions previously in existence between the former owner and the Natives, and to substitute labour conditions, under which even the chief, an old man, has been required to give service. The people were called upon to quit their houses, square buildings, timbered and thatched, and in connexion with this the owner gave less than one month's notice in the following terms: —

> "This is to notify I can let you have the school building
> no longer. I bought the farm and wish to receive the same
> at the end of your school quarter."

We desire to speak with all due respect of the self-governing Dominions of South Africa, but I think we may fairly ask the Colonial Secretary to help the Union Government to realize that there is a strong feeling in this country in favour of everything possible being done to secure just and reasonable treatment for the Natives. One may fairly ask the right hon. Gentleman to use all reasonable influence with the Union Government to secure for the Natives a fair quid pro quo for the loss of their former rights of land purchase, which would mean in some cases an extension of the native area, and if it were possible to suspend to some extent the operation of the Act until the Land Commission has reported. Having been connected with South Africa for a good many years, having travelled through it, and given a good deal of time to it, I desire to do what I can for the uplifting of the people of that country, and that is my reason for intervening in this Debate.

Other sympathizers, including the Member for Woolwich, rose in different parts of the House to support the foregoing appeal, but the Colonial Secretary stopped them by delivering his reply.

The RT. HON. L. HARCOURT: The hon. member for Tottenham (Mr. Alden) and the hon. Baronet the Member for Hackney (Sir A. Spicer) have drawn attention to the South Africa Land Act. It is not a sudden inspiration of the Botha Government. It is the outcome and result of a Commission appointed by Lord Milner some years ago, presided over by Sir Godfrey Lagden. The Commission was appointed

> "In view of the possible federation of the South African Colonies
> to gather accurate information as to native affairs so as to arrive
> at a common understanding on questions of native policy."

That Commission sat for two years. It had upon it representatives of every colony and territory. It arrived at what I believe was a unanimous (sic) report,* and this Act is practically doing no more than carrying out its recommendations. The Act has already been in operation for twelve months. The Commission of Inquiry, which was to be instituted under the Act, is now sitting. It is bound by the terms of its appointment to report within two years, and will probably report by Christmas next.** The whole of this Act is a temporary measure until that Commission reports. A native deputation has come over and seen me, and I believe many other members. That deputation left Africa against the advice of General Botha, and against almost the entreaties of Lord Gladstone. They knew that the Act would not be disallowed, because it had been announced months before in South Africa. The day the deputation saw me the period of twelve months during which that Act could be disallowed on my recommendation had already expired, and it is now an act which can only be suspended by the Government and Parliament of the Union of South Africa.

— * Col. Stanford (the Cape Colony representative on the Lagden Commission)
  and Messrs. Campbell and Samuelson (the Natal representatives)
  sent in two strongly-worded minority reports against such restrictions.
  Vide S.A. Native Affairs Commission, 1903–5, Vol. I. — Author. ** After Christmas the Commissioners' "terms of appointment" were altered
  from two years to three years. —

Sir W. BYLES: Does it forbid the holding of land by Natives?

Mr. HARCOURT: Perhaps the hon. member will allow me to complete my statement as the time is short.* The suspension of the Act would be worse than useless at the present stage. It would suspend the Inquiry which is taking place at this moment in the interests of the Natives themselves. I cannot believe that any further Commission is necessary, as the existing one seems to me both efficient and sufficient.

— * Mr. Harcourt would have shortened the time considerably,
  had he said "Yes" or "No", instead of replying in sixteen words. —

It is not clear why Mr. Harcourt made this statement as the Natives, in their petition to the King, never asked for a suspension of the whole Act. All that they wished was that the harshest clauses of the measure might be suspended, leaving the others in operation until the Commission rendered its report.

When Mr. Harcourt's reference to the Commission was made known in South Africa the Commissioners, then sitting in Pretoria, were informed of the plight of evicted Natives. The Commissioners replied that any grievance arising out of the operation of an Act of Parliament was beyond the scope of their enquiry, and that they could not consider such grievances. This was exactly what they had previously told the Natives at King Williamstown and elsewhere. At Harrismith the Commission heard the complaint of a son of Chief Wietzie, who, during the Basuto wars, had always remained loyal to the "Free" State Boers. The son had been evicted from the ground on which he and his fellow–tribesmen had resided for generations and he was forced to live on an urban location where it is impossible to do any farming. The President (Sir William Beaumont) said he was sorry to hear that a son of Wietzie found himself homeless, but he regretted that the Commission could not help him. Mr. Harcourt, therefore, must have been incorrectly informed regarding the functions of the Commission.

Yet another puzzle. After the appointment of this Commission in September 1913, there was a newspaper report to the effect that the Commission found the native difficulty most acute in the "Free" State, and that it had decided on setting aside without delay a strip of territory in the Western "Free" State as a native settlement. Immediately after the appearance of this report in the Press, angry meetings of the whites were held in Boshof and Hoopstad to protest against the proposals attributed to the Commission. In reply to these protests, Mr. Theron, the Minister of Lands, evidently speaking on behalf of the South African Government, not only repudiated the report but he also added significantly that "the Government had no intention of creating a native area in Hoopstad or anywhere else." So, where do we stand? Can it be wondered that the Natives are beginning to conclude that their position under the Union is hopeless?

But, to return to Mr. Harcourt, the Colonial Secretary also gave the Imperial Parliament a fresh explanation of the Natives' Land Act. It is a pity that we cannot reproduce his explanation side by side with the four explanatory circulars issued by the Union Government in 1913. Such a reproduction would show the discrepancy between the five explanations. We wrote to South Africa but could only secure one of these circulars, which purports to be an explanation of a previous explanatory circular — an explanation of an explanation. However, the definition of the Act, as given by the other three circulars, leaves, as far as we can remember, the root principle of the Act unexplained. Moreover, the statements set forth in these circulars are not in harmony; they have only one point of agreement, namely: that when Natives are driven out of their homes by the law, and are debarred by the same law from establishing other homes (the only provision made for them being that they should live as servants of the whites) the circumstances give them no ground for complaint.

Take for instance only two sentences in Mr. Harcourt's explanation. In the first of these, he appears to approve of the system of forced labour established by the Act; in the second, he denies the evictions that took place in July when he spoke, and those that took place subsequently. He seems to flatly deny not only what is admitted by Lord Gladstone and General Botha, but he likewise contradicts the terms of the Act itself. Indeed, if we had not been there and heard him we should have felt, on reading this part of his speech, that he had been misreported in Hansard. Thus —

If the Natives are farm labourers there is no limit to the number who may reside on white property. If not, they are not dispossessed until Parliament acts upon the report of the Commissioners, and then only when suitable land is provided by addition to a native reserve.*

— * At Downing Street Mr. Harcourt informed the Deputation
that he had the "assurance of General Botha" that the Natives
have too much land already. —

The Imperial explanation being as obscure as the Colonial explanations which preceded it, the reader's remedy is to fall back on the plain English of the Act (Chapter III), which alone has the force of law. Again Mr. Harcourt: —

If General Botha breaks his word I have no power to enforce it. I cannot bind his successors. If the Government of South Africa is not to be trusted in this matter they are to be trusted in nothing; and we know perfectly well that they can be trusted in these matters. NOTE WHAT HAS BEEN DONE WITH RESPECT TO THE INDIAN IMMIGRATION ACT. THIS WAS PASSED NOT FROM LOCAL DESIRE, BUT FROM IMPERIAL CONSIDERATIONS. THE PROVISIONS OF THAT ACT HAVE BEEN ACCEPTED BY THE COLONISTS AND BY THE REPRESENTATIVES OF THE INDIANS, WHO CONSIDER IT THE MAGNA CHARTA OF THE INDIANS IN SOUTH AFRICA. I think that that should be a sufficient guarantee as to the way in which General Botha proposes to act. General Botha, too, used THESE WORDS in Parliament: —

"He had told the deputation that he had given standing instructions to the magistrates throughout the country that if they found any one in their districts ejecting Natives from the farms they had to go and make inquiries and report to him. He had in all those cases which had been brought to his notice used the influence of his Department."

All we can say in regard to "these words" is that the Magistrates apparently ignored the "standing instructions" alluded to, for they allowed the officials of the Department of Lands to scatter the native tenants from Government farms at Standerton, Colworth and elsewhere and sent them adrift over the country, well knowing that they could find no other shelter.

On the 31st of January, 1914, the Magistrate of Ladysmith, presumably acting under instructions from one of General Botha's Departments, issued the following notice to 79 native families in his district: —

"To Vellem Sibisi, Kraal Head residing on one of the following farms, viz. Remainder of Brakfontein, Remainder of Weltevrede, etc.,

"Take notice in terms of Section 4 of Law 41 of 1884 that you are required to remove with your Kraal and inmates from whichever of the said farms you may be residing on, six months from this date, the aforementioned farms having all been purchased by Government for closer settlement purposes."

The Magistrate who so ruthlessly ejected these and other native families acted under the orders of the Government, who settled white people on the farms at the expense of a Treasury maintained also by native taxpayers. And it seems difficult to conceive how a Government which proved so indifferent regarding the fate of its own native tenants or of tenants on farms freshly acquired at the public expense, could be solicitous about the welfare of Natives evicted by private landowners. The statement, on the face of it, is incongruous.

In his heroic efforts to defend South Africa's giant wrong, Mr. Harcourt gave away his case when he referred approvingly to what he calls "the Magna Charta of the Indians in South Africa". Now, what is this "Magna Charta"? In 1913, when the South African Parliament was at the noontide of its "mad career", it passed this iniquitous land law to repress the native race; and also a law imposing the most humiliating limitations on British Indians. Yet it must be added that the Indian law was the milder of the two, as it did not prohibit Indian residents in South Africa from living on the land. The Rt. Hon. A. Fischer, Union Minister of the Interior, who died two years ago, called these two laws of 1913, "the Kafir law and the Coolie law".

As already stated, the London Committee of the Wesleyan Methodist Church asked to see Mr. Harcourt and inform him how drastically the "Kafir law" was operating against their converts and other Natives in South Africa, but Mr. Harcourt discreetly refused to see the Committee.

As for the Indians, no one in South Africa paid any heed to their complaints against the "Coolie law"; but their cry reached India and Lord Hardinge demanded the redress of their grievances. His Lordship insisted so forcibly that (unlike the Wesleyan missionaries) he could not be ignored. The result was that the South African Parliament, "not from local desire, but from Imperial consideration", was obliged in the next session (1914) to amend the "Coolie law" with a "Magna Charta of the Indians in South Africa", and Mr. Harcourt's reference to this episode conveys the suggestion that what is sauce for the Indian goose, with Lord Hardinge at its back, can be by no means sauce for the native gander without the backing of a Viceroy.

We cannot believe that to boast in one and the same speech about a "Magna Charta of the Indians" and dismiss the native appeal against a vital wrong is true Imperialism. For if Imperialism stands for the protection of a few thousand Indians in South Africa because they are supported by a Viceroy, and the neglect of the groans of five million Natives because (unlike a Viceroy) the missionaries who plead for them cannot enforce their claim with a political or diplomatic blow, then there would appear to be the suggestion of more fear than justice in Imperialism.

Mr. Harcourt further credits the Milner Commission, presided over by Sir Godfrey Lagden, with the origin of the Natives' Land Act. We do not wish to defend the policy of these two former South

African Statesmen, as we feel certain that they can take care of themselves. But we must say at once that we read the recommendations of the Lagden Commission ten years ago, as carefully as we have since read the controversy of the Natives' Land Act; and with the knowledge thus gained, we can safely tell the reader that that Commission never recommended that: —

1. "Except with the permission of the Governor–General", Europeans must be debarred from buying land from Natives (who have no land to sell), and Natives must be debarred from buying land or leasing land from Europeans, who alone deal in land. — (Sect. 1 of the Nat. Land Act).

2. When evicted Natives apply for the said "permission of the Governor–General" they should be told that that permission "will only be granted to a few exceptional applicants" and that it could under no circumstances be granted to Natives in the colony in which the applicants resided (The Government's reply to the "Free" State wanderers).

3. The Government should always take from three to six months to deliver this refusal, during which period applicants may have already become serfs or fled the country. (This has been the experience of all applicants within the writer's knowledge.)

4. There should be a fine of 100 Pounds or six months' hard labour on any farmer who provides the Native with a shelter while he is waiting for this disappointing reply to his application (Sect. 5 Nat. Land Act).

5. Native tenants to be hounded out of the Government farms long before the segregation takes place and that white people, who are not debarred from buying or leasing land for themselves, be settled thereon at Government expense. (See magisterial notice above.)

If Mr. Harcourt has been told by any one that the Lagden Commission recommended any of these pitiless iniquities, then we are afraid that his informer is a romancer of the superlative degree. The Lagden report was never discussed in any South African legislature, much less adopted by any Parliament in South Africa; indeed, it is detested because it recommended a Native Franchise for South Africa like the Maori Franchise of New Zealand.

One member of Parliament (Mr. Joynson–Hicks) said South Africa was a Home Rule country and he wondered what would happen if after Home Rule had been granted to Ireland some one asked the Imperial Parliament to interfere with Irish legislation.

We wonder who could have told this hon. Member that there was Home Rule in South Africa! There used to be Home Rule in the Cape Colony alone, but this has been swamped by the Act of Union, which has since established an oligarchic Government throughout the country. And if by Home Rule to Ireland it is intended to give the franchise to a selfish, greedy and tyrannical few; and give carte blanche to this few, telling them thereby to do what they wish with the rest of the population of Ireland, and telling them further that they will be accountable to nobody for any good legislation that they might enact on the one hand, or any maladministration that they might perform on the other hand as is the case in South Africa — if that be what is meant by Home Rule for Ireland, then God have mercy on the Irish.

When the reply of Mr. Harcourt was published in South Africa, supporters of this cruel law bubbled over with joy concerning it. One Dutch writer, after saying in a Dutch journal some very fine things about Mr. Harcourt, wound up a high–sounding eulogy by congratulating South Africa on having such a good Colonial Secretary at Downing Street. "Had Mr. Harcourt's predecessors been like him," said this writer to his readers, "South Africa would have been saved many tears." We doubt if Mr. Harcourt, the object of this appreciation, would feel flattered by it if he knew that all the black victims of this cruel law, and all their European sympathizers, stood firmly by the Imperial Government and by the Colonial Government in the present struggle, while the gentleman at whose instance it was introduced in Parliament, as well as the Dutch editor of the journal alluded to, are at present (May 1915) committed for trial on charges of high treason; and the proprietor of another Dutch journal, in which we read similar vaunting adulations of Mr. Harcourt, was fined 60 Pounds (so his paper says) for alleged complicity in the recent rebellion. These facts should impel the Rt. Hon. the Colonial Secretary to stop, look round and inquire "who's who" among his South African admirers.

Two members of the South African Parliament — Senator T. L. Schreiner and Mr. Wilcocks, M.L.A. — the former an opponent and the latter a supporter of the Natives' Land Act, recently discussed the Act from separate points of view; and both came to the conclusion that the measure was designed to keep the blacks in subjection. This conclusion is in harmony with the bitter experiences of the native races since this Act was enforced. Yet in the face of this unanimous testimony of different observers, Mr. Harcourt equivocates behind the irrelevant "assurances of General Botha" about a possible segregation, which question is not now before the country. Assurances on segregation only serve to confound the issue. If the Beaumont commission, or its successor, should ever report then the question of segregation may come before Parliament some time in 1926. The point before the country now is not segregation, but the Natives' Land Act of 1913, which is now scattering the Natives about the country. That is the measure against which the Native appeals for Imperial protection. Not the future segregation.

The only serious objection with which Mr. Harcourt apparently was able to charge the native deputation, and one which the Natives do not deny, is that they came to England against the "entreaties of Lord Gladstone" (who previously had twice refused to see them), and against the "advice of General Botha", by whose Cabinet the measure was enacted and enforced.

It is a pity that Mr. Harcourt did not at the same time tell the House of an authentic case where an aggrieved party ever sued for redress with the consent and advice of his oppressor. In this connexion, the scope of our reading being limited, our ignorance is possibly abysmal; but it must be confessed that we have never heard of such an interesting appellant and we are inclined to believe that there never has been one.

If General Botha wished to tell the whole truth, instead of making vague assurances to Mr. Harcourt, he would say: "I foresaw all the difficulties under which the Natives are suffering; and when Mr. Grobler proposed the summary stoppage of the sale and lease of land to Natives before the areas are segregated, I warned the House against this trouble, but the Hertzogites being too much for me I had to give in." Gen. Botha could go further and say to Mr. Harcourt: "If you will turn up page 579 of the South African Hansard (first column) reading from the top of the page, you will find my warning in these words: —

Unless they went slowly and carefully, there was a danger that they might take steps which would be unreasonable, unjust, and unfair on one section. For that reason, he regretted the amendment proposed by General Hertzog, because the amendment would have bad results if it were accepted. It would lead to an over–hasty measure of a most impracticable kind. This House would have to demarcate exactly and immediately those parts where the Natives would have to live, and he asked them: was this House able to do so? (Cries of "No".) It was all very nice to talk and take a map and draw lines on it. On the map they might be able to beacon off parts, and say, "This is for the Natives," but then, when they put their scheme into effect, they might find that the ground of many individuals had been taken away without any inquiries or any investigations having been made. (Laughter, and "Hear hear".) This House would expropriate the rights of many white people, and they would meet with the greatest opposition. Where were they going to put these people then? In the Transvaal, farmers certainly would not consent to this; he did not know the people of the Free State so well, but he doubted whether they would agree. (A Free State Member: "No, they certainly will not.") Instead of taking any steps like this, they should be practical, and not land themselves into greater difficulties than they could help. Governments before them had done their best. He agreed that the squatting of Natives should be put an end to as soon as possible, but they should not lose sight of the fact that many Governments before them had done their best to put an end to this squatting evil. He knew well how the Transvaal Government had, year after year, taken up this matter. But what did they find? Simply that when they had passed a Squatters Law they could only put it into operation in one small part of the country. (Hear, hear.) To introduce another Bill like that would simply mean deceiving the country — (hear, hear) — and the Natives. If they accepted the proposal of the Minister of Native Affairs to appoint a Commission to investigate the various conditions prevailing throughout the country, he thought they would be taking a step in the right direction. (Hear, hear.) However, care was essential, because they must prevent causing a sort of revolution through the country. What they wanted was a measure which would be acceptable to the white man as well as to the Native. (Hear, hear.)

These were General Botha's views when the Land Act was first mooted, but in defiance of his solemn warning, the Bill, when gazetted, provided that the eviction of native tenants should precede the Commission's inquiry; harsher and still harsher clauses were inserted in the Bill until the Act finally embodied all the proposals brought forward by General Hertzog. The promise to refer the Bill to a Select Committee was also broken, presumably as a result of pressure from the caucus. The Government could not face a Select Committee after this complete change of front as they must have known that reason was absolutely against them.

It might be asked: How could a Minister turn round afterwards and give "assurances" concerning the benefits of a measure which he had opposed before? To such a question we would hazard the following explanation: Our Prime Minister, on the one hand, is a British Privy Councillor and a General in the British Army; and, on the other hand, he is a simple Afrikander Boer, who only speaks Dutch in Parliament and addresses English audiences through an interpreter. And so in the eyes of General Botha, the British Crown Minister, if the Natives be treated justly, as British subjects should be treated, it is right; and, again, in the eyes of General Botha, the Afrikander Boer, if the Natives be treated harshly and barbarously, that too is right.

It is not unusual to find these two natures contending against each other in one and the same person, whenever the Prime Minister deals with native questions; then more often than not the Boer view, being that of his own nature, dominates the British sentiment, which is a fresh acquisition.

Having given above a striking extract from a speech on native policy, by the Rt. Hon. Louis Botha, Premier of British South Africa, we will now proceed to give an extract from another declaration by General Louis Botha, the Transvaal Boer. The Union Premier was giving evidence before the Labour Commission in Johannesburg and this is what he then said: —

11,302. Sir GEORGE FARRAR: You said that you would recommend the breaking up of Locations like Swaziland, Zululand and Basutoland and the putting of white settlers there? General BOTHA: I would suggest that these countries be given up to the white people to live in. . . .

11,337. The general tenor of your remarks is that there is sufficient labour, and it only wants a little patience to wait for it, that is all? I have distinctly stated that there is a greater amount of labour than has at present been obtained. But there are farmers who have farms, and have no Natives living on these farms. For these people it is difficult to obtain Natives because the Natives who are not living on the farms are in locations. If the locations were broken up the Natives would be made to live on farms.

11,338. You suggest that we should break up such land as Basutoland, Swaziland and Zululand? Yes, I say that such places are a source of evil. It is building up a Kaffir kingdom in the midst of us which is not only bad for the Kaffirs themselves but is a danger in the future.*

— * One of the Chiefs in these locations gave General Botha 200 bullocks
  to feed his troops engaged in crushing a rebellion of white men. —

11,339. But take Zululand, for instance; there is a quarter of a million people there. What would you do with them if you break up their territory? They would all live on the farms as the white people are doing now.

11,340. Oh, you want to cut up the land into farms, give it to the white people and retain the Kaffirs on the farms? Yes.

11,343. But what will the white people do with the Kaffirs, pay them wages or charge them rent for the ground or what? My opinion is that Kaffirs who now live in locations should work for the white people, and the land should be exploited. The white people would pay them for the work they did and this would civilize them.

11,344. A nation like the Basutos you would deal with in the same way? — Yes.

11,345. They at present occupy the land, we have had it in evidence before us to the effect that every inch of land in Basutoland is occupied and worked by the Kaffirs themselves as their own property? — That is just my argument . . . because there is opening for the Kaffirs there they go and live there without doing anything.

11,347. But they do something. They work the whole country, they have a lot of grain? — Yes, for themselves.

11,352. . . . I have shown you that Basutoland is fully occupied by Kaffirs, and they work it. Do you want to apply your scheme to Basutoland? — I do not know very much about Basutoland, I have never been there personally; but I am well acquainted with Zululand and also Swaziland, and I want to state this, that in my opinion it is not only a wrong policy, but also dangerous policy to have large tracts of country inhabited by uncivilized races, and to keep them there on the present terms.

11,353. But these Natives lived there from time immemorial. It was theirs before we came here. How can we drive them off the land now, and take it for ourselves? I think we are feeling very happy that we drove them from Johannesburg in the olden days. They lived in this country too just the same and the Kaffirs who became civilized under us have improved.*

— * `Transvaal Labour Commission', pp. 717–726. —

In the foregoing extract the reader has the root principle of the Natives' Land Act in a nut–shell. Not from hearsay "assurances" but from what fell from the Premier's own lips.

Mr. Jacob de Villiers Roos, head of the Union Law Department (who knows more about South African law than outsiders who have to rely on "assurances",) says in his evidence given before the Select Committee on Public Accounts, February 25, 1914, incidentally or accidentally: —

"A circular was issued by our Department, at the instigation of the Native Affairs Department, asking that prosecutors under the Natives' Land Act, before commencing prosecutions, should refer to the Native Affairs Department as otherwise IT WAS FEARED THAT AN UPHEAVAL MIGHT RESULT. The Transvaal Attorney–General drew our attention to this circular and said that it was an infringement of his powers. . . . When Mr. Beyers went away on leave Mr. Greenlees was appointed Acting Attorney–General, and he first drew the attention of the Minister to it. The Minister took no action until Mr. Beyers returned when the matter was again raised and then this circular was withdrawn."*

— * S.C. 1–'14, pp. 136–137. —

Now, what, in the name of common sense, does a supposedly civilized Government want with a law that it knows will cause "an upheaval"?

This Act should be abolished in the interest of the morality of the State and for the sake of the reputation of the Union Jack, because of the harm it does to the Natives and because its promoters have rebelled against the Crown. The Act has benefited no one; it has driven the Natives from the country to the cities, and has also disappointed the White Labour Party, who supported it in the belief that by its clause forcing Natives to work for white farmers it would keep the Natives away from the industrial centres.

It should be abolished in the interests of the Boers, for it has aroused the bitterest enmity of the blacks against the Dutch section of his Majesty's subjects.

Further, the Act should be abolished because it has lowered the prestige of the Union Jack in the eyes of the coloured subjects of the King, who have suffered and are still suffering untold misery under it. Perhaps nothing illustrates more clearly this changed feeling of the Natives than the present state of things in South Africa. Thus, if German South–West Africa had been annexed to the Cape before the Union, every Native, south of the Zambesi, would have approved of the step, whereas to–day, as a result of the Natives' Land Act, there is a different feeling extant. For now the Natives know that annexation to the Union will mean the elimination of the Imperial factor, and that as Capetown, like Pretoria, has ceased to represent British ideas of fair play and justice, such a change would in the annexed territory establish "Free" State ideals under the aegis of the Union Jack. The Natives of the Union shudder at the possibility of the Damaras, who are now under the harsh rule of the Germans, being placed under a self–governing Dominion in which the German rule will be accentuated by the truculent "Free" State ideas of ruling Natives. And they think that in the existing state of circumstances, Portuguese or French rule would be infinitely better for the Damaras than a Government which, although protected by the Union Jack, yet is inspired from Pretoria and Bloemfontein. And it is to be feared that the pernicious principles which Tommy Atkins is now fighting on the Continent to suppress, are going to be rigorously applied in a South–West Africa under Burgher rule. The prosperity of no State can afford to alienate the sympathy of any considerable portion of its tax–payers. And so, as 5,000,000 blacks have been alienated in their sympathies to the Union by this oppressive law, and as the Union Government is unable or unwilling to amend it, in the interest of the Union Government, no less than the 5,000,000 blacks, outside intervention becomes a necessity.

During three separate white men's upheavals in the last two years — two bloody strikes and a civil war — white revolters made frantic efforts to embroil the Union in a native rising, but the Natives very sensibly sided with the Government. The native leaders, in order to counteract this mischief–making, had to incur the expense of journeys by rail besides financing their own mission to reach the scene of the would–be native disturbance.

The time will come when these leaders will tire of spending their own money in paying fares to the Government Railways, to render free services to a Government which taxes them to pay other people lavishly for similar work, while it does not even tender them so much as a word of thanks.

Instead of the smallest recognition for our voluntary services, the Union Government repays our loyalty by persecuting our widows and fatherless children with the cold–blooded provisions of the Natives' Land Act. These cruelties are euphemistically described as the first step towards the segregation of white and black, but they might more truthfully be styled the first steps towards the extermination of the blacks.

When the war broke out, the Government promptly suspended the inquiries of the Commission, whose report is naively alleged to be pregnant with the fruits of the millennium, but the cruel evictions under the same law of the rebel Grobler are pursuing their course while the war lasts and the Union Government remains unconcerned. It was only when a whole tribe was evicted during the war that the Government interceded on behalf of the victims, but then, the only extent of the intervention has been to secure exemption for the chief of the tribe alone, on the condition that HE FORCED THE REST OF HIS TRIBE TO RENDER EVERY YEAR THREE MONTHS' LABOUR TO THE LANDOWNER. Yet these people could live happily on some other farm did not the Government prohibit their happiness at the behest of a rebel who, at or about the time of this enthralling compromise, was conducting treasonable operations against the Government.

The sublime ingratitude of the Union Government is wellnigh unbearable!

Chapter XVII The London Press and the Natives' Land Act

Slaves cannot breathe in England: if their lungs
Receive our air, that moment they are free;
They touch our country, and their shackles fall.
      Cowper.

The native deputation (thanks to Mr. H. Cornish, secretary of the Institute of Journalists) can truthfully assure their people, at the present critical state of their position, of the sympathy of the London Press. It is hardly necessary to mention that religious papers, to which the object of the deputation was made known, published some very encouraging articles on the same, and bespoke the deputation a cordial reception and a sympathetic hearing throughout the United Kingdom; but the mission might have been somewhat monotonous had we friends only and no enemies in the London Press. And a weekly paper with a yellow cover, called `South Africa', did its best to fill the role of an enemy.

It abused the Brotherhood Movement and the Aborigines Protection Society for taking up the cause of the deputation. The General Press Cutting Association, however, through whom we learnt of the attacks of `South Africa', did not tell us whether this journal also abused our other friends represented by the London Press. Such has been our good fortune in this respect that friends frequently congratulated us on the unanimity of the Press in our favour. In this we think they were right, as a cause with only one enemy could very well be depended on to take care of itself.

On one occasion some of our friends heard that the author was going to interview the fine–fingered editor of the `Westminster Gazette' by appointment, and they strongly advised us against doing so. "Why not?" we asked. "Oh," said our friends, "he edits the leading Government organ, and he is going to pump you of all information in order to use it against your cause and in favour of the Government." But we went — firstly, because we refused to believe that the editor of that great organ of British thought was capable of taking such a mean advantage of us; and secondly, because we were confident of being able to take care of ourselves against any kind of pump; and we can now say with satisfaction that, on the part of the British public, there was such a demand for back numbers of the two editions of the `Westminster Gazette' which contained a report of our interview and a photograph of the deputation that in a fortnight both issues were sold out of print. Further, it is safe to say that from the wide area from which inquirers wrote to us mentioning the `Daily News', it would seem that either that journal has a very big circulation or its readers are mainly interested in South African Affairs. And what, may be asked, are the qualifications of the newspaper `South Africa' which attempted to run counter to this overwhelming opinion in our favour?

Unlike some of its contemporaries, `South Africa' has not a single native contributor to its columns. Some London newspapers are in regular receipt of exchange copies from native newspapers published in South Africa, London papers which never claimed a monopoly over South African thought; yet here is a paper, South African in title and in pretensions, which cannot even boast of a South African native paper on its exchange list! What information, then, can the editors of such an exclusive London paper possess about an Act specifically enacted to operate against Natives? Logically, they would know absolutely less than next to nothing about such a law or its fell work. That alone should dispose of the qualifications of this enemy of the deputation, and his authority to speak on the subject of its mission.

The `African World' is an Anglo–African weekly which has native newspaper exchanges and several African correspondents both white and black. Its editor–in–chief was born in South Africa and was a journalist there before he came to reside in England; and it must be admitted that a paper with such connexions is in a better position to discuss the subject from both points of view. And so the `African World' says:

==

THE SOUTH AFRICAN NATIVE DEPUTATION

It must be admitted that the South African Native Deputation now in this country have gone about their business with decorum. They have not pressed themselves forward unduly, and, so far, the publicity given to them has been moderate in its tone, and the expressions by the members of the deputation have been equally moderate. Of course, their best friends discountenanced this visit, as we have noted from the South African Press, but it seems to be the general opinion that even though no appeal lies under the Union Constitution to the British Crown as regards native rights, an extraordinary anomaly seems to exist in this: That the Natives of South Africa within the Union appear to have fewer rights than those outside the Union, especially so far as an appeal to London on various matters affecting their interests is concerned. We are aware that Mr. Harcourt treated the deputation with the utmost discretion when he received them. We also know that Mr. Harcourt and General Botha are on very friendly personal relations, and under these circumstances, without wishing to dictate any action in the matter to the powers that be on both sides of the water, we would like to join our contemporary `The Globe'.

And what did `The Globe' say?

==

THE NATIVE APPEAL

The complaint of the South African Natives who have laid their grievances before certain members of Parliament amounts in effect to a complaint that Parliament is not Imperial. Their grievances are real and pressing, as anybody can discover who troubles to look up the recent proceedings of the Union Parliament, but they have no constitutional means of ventilating them. No native franchise exists in South Africa, and although certain members of the Union Senate are presumed to keep an eye on native questions their influence has proved ineffective. No appeal exists under the Union Constitution to the Crown as regards Native rights, for although this omission was pointed out at the time the Act of Union was debated in the Imperial Parliament and was adversely commented on, no steps were taken by the Colonial Office to rectify the constitution in this respect. We are, therefore, brought up against the extraordinary anomaly that Natives of South Africa within the Union have fewer rights than those outside — for the Basutos, who remain under direct Imperial control, have successfully appealed to London on various matters affecting their interests — or even than the Natives of Crown Colonies elsewhere, as the appeal of native landowners on the Gold Coast against recent legislation in that territory attests. In the latter case the appeal to the Colonial Office was successful in modifying the offending enactments; in the far more serious grievances of the South African Natives the Colonial Office has no constitutional title whatever. Nevertheless the relations between Mr. Harcourt and General Botha in other respects are notoriously so close and confidential that we may hope the Colonial Secretary will take the present occasion by the hand and urge upon the head of the South African Government the wisdom of dealing with native discontents in his own proper sphere before he prosecutes his claim for the inclusion of the Basutos and Rhodesia in the Union — a claim which both the black Natives and the white colonists have repudiated with all the emphasis at their command. General Botha could scarcely fail to give heed to private advice from the Colonial Office. In the case of the Natal Indians, whose grievances he recently redressed, he proved himself a man capable of taking a broad and generous view of a difficult question. There is no reason to anticipate until the contrary is proved, that he will fall below his own level in the present not less difficult or dangerous case.

==

VIEWS OF THE `DAILY NEWS'

"The South African National Congress, after resorting to every constitutional means of pressing their case against the Land Act on the Union Government, have sent five of their number to London in the firm conviction that the King of England, to whom they look as their natural defender and vindicator, will turn no deaf ear to their pleas. Two of the five — the Rev. J. L. Dube and Mr. Saul Msane — are Zulus; Dr. Rubusana is a Xosa; Mr. Mapikela, a Fingo; and Mr. Plaatje, the secretary of the National Congress, a Bechuana. All of them are men of obvious culture and with a striking command of the English language."

"Having failed to make any impression on the Union Government (`If we had votes,' Dr. Rubusana observed, `we could fight our own battles') the deputation has come to England in the hope of influencing the Imperial Government through the Colonial Secretary.

"What they ask for is:

"First, a suspension of the operation of the Act pending the report of the Delimitation Commission:

"Second, an inquiry into native grievances under the Act; and,

"Thirdly, an assurance that the Home Government will express its concurrence with certain promises made recently on behalf of General Botha, but obviously depending for their value on the continuance of his personal political supremacy.

Native Life in South Africa

Four Blacks to One White

"In carving out estates for themselves in Africa the white races have shown little regard for the claims of the black man," says the `Daily News'. "They have appropriated his land, and in appropriating his land have taken away his economic freedom, and have left him in a worse case than they found him. How the Native has been dispossessed may be illustrated by the facts in regard to the Union of South Africa. Here the blacks, as compared with the whites, are in the proportion of four to one; but they are in legal occupation of only one–fifteenth of the soil.

"Under the Natives' Land Act, which has brought the matter to a crisis, even the poor fragment of rights in the soil that remains seems doomed. For under the Act the Native is denied the right — except with the quite illusory `approval of the Governor–General' to purchase, hire, or acquire any rights in land from a person other than a Native. Under this provision, the Native whose tenancy expires, or who is evicted from a farm, is legally denied any career except that of a labourer. He cannot own, he cannot hire, he cannot live a free man.

A Legal Serf

"In the language of Mr. Dower, the Secretary for Native Affairs, he must `sell his stock and go into service.' He must accept any conditions the white farmer chooses or the mine–owner gives, and an ingenious clause encourages the white farmer to exact unpaid service from the native tenants. In a word, the Native is a legal serf in his own land.

"As British subjects, the deputation of Natives now in England have appealed to the Imperial Government for protection. They asked for its help to secure the suspension of the Act until the Land Commission report is before Parliament, and for machinery to inquire into and redress their grievances. They have got no satisfaction on these points.

"It is time that Parliament gave some attention to its obligations in regard to the South African Native. He has no vote and no friends — only his labour, which the white man wants on the cheapest terms. And the white man has got this by taking his land and imposing on him taxes that he cannot pay. In fact, the black man is `rounded up' on every side, and if, as the deputation suggest may be the case, he is forced to acts of violence, it will not be possible to say that he has not had abundant provocation.

Rights to the Soil

"There is only one principle that can be applied for his protection. It is the principle that he has rights in his native soil. Perhaps segregation is the only remedy now, but if so the reservations allocated to him in the Union area ought to have some relation to his needs. We cannot do much for him there, but we should do what we can."

Mr. Advocate F. A. Silva wrote to the `Daily News': —

==

AN APPEAL FOR JUSTICE

Sir, — Will you please allow me space, while appreciating your editorial of this date, to bring to the kind notice of your readers the distinction between "British justice as supposed to be" and "British justice as it is" with regard to the subject races, especially the black men?

If even the "hair" of a "white" British subject were to be touched in China or Japan or Turkey or Russia, the whole of the political parties of England, with their usual patriotism, will rise to the occasion, and with one accord demand the use of physical force against that country.

But here in South Africa, on the day the "Act" came into law, all agreements with regard to land were terminated, and thousands of the Natives found themselves ruined and homeless. From tenants they have become serfs.

If the Imperial Parliament looks with complacency on these tyrannical proceedings of a local Parliament, then the British public should not be surprised if the intelligent and thoughtful among the subject races of "Britain" consider "British justice" and "Russian tyranny" to be synonymous terms.

Let us draw attention to one more letter, by an Anglo–African to the `Daily News', which was typical of the rest: —

==

THE BLACK MAN'S BURDEN

Sir, — Those of your readers who, like myself, have some first–hand knowledge of the Natives of South Africa, know that this grievance voiced by the native deputation is a very real one. That such a deputation should have to come to England to urge such a plea is humiliating enough to them and to us. That their plea should be urged in vain would be disastrous to the last degree.

If the Natives' Land Act is the best thing the Union Government can do in the discharge of its responsibilities to the native tribes placed under its care by the King, then many of us would have to revise our faith in self–government as a fit instrument of national evolution; and would, moreover, strenuously resist the ultimate incorporation of the northern territories within the Union as being infinitely worse for the black man than even government under Chartered Company control.

One hopes that it is not yet too late for both Boer and Briton in South Africa to see that this debasement of the whole idea of self–government is to affront and discourage all in Great Britain who saw in the grant of its own political freedom to that great country a healing for its many woes. In the meantime Liberalism must back the native deputation at all costs, and it is well that `The Daily News and Leader' should lead the way.

==

ONE OBJECT OF THE S.A. WAR: THE LIBERATION OF THE NATIVE

One object of the South African War was to liberate the Native in the Transvaal. One result of it is that we have practically less opportunity to interfere in his behalf than we had under the Convention with the South African Republic. Interference in the internal affairs of a self–governing colony — in this case a colony in which a small number of white men govern a large number of black — has ceased to be within the realm of practical politics. But if this political interference is impossible, moral remonstrance is all the more in point. There is in all parts of the world a better and more enlightened as well as a duller and more callous public opinion, and the better opinion of a colony is powerfully reinforced by judicious expression of feeling in the mother country. There are occasions when that opinion should even be formally expressed by the Colonial Office or by a resolution of the House of Commons. Now, there is at present a deputation of South African Natives in this country appealing against the ratification of the Natives' Land Act of 1913. Mr. Harcourt has told them that he cannot interfere, nor can he any more than if he were an ornamental registering clerk. But he can if he chooses speak winged words to the South African Government, which, having alienated the entire white working population, is now exciting the same hostility among the blacks. The Act itself probably has a deeper motive. It prevents the sale of white men's land to the Natives or native land to the white men. This would have the effect of securing to the Native that very small portion of his own country which he has still managed to retain. This probably commended the measure to those who because they care for elementary justice are called negrophile, the colour of justice in a white man's eyes being apparently black. The other effect would be to prevent those Kafirs who are becoming educated and rising in the social scale from acquiring land. As in proportion to population the white man has by far the greater amount of land, it is clear that he does not come badly out of the bargain. However, it is not the Act itself of which the most serious complaint is made. What makes matters worse is the interim arrangement that pending the delimitation of native land by a Commission no Native whose lease of land has expired shall be able to renew it for a money rent or for any consideration whatever except labour service. It is contended that farmers are taking advantage of this prohibition to exact unpaid labour services from Natives, and are thus in effect reducing them to serfdom. It is clear that the position in which the Native is placed renders this only too possible, and it is an extraordinary thing that any such violent alteration of status should be made before instead of after the report of a Commission. For our part we cannot believe that men like Generals Botha and Smuts deliberately desire to reduce the Native to the condition of a semi-servile, landless labourer, and we would venture on behalf of the many Liberals who fought steadily for the right of South Africa to govern herself to appeal to them to extend a similar consideration to the people of whose destinies they have become responsible, and to suspend the operation of the Act until the administrative preparations for carrying it out with equity have been completed. — `Manchester Guardian'.

==

VIEWS OF THE "STAR"

We have always realized that one of the gravest problems of self-government in South Africa is the native question. On the one hand, South African Colonial opinion — by which is meant "white" opinion — will bitterly resent any shadow of dictation from Downing Street; on the other hand, the conscience of the British people cannot remain indifferent to any flagrant oppression of or injustice to the native races under the British flag. A very difficult question of this kind is raised by the deputation of South African Natives, which is now in this country, seeking to move the Colonial Office on the subject of the Natives' Land Act recently passed by General Botha. The ultimate object of General Botha's plan is the greatest exodus since the days of Moses; it is apparently to get rid of black landholders in areas in which the majority of the landowners are white, and to buy up tracts of land elsewhere from white landowners, in order to settle Natives upon them. In this way the black and the white races, so far as landholding is concerned, will be segregated into separate areas, with a reduction of possible cause of friction, and in some respects this is an excellent policy. But the trouble is that General Botha has passed the first part of his policy and has left the second part to the future. The Land Act provides that hereafter, "except with the approval of the Governor–General" — which proviso is mere leather and prunella — a Native shall not buy or hire any land from a person other than a Native. The effect of this is that at the termination of any existing tenancy a Native will have to relinquish his farm, and will not be able to hire or buy another from any white owner. If the Government had provided farms in the proposed native reserves for these men, their policy would be complete, but nothing has been done, and the fulfilment of that promise depends upon General Botha's continuance in office, and does not bind his successors. It is not surprising the South African Natives regard this Act as a means of driving them into the labour market either at the mines, or for white farmers. Mr. Dower, the Secretary for Native Affairs, addressing a meeting of Natives at Thaba Nchu, in the Free State, gave a strong hint of this when he said: "My best advice to you is to sell your stock and go into service." Here at home we hear a great deal about the "magic of property" and the importance of giving the worker an interest in the soil he tills; but in South Africa they apparently agree with the southerner in the `Biglow Papers' that

Libbaty's a kind o' thing
Thet don't agree with niggers.
It is clear that it is the duty of the Colonial Office to guarantee, in conjunction with the South African Government, the carrying out of the full policy as outlined by General Botha, and we hope occasion will be taken to urge action on these lines. — `Star'.

==

CAN BRITAIN PREVENT SLAVERY

A question of great importance and a question which may easily strain the links that bind the various parts of the Empire and the Mother Country, has arisen in South Africa owing to the operation of the Natives' Land Act passed last year by the Union Parliament. The Native question is by far the greatest problem South Africa has to solve, and its difficulties are so great that nobody has been able to advance any feasible scheme for its settlement, though there have been many suggestions as to the broad lines on which the matter may be settled. The Land Act is an attempt to establish modified segregation — i.e., confining the white man and the black to separate areas of the country. It is by no means a well–thought–out nor a very practicable enactment, and unfortunately has had the effect of greatly irritating the Natives throughout the Union. The Natives do not think they are being treated fairly, and have used every legitimate means to obtain a hearing. These means, however, are exceedingly meagre, practically non–existent, since they have no one to represent them, and as they have no vote they can bring no pressure on Parliament. Having failed in South Africa, they have sent a deputation to Great Britain, since, as they are British subjects, they consider that Great Britain should look after them. Arriving here, they find the Home Government cannot interfere in the internal policy of a self–governing colony, and so are left with no means of obtaining redress. It is surely impossible to admit that Great Britain can do nothing for the mass of the native population, although at the moment it appears to them that though they are subjects of the King he cannot even hear their appeal, and will do nothing for them, and has abandoned them, a state of affairs which is quite incomprehensible to them and leads them to depend solely on themselves to obtain redress — and that way rebellion lies. Britain is in an awkward position as she still has obligations to secure justice to the Natives. If South Africa were to enact slavery, would Britain still be able to do nothing to prevent it?

Ousting the Native

Surely Mr. Harcourt can suggest to the South African Government the necessity of appointing a Commission to inquire into the working of the Act, a Commission which would include Natives as well as whites. That the Natives have a material grievance is certain. The Act says that there shall be certain areas in which no Native can own or lease land, and similarly areas in which no white can own or lease land. That within a certain period the Natives owning land in the white area must sell out, and when their leases run out they shall not be renewed, similarly for the whites in the black area. Now at present no black area has been delimited, and the Commission performing this task will not report for a year or more; meanwhile the blacks are being turned off the land and have nowhere to go. The only course left to them is to hire themselves out as servants to the white; and, in fact, that is the real object of the Act. The farmers found that the Natives were acquiring land rapidly, and working for themselves rather than for the white man. There was a shortage of labour, and farmers wished to force the Natives to work for them rather than for themselves. This ejection with no other alternative is obviously most unfair, especially as there are indications that the native areas will not be delimited for a considerable time. The South Africans have always feared a combined action of all the native tribes, but surely by this Act they have chosen the simplest way of irritating every Native in South Africa. This condition of affairs is exceedingly grave, and, though the results are suppressed at present, there is no knowing what may happen if the British Government, whom the Natives regard as their final court of appeal, shows itself powerless. We know that the native question in South Africa is terribly difficult, but it is an obvious course to be pursued in order to maintain good relations between the two races that grievances should be fairly heard and dealt with justly. — `Review of Reviews'.

Chapter XVIII The P.S.A. and Brotherhoods

The Brotherhood must help not only the spiritual part of life,
  but also in social matters. They should always help the down–trodden,
  showing the brotherly feeling which was portrayed throughout
the life of Christ.
        Rt. Hon. A. Henderson, M.P.,
        President of the Brotherhood Movement, at Weston–super–Mare.

In a previous chapter we mentioned a yellow–covered newspaper which abused our English friends for supporting the appeal of the native deputation. It characterized the advocacy of the aims of the deputation by the Brotherhood as "Rubbish — a commodity which can always be picked up, and quite a lot of people spend much of their time in collecting it." "Why," exclaims this paper with indignation, "we had imagined that the `Brotherhood' movement was of a religious nature."

Our answer to this taunt is, that just because the Brotherhood movement opposes the Natives' Land Act it must be religious, for Anglican Bishops in South Africa have denounced this law in their episcopal charges (vide `Church Chronicle', 1913, October issues), and Anglican Bishops in South Africa are nothing if they are not religious. Nonconformist Ministers have condemned this law in their annual synods and conferences. Ex–Premier W. P. Schreiner, K.C., C.M.G., at present the London representative of the Union of South Africa, is the son of an old South African missionary. He was member of the Union Parliament when this law was passed and was one of the few senators who had the pluck to vote against it after condemning it; and it is monstrous to suggest that these pious and learned men could conspire to denounce a law just for the pleasure of denouncing it. And to our untutored mind it seems that if it be true that all these good men are working for the spread of Christ's Kingdom in South Africa, then we must be pardoned the inference that in the same country protagonists of this Act are working for the establishment of another kingdom. This inference grows into a belief when it is recalled that the men who are responsible for the recent commotion are the very men who forced this law upon the Government.

In the various reports of the South African Church Synods of 1915, the character of this "Church closing" law stands out in bold relief, and it is there revealed as an opponent of Christ and His work. Let us refer to only one of them. "The native work of the (Transvaal) District has been seriously hampered by the operation of the Natives' Land Act. As the result of evictions under the Act, some of the Churches on farms have ceased to exist." — Cape `Methodist Churchman', Jan. 22, 1915.

The numerous South African opponents of this law had no share in the recent upheaval, and the Brotherhoods by lending their platforms to a campaign in opposition to a law that emanates from such a quarter show that their cause, in addition to religion, is on the side of law, order, and constitutional liberty. We know, of course, that no doctrine of liberty would be acceptable in South Africa that did not also imply "liberty to ill–treat the blacks". Hence the Brotherhood propaganda, being colour–blind, explains the fury of the London mouthpiece of "lily–white" South Africa.

Early in July the deputation called at the Brotherhood headquarters in Norfolk Street, Strand, to explain to the National Brotherhood Council the object of their mission. Mr. William Ward, the national secretary, received the deputation in person; Mr. John McIntosh, secretary to the London Federation, Mr. W. Mann and other officers being also present. They invited the deputation to the Quarterly Meeting of the London Federation at Bishopsgate on July 14, 1914, after which the deputation received invitations to address meetings in various parts. Some of these engagements still remain unfulfilled. A list of the centres visited is given at the end of this chapter.

At the Bishopsgate gathering Mr. Will Crooks, M.P., was the "star turn". He welcomed the deputation and regretted the cold reception accorded to it by the Colonial Secretary. He added, however, that if they proceeded along the same moderate lines followed by Dr. Rubusana and Mr. Msane (the two members of the deputation who spoke that evening) he felt certain that they would do more good for their cause in the country than they did at the Colonial Office.

The `Brotherhood Journal', the newspaper organ of the movement said: —

==

Native Life in South Africa

Bear ye one another's Burdens

For Brotherhood men and women there can be only one response to their appeal. For Brotherhood is not only between man and man, but between nation and nation, and race and race.

In our movement, at any rate, there can be no colour bar to love and justice. If our Brotherhoods did not rise to a cause like this, we might well question the reality of their fraternal pretensions.

We are told that the problem has its difficulties. No doubt. But they can be overcome, if only our statesmen will act in a spirit of courage and faith. Surely empire means not only privilege and power and glory, but also responsibility and obligations. If it means only commercial profit, and injustice is to be done with impunity under the Imperial flag,

Of what worth is such an Empire?

This is a matter in which every one of our members should exert the force of opinion on the side of right. Let us open to our coloured brothers' cause our platforms and our hearts.

The five members of the deputation will be in this country for some months, and are prepared to address Brotherhoods and Sisterhoods, and to send information as to their case to any who wish it.

We doubt not that they will find in our midst not only a most sympathetic hearing, but active help in educating public opinion in this country, in order that a great wrong may be righted.

How unlike so many poor attempts at brotherhood, organized in the name of Christianity, especially in our part of the globe, where "they have made the welkin ring with the sorrowful tale of the unfortunate condition of the weak, but, like the rich man in the parable, they liked their Lazarus afar off," and considered their fraternal pretensions satisfied if they sent their dogs to lick his wounds. No, the Brotherhood movement is no such parody. It is practical Christianity which knows no distinction of colour or boundaries between nations. Our nine months' association with Brother Martin and Brother Timberlake, of the Shernhall Brotherhood, confirms this view; and our acquaintanceship with other members of this wonderful movement (which counts judges and members of Parliament as well as factory hands among its office-bearers) satisfied the writer that they are always ready to practise what they preach.

A noteworthy occasion in connexion with the campaign was our visit to the Southall Brotherhood on Sunday, March 14. We can hardly forget the day; it was on Crocus Sunday when thousands of Londoners went to Hampton Court in crowds to see the crocus bulbs in bloom. It was a glorious day and we remember it as the second day in 1915 on which the European sun shone through a cloudless sky from sunrise to sunset. Thousands of people attended at Hyde Park to witness the church parade, and still more thousands took advantage of the glorious spring day after a strenuous winter to flock to Epping Forest and other popular resorts.

In the afternoon we took part in an Imperial indoor demonstration organized by the "Southall Men's Own" at the Central Hall. Mr. William Cross of Hanwell represented England; Mr. T. Owens,

F.C.I.S., represented Wales; Mr. S. S. A. Cambridge, a black barrister, represented his homeland, British Guiana; Miss Ruth Bucknall, the celebrated lyric soprano, who artistically contributed the solos, represented Australia; while Scotland and the Emerald Isle were also represented in the orchestra and elsewhere in the hall; Mr. and Mrs. Lionel Boote, of Auckland, New Zealand, represented "the most English of the Colonies" (unfortunately the Indian representative could not reach Southall in time), and the writer represented South Africa, the baby member of the British family.

Among such intellectual giants, one was inclined at the outset to feel somewhat out of place, but thanks to the encouraging Brotherhood cheer which always accompany their reception of a speaker, the stripling soon finds himself at home, as is always the case on any Brotherhood platform, and that was how we felt that day.

Mr. W. Cross said, in part, that one of the most striking proofs of the unity of the Empire was shown in the splendid way that men had come forward to assist the Mother Country on the battlefields of Europe from all parts of our Dominions. The coloured men from India had come as free men and fellow-subjects to do their share. The Empire was composed of territories and people — once separated by race and creed, now united under one flag. There was a great resemblance between Brotherhood and Empire. In it all kinds of religion were represented, yet all were united in one great principle. It had been said the soul of Russia was pity, of France reason, and of Britain justice. No Empire could be built to stand unless based on justice and freedom. The principle of freedom underlay Empire as it underlay Brotherhood also. There was no limit to the Empire that was founded upon unity, toleration, justice, and liberty; it surely had no end. Similarly there was no frontier to the kingdom of Brotherhood, and they looked for a kingdom out-spanning far beyond the roll of British drums — the kingdom of Brotherhood — the kingdom of Christ.

Referring to the limitations of colour in South Africa, Mr. Cambridge said: "Have you no cattle and sheep in South Africa? Are there no birds? Have you not observed that they are of different colours and yet are not restricted in their flight on that account; and are you going to run counter to the work of nature in regard to human beings? The British Empire has a population of over 430,000,000, of which less than 100,000,000 are white, and there was a big problem to solve: `How to rule with justice and equity this great multitude of various races and creeds and consolidate them as fellow-subjects of one great and mighty Empire.' The future of the British Empire could be secured by following the high ideals of `Brotherhood' which were foreshadowed by Christ in the Bible, and by great writers such as Shakespeare and Addison. The fall of Rome was due to her failure to recognize the duty of welding her subjects together as brothers one and all under the Fatherhood of God. . . ."

It is a pity that the argument used by Mr. Cambridge would not go down with the majority of the rulers in South Africa. If it did one would remind them that even South African ladies pay higher prices for black silks than they do for white silks; that the value of domestic animals does not as a whole appear to be influenced by their colour: thus, whereas the fleece of white sheep commands a higher price in the South African wool market than the fleece of black sheep, their mutton has about the same flavour. Again of horned cattle, which give the same quality of beef, irrespective of colour; farmers will tell you of them that coloured cattle are among the best for farming and other purposes, while white bullocks are subject to sore eyes, and white cows continually suffer from erythema of the nipples ('Garget–mammitis'); yet we have not heard that this peculiarity had any influence on the quality of their beef or the quality of the milk they give. The springbuck, whence the best South African venison is obtained, has the colours of black, white and brown; and this blend has not prevented it from having the reputation of being the prettiest and most graceful antelope in the world. But argument in this respect is simply wasted on the ruling caste in South Africa: there, Mr. Cross's views about "freedom, liberty," etc., will simply be laughed out of court, unless he limits them to white men; so that one sometimes wonders whether Christ's metaphor about "casting pearls before swine" does not find an application here. Look at the weighty arguments delivered inside and outside Parliament against the Natives' Land Act. Surely no legislature with a sense of responsibility could have passed that law after hearing arguments of such force and weight against it; but the South African legislature passed that Act and seems to glory in the wretched result of its operation.

Mr. Boote expressed his pride in finding how shining was the native policy of New Zealand when contrasted with the native policy of South Africa. "Why," said Mrs. Boote to us, with evident satisfaction, "we have got Maori members of Parliament and our country is all the better for it." She had every justification to look pleased at the comparison which reveals the justice of her country's rule, for we remember how the women of New Zealand got the vote. The white members of Parliament in New Zealand were equally divided on the Women's Enfranchisement Bill; but for the native members, there would have been a tie, as was the case in South Africa three years ago, when the white members of the South African Parliament, as seemed likely there, wheedled the Women's Suffrage Bill out of the House. Happily for Women's Franchise in the Antipodes the Maori members voted solidly for the Bill and secured the passage of a reform which, judging by the satisfactory results in Australia and elsewhere, gave the lead to the rest of the Empire.

It was at Hammersmith, where the chairman after hearing our story of the operation of the Natives' Land Act, in moving a resolution, in a sympathetic speech, asked: "Why did we spend 240,000,000 Pounds and kill 10,000 men in the South African War if this is the result?" He asked the permission of the audience to change the last hymn on the programme and sing the Brotherhood Song of Liberty.

As the newspaper 'South Africa' seems to insinuate that the Brotherhood movement by allying itself with our cause had deviated from its aims and objects, we would explain that the chairman did not run out of the meeting to borrow a book from somewhere containing that song. The song is No. 26 of the 'Fellowship Hymnal' — the hymn–book of the P.S.A. and Brotherhoods.

At subsequent meetings it had often been our pleasure, after delivering the message from the South African Natives, to sit down and hear the chairman give out that hymn, and the orchestra lead off with the tune of Costa's March of the Israelites. A pleasant variety was lent to it at the Victoria Brotherhood in Monmouthshire, which we visited on the first Sunday in 1915. There the chairman gave out the now familiar hymn, and the grand organ chimed the more familiar tune of "Jesu, lover of my soul" (Hollingside's), and the variety lent extra freshness to the singing of the Brotherhood Song of Liberty, which is reproduced: —

Men whose boast it is that ye
Come of fathers brave and free,

If there breathe on earth a slave,
Are ye truly free and brave?
If ye do not feel the chain
When it works a brother's pain,
Are ye not base slaves indeed —
Slaves unworthy to be freed?

Is true freedom but to break
Fetters for our own dear sake,
And with leathern hearts forget
That we owe mankind a debt?
No! true freedom is to share
All the chains our brothers wear,
And with heart and hand to be
Earnest to make others free.

They are slaves who fear to speak
For the fallen and the weak;
They are slaves who will not choose
Hatred, scoffing, and abuse,
Rather than in silence shrink
From the truth they needs must think:
They are slaves who dare not be
In the right with two or three.

      J. R. Lowell.

P.S.A. and Brotherhood Societies Addressed by the Deputation
    and the Order in Which They Were Visited

[Modified from original table format]

[a] Society. [b] Name of President or Secretary.
    [c] Where Meetings are Held. [d] By Whom Addressed.

---

[a] 1. London Federation of Brotherhoods [b] Mr. John McIntosh [c] 230, Bishopsgate, E.C. [d] Mr. Saul Msane, Dr. W. B. Rubusana

[a] 2. Tooting Brotherhood [b] Rev. E. Aldom French [c] Wesleyan Central Hall, Tooting, S.W. [d] Mr. Saul Msane, Dr. W. B. Rubusana

[a] 3. Willesden Green Men's Own Brotherhood [b] Mr. H. J. Weaver [c] Baptist Church, High Road, Willesden Green [d] Mr. Sol T. Plaatje, Mr. T. M. Mapikela

[a] 4. Westbourne Park Brotherhood [b] Dr. J. Clifford, MA.DD. [c] Baptist Church, Bayswater, W. [d] Dr. W. B. Rubusana

[a] 5. Willesden P.S.A. [b] Mr. W. Springbett [c] Primitive Methodist Church, Willesden Green [d] Dr. W. B. Rubusana, Mr. T. M. Mapikela

[a] 6. East Ham Brotherhood [b] Rev. W. H. Armstrong [c] Central Hall, Barking Road, East Ham [d] Dr. W. B. Rubusana, Mr. T. M. Mapikela

[a] 7. Tooting Graveny Brotherhood [b] Mr. A. Riding [c] Central Hall, Tooting, Broadway [d] Mr. Saul Msane

[a] 8. Men's Brotherhood [b] Rev. A. Clifford Hall [c] Congregational Church, Greenwich Rd., S.E. [d] Mr. Saul Msane

[a] 9. Hammersmith Brotherhood [b] Mr. J. W. Butters [c] Albion Congregational Church, Hammersmith [d] Mr. S. T. Plaatje

[a] 10. Shern Hall Brotherhood [b] Mr. W. H. Jennings [c] United Methodist Church, Whipps Cross [d] Mr. S. T. Plaatje

[a] 11. Swanscombe Brotherhood [b] Mr. E. Pallant [c] Wesleyan Church, Swanscombe, near Northfleet [d] Mr. S. T. Plaatje

[a] 12. Clifton Brotherhood [b] Rev. F. Hastings [c] Congregational Church, Peckham Rye [d] Mr. S. T. Plaatje

[a] 13. Abertillery P.S.A. [b] Mr. Wm. Davies [c] The Pavilion, Abertillery, South Wales [d] Mr. S. T. Plaatje

[a] 14. Abertillery P.S.A. [b] Mr. E. Jefferies [c] Wesleyan Church, Abertillery, South Wales [d] Mr. S. T. Plaatje

[a] 15. Barking Brotherhood [b] Mr. W. Barnard [c] Wesleyan Church, Barking, Essex [d] Mr. S. T. Plaatje

[a] 16. Willesden Green Men's Own [b] Mr. C. E. Pink [c] Baptist Church, High Rd., Willesden Green [d] Mr. S. T. Plaatje

[a] 17. Victoria Brotherhood [b] Mr. J. W. Hall [c] Wesleyan Church, Newport, Monmouthshire [d] Mr. S. T. Plaatje

[a] 18. Marsh Street Men's Own Brotherhood (Men's Meeting) [b] Mr. E. K. Fuller [c] Queen's Cinema Electric Theatre, Walthamstow [d] Mr. S. T. Plaatje

[a] 19. Greenhithe Brotherhood [b] Mr. S. W. Lineham [c] Wesleyan Church, London Rd., Greenhithe [d] Mr. S. T. Plaatje

[a] 20. Marsh Street Men's Own (Evening Meeting: Mixed) [b] Mr. W. F. Toynbee [c] Queen's Cinema Electric Theatre, Walthamstow [d] Mr. S. T. Plaatje

[a] 21. Dartford P.S.A. [b] Mr. H. Keyte [c] Primitive Methodist Church, Dartford, Kent [d] Mr. S. T. Plaatje

[a] 22. Southall Men's Own Brotherhood [b] T. Owen, Esq., F.C.I.S. [c] Central Hall, Southall, W. [d] Mr. S. T. Plaatje

[a] 23. Lloyd's Park P.S.A. [b] Rev. R. P. Campbell [c] United Methodist Church, Lloyd's Park [d] Mr. S. T. Plaatje

[a] 24. Men and Women's Meeting [b] Mr. F. Mercer [c] Independent Church, Edmonton, North [d] Mr. S. T. Plaatje

[a] 25. Chiswick Brotherhood [b] Mr. D. J. Hawkins [c] Brotherhood Hall, Turnham Green Terrace [d] Mr. S. T. Plaatje

[a] 26. Abney Brotherhood [b] Mr. W. A. Procktor [c] Abney Church, Stoke Newington [d] Mr. S. T. Plaatje

[a] 27. Uxbridge P.S.A. [b] Mr. W. Ashton, J.P. [c] Old Meeting House (Congl.), Uxbridge [d] Mr. S. T. Plaatje

[a] 28. West Ealing P.S.A. [b] Mr. S. Garrard [c] Primitive Methodist Church, West Ealing [d] Mr. S. T. Plaatje

[a] 29. New England P.S.A. [b] Sir Richard Winfrey, M.P. [c] P.S.A. Hall, Peterborough, Northampton [d] Mr. S. T. Plaatje

[a] 30. Shern Hall Brotherhood [b] Rev. James Ellis [c] United Methodist Church, Walthamstow [d] Mr. S. T. Plaatje

[a] 31. Leighton Men's Meeting [b] Mr. G. F. Drew [c] Corn Exchange, Leighton Buzzard, Bedfordshire [d] Mr. S. T. Plaatje

[a] 32. Pembury Grove P.S.A. [b] Mr. Ernest Prior [c] United Methodist Church, Clapton [d] Mr. S. T. Plaatje

[a] 33. Shepherd's Bush Brotherhood [b] Mr. F. C. Simpson [c] Shepherd's Bush Tabernacle (Baptist) [d] Mr. S. T. Plaatje

[a] 34. East Ham Brotherhood [b] Mr. G. Sorrell [c] Central Hall, Barking Road, East Ham [d] Mr. S. T. Plaatje

[a] 35. Botwell Brotherhood [b] Mr. J. Matson [c] The Cinema, Hayes, Middlesex [d] Mr. S. T. Plaatje

[a] 36. Kingsland P.S.A. [b] Mr. J. Harding [c] Congregational Church, High Street, Kingsland [d] Mr. S. T. Plaatje

[a] 37. Heathfield Brotherhood [b] Mr. Hy. H. Castle [c] Recreation Hall, Heathfield, Sussex [d] Mr. S. T. Plaatje

[a] 38. Men's Own Brotherhood [b] Rev. A. Hallack, M.A. [c] Angel Street Church, Worcester [d] Mr. S. T. Plaatje

[a] 39. Greenwich P.S.A. [b] Rev. W. T. Penny [c] Central Hall, London Street, Greenwich [d] Mr. S. T. Plaatje

[a] 40. Hither Green P.S.A. [b] Mr. P. Duff [c] Congregational Church, Torridon Road [d] Mr. S. T. Plaatje

[a] 41. Whitefield's Men's Meeting [b] Rev. W. Charter Piggott [c] Whitefield's Tabernacle, Tottenham Court Road [d] Mr. S. T. Plaatje

[a] 42. North End Brotherhood [b] Mr. Elwin Wrench [c] North End Hall, Croydon, Surrey [d] Mr. S. T. Plaatje

[a] 43. Trinity Men's Own [b] Mr. A. J. Walker [c] Congl. Church, Victoria Park, Sth. Hackney [d] Mr. S. T. Plaatje

[a] 44. Acton Brotherhood [b] Mr. James McIntosh [c] Congl. Church, Churchfield Rd., Acton, W. [d] Mr. S. T. Plaatje

[a] 45. P.S.A. Brotherhood [b] Mr. W. G. Brown [c] Wesleyan Church, High Rd., Tottenham [d] Mr. S. T. Plaatje

[a] 46. Northampton Men's Own [b] Rev. R. Morton Stanley, M.A., B.D. [c] Doddridge Church, Northampton [d] Mr. S. T. Plaatje

[a] 47. Cheshunt and Waltham Cross P.S.A. [b] Mr. A. W. Ashmead [c] Drill Hall, Waltham Cross [d] Mr. S. T. Plaatje

[a] 48. Staines P.S.A. [b] Mr. R. C. Edwards [c] Town Hall, Staines, Middlesex [d] Mr. S. T. Plaatje

[a] 49. Snell's Park P.S.A. [b] R. Green, Esq., C.C. [c] Congregational Church, Upper Edmonton [d]

Mr. S. T. Plaatje

[a] 50. Camberwell P.S.A. [b] Mr. H. A. Spong [c] Masonic Hall, Camberwell, Surrey [d] Mr. S. T. Plaatje

[a] 51. Norbury Brotherhood [b] Mr. J. L. Moody [c] Wesleyan Church, London Rd., Norbury [d] Mr. S. T. Plaatje

[a] 52. Hastings Brotherhood [b] Mr. A. G. Strickland [c] Congregational Church, Hastings, Sussex [d] Mr. S. T. Plaatje

[a] 53. Evesham Men's Own Brotherhood [b] Mr. G. H. White [c] Cowl St. Church, Evesham, Worcestershire [d] Mr. S. T. Plaatje

[a] 54. South Bank Brotherhood [b] Mr. T. Bosher [c] South Bank-on-Tees, Yorkshire [d] Mr. S. T. Plaatje

[a] 55. Tees-side Brotherhood [b] Mr. T. Summers [c] Wes. Church South Bank, Yorkshire [d] Mr. S. T. Plaatje

[a] 56. Shepherd's Bush, P.S.A. [b] Rev. W. G. Davis [c] Wesleyan Church, Shepherd's Bush [d] Mr. S. T. Plaatje

[a] 57. Stockton United [b] Mr. W. Weighell [c] Baptist Tabernacle, Stockton-on-Tees [d] Mr. S. T. Plaatje

[a] 58. Wembley Brotherhood [b] Mr. H. W. Hagger [c] Union Hall, Wembley [d] Mr. S. T. Plaatje

[a] 59. Watford Men's Own [b] Mr. A. G. Baker [c] Beechen Grove, Ch. Watford, Hertfordshire [d] Mr. S. T. Plaatje

[a] 60. Clerkenwell Men's Own [b] Mr. R. G. Pursaill [c] Peel Institute, Clerkenwell Green [d] Mr. S. T. Plaatje

---

In addition to the Brotherhoods and P.S.A.'s, we are indebted to
the Sisterhoods, Adult Schools and several Church bodies who gave us
many occasions to speak, the response to our message being most gratifying.

Chapter XIX Armed Natives in the South African War

Oh, where is he, the simple fool,
 Who says that wars are over?
What bloody portent flashes there,
 Across the Straits of Dover?

141

Nine hundred thousand slaves in arms
 May seek to bring us under
But England lives and still will live,
 For we'll crush the despot yonder.
Are we ready, Britons all,
 To answer foes with thunder?
    Arm, arm, arm!

The Gallant Bakhatla Tribe

When Bechuanaland was invaded by the Republican forces at the outbreak of the Boer War, the British Police Force in the Bechuanaland Protectorate, finding themselves hopelessly isolated in that far—away region, decided to evacuate Gaberones and effect a junction with Colonel Plumer's force which was then coming south from Rhodesia. The British Commissioner, before leaving Gaberones, advised the Native Chiefs of the Southern Protectorate to make the best terms possible with the invaders until the Transvaal Republic was conquered by the advancing British Army.

Chief Lentsue of the Bakhatla, acting entirely on his own responsibility, sent his brother Segale with a message to the Dutch Commandant, reminding him that the war was a white man's war, and asking him at the same time not to traverse his territory with armed Boers; he also added that any invasion of his territory would be resisted with all the means at his disposal. Naturally, this message was treated with the contempt that a Boer would habitually treat any frankness on the part of a "Kafir", and the Boers, in utter disregard of this warning, invaded Bakhatla territory. Chief Lentsue was not in a position to attack the Boers at the beginning of the invasion. He had the men but hardly enough ammunition to last for a whole day, so he had to bide his time, scheming the while to secure an arsenal. The Dutch contempt for Lentsue's threats advanced by 100 per cent when they overran his outer villages on two occasions and he failed to offer any resistance, but they had not calculated that his Intelligence Department and War Office were hard at work in order that his threat to the Boers might not come to naught. Accordingly on a certain day a convoy of huge buck—wagons, each drawn by sixteen African bullocks, carrying ammunition to the Dutch troops in Bechuanaland, meandered its way slowly in the direction of the Marico River, escorted by a squadron of mounted Burghers. All of a sudden they were surprised and disconcerted by a fusillade of musketry, and the situation grew in gravity from the fact that whichever way the members of the convoy scampered, they appeared to be running from the frying—pan into the fire. The ruse was swift and successful, indeed so successful that the train of ammunition and provision wagons proceeded on its way to Lentsue's town, Mochudi, but under a different escort.

What had happened was this: The sub—chief Segale, who has since been known as Lentsue's fighting general, had closely watched the movements of the Dutch and studied their plans, till he was able to anticipate the coming of this convoy and to waylay it. He captured enough ammunition in this and succeeding attacks to enable the Chief Lentsue to arm his men. Thus they repulsed two invasions of the Boers, followed the enemy into his territory, and came home with numbers of head of cattle, and Lentsue's territory was never again invaded by the Boers.

This isolated action of the Bakhatla Chief and people in a remote corner of the Empire, on the boundaries of the late Boer Republic, had its moral and material value. The Boers, who virtually owned the whole of Bechuanaland to the south, except Mafeking town, found that it would pay them better to adopt a friendlier attitude towards the other Bechuana tribes. Thereby a Dutch Field Cornet pronounced all the Bechuana Chiefs as the original Afrikanders — with the exception of Lentsue of the Bakhatla, and Montsioa of the Barolong in Mafeking. These two chiefs, the Field Cornet said, were traitors to their country as they had joined the foreign Rooineks against their black and white fellow Afrikander. But the armed Burghers ceased to help themselves to native property, and the Government's huge compensation bill at the end of the War became less formidable in consequence. Furthermore, the task of that unacknowledged hero — the native dispatch runner — became so appreciably easier that an almost regular bi-weekly communication was maintained between headquarters at the Cape and the siege garrison at Mafeking, for the native runners after crawling through the lines of the investing Boers, under cover of the night, could move through the peasant villages with much less danger of detection by Boer patrols.

But it must be confessed that Chief Lentsue's defensive activities were wholly illegal, inasmuch as the Boers, although they had declared war against Lentsue's sovereign Lady, Queen Victoria, were not at war with him. It was defined, by an uncanny white man's mode of reasoning, that the war was a white man's business in which the blacks should take no part beyond merely suffering its effects. The Natives' retort to this declaration was in the words of a Sechuana proverb, viz., "You cannot sever the jawbones from the head and expect to keep those parts alive separately." It was this principle, we presume, that guided Lentsue's action. Still from the standpoint of white South Africa, the Chief's operations were a purely filibustering adventure; and while it seemed difficult to indict Lentsue on any definite charge, some of his men were arrested for having taken part in a cattle-raiding expedition in Transvaal in the course of which they shot and killed a German subject of the Transvaal Republic. These men were tried at Pretoria after peace was declared, and three of them were sentenced to death. All through the trial the Chief stood by his men, who pleaded justification. He accompanied them in the first instance to Pretoria, and afterwards paid for their defence at the trial, and it was evident that he took the verdict and sentence very much to heart.

If the verdict strained the loyalty of the Bakhatla, it had the effect of satisfying the Boers across the Bechuana border, in the Western Transvaal, who had to live down the sad memory of a victory gained by a black chief over their white army and of their purposes thereby. From a Dutch point of view nothing could be more humiliating than that black men should have gained such a signal success over them, and they are constantly crying out for the repression of Lentsue and his "proud" Kafirs. The Boers' demand that the Union authorities should make the thraldom of the Natives more effective, forgetting that the armed forces of the Boers when left to themselves during the temporary British evacuation of Bechuanaland were unable to do it. Notwithstanding this fact, the newspapers, especially the Rand Sunday Press, seem always to have open spaces for rancorous appeals to colour prejudice, perhaps because such appeals, despite their inherent danger, suit the colonial taste. Preceding the introduction of the Natives' Land Act, the clamour of a section of the colonists and most of the Transvaal Boers for more restrictive measures towards the blacks was accompanied at one of its stages by alarming reports of "Native disaffection", "Bakhatla insolence", and similar inflammatory headlines. One Sunday morning it was actually announced in the Sunday Press of Johannesburg that the Bakhatla had actually opened fire on the Union Police and were the first to draw blood. Our own inquiries proved that the British Protectorate, in and around Lentsue's territory, where the Bakhatla dwell, was abnormally quiet. All that had happened was that two Dutch policemen had unlawfully crossed into Bechuanaland with firearms; that the Natives had disarmed them and taken them to their chief, who in turn handed them over to the British authorities at Gaberones, where they were tried and sentenced.

It is not suggested that Sunday papers in giving publicity to disturbing reports lend their space to what they know to be untrue; but the fact remains that, right or wrong, their editorials seem ever ready to fan the glowing embers of colour prejudice into a blaze; and after arousing in this manner a most acute race feeling, the editors, upon discovering their mistake, if such it was, did not even trouble to tell their readers that they had unwittingly published exaggerated accounts — since after a fair trial before the British tribunal at Gaberones, the offending Union Police were fined 50 Pounds. The fact is that while under the quasi-Republican laws of the Transvaal a native policeman dare not lay his "black hands" on a "lily-white" criminal, even if he caught him in the very act of breaking the law: in British Bechuanaland, "there shall be no difference in the eye of the law between a man with a white skin and a man with a black skin, and the one shall be as much entitled to the protection of the law as the other," and so in spite of scaremongers' ravings to the contrary, Chief Lentsue proved himself once more on the side of the law of his Empire.

> Go mokong-kong ko Tipereri,
> Go mokong-kong gole;
> Go mokong-kong ko Tipereri,
> Go mosetsana montle.
> Dumela, Pikadili,
> Sala, Lester-skuer,
> Tsela ea Kgalagadi, Tipereri,
> Pelo ea me e koo.
>   "Tipperary" in Rolong.

The Barolong and the War

The Barolong and other native tribes near Mafeking were keenly interested in the negotiations that preceded the Boer War. The chiefs continually received information regarding the mobilization of the Boer forces across the border. This was conveyed to the Magistrate of Mafeking with requests for arms for purpose of defence. The Magistrate replied each time with confident assurances that the Boers would never cross the boundary into British territory. The Transvaal boundary is only ten or twelve miles from the magistracy. The assurances of the Magistrate made the Natives rather restive; the result was that a deputation of Barolong chiefs had a dramatic interview with the Magistrate, at which the writer acted as interpreter. The chiefs told the Magistrate that they feared he knew very little about war if he thought that belligerents would respect one another's boundaries. He replied in true South African style, that it was a white man's war, and that if the enemy came, Her Majesty's white troops would do all the fighting and protect the territories of the chiefs. We remember how the chief Montsioa and his counsellor Joshua Molema went round the Magistrate's chair and crouching behind him said: "Let us say, for the sake of argument, that your assurances are genuine, and that when the trouble begins we hide behind your back like this, and, rifle in hand, you do all the fighting because you are white; let us say, further, that some Dutchmen appear on the scene and they

144

outnumber and shoot you: what would be our course of action then? Are we to run home, put on skirts and hoist the white flag?"

Chief Motshegare pulled off his coat, undid his shirt front and baring his shoulder and showing an old bullet scar, received in the Boer–Barolong war prior to the British occupation of Bechuanaland, he said: "Until you can satisfy me that Her Majesty's white troops are impervious to bullets, I am going to defend my own wife and children. I have got my rifle at home and all I want is ammunition."

The Magistrate duly communicated the proceedings to Capetown, but the reply from headquarters was so mild and reassuring that one could almost think that it referred to an impending Parliamentary election rather than to a bloody war. But the subsequent rapid developments of events showed that the Natives of Mafeking were in advance and that those at headquarters were far behind the times. In a short time after the interview of the chiefs with the Magistrate, the Boers, following the terms of their ultimatum, crossed the border between the Cape and Transvaal, cut the lines of communication north and south of Mafeking and, before any arms could reach this quarter, Mafeking (a little village on the banks of the Molopo) was surrounded, with Montsioastad, a town of 5,000 native inhabitants. The population of these places was largely increased by refugees, both white and black, from outside the town, and also from the Transvaal.

At this time of the investment General Cronje sent verbal messages to the chief advising him not to mix himself and his people in a white man's quarrel. This view of General Cronje's was, at the beginning of the siege, in accord with local white sentiment. The European inhabitants of the besieged town had a repugnance to the idea of armed Natives shooting at a white enemy; but the businesslike method of General Cronje in effecting the investment had a sobering effect upon the whole of the beleaguered garrison; the Dutch 100–pounder Cruesot especially thundered some sense into them and completely altered their views.

The Barolong youth had his baptism of fire on October 25, 1899, when General Cronje tried to storm the garrison by effecting an entry through the native village. He poured a deafening hail of nickel into the native village. The Natives who were concealed behind the outer walls of Montsioastad waited with their rifles in the loopholes, according to Captain Marsh's instructions, till the Boers were quite near to them, then returned the fire with satisfactory results. After this encounter the whites, for the first time, regretted that there were not any arms in the place with which to arm all the Natives. As this attack was unmistakably severe and a Red Cross wagon moved around the Boer lines in the afternoon, it was feared that the native casualties were heavy, and medical aid was offered by the white section of the garrison. But all were agreeably surprised to find that beyond slight damages to the housetops there were no casualties among the Barolongs. The following was the only injury: A shell burst in front of Chief Lekoko as he was engaged in repelling the Boer attack, but no fragments of it touched him. One piece of shell, however, struck a rock and a splinter of the rock grazed his temple. At best only a few rounds of ammunition could be handed out to those of the Barolongs who used their own rifles, and it is doubtful if so little ammunition was ever more economically used, and used to greater advantage.

The investment of Mafeking was so effective that only certain Natives could crawl through the Boer lines at night. Throughout the seven months of the siege only one white man managed, under the guidance of two Natives, to pass into the village. All the dispatches which came into and out of Mafeking were carried by Barolong runners. Before the Boers moved their stock into the far interior of the Transvaal, the Barolongs continually went out and raided Boer cattle and brought them into the besieged garrison. Often the raiders had to fight their way back, but sometimes as they returned with the cattle in the night the Dutch sentries preferred to leave them alone. The result was that General Snyman, who commanded the besiegers after General Cronje went south, issued a general order authorizing the shooting dead of "any one coming in or out of Mafeking", armed or unarmed.

At his village called Modimola, ten miles outside the beleaguered garrison, there lived Chief Saane, uncle of the Mafeking chief. Being apparently harmless he was not for some months molested by the Boers. Later, however, they rightly suspected him of supplying the garrison with information. They then took him and his followers to Rietfontein, where they placed him under surveillance, but Chief Saane proved even more useful in captivity than in liberty. He used the seemingly inoffensive young men of Rietfontein, to glean all first–hand information from the Boers, who still had command of the lines of communication. Then he sent the news in verbal messages to his nephew, the paramount chief in the siege, who in turn communicated it to Her Majesty's officers in command. By means of this self–constituted intelligence bureau the garrison learnt of the surrender of Cronje — a happy consummation of the battle of Paardeberg — shortly after the good news reached their besiegers; and when official confirmation came from the Cape, more than a week later, Chief Saane's messengers were there again with fresh news of the surrender of Bloemfontein. This news, as might be well supposed, was glad tidings to the besieged people. They were in fact the truths that King Solomon thus sets forth: "As cold water is to the weary soul, so is good news from a far country," for, in those days, before the invention of aeroplanes and Marconigrams, no country in this wide world was further than a besieged garrison.

Among the first civilian bodies raised in Mafeking for purposes of garrison defence was the "Cape Boy Contingent", a company of mixed classes in varying degrees of complexions. Sergt.–Major Taylor, a coloured bricklayer, who led the contingent and directed the crack snipers of that company, was killed during the fourth month of the siege, by a fragment of a huge shell in the outer trenches.

His funeral was attended by General Baden–Powell and other staff officers, and was probably the only funeral of a coloured person in the South African war that was accorded such distinguished military attendance.

The language of the Cape coloured or mixed people is the same as that of the Boers, viz., the Cape Dutch. At times during the siege our advance lines and those of the Boers used to be less than 100 yards apart, and when the wily snipers of both sides saw nothing to snipe at, they used to exchange pleasantries at the expense of one another, from the safety of their entrenchments. Sometimes these wordy compliments made the opponents decidedly "chummy", to borrow a trench phrase. In that mood, they would now and again wax derisive or become amusing, bespeaking the fates of one another or the eventual outcome of the war. Whoever got the worst of the argument used to cut off communication with an unpleasant remark; but when it was mutually amusing, both sides enjoyed an advantage and each joined heartily in the resulting merriment. On more than one occasion a convivial Dutchman momentarily forgot the martial aspect of the mutual hilarity and complied with an equally convivial coloured man's exclamation to "kyk hier, jong" (look here, old fellow), and directly he "kyked" the snipers did to him that which from the enemy's point of view would amount to "devil's work".

The reader of these reminiscences will perhaps permit us to pay a tribute to the Dutch Burghers who, under General Snyman, besieged Mafeking. Whatever we may say against them, in other ways, this much must be said in their favour, namely, that they left us entirely alone on Sundays. Such an opportunity gave the Mafeking people a chance to get about, to have a thorough wash–up, and to keep the Sabbath holy. Snipers put down their rifles on Sunday mornings, declared a day's peace among the contending forces between the opposing trenches, and pointed out to one another landmarks beyond which the opposing sentries might not cross, since to wander past these beacons would mean a sudden resumption of hostilities. But as the landmarks were religiously respected there seldom was any occasion to desecrate the Sabbath by the clash of arms. We had thus a whole day's recreation, when the trenchmen used to visit their families in the women's camp and make all–round preparations for another week's bombardment.

The "Cape Boys" fought with distinction and maintained their reputation right up to the end of the siege. Visitors to Mafeking may now see near the obelisk in front of the pretty town hall of the famous siege town, a five–pounder gun "captured by the Cape Police during the siege". This gun was seized by the coloured Sergeant Bell and two other subalterns of the "Cape Boys" contingent; their contingent was then under the command of Lieutenant Currey of the Cape Police.

Besides the brave coloured men who fell during the defence of Mafeking, one painful effect of the siege, in connexion with this contingent, was that of Mr. Swartz, who was blinded by an exploding Boer shell and has never been able to regain his eyesight.

Ukude, ukude Tipperary,
 'Kude mpela ku hamba,
Ukude, ukude Tipperary,
 Nentombi 'nhle ng' asiyo.
Hlala kahle, Piccadilly
 Nawe Leicester Square
Ikude lendlhela yase Tipperary
 Kona 'po nhliziyo yami.
          "Tipperary" in Zulu.

Two other small companies who filled their posts without reproach were the Fingo contingent and the Black Watch, so–called, presumably, from the jet–black colour of the members. The "Black Watch" included Mozambique and Zambesi boys, Shangaans and others from among the blackest races of South Africa. The greatest disaster sustained by this company was when a party of thirty–three of them dashed into the Boer lines on an ill–starred attempt to loot cattle from the enemy's herds. After their night's dash out of the garrison they got to a hiding place for the day, but they were followed there and were surrounded by a Boer commando, which peppered them with a maxim and a big gun. They fought up to the last cartridge, but were helplessly outnumbered and outranged by the Boers, who killed them to a man.

Cattle–raiding was a dangerous business in which the crafty Barolong, who belonged to the country, alone were well versed. A subtle warrior among the Barolong, named Mathakgong, was a regular expert in this business. He led the occasional Barolong dashes into the Boer lines in search of beef and he invariably managed to rush his loot into Mafeking. He did this throughout the seven months' siege with the loss of only two men. The only misadventure of this intrepid looter was when he attempted to rush in an unusually large drove of cattle which Colonel Plumer had been buying and collecting at his Sefikile camp about forty miles north of Mafeking for the besieged garrison. Dutchmen tell us that for days they had learnt that Colonel Plumer was arranging to send cattle into Mafeking. They even knew the exact number — 100 head — and so they sent scouts to the north every day to watch the roads and warn the besiegers of the event. Hence, although they had left Mafeking unobserved, when Mathakgong's party approached Mafeking on the return trip with the cattle, a strong Dutch force was waylaying him and waiting to give him and Colonel Plumer's cattle a hot reception. They opened a rattling fusillade upon the cattle drivers, which could be heard from Mafeking. Over half of the cattle were killed in the ensuing fight, and the remainder, like the fat carcases of the dead bullocks, fell into the hands of the Boers. The drivers escaped with only two wounded out of the party of twelve. They said that they owed their escape almost entirely to the carcases of dead cattle, which they used as ramparts.

When Mathakgong heard subsequently how the Boers had planned to annihilate him and his small party, he became very indignant at what he called "the clumsy European method of always revealing their intentions to the enemy."

Away out in Basutoland, "the Switzerland of South Africa", the Paramount Chief Lerothodi offered to send an army on Bloemfontein while the "Free" Staters were engaged in the British Colonies of Natal and the Cape, which they had invaded. Lord Milner strongly forbade him from taking that step, and it was all that Sir Godfrey Lagden, the British Resident in Basutoland, could do to restrain the Basuto warriors from swooping down upon the Orange "Free" State.

On one occasion, however, the Basuto mountaineers were quickly mobilized. Word reached Maseru that General De Wet, whose guerrilla career was then at the height of its fame, was seriously harassed by Imperial troops in the "Free" State, and that it was feared he would escape through Basuto territory. In such a case it was ruled that the Basuto would be justified in opening fire upon the trespassing commandoes, but not until the Boers actually set foot upon Basuto territory. Therefore the Basutos, in anticipation of this violation of their territory, under the leadership of Councillor Philip Modise, made a record turn–out in one night, in a mountainous country, without telegraphic communication, and where all the orders were conveyed by word of mouth by men mounted on the sure–footed Basuto ponies; so that at daybreak as the Boers at the frontier near Wepener awoke, they found the Basuto border to be one mass of black humanity. The Basutos made strong appeals to Maseru for permission to cross the border and rush the Boers, and again they were forbidden. At length General De Wet, amid a rain of British shells, withdrew his commando and carried his operations elsewhere.

General De Wet, in his book on the South African War, admits that he was once hopelessly cornered and that then his only safe way of escape lay through the territory of the Basuto. He next proceeds to give his reason for not violating Basuto territory: it is that the Basutos showed no hostility towards the Boers, and that he had no wish to provoke them. No mention is made that armed Basutos barred his way, but if General De Wet's restraint were voluntary it would be the first instance in history that a Boer general had shown any regard concerning the rights or feelings of the Natives.

General Botha has on several occasions mentioned the loyal assistance rendered to the Transvaal Burghers by the Natives of the Transvaal. We may also mention the case of Chief Mokgothu, of the Western Transvaal, who with his headmen was detained at Mafeking after the siege. In fact that chief died in the Mafeking prison where he was interned with the Republican political prisoners for participating in the war on the side of the Republic.

On another occasion General Botha (obviously referring to Natives other than those around Mafeking) unwittingly paid a tribute to the valour of British Natives during the South African war. Speaking in the Nieuwe Kerk, at Middelburg, Holland, the General said: —

The Kaffirs turned against us and we not only had to fight against the English but against the Natives as well . . . when the attacks of the Kaffirs increased, our cause became dark and black. . . . All these facts taken collectively compelled us to discuss terms of peace.*

— * "De Boerengeneraals in Zeeland", p. 29. —

The southern defences of Montsioastad were maintained by the Barolong, under their own chief Lekoko, in their own way and with their own rations and rifles. These were only supplemented by supplies of ammunition, of which there was not too much in the garrison. And the only instructions which Major Godley and Captain Marsh gave the defenders was to "sit tight and don't shoot until the enemy is quite close."

The rest of the native population in the besieged town was under the fatherly care of Mr. C. G. H. Bell, the civil magistrate. And the harmonious relation between white and black as a prevailing characteristic of the population of the garrison throughout the siege was largely due to the tactful management of Major Lord Edward Cecil, D.S.O., Colonel Baden–Powell's chief of Staff. At the end of the siege, Lord Roberts sent General Sir Chas. Parsons to thank the Barolong for the creditable manner in which they defended their homes throughout the siege. The veteran soldier evidently thought that he had not done enough in the matter, so later on he sent Major the Hon. Hanbury Tracey from Pretoria with a framed address to the Barolong chiefs, written in gilt letters.

Colonel C. B. Vyvyan, who was escorted to Montsioastad by a squadron of the 4th Bedfordshire Regiment, headed by their band playing patriotic airs, presented the address in the presence of a large gathering of Barolongs and European visitors. The ceremony was described by the `Mafeking Mail' as follows: —

Within the square, seated on chairs and stools, were the Barolong men, whilst the women, attired in their brightest dresses, took up positions wherever they could get a view of the proceedings. On the arrival of the Base Commandant (Lieut.–Colonel Vyvyan) and the Resident Magistrate (Mr. C. G. H. Bell), a Union Jack was hoisted to the accompaniment of a general cheer. A large number of civilians and several military officers witnessed the ceremony, among them being the Mayor (Mr. A. H.

Friend), Mr. W. H. Surmon (Acting Commissioner), Lieut.–Colonel Newbury (Field Paymaster), Major the Hon. Hanbury Tracey (the officer who brought the address from Pretoria), and Major Panzera.

Mr. Bell, addressing the assembled Natives, said: To–day is an historical one in the history of the Barolongs as represented by Montsioa's people. I am sure it must be most satisfactory to you all who have so bravely assisted in the defence of Mafeking to have this honour conferred upon you, which is unprecedented in the annals of the history of the native tribes in this country. The Field–Marshal commanding Her Majesty's troops in South Africa has expressed in the address which is about to be presented to you his thanks for the services you rendered during the siege — an honour which I am sure you will appreciate at its full value, and which I can assure you is fully recognized by the Europeans who took part with you in the defence of the town. On many occasions bravery was displayed by both Europeans and Natives. We have fought and risked our lives together; we have undergone privations; we have eaten horses and various other animals of a like character; we have seen our friends fall, shattered by shells; and we have endured hardships and trials which very few men endure more than once in a lifetime. We have fought together for one common object. We have attained that object, and it is now impossible for us to do otherwise than experience a feeling of fellowship which is accentuated by the proceedings of to–day. You Barolongs at the commencement of the siege declared your determination to be loyal to the Queen, and when we had a meeting here shortly before war broke out you were assured by General Baden–Powell that if you did remain loyal your services would not be forgotten, and the Field–Marshal has endeavoured to–day to convince you of the truth of that statement. There are certain names mentioned on the address; but I cannot help, while talking to you now, mentioning the names of other persons who were of great assistance to us during the siege. It was altogether impossible to include the names of everybody on the address, and some of you may think that your names are not there because you have been overlooked, but that is not so. I will just mention the names of a few which, had there been room, might have appeared. First, there is Saane, who remained outside and assisted our dispatch runners, and who when he heard news sent it to us. It is only those who suffered from news hunger at the time can understand the pleasure we experienced at the assistance continually rendered to us by Saane. Then there is Badirile, who so bravely commanded his young men on the western outposts, and who on many occasions went through determined encounters with the enemy. Then again there is Joshua Molema, Motshegare and Mathakgong, all of whom did good service. Then there was Dinku, who on the day Eloff came in and when the enemy was behind him, stuck to his little fort, and who during the attack was wounded by a shell, which has since caused his death. His memory will not fade away amongst you Barolongs, as he was well known as a brave man.

Colonel Vyvyan then stepped forward and said: Chief Wessels and men of the Barolong nation, — Lord Roberts, Commander–in–Chief of the British Army in South Africa, has sent a special officer from Pretoria to bring you his greeting and to deliver to you a mark of his approval and the approval which he expresses on behalf of the Queen. Gathered here to–day are subjects of the Queen from various parts of her wide dominions — men who have come overseas from England, from Australia, from Canada, and from India — and they are here this afternoon to meet her native subjects of the Barolong tribe; whilst we, the officers and soldiers of the Queen who fought in Mafeking, wish to show what we think of our friends and neighbours down here in the stadt. You have done your duty well. You will remember that some time ago an officer was sent by Lieut.–General Baden–Powell to thank you for your services, and now the greatest General of all has sent you a special mark of his esteem in the form of this letter, which I shall read to you:

V [Crest of Queen Victoria] R.

"The Chief Wessels, Lekoko, and the Barolong of Mafeking.

"I, Frederick Sleigh Baron Roberts, K.P., G.C.S.I., G.C.I.E., V.C., of Kandahar and Waterford, hereby testify my approbation of the loyalty to H.M. Queen Victoria, and the good behaviour of the Barolongs under the leadership of Wessels, Lekoko, and the headmen Silas Molema and Paul Montsioa, throughout the long and trying investment of Mafeking by the Boers, from October 13, 1899, to May 17, 1900, and I desire to congratulate these leaders and their people on the successful issue of their courageous defence of their homes and property against the invasion of the enemy.

"(Signed) Roberts,
Field–Marshal. "Pretoria, July 1, 1900."

Addressing Chief Wessels, and at the same time handing him the letter, the Colonel concluded: I give you this on behalf of Lord Roberts and the Queen. You are to accept it on behalf of your nation. You are to keep it and show it to your children and tell them why it was given to you and that they are to be proud of it.

The Colonel held out his hand, which Wessels gripped very cordially. The band played the National Anthem, and the Barolongs joined in one of their native cheers.

Wessels then rose, and taking off his white helmet, replied on behalf of his tribe.

Replying to the address and speeches Chief Wessels Montsioa asked the officers to convey to Lord Roberts the gratitude of the Barolong for the relief of Mafeking, adding: "I have gone to extremes into which my forefathers scarcely ever went in defending their homes. I have eaten horseflesh, donkey and mule flesh, and had the relief column not come when it did, I was going to eat dog flesh, if by that means I would have been enabled to hold up a gun and keep the enemy out of doors, until Lord Roberts sent relief."

Mr. Chamberlain, who visited Mafeking two years later, inspected the old siege position and addressed the largest meetings we had ever seen in Mafeking. He said to the thousands of assembled Barolongs: "You ask in your addresses that the conditions secured to you, when you were transferred from the Imperial Government to the Colonial Government should remain as they are. I do not think that Sir Gordon Sprigg or any one who may succeed him will alter them in any respect, and should any one attempt to alter these conditions, you will have your appeal to His Majesty's Government." This was said in the presence of Sir Gordon Sprigg, the Cape Premier of the day, Mr. Thomas L. Graham, the Cape Attorney–General (now Judge of the Supreme Court at Grahamstown), and Sir Walter F. Hely–Hutchinson, Governor of the Cape Colony. But what must be the feelings of these people, and what must be the effect of these assurances upon them now that it is decreed that their sons and daughters can no longer settle in the Union except as serfs; that they no longer have any claim to the country for which they bled, and that when they appeal to the Imperial authorities for redress of these grievances, they are told that there is no appeal?

A promise of a farm was made to the Fingo and Kafir contingent, but that promise still remains unfulfilled.

When His Royal Highness the Duke of Connaught visited Mafeking in 1906, he was touched by the grateful references which Chief Lekoko made to the benign rule of His Royal Highness's late illustrious mother. And he assured the assembled Natives, in the name of His late Majesty King Edward VII, that the death of their beloved Queen would "not alter their status in any manner whatsoever as His Majesty took the same deep interest in the welfare of the native population as the late Queen did." In view of this statement by His Royal Highness, Chief Lekoko congratulated his people on having had the honour of receiving "assurances of Imperial protection, not from an Imperial official, but from the lips of His Majesty's own brother, and in the King's English," the Barolong felt that they were reclining on a veritable rock of ages.

Since the inauguration and meeting of the first Union Parliament, laws have been enacted which threaten to annul all this. As far as the Barolongs are concerned, the Colonial Government is not the only aggressor.

In the early 'nineties a British Boundary Commission awarded the territory of Mokgomana to a northern tribe. The award caused great dissatisfaction amongst the Barolong; accordingly they sent a deputation to the High Commissioner about the award. It was only after they announced their unalterable intention to assert their claim to that territory by means of the sword, that the Imperial authorities, in the name of the Queen, re-considered the former decision, and that Sir Hamilton Goold Adams restored that land to the Barolong, under date March 11, 1896. But the Colonial Office, completely ignoring Sir Hamilton Goold Adams's signature on behalf of the Queen, and without referring the matter to the native inhabitants in any way, lately confiscated that territory and declared it the property of the Crown. In consequence of this high-handed proceeding there is much bad blood among the Barolong.

It might be said in support of this act of the Colonial Office that strangers will not be settled in the territory, but Sir Garnet Wolseley once declared that "as long as the sun shines in the heavens, Zululand shall remain the property of the Zulus." The sun is still shining in the heavens, and right up to the time of the outbreak of the European War in 1914, the Union Government were very busy cutting up Zululand and parcelling it out to white settlers under the Land Settlement Act of the Union (for white men only), parcels of land to survey which black taxpayers are forced to pay, but which under the Natives' Land Act no black man can buy; and what is true in regard to Zululand, British Kaffraria, East Griqualand and other native territories, is equally so in regard to Bechuanaland.

Chapter XX The South African Races and the European War

Oh! the Battle-bow is strung,
The Banner is outflung:
From lowlands and from valley,

From mountain–tops, they rally!
      L. J. Coppin.

Africa is a land of prophets and prophetesses. In the course of our tour of observation on the ravages of the Land Act, we reached Vereeniging in August, 1913, and found the little village astir because the local pastor, Rev. S. H. Senamela, was returning from a certain funeral service. To many of the people of the place the event seemed to be a momentous one, affecting as it appeared more people than would be ordinarily the case. The person whose death and funeral caused all this stir was a black seeress of Vereeniging, of whom it was said that in her lifetime she prophesied the Anglo–Boer War and some such situation as that created by the Natives' Land Act. Before breathing her last, this interesting lady (whose sayings carried great weight among the surrounding native peasants and the Dutch neighbours on the farms of that neighbourhood) had, it was said, uttered her last prophecy. It was to the effect that a great war would take place in the near future, amongst the white peoples of the country, that there would be much bloodshed, but that the survivors would live very peacefully with the native population. We are sorry now that we did not care to listen to the whole story when it was related, and we very much wish that we had remained to interrogate the narrator as to whether the black population that would thus remain to share life with the white survivors in South Africa would be a contented one, or whether they would be living in chains, of which the thraldom of coming events appears to be casting its shadow before. But at the time it sounded parlous to think that anything could interrupt the calm of the tolerant British colonists and egg them against their Dutch rulers, who call them foreign adventurers. Nor could we conceive of any reason why the Boers, who have now more freedom than they ever dreamt of possessing under their own flag, including the right to partially enslave the blacks, should suddenly rise up against the English, whose money and brains are ever at the beck and call of the Dutch! Here, however, is the war, predicted by the late native seeress, and evidently we have to make the best of it.

The writer was in London at the end of July, 1914, when there were many disquieting reports about the activities of suffragettes, and when there were still more serious reports about the unlawful mobilization of volunteer armies in Ireland.

It was in this exciting period that attention was at once transferred from Ireland to the Continent of Europe. There it seemed that every moment was ticking to drive us towards the greatest war that the world ever saw. And though matters grew hourly more serious, it did not then occur to the writer, a stranger then of only six weeks in London, that after seeing the capital of the Empire under conditions of peace, he was soon to see it under a war cloud filled with all the horrors of the approaching war storm and all the signs of patriotic enthusiasm. We were about to see Mafeking over again, but through the biggest magnifying glass.

To walk along Oxford Street of an afternoon and see the multitudes of well–dressed women pouring into the streets from the underground stations (the "Tube" and the "Met", as they are called in the vernacular), round Charing Cross and Piccadilly, and see them walking up and down the thoroughfares and looking at the wares displayed in the dazzling shop windows; or to come down Bishopsgate of a morning and see the stupendous swarms of white men rushing to and fro along the pavements of Threadneedle Street, crowding the motor–buses round the Mansion House, St. Paul's and Ludgate Circus — yet all this throng so well regulated by the City Police that nobody seems to be in the other's way — the disproportion of men and women in the East and West respectively forming a partial segregation between the sexes: to see these myriads of humanity gave one the impression that if the Garden of Eden (whose whereabouts has not yet been defined) was not actually in London, then some very fertile human germ imported from the Garden must have been planted somewhere in the vicinity of Trafalgar Square, or the Elephant and Castle. These great masses of people when the war broke out were swept over, as already indicated, by a wave of patriotism, and sections of them reinforced by a regular inflow from the provinces, and foreign tourists — Americans, Scandinavians, Orientals and Colonials — rushing back from the danger zone on the Continent, stranded in London with their pockets bulging with useless credit notes, all these joined the buzzing groups in Fleet Street in scanning the latest telegrams posted at the windows of the newspaper offices, or, going to Hyde Park, they listened to the open-air speeches delivered there. In this gamut of personalities and nationalities there were, at first, faint murmurs by some of the English against their country joining the strife and in favour of her remaining neutral and leaving the Continentals to "stew in their own juice". But when German seamen laid mines in the English Channel, and capped their deeds by sinking the `Amphion' and the `Pathfinder', with hundreds of officers and men, the "protestants" found that their efforts were out of date and that their arguments could have held water in the good old days, before the declaration of war, but not after. For the silent determination of the London crowds, of both sexes and all colours, was so emphatic that one could almost read it in their thoughts, and see it, as it were, percolating through every fibre of their systems. If the weaker races of the world — (and which race is weaker than the coloured?) — are ever to enjoy rest, then the great Powers must avenge the violation of the neutrality of Belgium.

Early in August, we left London to visit the Scottish capital, and as far as the swiftness of the North British Railway would allow a glimpse, the country towns and villages of the north appeared to be swarming with Territorials in khaki. A painful sight at some of the stations was the number of restive horses forced into the railway trucks by troopers — beautiful, well-fed animals whose sleek appearance showed that they were unaccustomed to the rough life to which the Tommies were leading them. Further, it was sad to think that these noble creatures by their size were to be rendered easy targets for the marksmen of the enemy's forces, and that they would in addition be subjected to the severity of inclement weather conditions, to which they likewise were unaccustomed.

At Edinburgh, the Cameron Highlanders marched along some of the streets in their battalions, flinging the Highland kilt like the plaited reeds of so many thousands of Bojale* girls. Handsome young Scotchmen, all of them, and it was shocking to think that these fine young fellows in the flower of their youth were going to be fired at with a set purpose to kill them as if they were a flock of springbuck on a South African veld. Surely it is time that civilization evolved a less brutal and less savage form of warfare! On Sunday evening we attended divine service at St. Giles's Cathedral, and the critical political situation permeated the entire service. This feeling was not lessened by the announcement that one of the gallant boys who sank with the `Amphion' was a son of one of the sidesmen of St. Giles's. It was war as unmistakable as it was grim.

— * Bechuana circumcision rites. —

After the declaration of war between Great Britain and Germany, the Irish tension at once died away. The self-constituted opposing armies of Dublin and Belfast, or rather Ireland and Ulster, came forward and offered themselves and their arms to the Imperial authorities. They were anxious to proceed at once to the Continent and assert British prestige on the battlefield; the suffragettes likewise at the outbreak of the war declared a truce and offered their humble services to the Empire. "More power to their hatpins!" But how about South Africa, the baby–member of the British family? Where does she come in?

Within a week after the outbreak, Mr. Harcourt sent the following dispatch to the Governors–General of Canada, Australia and New Zealand: —

Please communicate to your Ministers the following message from His Majesty and publish: "I desire to express to my people of the overseas Dominions with what appreciation and pride I have received the messages from their respective Governments during the past few days. The spontaneous assurance of their fullest support recalls to me the generous self–sacrificing help given by them in the past to the Mother Country. I shall be strengthened in the discharge of the great responsibilities which rest upon me by the confident belief that in this time of trial my Empire will stand united, calm, resolute, trusting in God. — George R.I."

More offers of men and money came from the Dominions; and when such well–deserved Royal encomiums are showered on the already laurelled heads of other dominions, a self–respecting South African like ourselves walked the streets with a drooping head. And when our kinsmen in West Africa under the leadership of British officers, annexed German Togoland rather early in the campaign, we found these questions reverting in our thoughts: What is our Government doing? When is it going to move? Surely our Prime Minister, who is also Minister of Native Affairs, should now postpone the constant pampering of the back–velders, hang colour prejudice for a more peaceful time, call out the loyal legions — British, Boer, and Black — and annex German South Africa without delay! As a British General and Minister of Native Affairs, he should himself lead the black contingents and leave the whites to be led by their regular officers.

At the beginning of August, a special meeting of the South African Native Congress was called at Bloemfontein, first to express its disappointment at the cold reception given to the native deputation by the Imperial Government; and secondly, to express its thanks to the British public for the kind reception given to the deputation; and thirdly, to devise ways and means for the deputation to tour the United Kingdom on a mission, revealing to the British people the manner in which the Colonial Government discharges its trust to the coloured people.

Many of the delegates to the Congress had travelled long distances by rail and road, but on their arrival at Bloemfontein it was only to learn that war had broken out between Great Britain and Germany. Hence the Native Congress, in view of the situation, resolving itself at once into a patriotic demonstration, decided to hang up native grievances against the South African Parliament till a better time and to tender the authorities every assistance.

Mr. Dube, the president of the Congress, who had just returned from England in time for the conference, proceeded direct to Pretoria with the Executive, to lay at the feet of the Government this offer of service made by the Native Congress. Offers of service poured into the administrative capital from native chiefs and people in all parts of the country. Magistrates who held meetings in their districts on the instructions of the Government to explain the situation to the Natives received similar offers. And besides all these, offers of service also came from the Zulu chiefs and headmen, from Chief Dalindyebo of the Tembus, Marelana of the Pondos, and from Griffiths of Basutoland. In Bechuanaland, the veteran Chief Khama and other Bechuana chiefs offered the services of native warriors as scouts in German South West Africa, and the Swazi princes offered a Swazi impi, besides undertaking to help in any other manner, as they did in the campaign against Sekukuni in the 'seventies. The members of the native deputation in England were longing to catch the first steamer back to South Africa to join their countrymen and proceed to the front. But while all these offers were gratefully acknowledged, none were definitely accepted. Surely there must be something wrong. Is it that the wretched South African colour prejudice is exerting itself even in these critical times?

At Pretoria, Captain W. Allan King, the popular Native Commissioner of the Pretoria District, held a meeting of Transvaal Natives, which amongst others was attended by His Worship the Mayor of the Union capital; and there again native offers of service were tendered. Mr. Makgatho, the chairman, in his denial of the report that appeared in the newspapers to the effect that "South Africa could not take the field as she had a native menace to watch", voiced the prevailing feeling of the Natives. Captain King, however, assured the Natives that no such slanders were uttered by the Government. He further reminded them that the Imperial Government was face to face with the biggest struggle that ever took place since the foundation of the world; and that there would be fighting on land, in the air, on the water and under the water. He urged the Natives to go to work as usual and see to it that there was no slackening of industries. He also made a plea for the abiding respect of the Natives to the German missionaries of the Transvaal, having regard to what those good men had done in bygone years for the evangelization of the Natives of that Province. How little did any one dream at the time that he was thus pleading for others, that Captain King would be among the victims of the war; and that he would fall, not from a German bullet, but from one fired by one of the Dutch traitors, in a brisk fight to quell the recent Boer rebellion.

  Ku mugama e Tipperary,
  E malandalahla;
  Ku mugama e Tipperary,
   Kwe sona standwa sam.
  Bhota, Piccadilly,
  Sala, Leicester Square,
  Kude le–le–le, e Tipperary
  'Ntliziyo yam ikona.
        "Tipperary" in Xosa.

White men wrote to the newspapers that as France, our great Ally, was using Native African troops, there could be no objection against England doing the same — as if England had rejected the assistance of her coloured subjects pending a decision by France. A well-known Natal campaigner wrote to the authorities offering to raise a crack Zulu regiment composed of men who had formerly fought for the old flag against their own people. He said he felt certain that those Zulus could give as good an account of themselves against any regiment in the field as any force yet mobilized; but there was no definite acceptance of these offers by the Government. The native uncertainty that arose from this attitude of the South African Government went on until October, when our colleagues of the native deputation returned home from England and threw themselves into the vortex of the martial enthusiasm that was then sweeping through the country, and as no offers were accepted by the Government, Dr. Rubusana made to it the following further offer: —

The Right Hon. the Minister of Native Affairs, Pretoria, Transvaal.

Sir, — Coming as I do so near from the scene of operations in Europe, I feel that something more practical than mere lip–loyalty is required from those who boast of the fact that they are British subjects, and are loyal to the British Crown, more especially during this present crisis. That being so, I am prepared to raise, if you deem it necessary, a native levy of 5,000 able–bodied men to proceed to German South–West Africa, provided the Government is prepared to fully equip this force for the front. I should, of course, be prepared to accompany them.

I have the honour to be, Sir,
Your obedient servant,
W. B. Rubusana.

==

Reply.

Union of South Africa,
Department of Defence,
Pretoria.
November 2, 1914.

Sir, — With reference to your letter of the 20th ultimo, I am directed to state that the Union Government greatly appreciates the loyal sentiments which are being expressed by the native citizens of the Union.

I am, however, to refer you to the provisions of Section 7 of the South Africa Defence Act, 1912, and to state that the Government does not desire to avail itself of the services, in a combatant capacity, of citizens not of European descent in the present hostilities. Apart from other considerations the present war is one which has its origin among the white people of Europe and the Government are anxious to avoid the employment of its native citizens in a warfare against whites.

I have the honour to be, Sir,
Your obedient servant,
H. B. M. Bourne,
Secretary for Defence. Dr. W. B. Rubusana,
East London, C.P.

General Botha was once confronted with a definite request to reconcile two conflicting declarations of policies enunciated by two members of his Cabinet, and in reply to that request he gave the following highly diplomatic explanation: "The one Minister has said things which should not have been said, and the other Minister had said things which should have been said in a different way."

Native Life in South Africa

If there is one document which contains things that should not have been penned, or that should have been differently worded, surely it is the document we have just quoted. Fancy refusing native assistance in the present world's war on the ground of colour! For weeks before Dr. Rubusana sailed from Europe the Turcos and Algerian and Moroccan troops had been doing wondrous deeds on the Continent for the cause of the Allies. These coloured troops also included a regiment of wealthy Natives from North Africa who had come to fight for France entirely at their own expense — a striking evidence of what the Empire is losing through the South African policy of restricting native wages to one shilling a day, in a country where the cost of living is about the highest in the world. The Union Government rejected the native offer a week after Lord Roberts laid down his life, having delivered the appreciation of a grateful Empire to the gallant Indian regiments who with distinction were participating in the same war; and a month after the first German General Freise was captured in the course of a daring charge by North African Natives from the French Colonies; ten days after the Germans at Tsiengtau had surrendered to the British and Japanese forces; and nearly three weeks after the Germans had successfully involved Turkey in the strife; and while the Canadian troops on Salisbury Plain included Red Indians. Where, then, is the wisdom of telling Dr. Rubusana, who knows all these facts, that the Government's rejection of the native offer is due to the fact that the present struggle is an all—white one? The truth of the matter is that the South African Government worships an idol, which was best described by Sir Gordon Sprigg as "the demon of ignorance and prejudice", and the claims of this fetish in South Africa precedes those of the Empire.

Under the old Republics we had a law which since the Union has become the unwritten law of South Africa. In this law it is laid down that a coloured policeman shall not lay his black hands on a white man even if he found him red—handed in the commitment of a crime. The duty of a coloured policeman in such circumstances would be to look around for a white constable and report the misdemeanour to him. Rather than suffer the humiliation of a black official taking a white criminal into custody white South Africa would prefer to have the country overrun with white criminals, ergo, if the safety of the Crown is at stake and it could be saved only by employing black men, we would much rather let the Crown go than suffer the humiliation of seeing black warriors resisting a white enemy. If there is one point upon which white South Africa is agreed, it is that the claims of South Africa come first and those of the Empire afterwards. The "bitter—enders" go further: they say that "the Empire comes handy only in so far as it is useful to us, but when we have sucked it dry, like an orange, it must be thrown away."* It may be that the blacks have their reasons for objecting to these creeds: they would prefer Imperial lines all the time, for Imperial lines are benevolent while South African lines are cruel; consisting largely of repression and slavery.

— * General Botha's reply to General Hertzog on the Ministerial crisis of 1912. —

There is a talk in South Africa, which unhappily is not confined to Dutch—speaking South Africans. It advocates the elimination of the Imperial factor, because that factor is said to interfere with colonial liberties, among which is the right to "correct" a Native in a manner that a colonial deems fit. Thus, under the inconvenience of the "pestilential Imperial factor", a colonial Magistrate was forced to fine General De Wet the sum of 5s. on his pleading guilty to having horse—whipped a Native. Under German rule, which threatened the Union, the liberty of chastising the Native according to colonial ideas would be extended, for the German method is that of the old "Free" State, where a Native used to be tied to a wagon—wheel and whipped. If he dies in consequence of the beating, his death was but a nominal offence. This state of things explains the determination of the native races to fight for the retention of the Imperial factor, or for what vestige of it still remains in the country.

A native clergyman sends us the following letter. We are not quite certain if the reverend gentleman desired to enlist as a private or as a chaplain; anyway, this is what he says:

Can it be really true that we, too, belong to the British Empire? This war is growing in such dimensions that it is even affecting the King's household. The Prince of Wales has gone to the front, and His Majesty the King has also gone, yet we are told that we are not worthy on account of our colour to fight for our King and Empire. White men only must defend the King's Dominions while we remain behind with the women and children. Surely it cannot be the wish of the loyal Boers that we must not defend our Empire; it is only the wish of the rebels, and it seems that our Government will continue to study their feelings even while they are engaged in shooting down loyal people.

It would seem that the South African Government is so deeply in love with the Natives that they are scrupulously careful lest the Natives should singe so much as a hair in the present struggle, and that white men alone may shoot and kill one another. But, in point of fact, black men ARE required by the Union Government to proceed to the front as Government wagon drivers, driving provisions and ammunition wagons, and acting as orderlies to the white burghers. In these capacities they are exposed to all the risks and horrors of the war, yet even if they are shot, they must not, under any circumstances, be mentioned in the casualty lists, nor must they carry arms, lest their behaviour should merit recognition; their heroic deeds and acts of valour must, on account of their colour, not be recorded. These native drivers are classed with the transport mules, with this difference, that while the owner of a mule receives monetary compensation for each animal that falls on the battlefield, or is captured by the enemy, the Government's interest in the black driver ceases when he is killed.

Suppose the services of these muleteers were recognized in a combatant capacity, some one might get it into his head to ask: "Why should loyal fighting taxpayers be debarred from the rights of the franchise that are liberally bestowed on white rebels and their relations, some of whom are said to contribute nothing towards the upkeep of the State?" So then to refuse these Natives the right to carry arms in defence of the Empire, and to send them to the front without arms, is to deprive such inquirers of this and similar arguments.

On St. Patrick's Day, the `Westminster Gazette' appeared with a leading article, from which we make the following extract: —

It will be impossible, when we have had the assistance of the Indian Army in Europe, to restrict the promotion of its officers in the manner laid down hitherto. It will also be impossible to restrict Natives of India WHO HAVE PROVED THEIR ABILITY AND EXPERIENCE BY LONG SERVICE in their own country TO POSITIONS IN WHICH THEY ARE SUBORDINATE TO THE RAWEST NEW ARRIVAL FROM THE COVENANTED SERVICE. All these discriminations which rest simply on race and are justified by no natural disability will have to be swept away, and new and more generous conditions laid down for the whole Indian public service.

Surely what is true in regard to the Indian public service is equally so in regard to that infallible South

African taxing machine, the adjunct of the Union Civil Service, which is officially called the Native Affairs Department. There, raw recruits serve their apprenticeship while lording it over Natives who have proved their ability and experience by a quarter of a century's service in their own country. It is to prevent the application to South Africa of broad—minded views like those expressed by the `Westminster Gazette' that native Africans must not serve against the Germans. Therefore it seems to have occurred to the authorities that the best course is to engage the Natives in a capacity in which their participation will demand no recognition. These statements are not mere empty phrases, for the writer recently caused inquiries to be made through the Department of Native Affairs in South Africa as to whether there were any Coloured People who had been killed or wounded while on active service at the front. And the result was a long list of killed, wounded, and captured up to the end of October, 1914, among Natives and Coloured People who had not been mentioned in the casualty lists.*

— * When the enemy airmen attacked the British camp at Garub (G.S.W.A.),
  on March 27, 1915, and dropped bombs on General Botha's guns,
  Reuter says, "only one Native was slightly wounded." —

This deference to South African prejudice would at least seem reasonable if the King's enemies also had colour scruples. But so far from that being the case, Natives living far away from defended centres are always the first to suffer when a white man's war breaks out. In fact they are always subjected to indignities from which they would be immune if they had arms. One of the first steps taken by the "Free" State rebels under General De Wet during the recent rebellion was to dash for the nearest native owner of horses and annex their mounts. The unarmed proprietor's recourse in that case was to take to his heels and leave the rebels to plunder his stock. Any hesitation to run away has involved some unfortunate Native in the danger of being horsewhipped into the service of the King's enemies, and if he took the first opportunity to escape from the rebel commando, a detection of his act would positively have meant a bullet behind his neck.

The late Dean Green of Natal, writing years ago, said: —

"Every chief should have his own militia and police. Our common human nature tells us that it is the duty of every one capable of bearing arms to fit himself to be able to defend his country and Government. Were the Government to refuse permission to the chief to enrol his young men, it would inflict a wrong on them, against which their manliness would revolt. Our Government, however, is not established to alienate from us the native races, but to attach them to us by giving them full freedom to exercise under restraints of Christianity all those instincts and desires which are proper to their manhood.

"The Houssas and Soudanese on the north, the negro tribes on the west, form part of the Imperial forces, and have shown themselves true, brave, and useful troops. On no possible ground of justice can the loyal Bantu tribes be placed under a ban, and refused to serve in the ranks for the defence of the Empire. A youth debarred from the legitimate opportunities of exercising his manly energies will become riotous and unruly, and addict himself, for the sake of excitement, to sheep—stealing, etc."

The `Christian Express', which has always acted as the mediator between the overbearing section of

Colonial opinion on the one hand and the subject races on the other, tried to allay the disappointment of our people with the excuse that the Government refused the native offer on the ground that it desired to use men from the more advanced races who are capable of being more easily trained.* In the face of historical records, however, this argument will not hold a drop of water. British archives are overloaded with instances of the valour and tractability of the aboriginal races of South Africa no less than those of their nephews, the Cape Coloured People. Not having enough space to enumerate them at length we may only refer to two instances of recent date.

— * The `Express' is now advocating the raising of an army of 100,000 Natives. —

During the South African war, the writer was asked by the military authorities to recruit twelve young Natives to act as scouts in the Western Transvaal. The young fellows were handed to Sergt. Clemens of the Cape Police for training. Three days after they were enrolled we met the Sergeant, who was highly pleased with his "raw recruits". He told us with evident satisfaction that, after he had given them oral instructions in the handling and use of firearms, he took them to the range to try them at shooting; and all but two of them hit the bull's eye with the first attempt. This is but one isolated instance which is typical of the rest.

It is doubtful if any white man is a greater authority on the character of the Zulus than Mr. R. C. Samuelson of Natal. Writing on the outbreak of the European war and the advisability of raising native levies, he said: —

During the late rebellion I was captain and adjutant of 350 men composed of men, half of whom were Christians and the other half heathens of the Amangwane, a section of the Amabomyu tribe, who at the beginning of the rebellion were raw recruits, but who, after three months' drill and manoeuvring, were as expert in their drill and use of the rifle and riding as any corps in the field. In all my dealings with all these men and many more, I found them most attentive, most orderly, most careful about their arms, most alert on duty, perfectly reliable, and in and out loyal to the Government and those they were under. Having been a volunteer for many years, and a cadet at college in the Cape, I can safely say that I never found our people as a body so easy to manage and train in the military art, and so orderly and attentive as these natives were.

I had the honour to be called upon to summon 50 of the Zulu war and Boer war heroes to be reviewed by the Duke of Connaught; many of these had the Zulu war medal on, which the Duke took special notice of, but the Boer war medal was not there. These people were highly complimented by the Duke, and afterwards gave a free concert to the Royal party in the Maritzburg Town Hall, which was attended by immense crowds, the chief song of the evening being a Zulu song specially prepared by these men, and set to music by them, in honour of the Royal party, which was also embossed and presented to the Royal party. The Royal party expressed their appreciation by sending forward to me one of the officers in waiting on them to thank the singers.

"Izwe Lakiti" Aug. 12, 1914.

The writer has received several letters expressing the native resentment of the idea that they should fold their arms and cogitate while other British subjects, irrespective of colour, are sacrificing their

161

lives for the defence of the Empire in this, the darkest period of His Majesty's reign. Our reply to each of these letters was that the natives should subscribe, according to their small means, to the several war funds; and our latest information is that they are subscribing to the Prince of Wales' Fund, the Governor–General's and the Belgian Relief Fund. When we last heard from home the Basutos had given 2,700 Pounds to the National Relief Fund, the list being headed by Chief Griffiths with a donation of 100 Pounds. Chief Khama of Bechuanaland gave 800 Pounds, Chief Lewanika of Barotseland 200 Pounds, Chief Lekoko and two other Chiefs, each 30 Pounds, while the Zulus, Tembus and Pondos were still collecting. At Kimberley the Natives gave concerts for the benefit of the Mayor's Relief Fund. At their Beaconsfield concert the Kimberley Band under Herr Carl Rybnikar, known as the best volunteer band in South Africa, attended and gave selections; and Chief Molala of the Batlhaping gave General Botha 200 bullocks to feed the Union troops.

In April 1915 the Minister of Native Affairs gave the following testimony of native loyalty and co–operation. Speaking from his place in Parliament Mr. Malan said — "he thought it his duty to say that the attitude of the large number of the Natives entrusted to their care, all through the troubles, had been most exemplary and most patriotic. There was one exception to which he would refer,* but from the commencement, from all parts of the Union, resolutions came to the Government of expressions of loyalty on the part of the Natives, and of their support in the measures Government was taking in connexion with the war. They (the Natives) gave oxen and supported liberally, according to their means, the different patriotic funds which had been established, and generally gave the Government every assistance. The Government had been able to enrol between 23,000 and 24,000 Natives for service in German S.W. Africa, in building railways and in transport work. The chief of the Tembus had volunteered to send his own son to German S.W. Africa for the purpose of superintending the members of his tribe, a large number of whom had volunteered for the front. All that spoke well for the Natives, and he would be neglecting his duty if he did not testify to that."

— * The "one exception" referred to by Mr. Malan was the Hlubis
   of Matatiele district, who forcibly resisted the cattle dipping regulations
   because, they said, the frequent dipping killed their cattle. —

In opening the Rhodesian Legislative Council, on April 28, Mr. Administrator Chaplin concluded by saying that the behaviour and attitude of the native population since the outbreak of the war left nothing to be desired. All information available showed that any attempts by emissaries of the enemy to stir up trouble would fail to meet with support. "Numerous expressions of loyalty to His Majesty have come from leading Chiefs, taxes are readily paid, and perfect order has been maintained."

What a happy land in which to live South Africa would be if, instead of the present god of colour prejudice, we had some such confidence as is reposed in the blacks by the British authorities in East Africa and elsewhere. The naughty white piccaninnies who always insult inoffensive black passers–by would be taught that the Native is a useful neighbour whose strong right arm may be depended upon in times of trouble, instead of being taught, as they are taught in Transvaal, that every man Jack of them is a black peril monster who must not only be discriminated against, but who must be indiscriminately insulted and repressed. The following dispatch, published in the `Daily Chronicle', illustrates the confidence of the British authorities in East Africa towards the blacks: —

==

East African Battle won by Native "Non–Com".

About the end of September the Germans advanced 600 strong, with six machine guns, from the Vanga side. They were held at Margerini on September 25 by Captain Wavel's Arab Company, and some King's African Rifles under Captain Stoner arrived from Jubaland on the 27th, none too soon to reinforce Captain Wavel, the enemy in the meanwhile having become very aggressive.

The German plan of attack was to destroy the Salisbury bridge, which connects Mombasa island with the mainland, thus securing one of the most important strategical positions in East Africa.

The "Koenigsberg" did not arrive, perhaps because of the nearness of British warships, and the little British force of 300 men dislocated the land operations of the enemy. "C" Company held off the Germans until October 2, when they were reinforced by Indian troops. The Jind Infantry behaved particularly well at Gazi, where they had to face a very heavy fire from the six machine guns of the enemy.

The King's African Rifles deserve special mention. Major Hawthorn, who was in command, and all the European officers, were wounded early in the engagement, thus leaving the little force leaderless.

Colour–Sergeant Sumani quietly took charge, and led on his men as if nothing had happened. He gave the order to charge, and the enemy broke and fled. This incident has not yet appeared in the bald official announcements, but it is hoped the splendid conduct of the native colour sergeant will receive recognition.*

— * Sergeant Sumani has since been decorated with the D.S.O. —

Chapter XXI Coloured People's Help Rejected / The Offer of Assistance by the South African Coloured Races Rejected

The Africans and their descendants in America have proven to the world
  that they do not lack courage and military ardour. This the French
  have recognized by enlisting them in their present struggle.
  We hope for the sake of the Africans that they will give
  a good account of themselves, but the coloured race is like the Irish
  who are invincible in fighting for other nations, but not for themselves.
        An American on the Great War.

The African Political Organization was early in the field. Dr. Abdurahman, its president, during the first week of the war, had a force of 3,000 coloured men at Capetown ready to take the field against the Germans. These men included those who had fought for the British flag, side by side with the British troops in the Matabele wars and other South African campaigns in various capacities. In a few days the number of this force rose to 5,000 able–bodied men ready to go to the front. A definite offer of the service of this force was communicated to the Union Government, who replied that the offer was under consideration.

Mr. William Hosken, the famous Johannesburg politician, member of the Transvaal Parliament before the unification of South Africa — a gentleman whose legislative talents are now unfortunately in abeyance, because his liberal views on colour are too advanced for the palates of the lily–white voters of his State — offered to pay the cost of recruiting such a coloured force. Application forms were scattered throughout the country, asking volunteers to send in their names and addresses to the A.P.O. headquarters signifying their intention to serve as units of the Hosken Division. Our old friend Mr. N. R. Veldsman, a coloured political organizer of considerable ability, who had been in retirement for the past year or two, came forward, took his place among the coloured leaders, and addressed patriotic meetings at Saron and other Cape districts on behalf of the recruiting movement.

==

PATRIOTIC DEMONSTRATION

The City Hall, Capetown, was packed on Monday night, August 31, 1914, with coloured citizens of Capetown, who had assembled to express their loyalty to King George and their determination to support the Government during the present crisis.

Sir Frederick Smith, who presided, thought the coloured people had taken a wise course in calling that meeting to tender their assistance to the Government while Britain was engaged in war. He was confident that that demonstration would receive the grateful appreciation of the Prime Minister, his Cabinet, and also of H.M. King George.

Dr. Abdurahman said that the coloured people had met in public meeting on many occasions, but never in the history of South Africa had they been called together on a more solemn occasion, nor at a more critical juncture, and never when the issues were fraught with greater consequences.

The coloured people had many grievances, but all that must be forgotten while danger was threatening the very existence of the Empire. If the Empire fell, South Africa would fall, Capetown would fall, and Capetown might even be laid in ruins.

Although England was engaged in a life and death struggle, South Africans felt secure and could sleep in peace. That security was due to the supremacy of the British Navy. They had met that night to decide how they could assist the Empire. He moved the following resolution:

"That the coloured citizens of Capetown, in mass meeting assembled, under the auspices of the A.P.O., hereby express their loyalty to H.M. King George V, and take this opportunity of placing on record their recognition of the fact that the security that they at present enjoy is due primarily to the supremacy of the British Navy; and further, they pray that Britain's efforts during the war will be crowned with success. That a copy of this resolution be forwarded to H.E. the Governor–General for transmission to H.M. the King." (Applause.)

Mr. J. C. Carelse, in seconding the resolution, remarked that that was not the time to consider their own troubles, but to show the enemy that they stood together as a united Empire against any foe who dared to lower the Union Jack. The resolution was adopted with enthusiasm.

Mr. N. R. Veldsman appealed to the coloured people to assist those who as a result of the war might suffer. The coloured people should spend less on bioscopes and trivialities, and contribute to a fund which it was proposed to raise. He moved the following resolution:

"That, in order to alleviate the suffering which inevitably accompanied war, an appeal is hereby made to the coloured citizens of the Union to contribute to a fund to be administered by the following committee: The Rt. Rev. Bishop J. A. Johnson, Mrs. Wooding, Mrs. Abdurahman, Mrs. Gow, Dr. Gool, Dr. Abdurahman, the Rev. F. Gow, Messrs. C. J. Carelse, S. Reagon, N. R. Veldsman, S. F. Geyer, P. Grever, H. Hartog, B. Baron, H. Cressy, A. Arendze, H. J. Gordon, R. Hoedemaker, W. A. Roberts, M. J. Fredericks, Fred Hendricks, H. A. Gamildien, Pfieffer, and George Fife."

The Rev. Mr. Gow seconded the resolution, and said that although the spirit of war was in the air, there was also a spirit of helpfulness in the air. They should at this period forget race and creed and contribute to the fund.

Mrs. Wooding, who spoke in support of the resolution, remarked that the coloured women would be found ready to do their duty whenever the call went forth. The best way to show loyalty to the Empire was by rendering some service. The resolution was unanimously adopted.

Dr. Gool said that another way of giving practical assistance to the Empire was by raising volunteer corps for active service. He moved:

"That the offer made through the A.P.O. to raise volunteers for active service at home or abroad be approved, and that this meeting tenders to the Union Government its loyal support during the present crisis."

Mr. S. Reagon, who seconded, said that they were excluded from the Defence Force. But as the Empire was endangered he hoped an opportunity would be given the coloured people to take a part in the fighting line.

The resolution was agreed to. The sum of 37 Pounds was raised during the evening.

Mr. H. Seymour rendered some patriotic selections on the organ. The meeting concluded with the singing of the National Anthem.

At Johannesburg, Mr. Koopman presided over a crowded meeting of the Rand branches of the Coloured Organization, which unanimously endorsed the proposal to raise the corps. Similar meetings, under the respective chairmanship of Mr. Keiler, Mr. Samuels, and Mr. I. Joshua, were held by the Pretoria town and country branches and at Kimberley. At Pretoria, Revs. G. Weavind and Mr. Hanford, both missionaries, also spoke offering to associate themselves with the coloured people in any benevolent efforts undertaken to alleviate the distress that might follow the outbreak of the war. Port Elizabeth and other district branches also moved in the same direction. Capetown, the headquarters of the Organization, was the centre of these activities, and a number of coloured women wrote to the A.P.O. secretary offering their services as nurses to accompany the coloured volunteer force to German South–West Africa, so that the coloured people, as the A.P.O. newspaper puts it, "have closed their book with its ugly record against the Botha Government, and offered the Prime Minister their loyal support during the war."

But while these things were in progress, the Union Defence Force, which had mobilized near the German frontier under Colonel Maritz, rebelled against the Crown, and with their arms and ammunition they joined the Germans. This act of rebellion occasioned the greatest alarm among the coloured population near the boundaries of German South–West Africa. And they appealed to the Government for arms to protect their homes and properties. They remembered what happened during the Boer War, when the Dutch inhabitants of those districts joined their kinsmen from across the Vaal, and how that Natives who were armed always remained free from molestation. That their present fear was not groundless the following declaration shows: —

I herewith declare that my brother and I were on a visit to the farm Groen Doorn, Cape Province, on the morning of September 16, 1914.

When we got opposite the police camp, we were surprised to see the camp invaded by Germans. The Germans then beckoned us to come up, and told us that we were prisoners, and that we must go with them to the station of Ukamas. My brother on hearing that turned his horse and galloped back. The Germans called on him to halt at once, but he did not stop. Then they fired at him, and shot him dead.

My brother was left lying where he fell. After he was shot I asked if I could go to him, but the Germans would not allow me. Afterwards I was taken to the German camp, where I found all the coloured people of Groen Doorn that were captured by the Germans. Two old women who were too weak to walk all the way were left half–way without either food or water; one of the two was a cripple, and the other an old woman between sixty and seventy years of age.

I stayed at the German camp at Nakob till the first German patrol went back to Groen Doorn to guard. Then that same evening I ran away from the German camp, and fortunately got safe home to my house at Nudab.

I again declare that this story is an exact reproduction of what I have seen with my own eyes.

     (X his mark)
     Jacobus Bezuidenhout. Witness: T. Kotzee.
Signed at Keimoes this 6th day of October, 1914.

This statement was conveyed to the Union Government by Mr. M. J. Fredericks, secretary of the African Political Organization. With it there was a request by a meeting of coloured people at Calvinia and adjacent districts near the German frontier asking for arms. General Smuts replied, regretting the situation in which the coloured residents of the districts of Calvinia, Kenhardt, Keimoes, and Upington found themselves; and said that he hoped the Union forces would ere long remove the cause of their anxiety. He added that the question of arming coloured citizens had been carefully considered by the Government, but that, for reasons already published, their request for arms could not be complied with.

Finally General Smuts expressed regret at the shooting of the brother of Jacobus Bezuidenhout. "Apparently the deceased had been shot because he attempted to escape, and in the circumstances," added the General, "the Germans were clearly justified in shooting him."

If General Smuts is right in his concluding remarks, then the Germans are quite justified in pillaging Belgium, as the reason they ravaged that country was because the Belgians refused to comply with a plain request to allow German troops to proceed through Belgium to France. But whatever the view of the South African Government might be on these subjects, we would like to point out that it is against a coloured man's grain to obey the orders of a man, no matter who, if he is at war with the coloured man's chief. It would be nothing unusual for a German to order a coloured man about in times of peace, but once war was declared, it became an outrage upon the traditions of the blacks to obey Germans who were now the enemies of their country.

General Smuts will no doubt remember his own operations in 1901, before he became a British subject. How he then invaded Cape Colony, and got a number of recruits from among the Dutch inhabitants of certain Cape districts. How eventually, when he came to the district of Calvinia, his burghers, reinforced by rebels, found a coloured blacksmith there, by the name of Abraham Ezau. How the burghers demanded certain information from this man, and he refused to supply enemies and rebels of the Crown with any information. That the man was severely ill-treated and tortured, but that he would not disclose anything. And how that a gang of Boers dragged this coloured man out of the town and shot him down; that they also looted Abraham Ezau's shop and took away the murdered man's tools, which his widow never recovered, and for which the writer has been informed she never received any compensation. The Cape Government, prior to the Union, erected a tombstone over the grave of this man, who sacrificed his life for it rather than betray his country. And the sight of that memorial stone was no doubt a grim reminder to the inhabitants of Calvinia of what would happen if the rebels invaded Calvinia once more.

> Burra dur hai Tipperary
> Bahoot lumbah koouch wo
> Burra dur hai Tipperary
> Sakki pas pownchenay ko
> Ram ram Piccadilly
> Salaam Leicester Square
> Burra, burra dur hai Tipperary
> Lakin dil hoaye phus-gayah.
>> "Tipperary" in Hindustani.

The Natives and the Cape coloured Afrikanders were not alone in tendering loyal offers of service to the Government. The Indians of Natal and other coloured residents likewise offered their services to the Government, besides subscribing liberally according to their means to the various war funds. The St. Helenians of Capetown passed the following resolutions, which Mr. S. Reagon, the secretary, forwarded to the Government: —

(1) That this meeting of St. Helenians expresses its unswerving and devoted
    loyalty to His Majesty King George and His Governments.

(2) That it expresses its full confidence in the Union Government
in the present crisis through which the Empire and Union are passing,
and congratulates General Botha, and expresses its deep appreciation
of his practical patriotism in having taken command of the Union Forces
in the field.

(3) That the services of the Association and its members be hereby offered
to the Union Government in whatever manner they may be of assistance
to ensure the triumph of the Empire and for the maintenance
of law and order.

Shortly after the outbreak of the present war, Dr. Abdurahman offered the Government the services of the 5,000 coloured warriors recruited through the A.P.O., and General Smuts replied that the offer was under consideration. Meanwhile the A.P.O. recruiting agency had been continuing its work, and no fewer than 13,000 coloured men had sent in their names and addresses and signified their intention to take the field. So Mr. Fredericks, the secretary of the A.P.O., wrote once more to General Smuts, on October 23, offering the services of these men in the name of the Coloured People's Organization. This offer brought forth the following definite reply, which is couched in identical terms to the one sent on the same date to Dr. Rubusana, who wrote offering the services of 5,000 Natives: —

==

Department of Defence,
Pretoria,
November 6, 1914.

Sir, — With reference to your letter of the 23rd ult., I beg to inform you that the Union Government greatly appreciates the offer of service of the Cape coloured people.

I am, however, to refer you to the provisions of Section 7 of the South African Defence Act, 1912, and to state that the Government does not desire to avail itself of the services in a combatant capacity of citizens not of European descent in the present hostilities. Apart from other considerations, the present war is one which has its origin among the white peoples of Europe, and the Government is anxious to avoid the employment of coloured citizens in a warfare against whites.

No doubt the Government of British South Africa was actuated by the loftiest motives in rejecting voluntary offers of service from citizens of non–European descent; but it is clear that such a reply at such a time ought not to please many people in Great Britain who had to offer the cream of British manhood to defend their portion of the Empire, and then to offer in addition more men to lay down their lives for the safety of the Colonies, including South Africa, a land with thousands of able–bodied and experienced warriors who are willing to defend their own country. For the same reason this decision ought not to please our French Allies, who, besides sacrificing men and money on the battlefields of Continental Europe, must provide more men and money to guard their colonial possessions in different parts of the globe. This decision ought not also to cheer any one in Belgium, where fathers and mothers and their children are separated and starving, a nation living practically in exile, or in bondage, its brave monarch sojourning in foreign territory. On the other hand, if there is any one place where this decision of the Government of British South Africa would be hailed with the liveliest satisfaction, it is certainly Berlin, and that particularly after the bitter experiences of German troops in encounters with native African troops, both in Continental Europe and in East and West Africa.

Similarly this decision of the South African Government ought not to please the Boers themselves, inasmuch as, finding the request for volunteers amongst the whites failed to secure sufficient men, the Union Government had perforce to resort to coercion, in that some 300 Boers who refused to enlist for service in the expedition to German South West Africa were fined or imprisoned. This course, which is practically conscription, would have been unnecessary had the Union Government accepted the offered service of the 18,000 and more volunteers whom it curtly rejected.

The coloured people, judging by the letters that many of them have sent to the Press, felt humiliated to find that during the Empire's darkest hour a Government to which they pay taxation is publishing decisions that ought to wound the feelings of the Allies' sympathizers and give satisfaction to the enemy.

It is just possible that the Government refused the offer of the coloured people in deference to the wishes of a section of the white people of the Union; but judging from the African Press, that section, although somewhat noisy, was an infinitesimal one. This section, as is shown from the extract below, also discussed the voyage of the Indian troops to Europe. The `East Rand Express', a paper published in one of the most important suburbs of Johannesburg, said: —

==

COLOURED TROOPS AND THE WAR

The news that Great Britain intends to employ Indian native troops against the Germans has come as a shock to many South Africans. We can but hope the news is incorrect. In our opinion it would be a fatal mistake to use coloured troops against the whites, more especially as plenty of whites are available. From the English standpoint there is probably nothing offensive in the suggestion. Most Home people do not seem to see anything repugnant in black boxers fighting whites, but they have not had to live in the midst of a black population. If the Indians are used against the Germans it means that they will return to India disabused of the respect they should bear for the white race. The Empire must uphold the principle that a coloured man must not raise his hand against a white man if there is to be any law or order in either India, Africa, or any part of the Empire where the white man rules over a large concourse of coloured people. In South Africa it will mean that the Natives will secure pictures of whites being chased by coloured men, and who knows what harm such pictures may do? That France is employing coloured troops is no excuse. Two blacks in any sense do not make a white. The employment of native troops against Germany will be a hard blow on the prestige of the white man.

These emotionalists urge the Imperialists against the use of black warriors for the simple reason that it would give them (the emotionalists) "a shock". So that the agony of British troops and the anxiety of British wives and mothers is not to be lessened, nor the perils of non–combatants greatly minimized, or the war hastened by a decisive concentration of the Empire's forces on the battlefield, because of the "shock" it would give the emotionalists for black to fight against white. The common−sense view would show the advantage in permitting all subjects, including the coloured races of South Africa, to take part in the struggle and thus enable the authorities to place more men on the Continent, instead of sending drafts of Imperial troops to take the places of men at the outposts of the Empire, who are disqualified solely by their colour.

Last New Year the author received a letter from a well−known British mother conveying her well−wishes besides the following moving particulars: —

We are almost beside ourselves with grief over this awful war. My young nephew has been home on a nine days' holiday at Christmas and he has now returned to the front. He has been awarded the D.S.O. for blowing up a bridge and so delaying the Germans in the march upon Paris. My cousin, Mrs. ——, has lost her two only sons — both killed on the same day — December 21. Besides other English friends and relatives fighting on the British side, I have also a young German cousin fighting on the other side. He has been so badly wounded in his throat that the vocal chords have received such an injury as to lead to the loss of his voice, and his career as a barrister is probably at an end. His poor mother is a widow and has only one other son, who is very delicate.

The writer has during the past six months come across instances of the loss of an only son, but all these agonies count as nothing to your colourphobic emotionalists, who must, at any price, be spared their "shock" regardless of the sufferings of others. Now ask these men what they would offer the Empire as a substitute for the coloured troops whose employment against the enemy gives them "the shock", and you will find that they have nothing to offer but their colour prejudice.

What, for instance, could the leader−writer of the `East Rand Express' offer to the Empire in place of the generous help rendered to it by the Maharajah of Mysore, a lad of only eighteen years of age, who besides the services of his men gave the "trifle" of 330,000 Pounds, or in place of the present of the Nizam of Hyderabad, who contributed 396,000 Pounds towards the cost of the Hyderabad contingent; or the Maharajah Scindia of Gwalior, who handed to King George, as a Christmas present for the troops, a "tiny fleet" of forty−one motor−ambulances, four motor−cars for officers, five motor−lorries and repair wagons, and ten motor−cycles; or to come nearer home, and to deal with a more modest gift, the two hundred bullocks which Chief Molala Mankuroane, near Kimberley, gave General Botha to feed the Union troops?

And when these liberal sacrifices are made by black men for the safety of the Empire, INCLUDING BRITISH SOUTH AFRICA, one is constrained to ask: Where are those loud−mouthed pen−men who, possessed of more pretension than foresight, wrote bombastic articles in the Transvaal Press before the war, threatening that "South Africa will cut the painter", and "paddle her own canoe", if men and women in Europe made themselves a nuisance by advocating ideas of justice in favour of the blacks? General Botha confessed last September that the South African Government tried to, but could not, borrow more than 2,000,000 Pounds; that the Imperial Government had come to the rescue and "helped the Union out of its embarrassment with a loan of 7,000,000 Pounds" of British money. When from his seat in the Union House of Assembly the Prime Minister announced this failure, why did not these secessionists come forward and display their "paddling" capacity? What has suddenly become of them?

Is it not about time that the Empire recognized the unprofitableness, and even the ruinous policy, of these gentlemen, and that it ceased paying so much attention to those whose views are distorted by colour prejudice, whose object is to inflict unnecessary harm on the minds, bodies and spirits of loyal subjects of the Crown? One cannot help saying that if their career in this respect is not checked, their evil policy will land the Empire in a tangle of difficulties from which its rescue will require the highest statesmanship, much expenditure of treasure, if not also the shedding of blood.

We have already stated that coloured men ARE serving the Empire at the front, but mainly in capacities that do not involve their recognition. We have recently read of the trial of two coloured men at Willowmore, in the Cape Province. They were said to have expressed the view that if coloured persons are not fit to fight for the Empire "in a war originating entirely among Europeans", they could not be considered fit to drive military wagons in the same war. Recruiting of military drivers was in progress at the time, so they were charged under martial law, and sentenced to nine months, with hard labour, for obstructing the recruiting work. In this case our difficulty is that, not being a lawyer, we are not able to draw the fine distinctions between legal phrases. But to our untutored lay mind it seems that if to give expression to such logic (whereby ten drivers may think twice before enlisting) is a crime under martial law, then it should be over ten times more criminal, under the same law, for a Government to refuse the offer of service, in the same war, of 18,000 warriors and thereby barring the enlistment of a possible 80,000.

One of the best replies to colour sentimentalists which we have ever read on this subject is quoted from the `New York World' by the `Crisis' (Professor Du Bois's paper) of the same city. Says the `New York World': —

The German Ambassador has announced to the United States that he is "unconditionally opposed" to the use of coloured troops. This is a curious prejudice on the part of the diplomatic representative of a Government that is seeking to bring Turkey into the conflict and trying to persuade the Turk to instigate a "holy war" in Egypt and India against all non–Mohammedans.

When Germany went to war with the British Empire she must have expected to fight the British Empire, and not merely a selected part of the population, the colour of whose skin happened to meet the approval of Berlin.

It is natural enough that Great Britain should bring up her Indian troops, who, by the way, are as completely identified with the Aryan race as the Prussians. But no matter what their race may be, they are part of the Empire and part of Great Britain's regular military power.

If Germany were at war with the United States her troops would have to meet our Negro Cavalry, than whom there are no better soldiers in uniform.

German denunciation of the Indian troops is as futile as German denunciation of the Japanese as "yellow–bellies". It is too late to draw the colour line in war. That line was erased more than fifty years ago by Abraham Lincoln in that noble letter to the Springfield Convention: "And there will be some black men who can remember that, with silent tongue and clenched teeth and steady eye and well–poised bayonet, they have helped mankind on to this great consummation."

One South African writer to the Press had humanitarian reasons against the employment on the Continent of coloured troops from India. He said that 70,000 of them will be like a morning meal to the trained soldiers of Germany. This sympathetic view does not appear to be shared by German writers to the `Berliner Tageblatt', who have a high regard for the ferocity of "these Eastern devils". Apparently this is the only German view which is in harmony with the dispatches of Generals French and Joffre. His Majesty the King has since been to the front, where, in the presence of H.R.H. the Prince of Wales, Sir Pertabh Singh and other high Imperial officers, His Majesty personally decorated Havildar Darwan Sing Negi (an Indian) of the 39th Garhwal Rifles, with the Victoria Cross, and we need hardly add that V.C.'s are not awarded for fun.

On the first Saturday in March, 1915, King George went to Aldershot and acted as starter in the big military race in which over 500 soldiers competed. Her Majesty the Queen was also present and graciously distributed the prizes. The race was won by Private Stewart, a black trooper from Jamaica. Even the Coldstream Guards have their coloured private in training for the front; but South Africans inform you that the heavens will fall if coloured troops are sent against the white Germans, who, from the beginning, never scrupled to send black warriors against the British.

In regard to the award of the V.C. to Indians, many writers sent letters to the Press claiming that it was unprecedented for coloured warriors to wear the V.C. Whitaker and similar publications might have told them that a Native African sergeant of the West Indian Regiment wears the V.C. won on the Gambia River as long ago as 1892.

Chapter XXII The South African Boers and the European War

I slept and had a vision; and what was it about? For lo and behold,
   the sky was covered with a dark cloud on which was impressed
   the number 15, and blood issued from this cloud. Thereupon I beheld
   General Jacobus De la Rey returning to his Lichtenburg home
   without a hat on his head, and he was closely followed by a carriage
   full of flowers.
         Niklaas Rensburg (the Boer Prophet).

When the war broke out, there was no question, as far as one section of the whites were concerned, as to the duty of South Africans, but the majority of the unofficial Dutch and German sections were for remaining neutral and taking no part whatever in the struggle, either for or against the Crown. Among the Backvelders there appeared to have been some misunderstanding as to whether the South Africans were subjects or merely friends of the British Government. This bewilderment became more confusing during the interval between the outbreak of the war and the meeting of the Union Parliament. All kinds of ideas were expressed in the Press. The progressive section, mainly English, urged not only that South Africa had no alternative but to join the struggle, but they actually raised volunteer corps, which they proceeded to equip for service in Europe.

The regular volunteer forces of the country went forward at an early period of the campaign, and took the German ports. In connexion with the mobilization of these forces a regrettable catastrophe must be recorded here. The long train in which the Kaffrarian Rifles, mostly English, were going from

King Williamstown, via Capetown, to the front, was derailed near the Hex River, and the gallant Riflemen had eight killed and about a hundred wounded. They are sons of the old English settlers of the Eastern Province, and some are members of European families who are very popular with the Natives of the Cape, so that white and black alike felt deeply the result of the catastrophe. General Lukin, who was in charge of the advance forces, quickly went up the South–Western Coast, and forced the enemy to evacuate his ports and retreat inland towards Windhuk, the capital of the German Colony. General Beyers and the rest of the Defence Forces which were entrusted with the land operations also mobilized. The mobilization of this force took an extraordinarily long time, but it was satisfactorily explained that the marshalling of the citizen forces had to await the sanction of Parliament, which did not meet until September 10, 1914.

A special session of the Union Parliament took place on this day, at which General Botha, the Union Premier, made a great speech.

In the course of his speech General Botha said that the Imperial Government had informed the Government that certain war operations in German South–West Africa were considered to be of strategic importance. The Imperial Government added that if the Union Government could undertake these operations they would be regarded as of great service to the Empire. The Empire to which South Africa belonged was involved in one of the greatest and cruelest wars which had ever befallen humanity. General Botha continued:

The Government, after careful consideration, had decided to comply with the request in the interests of South Africa as well as of the Empire. (Cheers.) There could only be one reply to the Imperial Government's request. There were many in South Africa who did not recognize the tremendous seriousness and great possibilities of this war, and some thought that the storm did not threaten South Africa. This was a most narrow–minded conception. The Empire was at war; consequently South Africa was at war with the common enemy. (Cheers.) Only two paths were open — the path of faithfulness to duty and honour — (cheers) — and the path of disloyalty and dishonour. A characteristic of the South African people was their high sense of honour, and they would maintain their reputation for honourable dealing untarnished. (Cheers.) To forget their loyalty to the Empire in this hour of trial would be scandalous and shameful, and would blacken South Africa in the eyes of the whole world. Of this South Africans were incapable. . . .

With regard to the operations in South–West Africa, General Botha declared that there could be only one response to the Imperial Government's wishes unless they wished to contemplate a situation much more serious than that which now confronted them. The mode of operations could not be discussed in the House; it must be left to the commander of the Union forces.* The Government had summoned Parliament so that the representatives of the people should know exactly what had happened.

— * General Beyers. —

He wished them to understand the seriousness of the position, and to accept the responsibility which they would be called upon to accept. He placed himself with confidence in the hands of the House. General Botha detailed the German entry into Union territory at Nakob. This force was entrenched in kopjes in Union territory at the present time. He also described an affair at Schuitdrift in August. In addition to this, armed German forces were on the Union frontier in large numbers before there was any question of Union mobilization. The Premier said he quoted the foregoing to show the hostile attitude adopted by Germans in the neighbouring territory.

He next referred to the White Paper on the diplomatic proceedings on the eve of war. These documents, he declared, showed that if ever Great Britain entered upon a war with clean hands it was this war. It was abundantly clear that Great Britain did not want war, and did her utmost to maintain peace; but war was forced upon them. Only when it became impossible, without loss of prestige and honour, to remain out of war did the Imperial Government take that supreme step. (Cheers.) By the Imperial Government's decision the whole Empire was involved in the war. (Cheers.) He emphasized that the war was not a war of aggrandisement or for the acquisition of land, but that it was undertaken out of a sense of duty and in discharge of solemn treaty obligations to defend other nations who were being trampled upon, and whose territory was being violated. He wished the House to realize that South Africa's future was being decided on the battlefields of Europe. . . .

He appealed to South Africans to be tolerant with each other at the present time. No one could blame the Dutch South African who did not feel exactly as the British South African felt. It did not follow that Dutch South Africans were disloyal. There was no question of disloyalty. Although there might be many who in the past had been hostile towards the British flag, he could vouch for it that they would ten times rather be under the British flag than under the German flag.

Great confidence had been reposed in the people of South Africa. They had received a constitution under which they could create a great nationality. Great Britain had given them this constitution, and ever since had regarded them as a free people and as a sister State. As an example of how the Imperial Government treated them, General Botha said that last July the Union Government wanted to raise a loan of 4,000,000 Pounds. They had raised only two millions. As things were it would be fatal to go into the money market just now, so the Imperial Government had now come to the assistance of the Union Government and had lent the Union 7,000,000 Pounds. (Loud cheers.) That was the spirit of co–operation and brotherhood which invariably animated the Imperial towards the Union Government. Notwithstanding its own difficulties, the Imperial Government had come forward and helped the Union Government out of its embarrassment. (Cheers.)

In conclusion, the Premier said he felt it was the duty of South Africa to assist in relieving the sufferings and privations inflicted by the war. The Government therefore proposed to offer South African products like mealies and tobacco for the soldiers, and brandy for medical purposes. The farmers had already come forward with offers of products, and the Government would undertake their dispatch. General Botha indicated that the matter would be dealt with more fully later, and closed his speech with an eloquent expression of his belief that South Africa would acquit herself honourably in the eyes of the world.

Opposition Views

Sir Thomas Smartt, Leader of the Opposition, said the message which the Prime Minister by his speech had given to the Home Country would send a thrill of pride through the Empire — a thrill of pride at knowing that in the day of danger South Africa had been true to her trust and had remembered her obligations as well as her privileges of free citizenship. (Cheers.)

Mr. Cresswell, the Labour Leader, urged that an expedition should be sent to fight side by side with the Allies on the Continent.

General Hertzog said that General Botha's motion had come as a great surprise, and moved the adjournment. Other members supported General Hertzog, but the motion for the adjournment was rejected by 85 votes to 12.

After this short session of Parliament, enthusiastic meetings were held throughout the country. Those in the cities were mainly attended by citizens of English descent. Strong resolutions of confidence in the Union Government, and of approval in the proposed expedition to German South–West Africa, were passed at these meetings. At country meetings, however, the enthusiasm was in the opposite direction. There, the resolutions condemned the Government's military policy, and General Botha was roundly accused of not taking the country into his confidence. When the loyalists urged that the Parliamentary representatives of the critics, who, by the way, enjoy manhood suffrage, had authorized the Government policy, the growlers replied that their members did not consult their wishes.

General Botha made it as plain as the Dutch language could put it that the Germans had been in camp near Nakob in their own territory. That they left their Nakob base on the German side of the Border and came over to the Union territory for water, and proceeded to entrench themselves amongst the ridges and kopjes which commanded the water–holes, and that in addition to the duty of the Union as part of the Empire, this military trespass on the part of the German forces further strengthened the case for an expedition into German South–West Africa.

At these Backveld meetings the story about the Germans crossing the border was characterized as a bit of ministerial concoction. Clever geographical students, who mounted the platforms with maps in their hands, were reported to have demonstrated to the satisfaction of their auditors that the new map showing the German position was falsified by the railway surveyors and that Nakob Sued was clearly depicted in the old maps as laying in German territory. The Dutch reporters, however, do not state that the ridges and kopjes referred to by General Botha were also stated to be on the German side of the line according to the old maps. So that the position was like this: at first the Boers would not sanction an expedition against the Germans until the latter invaded Union territory, and when the Government proved by means of police reports that the Germans had actually crossed into Union territory the critics accused the Ministry of telling untruths. This, then, must have been the cause of so much delay in mobilization, and which Ministers had to contend against. It must be added, however, that most of the meetings mentioned took place in Transvaal. At the Cape the discontent was almost insignificant, whilst as much of it as had existed promptly ranged itself on the side of the Government when the "Free" State and Transvaal hoisted the standard of rebellion.

Matters went ahead somewhat after the meeting of Parliament. But a rude awakening awaited the people of the Union, if not the peoples of the Empire, when they got up one September morning and read the following correspondence relating to the resignation of General Beyers, the head of the Union forces: —

==

GENERAL BEYER'S EXTRAORDINARY ATTITUDE

Ex–General Beyers to General Smuts
   Pretoria,
   September 15, 1914.

Honourable Sir, — You are aware that during the month of August last I told you and General Botha by word of mouth that I discovered the sending of commandos to German South–West Africa for the purpose of conquering that territory. I was on the point then of resigning, but hearing that Parliament would be called together I decided to wait, hoping a way out of the difficulty would be found. To my utmost surprise, however, Parliament confirmed the resolution adopted by the Government — namely, to conquer German South–West Africa, without any provocation to the Union from the Germans. The Government must be aware that by far the great majority of the Dutch–speaking people of the Union decidedly disapproved of our crossing the frontier, and that two conferences of commandants recently held at Pretoria bore eloquent testimony to this. I challenge the Government by an appeal to the people, without making use of compulsion, to obtain another result.

It is said that Great Britain has taken part in the war for the sake of right and justice, in order to protect the independence of smaller nations, and to comply with treaties, but the fact that three Ministers of the British Cabinet have resigned shows that even in England there is a strong minority who cannot be convinced of the righteousness of a war with Germany. History teaches us, after all, that whenever it suits her interests, Great Britain is always ready to protect smaller nations, but unhappily history also relates instances in which the sacred rights of independence of smaller nations have been violated and treaties disregarded by that same Empire. In proof of this I have only to indicate how the independence of the South African Republic and Orange Free State was violated, and of what weight the Sand River Convention was. It is said that war is being waged against the barbarity of the Germans. I have forgiven, but not forgotten, all the barbarities perpetrated in this our own country during the South African war. With very few exceptions, all farms, not to mention many towns, were so many Louvains, of which we now hear so much.

At this critical moment it is made known in Parliament that our Government was granted a loan of 7,000,000 Pounds by the British Government. This is very significant. Any one can have his own thoughts about this. In the absence of legitimate grounds for the annexation policy of the Government you endeavour to intimidate the public by declaring that the Government are in possession of information showing that Germany has decided, should the opportunity arise, to annex South Africa. My humble opinion is that this will be hastened if from our side we invade German territory without having been provoked thereto by the Germans, and as to the alleged German annexation scheme, this is nothing more than the result of the usual native suspicion attending such matters. The allegations made in Parliament — namely, that the Germans have already violated our frontier — are ungrounded. See the report of the Information Bureau, corroborated by Colonel Maritz* and his officers, who are on and near the frontier. Apparently the Government longed for some transgression by the Germans of German South–West Africa, and have been disappointed in this, for so far not a single German soldier has crossed our frontier, as you know very well. The report is perfectly correct regarding an involuntary transgression of the frontier some time ago and the tendering of an apology for so doing.

— * Maritz was at this time on active service, nominally as a Colonel
   at the head of a British regiment, but in reality as a General
   in the German Army, using British arms, stores, railways, and telegrams
   in the service of the Kaiser. —

Whatever may happen in South Africa, the war will be decided in Europe in any case, so if Germany triumphs and should decide to attack us, then even Great Britain would be unable to help us. We shall at least have a sacred and clean cause in defending our country to the utmost provided we stay inside our borders. Meanwhile, in case we are attacked, our people will arise as one man in defence for its rights. Besides, I am convinced that a commando of about 8,000 Germans, as at present stationed in German territory, will not be so foolish as to attempt an attack on our country. I have always said, and represented at Booysens recently, that if the Union is attacked Boer and Briton will defend this country side by side, and in such case I will deem it a great honour and privilege to take up my place at the head of our forces in defence of my fatherland. I accepted the post of Commander–General under our Defence Act, the first section of which provides that our forces can only be employed in defence of the Union. My humble opinion is that this section cannot thus be changed by informal resolution of Parliament, such being contrary to Parliamentary procedure. So the Defence Act does not allow us to go and fight the enemy over the frontier, and to light the fire in this way. But should the enemy penetrate into our country it will be our duty to drive him back and pursue him in his own territory.

In his speech General Botha speaks about the help we had from the Belgians and French after the South African War. That assistance is still appreciated by us and by all our people, but we must not forget that the Germans also were not behindhand, and have always been well–disposed towards us. So why should we deliberately make enemies of them? As circumstances are, and seeing no way of taking the offensive, and as I sincerely love my country and people, I must strongly protest against the sending of Union citizen forces over the frontier. Who can foretell when the fire the Government has decided to light shall end? For the reasons enumerated above I feel constrained to resign my post as Commandant–General, as also my commissioned rank. For me this is the only way of faith, duty, and honour towards our people, of which mention was made by General Botha. I have always tried to do my duty to my best convictions, and it sorely grieves me that it must end in this way.

> I remain, etc.,
> (Signed) C. L. Beyers.

==

General Smuts to Ex–General Beyers
   Pretoria,
   September 19, 1914.

Sir, — It was with regret that I received your letter of the 15th inst. tendering your resignation as Commandant–General of the Union Defence Forces and as officer of the Union. The circumstances under which the resignation took place and the terms in which you endeavour to justify your action tend to leave a very painful impression. It is true that it was known to me that you entered objections against war operations in German South-West Africa, but I never received the impression that you would resign. On the contrary, all information in the possession of the Government was communicated to you, all plans were discussed with you, and your advice was followed to a large extent. The principal officers were appointed on your recommendation and with your concurrence, and the plan of operations which is now being followed is largely the one recommended by yourself at a conference of officers. My last instructions to you before I left for Capetown to attend the special session of Parliament were that in my absence you should visit certain regiments on the German border, and it was well understood between us that immediately the war operations were somewhat further advanced and co-operation among the various divisions would be practicable you should yourself undertake the chief command in German South West Africa. The attitude of the Government after this remained unchanged, and was approved by Parliament after full discussion.

One would have expected that that approval would make the matter easier for you, but now I find that you anticipated that Parliament would disapprove the policy of the Government, and that your disappointment in this became the reason for your unexpected action. In order to make your motives clearer the reasons for your resignation were explained in a long political argument which was immediately communicated to the Press and came into the hands of the Government long after publication. I need not tell you that all these circumstances in connexion with your resignation have made a most unpleasant impression on my colleagues and myself.

But this unpleasant impression has even been aggravated by the allegations contained in your letter. Your bitter attack on Great Britain is not only baseless, but is the more unjustifiable coming as it does, in the midst of a great war, from the Commandant-General of one of the British Dominions. Your reference to barbarous acts during the South African War cannot justify the criminal devastation of Belgium, and can only be calculated to sow hatred and division among the people of South Africa. You forget to mention that since the South African War the British people gave South Africa her entire freedom, under a Constitution which makes it possible for us to realize our national ideals along our own lines, and which, for instance, allows you to write with impunity a letter for which you would, without doubt, be liable in the German Empire to the extreme penalty. As regards your other statements, they have been answered and disposed of in Parliament. From these discussions it will be apparent that neither the British Empire nor South Africa was the aggressor in this struggle. War was, in the first instance, declared by Austria-Hungary, and thereafter by Germany, under circumstances in which the British Government employed its utmost powers to maintain the peace of Europe and to safeguard the neutrality of Belgium. So far as we ourselves are concerned, our coast is threatened, our mail-boats are arrested, and our borders are invaded by the enemy. This latter does not occur, as you say, in an involuntary manner and with an apology, which latter, at any rate, was never tendered to our Government. Under these circumstances it is absurd to speak about aggressive action on the part of the Union, seeing that together with the British Empire we have been drawn, against our wish and will and entirely in self-defence, into this war. As regards your insinuation concerning the loan of seven million pounds which the British Government was kind enough to grant us, and for which the public of the Union, as evidenced recently in Parliament, are most grateful it is of such a despicable nature that there is no necessity to make any comment thereon. It only shows to what extent your mind has been obscured by political bias. You speak about duty and honour. My conviction is that the people of South Africa will in these dark days, when the Government, as well as the people of South

Africa, are put to the supreme test, have a clearer conception of duty and honour than is to be deduced from your letter and action. For the Dutch–speaking section in particular I cannot conceive anything more fatal and humiliating than a policy of lip–loyalty in fair weather and of a policy of neutrality and pro–German sentiment in days of storm and stress. It may be that our peculiar internal circumstances and our backward condition after the great war will place a limit on what we can do, but nevertheless I am convinced the people will support the Government in carrying out the mandate of Parliament, and in this manner, which is the only legitimate one, fulfil their duty to South Africa and to the Empire and maintain their dearly won honour unblemished for the future. Your resignation is hereby accepted.

(Signed) J. C. Smuts.

When the war broke out, the Natives of South Africa, who, in many instances, are much better in touch with the backvelders than the Dutch editors who reside in towns, fully expected a general revolt among the unofficial section of the Boers. But when Holland declared her neutrality the Natives began to breathe more freely, as that declaration led them to believe that the Boers would not now rise. When General Beyers's resignation was published, however, the Natives again felt that the outbreak was only a matter of days. In the country, especially the Orange "Free" State, our people are helplessly mixed up with the Boers, and it can readily be understood that they felt somewhat insecure, notwithstanding the Government's assurances. One native farmer sent the following letter to the author in England: —

I am glad to find that your newspaper, the `Tsala ea Batho', is as up to date in your absence as when you are at home. It was the first to publish General Botha's statement to the Natives (about the war), and again the first to comment on the treacherous resignation of General Beyers. The resignation was handed to the Government on the 15th, and the `Tsala' commented on it on September 19, before the daily papers. I think that the daily papers were still trying to reconcile their previous articles about the loyalty of ALL WHITE SOUTH AFRICANS with the resignation. The fact that General De la Rey was shot while travelling in the same car with General Beyers on the same day that Beyers resigned is cited as a further proof of the unswerving loyalty of all the Boers. One cannot understand how these white folks reason; but the attitude of the Imperial Government and of the Union Government is incomprehensible. Fancy telling the loyal Rhodesians to come and fight under a man like that! General Botha ought himself to go to the front, if a civil war is to be averted, leaving General Smuts to watch the next Dutch move and nip it in the bud.

One of the tragedies of the first few weeks of the war was the death of Senator General De la Rey of Lichtenburg, who was accidentally shot by a "Rand" policeman on the night of September 15, while travelling with General Beyers in a motor–car.

His funeral took place on September 20, at Lichtenburg, and was attended by a large number of Boers, including the Prime Minister, General Smuts, General De Wet, and other Dutch generals. Mourners and their friends came to Lichtenburg by the ordinary train and by the special train which conveyed the body from the Rand. They came in all manner of vehicles from the surrounding farms, and, for the first time, the Dutch Reformed Church at Lichtenburg opened its doors to the blacks, who came to pay their last respects to, and view the body of, a popular Boer, known among the Bechuana as Koos La Rey. A commando of 400 Burghers came from Wolmaranstad on horseback. English merchants from Johannesburg were also present, including Senator Tucker, representing the Unionist party. The body was draped WITH TWO FLAGS — the flag of the old Transvaal Republic and of the old "Free" State Republic. Besides the officiating clergy, three Dutch statesmen also spoke at the funeral service, viz., Generals Botha, Beyers, and De Wet.

The loyalists returned from the funeral service to their path of duty, while the sullen section of the Dutch remained at Lichtenburg to fan the embers of rebellion — though it must be added that the operations at Lichtenburg were more or less in camera.

At 8 o'clock on Monday morning, September 21, the day after General De la Rey's funeral, General Kemp, standing on General Beyer's motor–car, presided over a gathering of from 800 to 1,000 Boers. The Rev. Mr. Broeckhuizen opened the meeting with a short prayer. A verbatim report of this prayer appeared in the Dutch papers as follows: "Lord, we thank Thee that Thou rulest our nation through these dark days and stormy circumstances. We have buried our hero and have gathered to speak in his spirit. We thank Thee for such a man as General Beyers, beside whom his friend was shot. We thank Thee also for General De Wet and General Kemp, and that Thou hast given us such men to lead us. We stand for our people. Help us, O Lord, towards the salvation of our people and the salvation of our fatherland. Amen."

The three personalities mentioned in this prayer became active participants in the rebellion, and so did the reverend gentleman who prayed. In fact the latter sent a letter to his congregation three months later from the Johannesburg prison, resigning his pastorate at Pretoria.

In opening the meeting the chairman disclaimed all ideas about a revolution. They had come to consider calmly a decision by the Union Parliament to invade German South West Africa; but while he was speaking, some one produced a flag of the old Free State Republic, and General Kemp rebuked the person for this puerile action. Whether the rebuke was due to the fact that the Boers had not yet then made up their minds to rebel, or because Maritz's plans with the Germans on the south–western frontier had not yet matured, we do not know. Anyway, General Beyers, in supporting the chairman, added that his cause was a clean one and there was no necessity for nonsensical flag–waving. They were there, he said, to pass a calm resolution and forward it to the Government.

One Mr. van der Hoff inquired why General Beyers resigned. The chairman replied that the reasons were clearly set forth in the letter of resignation. At the request of the gathering the Rev. Mr. Broeckhuizen read the letter aloud, the reading throughout being punctuated with cheers. It does not appear, however, that General Smuts's reply was also read, presumably because there was no call for it.

General Liebenberg wanted to know what the situation was that morning; then he proceeded to say: "The enemy is already inside our borders. Some one had disturbed a beehive and the result is what might have been expected. We have three generals before us" — (apparently in addition to the speaker) — "yesterday we buried the dearest of them all. I want a reply from Generals De Wet and Beyers. We are British subjects, and it is not improbable that the Government might instruct their officers to call us out to–morrow."

General De Wet, the man of the hour, then stepped on to the motor-car to speak, prefacing his speech with the remark that he could not help remembering his brother buried the previous day. Then, in beginning his speech, he said: "Burghers and Brethren, — If there be any one present who is not a brother, let him walk away. Since nobody is leaving I conclude that we are brothers all. If there be any stepbrothers here, they are all welcome, but a traitor always reminds me of Judas." Proceeding, he said that "the Germans had been made enemies by the Government. The fire was already burning, so let us adopt a calm resolution, expressing the will of the people. Not that I wish to praise my people, but we are not going to soil our hands, no not even to show our loyalty. Let us be cool, remembering that we have many sympathizers in South Africa and elsewhere. If any one wished to gnash his teeth and hath no teeth his best course is to consult the dentist for a set. Better an hour too late than a minute too early. We do not all reside near a telephone or a telegraph office and cannot be conversant with what goes on at the frontier. Even when Generals Beyers and Kemp are asleep, keep a watch and remain cool. I believe there are numerous Christians among us. When it is time the whole of the people will rise up like to-day."

Some one wished to know if it was possible to recall the forces already at the border. That, said the chairman, would be decided later.

The Rev. Mr. de Klerk said General Beyers's letter translated the real feeling of the people. Even though Generals Beyers, Kemp, and De Wet had resigned, they still remained Generals. They honoured other officers who had the pluck to resign with General Beyers (whose names the Government had not published but had suppressed), including Lieutenant Kol Bezuidenhout. One Field Cornet to the speaker's knowledge had resigned, but his name had not been announced." The reverend gentleman then betrayed his flagrant ignorance of South African history when he said: "Our people were never known to have robbed any one of land. All (?) their land had been acquired by means of purchase or barter. The history of South Africa was a spotless one." After stating that the Afrikander must express his disdain with respect to the Jameson raid and the unrighteous annexation of the Republics, he concluded: "Blood is flowing in Belgium, but is it in the interest of South Africa to draw the sword on that account? It may be in the interests of the Empire; but the hem of my coat is nearer to my body than the coat itself. The sending of troops to Damaraland is nothing but an attack upon a people that had done us no harm. I believe it to be our duty to sit still."

Rev. Mr. Van der Merwe, who said he spoke on behalf of the young people, said all their officers should resign like General Beyers and others. He hoped that any officers present would resign before noon that day.

General De Wet pointed out that the appointment of any Jack, Tom, and Harry might follow such wholesale resignations, for although he lived in the "Free" State he held a share in the affairs of that (Transvaal) Province.

General Beyers: "I consider my own resignation a sufficient protest. The other representatives of our people should remain at their posts." (Cries of "No, no, no.")

Rev. Mr. Broeckhuizen implored the people to stand by their Commander-in-Chief, General Beyers, as he himself was going to do, no matter how barking lap-dogs raved. Despite any letters that some fellows might write to the papers to the contrary, the world must know that the people stood behind General Beyers. Although he was still going to suffer — (as he truly did) — they should support him till everything was in order.

As a parting shot General Liebenberg said: When peace was declared in 1902 he had such implicit faith in the late General De la Rey that he (General Liebenberg) remained quietly on his farm and was always obedient to him. He expected these troubles since 1912. And now it had become impossible to keep quiet much longer. According to the latest accounts the Germans were 150 miles across the boundary. (A voice: "We will beat them back.")

The speaker: "The same thing was said when they were in Belgium, but they are now marching on Paris."

A revised resolution was then put: it declared the reported action of the Government to be "in conflict with —

"1. The wishes of the overwhelming majority of the population of the Union." (An extravagant assertion considering that there are six million people in the Union and that the meeting only represented a section of the half a million Boers.)

A reply was demanded from the Government before September 30, so as to get it in time for consideration at a subsequent people's gathering.

When this was carried, General De Wet said in parting: "If there be still a few lap–dogs here, friends, don't take any notice of them. They have now no teeth. We are now more united than when the difference between the Government and `the People' first began." (Obviously General De Wet was here alluding to the rupture between the Government and General Hertzog in 1912, when, to the disgust of himself and his followers, the latter was forced to leave the Ministry. One reason why the Natives' Land Act was passed was in order to "dish the Whigs" and placate the Hertzogites.)

* * * * *

On September 24, General De Wet held another meeting at Kopjes, Orange "Free" State. The Resident Magistrate of Parys attended the meeting and read a telegram from the Government announcing that no Burghers would be forced to proceed to the front; that only volunteers would be asked to serve. This wire, however, did not satisfy the Burghers. They contended that the expedition to German South–West Africa was a policy of setting the prairie on fire, and it did not matter who the originator of the fire was, for when it was raging the Burghers would be called upon to quench it.

After the meeting had passed votes of condolences to Mrs. De la Rey, General De Wet said he was opposed to a war against a nation that had done him no harm. Whether or not the Government used volunteers, "who," he asked, "would be responsible for the harm that is likely to follow a provocation of the Germans? This expedition is to coax them into our country. You may go if you like," added General De Wet emphatically, "but I won't."

Now, the Boers in certain respects are not unlike the Natives; thus when a grey-haired Native, or a Boer, addresses a crowd of his compatriots and says to them, "You may do such and such a thing if you like, but I will not," it is understood by them to be a roundabout way of saying, "Take my advice and don't." And so when such a declaration is made by a man as influential amongst his people as General De Wet, it is not surprising that the crowd shouted in response, "We won't go. Let the authorities adjust the result of their own bungling. Ninety-two men in Parliament voted for the expedition without consulting their constituents, and we are not satisfied." Thereupon some one shouted, "Where is Mr. Van der Merwe?" Others said, "Call him; perhaps he is in the crowd." So the stentorian voice of a Boer equipped with a powerful pair of lungs called out, "Van der Merwe! Van der Merwe!! Van der Merwe!!!" and then announced "He is not here."

Mr. Van der Merwe is the Parliamentary representative of the district where the meeting was held.

In conclusion, General De Wet said: "Here is the Magistrate and there is the prison. If I have said anything that I cannot substantiate I will willingly surrender myself into their hands."

The motion against the expedition was then put, 512 Boers voting for it and only two against it.

* * * * *

Es ist sehr weit nach Tipperary,
  Es ist sehr weit zu gehn;
Es ist sehr weit nach Tipperary,
  Meinen liebsten Schatz zu sehn.
    Leb' wohl, Piccadilly,
    Adieu, Leicester Square,
Es ist sehr sehr weit nach Tipperary
  Doch dahin sehnt mich sehr.
          "Tipperary" in German.

On September 29, General Botha addressed his constituents at a Transvaal station called Bank, on the Kimberley–Johannesburg line. A thousand Burghers met the Premier as he left his special travelling saloon for the place of the meeting and gave him a rousing reception. Before General Botha spoke, he permitted his opponents (to the evident displeasure of the majority of the audience) to unbosom their alleged grievance. Appreciative addresses were read expressing confidence in the Government and approval of the expedition to German South West Africa. Addresses opposing the expedition were also read; they included one that was said to be a petition from Boer women, strongly objecting to the expedition. The reading of these addresses took up much time and must have tried the patience of the Premier's admirers who were anxious to hear the speech of the day. They called on the readers to "Shut up!" but the Prime Minister urged them to give both sides a chance.

After these lengthy preliminaries, the Prime Minister amid cheers delivered a speech justifying the projected invasion of German South West Africa, in obedience to the desire of the Imperial Government. He reminded the Boers that the expedition had been voted for by a Parliament elected by them. He added that he personally would always lead his people along the white man's path of honour and Christianity, and that he would never choose the coward's way of disloyalty and treason. The whole of the speech might be summed up in a few lines taken out of General Smuts's reply to General Beyers: "I cannot conceive anything more fatal and humiliating than a policy of lip–loyalty in fair weather and a policy of neutrality and pro–German sentiment in days of storm and stress."

The Prime Minister further asked what reliance could be placed on Germany who ravaged Belgium. He pointed out that when the late President Kruger arrived in Europe — a fugitive from his country — the French and the Belgians welcomed him, while the Kaiser would not even see the old man.

General Botha made some remarks at this meeting which displeased the coloured loyalists. Without wishing to defend the Premier, the remark, in our opinion, was justifiable. It was more of a recruiting speech than a declaration of policy, and naturally he had to appeal to the sentiments of his hearers. Nothing goes down so easily with the northern Boers as colour prejudice, and in the circumstances General Botha was justified in denouncing the neutrality party, who advocated a policy of "sitting with folded arms until German South West Africa fell into their lap like a ripe apple. The Imperial Government," he went on to say, "could send a force of 50,000 coolies* to capture the German Colony, and tell them that, after the war, they could make a coolie settlement there. Would this have been in the interest of the country? (Cries of No, no.) But instead, the Imperial Government had asked the Union to do the work, and I am proud to have been asked."

— * A contemptuous term for British Indians. —

Nor could Englishmen, having regard to the circumstances, very well take umbrage at another remark of General Botha's in the same speech. It was, we believe, a clever appeal to the feelings of Backvelders when he said: "Can you rely on the Kaiser's promises? In the South African war, WHEN I GAVE THE ENGLISH A SOUND THRASHING at Colenso, what did the Kaiser do? He sent a telegram to Lord Roberts advising him how to stab me in the back, by marching across the `Free' State."

The danger that would follow a German victory in South Africa was so lucidly put by the Premier that many waverers were at once imbued with the patriotic spirit. Carping criticism, it is true, continued, but many wobbling defence officers resolved to follow General Botha to the uttermost. The opposition, on the other hand, told the Boers that the official element among them who supported the Government did so, not through patriotic motives, but for the sake of their jobs. The most credulous section among the Boers seemed to believe that the Germans would never invade British South Africa. This section at first was baffled by the contention of the neutrality party that the Government was maligning the Germans; but they were soon disillusioned.

On September 26, Colonel Grant took possession of some water–holes on the line of advance. This step was essential to the success of the proposed expedition. The enemy retired, but only to mount their artillery on some ridges overlooking the camp of the advancing British forces. From those positions the enemy shelled our troops till their ammunition was exhausted. The British casualties amounted to sixteen killed, forty–three wounded, eight missing, and thirty–five captured. These figures would be insignificant on the battlefields of Europe, but to lose so many men in only one attack in South Africa was almost appalling. This reverse having brought home to the waverers the danger of procrastination, a fresh spirit set in among the passive loyalists. But the opposition was busy.

* * * * *

On the same day that General Botha carried the day at Banks, Commandant Vermaas addressed over 100 Burghers at a Transvaal farm called Korannafontein. There were present such notable Dutchmen as Mr. Sarel Du Plessis and Mr. Cornelius Grobbelaar. They were so provocative that Commandant Vermaas asked the meeting with some warmth: "Who do you believe about the occurrences at the German frontier, the Government who receive all the police reports, or General Beyers? All I can say is that you will weep when General Botha gets shot, for I know what he did for this country. And if you disbelieve the Government, what will be the use of telling you that the Germans were the aggressors?"

Sensible speeches were delivered by Mr. D. Louw and others. This speaker deeply regretted the resignation of General Beyers, and said: "He had charge of all the Defence secrets and it cost us much money to let him travel about this country and abroad; and at a critical moment, when we are face to face with trouble he tenders his resignation." The meeting, however, insisted that the Union Government were the delinquents. The Germans, they said, had crossed the border accidentally, for which little relapse they had tendered a suitable apology. Some speakers said that the Ministry's ambitious annexation policy was actuated by a desire for posthumous fame regardless of the blood of Afrikanders, which was more precious than the deserts of German South West Africa. The issue would be decided on the battlefields of Europe, so why the premature invasion, and why the forgery of the railway map in respect to the position of Nakob where the German forces are? "Supposing the Germans win in Europe," asked one of the speakers, "what would be our position after the raid? We prefer to follow General Beyers."

While Commandant Vermaas, the Government emissary, was still speaking, some one shouted: "Three cheers for General Hertzog!" These were vociferously accorded.

At this stage one of the young bloods came out with a brand–new defence of Germany's desertion of the Boer cause during the South African war. Germany, he said, had a ten years' treaty with England and could not go to war against the British, who were there again too smart for us. When Queen Wilhelmina was in Germany the Kaiser said to her: "Tell the Transvaal not to declare war against England just yet ——."

Commandt. Vermaas: "And you call it friendship. Why promise us help when they had a treaty with England?"

After some dialogues, in which the Bible was quoted on both sides, for and against the expedition, a resolution was adopted, by eighty–nine votes to twenty–three, against the invasion of German South–West Africa.

An aged Dutch gentleman remarked that the late Republican Government made a mistake in first sending an ultimatum to the English, and in attacking German South–West Africa the Union

Government was repeating the same mistake.

* * * * *

Oom: Who set this ancient quarrel new abroach?
    Speak, nephew, were you by when it began?

Neef: Here were the servants of your adversary
     And yours, close fighting ere I did approach:
    I drew to part them; in the instant came
    The fiery Tielman, who swung about his head
     And breathed defiance in my ears . . .
    While we were interchanging, thrusts and blows
    Came more and more, and fought on part and part
    Till the Judge came, who parted either part.

According to `Het Westen' of Potchefstroom, over a thousand Burghers packed the Lyric Hall on Friday, October 2, 1914, to hear General De Wet speak against the invasion of German South West Africa. Apparently this was an attempt by the Backvelders to challenge the enthusiasm of the townspeople in the various centres who had been passing loyal resolutions in favour of the expedition and of confidence in the Union Government. Not all the supporters of the Backvelders' cause could gain admission to the hall, which was packed almost to suffocation before the hour of meeting. Several prominent "Free" Staters were on the platform with General De Wet. A rabble of roughs had been brought from the outskirts of the town by opponents of the cause, so the paper says, to interrupt the proceedings and to create disturbance. They waited outside and were "responsible for a state of things which is wholly unknown in the history of South Africa."

Admission was by ticket, and everything was in order up to eight o'clock, when Commandant Erasmus took the chair. General De Wet was carried shoulder high into the meeting amid thunderous applause. The local police force had had timely notification that the meeting was arranged for, but the paper complains that only seven of them were to be seen about the building, and these seven apparently were seized with a blindness of a mysterious kind, for they saw nothing of the disturbance that occurred during the meeting, except when it was thought necessary to arrest an Afrikander.

The chairman having opened the meeting, Professor Duvenage welcomed the visitors from near and far, including the ladies in the gallery. The professor, alluding to the English meeting which took place in the town hall a few evenings before, observed it was not interrupted by any one. This meeting, he said further, had been called to discuss the South African aspect of the war. It had nothing to say about the operations in Europe; all that they wished to protest against was the invasion of German South West Africa. Hereupon dead cats, brickbats, stale eggs and other things were hurled into the hall through the windows, occasioning an indescribable commotion. Angry Afrikanders jumped out of the windows and seized some of the offenders and administered such a sound thrashing to one of them that he only escaped serious bodily harm by lying down.

The dead cats, bricks, etc., were picked up and thrown out of the window; but, as the interrupted meeting was about to proceed, some one disconnected the electric cable and plunged the building in darkness. The confusion became confounding. Matches were struck in several parts of the hall, and it was with considerable difficulty Generals De Wet and Kemp were heard suggesting an adjournment of the meeting to the Dutch Reformed Church Square. The crowd passed out of the Lyric Hall and marched in the direction of the Dutch Reformed Church Square, closely followed by the hooting band of interrupters.

A handy carriage procured from somewhere served as a platform and, under the light of Africa's silvery moon, 1,500 Burghers crowded round the improvised platform while the turbulent interrupters screeched some English national airs. General Kemp, who warned the crowd against the danger of being struck by missiles, asked them to squat on the ground, so as to be better able to hear General De Wet. The guerrilla General, having stepped upon the carriage–platform, said to the audience: "Yes, sit down flat so that those disturbance–makers may hurl their missiles at me on top of the carriage. (Laughter.) Some of those who came to interrupt peaceful Afrikanders may yet become children of death before the evening is far gone. (Boos from the opponents.)

"That may be European or Downing Street civilization, but it is unknown in South Africa; but let us hope that folks with such upbringing will yet live to change their manners. Those who are standing against the wire fence are asked to come nearer and not be afraid, if not, then let them go to their homes, wherever those may be, and leave us alone. I promise you that within a year this disrespectful crowd will have been taught to respect the rights of Afrikanders. That I promise you, and the Afrikander will do it with his own hands. (Loud cheers.) If I am wrong in this, there is your jail, your police and the Magistrate, and let them punish me if I am guilty." (Voices: "They dare not touch you!").

Proceeding the General went on to refer to an article of the `Volkstem', the Ministerial organ of Pretoria. The `Volkstem', he said "had for long been crowing King, King, but the sun will rise when the cock will cease to crow. (Laughter.) The Government has now issued regulations under which we may not speak, but, friends, bear in mind, and the `Volkstem' must know, that we have not yet a Popedom, and we are not yet in Russia, for you will search in vain for the truth in a newspaper." — (We would very much like to know the opinion hereanent of the Backveld newspaper organ in which we read of this meeting. — Author.) — "Friends, a newspaper can do a lot of harm, and much of the condition in which our country finds itself may be attributed to the `Volkstem' — that Government adulator (`de regeering se vetsmeer' document).

"Whereas our people could freely express their views, the Government now wants to prevent an expression of their bitter feelings over the land–robbery now engaged in at German South West." (At this stage, an egg thrown from the back of the crowd fell uncomfortably near the speaker and aroused some angry remarks in the crowd, but the speaker continuing said: "Never mind, friends, I have another coat. The Government talk of calling out volunteers only; but many children were surreptitiously torn away from their mothers, and many were taken against the will of the parents. I am ready to bow under the law, but not when it is broken by the Government. Our law authorizes us to defend our borders, not to wage war outside." After some more quarrels, interruptions, blows and fights in several parts of the crowd, the police arrested a Burgher. But some men who surrounded the police rescued the prisoner and, it was said, assaulted a policeman.)

Proceeding with his speech after the interruption, General De Wet said: "We can never thank the English sufficiently for their gift of self–government under a free constitution approved by His Majesty the King; but it was not implied thereby that we should go and commit a theft." More interruptions, during which it became impossible for the speaker to continue. In the turmoil cheers were given for General De Wet, who, resuming at length, remarked: "You fellows, along the wire fence, the Lord have mercy on you when I turn my back. You will be responsible if blood flows in this meeting to–night. As I have had a better up–bringing I am keeping the people back from tackling you. I have not been brought up in what they call Waaihoek at Bloemfontein. It was not General Botha's place to get this country to snatch chestnuts out of the fire for England. They bluff us with the statement that the coolies* might be asked to come and take German South West Africa for themselves. Well, let it be so. They will be in their proper surroundings there amongst the Hottentots. And if it amounts to that, Kafirs armed with assegais can be sent against them, for as it now happens the Kafir has got to work for the coolie in Natal."

— * Contemptuous South African term for British Indians. —

After more disturbances, the General said he was not so certain that the police were doing their duty, and he would have to report them to the Government. These men were paid out of his pocket and the pockets of other Burghers, but the people got no protection from them. And when in self–defence an Afrikander remonstrates with the hooligans, he is arrested. He thought there was a Magistrate present, and can they not get protection?

Assistant Magistrate Cronin then ascended the carriage and said: "I expect you all to give the Burghers a fair opportunity to speak."

Concluding General De Wet said: "It was not a question of Hertzog v. Botha. The burning point was German South West Africa. The reason why the people were unarmed was because the Government did not trust them. Things being so, they should not be surprised that the people had no confidence in the authorities. Many had guns but no cartridges; how then could the country be expected to defend itself?"

Mr. Paul Schutte moved the resolution which was put to the meeting, protesting against the expedition to German South West Africa. "At this time," says the Dutch paper that reported these proceedings, "the throats of the interrupters, not being made of steel, had become so hoarse and weak that their interruption was ineffective, except, perhaps, when they dealt out blows."

Mr. Paul Schutte said, in moving the resolution, that the hand of God was pressing heavily on the land: poverty, misery, and the drought finishing the people. Was it not dangerous for the Government to embark on such an undertaking without the backing of the unanimous will of the people?

Mr. Serfontein (presumably one of the two members of Parliament of that name) said he was going to speak the whole truth, and nothing but the truth.

He said he would give documentary proof that a map has been forged; he did not know by whom. It is said that Nakob is in Union territory, yet according to the original Government map, that place was on German territory. "There is the map," he said, apparently flaunting it, "satisfy yourselves."

Proceeding he said: "General Tobias Smuts had declared that he knew the Government decision was against the wishes of his constituents, yet he wanted to support the Government in favour of the war. General Beyers, who knew all the circumstances, denies that Nakob is in Union territory. In these circumstances, how can we, as Christians, ask God to guide us in the undertaking?"

Professor Postma and the Rev. Mr. De Klerk, the two next speakers, quoted the Bible to show that to proceed against German South West Africa was forbidden by Providence. Mr. Furstenburg, who followed, called on the Burghers to maintain the high character of their people. After a few words of thanks from General Kemp to the audience for their attendance, the 1,000 Burghers, amid interruptions, signified their objection to the expedition by standing on one side. This act closed a most exciting meeting.

One of the opponents, the paper says, smacked a Dutch lady on her mouth and caused it to bleed. She coolly turned round and gave him such a heavy blow with her fist that he collapsed, saying in the purest English accent as she did so: "It takes but one woman to fight a Britisher." Another of the interrupters had to be taken to the hospital.

Commandant Els and Mr. Rocco de Villiers, the "Free" State lawyer, on their way to the meeting, had a mishap with their motor-car, fifteen miles distant, so that they reached Potchefstroom on foot, after the meeting.

"Three cheers for our brown people," shouted one of the disturbers. "You have forgotten the coolies," retorted a Dutch lady.

After the meeting, the opposition formed itself into a procession and marched through the town. They also delivered short speeches confirming what had been done at a previous meeting of townspeople, which supported the expedition. They booed General De Wet and his followers, and dispersed after giving cheers for Generals Botha and Smuts and singing the National Anthem.

One item on the programme of the meeting was an address which should have been presented to General Beyers, the ex-Commander-in-Chief, but as for some reason or other he was not present, the address was sent to him instead. It congratulated him on his resignation, a step which the signatories were sure he would never regret, as it was in accord with the peace-loving and the most pious part of his people, who resent the "capture" of German South West Africa. Further, they thanked him for coming to address them and hoped he would deliver a speech that would shut the mouths of mischief-makers who accused him of being a German agent.

A similar drama was enacted at Johannesburg during the following week, when General De Wet carried his campaign of protest into the stronghold of the sections in favour of the Government expedition. His meeting at the Lewis Cinema was only in progress a few minutes when bricks, etc., came through the fanlights, and the lights went out. The meeting was adjourned to Church Square, where supporters of the Government gained the upper hand and overpowered the "neutral" party so completely that General De Wet, Mr. Serfontein and Rev. Mr. Postma could not be heard. Cheers

189

were continually given for the King, for Generals Botha and Smuts, and the speeches were drowned by the patriotic airs sung by the throng, and the meeting proved a complete fiasco.

Chapter XXIII The Boer Rebellion

Arm, arm, Burghers; we never had more cause!
The Goths have gathered head; and with a power
of high–resolved men, bent to the spoil,
They hither march amain, under conduct
Of Manie, son to old Gerit Maritz,
Who threats in course of his revenge, to do
As much as ever Black Bambata did.

The following telegram was published by the South African Government: —

==

October 13, 1914.

Ever since the resignation of General C. F. Beyers as Commandant–General of the Citizen Force, there have been indications that something was wrong with the forces in the north–west of the Cape Province, which were placed under the command of Lieutenant–Colonel S. G. Maritz.

The Government at once arranged to send Colonel Conraad Brits to take over the command from Lieutenant–Colonel Maritz.

On the 8th instant Colonel Brits sent a message to Maritz to come in and report to him. To this message Maritz replied in a most insolent manner that he was not going to report to anybody. All he wanted was his discharge, and Colonel Brits must come himself and take over his command.

Colonel Brits then sent Major Ben Bouwer to take over the command.

An Ultimatum

On arrival at Maritz's camp, Major Bouwer was taken prisoner with his companions, but personally was subsequently released and sent back with an ultimatum from Maritz to the Union Government to the effect that:

Unless the Government guaranteed to him before ten o'clock on Sunday morning, October 11, that they should allow Generals Hertzog, De Wet, Beyers, Kemp, and Muller to meet him where he was, in order that he might receive instructions from them, he would forthwith make an attack on General Brits's forces and proceed further to invade the Union.

Major Ben Bouwer reported that Maritz was in possession of some guns belonging to the Germans, and that he held the rank of General commanding the German troops.

190

He had a force of Germans under him in addition to his own rebel commando.

He had arrested all those of his officers and men who were unwilling to join the Germans, and had then sent them forward as prisoners to German South West Africa.

Major Bouwer saw an agreement between Maritz and the Governor of German South West Africa guaranteeing the independence of the Union as a republic, ceding Walfish Bay and certain other portions of the Union to the Germans, and undertaking that the Germans would only invade the Union on the invitation of Maritz.

Major Bouwer was shown numerous telegrams and helio messages dating back to the beginning of September. Maritz boasted that he had ample guns, rifles, ammunition, and money from the Germans, and that he would overrun the whole of South Africa.

In view of this state of affairs the Government is taking the most vigorous steps to stamp out the rebellion and inflict condign punishment on all rebels and traitors. A proclamation declaring martial law throughout the Union will appear in a Gazette Extraordinary to-day.*

— * "U. G. No. 10–'15", pp. 22–24. —

This treachery was more fully described by a Cape Attorney — a subaltern in the Citizen Force under Maritz — in the following letter to the `Transvaal Leader':

"We arrived at Kakamas," he writes, "after a long and wearisome trek through Bushmanland, a company of about eighty, consisting mostly of raw farmer youths.

"We remained in camp for about six weeks, and, in the first week of October, orders came from Maritz for 200 troops, comprising the Calvinia, Clanwilliam, and Kenhardt men, to strike camp and trek toward the German border.

"Two days later the remaining men in camp, consisting of the Kakamas members of the Defence Force, some Kakamas Volunteers, and our own troop, altogether about 300 men, likewise trekked in that direction. After two days' riding, we came to a farm called Blokzijnputs, where we met the first 200 men.

"The village of Keimoes was crowded with German troops; our men and officers were walking and talking among them on the friendliest possible terms, and the German and the old Transvaal Republican flags were flying side by side.

"In a very short time we were made fully aware of the position. The act of treachery which led up to it was being freely discussed by everybody, and then I realized that `we' — I say `we', for I never for one second doubted that most of our men would refuse to turn rebels — had been caught like rats in a trap.

"But a further shock awaited me. About half an hour after our arrival we were summoned to fall in before Maritz, who then addressed the crowd.

"He first spoke about the Government wishing to force him over the border with a lot of untrained and unarmed youngsters, and went on to say that he refused to sacrifice their lives.

"After a bitter attack on the characters of Generals Smuts and Botha, he denounced the British Empire as a whole, and wound up by declaring himself an out and out rebel.

"He stated that he was going to fight against the Union and Imperial Governments for the independence of South Africa, and called upon all who were unwilling to follow him, or `had the English feeling in them', to stand on one side.

"Ten Loyal out of Six Hundred"

"This speech was followed by a short speech in German by the representative of the Governor–General of German South–West Africa.

"Then followed a scene which can never be forgotten by those who witnessed it. All our men started to shout, cheer, and throw up their hats — all except ten of us, who stood there looking, I suppose, more dead than alive. Just imagine, out of 600 men actually trekking towards the border to invade German territory only ten refused to turn rebels.

"However, after recovering somewhat, we approached our captain (Beukes) and told him we were not going to join Maritz, and asked him to see that we were not sent to Windhuk. This Maritz had given us to understand was the only alternative to joining him."

The writer proceeds to state that after being kept prisoners for some time they were set free forty miles from a Union troop frontier post. — `Central News'.*

— * See also Appendix to the "Report of the Select Committee on Rebellion",
S.C. 1–'15. —

In the "Free" State

General De Wet organized large commandos and took possession of the town of Heilbron, held up a train and captured Government stores and ammunition, some prominent Burghers being among his active supporters; so much so that, a week later, when President Steyn was endeavouring to get him to Bloemfontein, in order to persuade him to discuss terms of peace with General Botha, he had no fewer than 3,000 men under him.

General De Wet publicly unfurled the rebel banner in October, when he entered the town of Reitz at the head of an armed commando. Some of his men assaulted the postmaster, who was in the act of telegraphing the news to the capital, and destroyed his instruments. The guerrilla General addressed an open–air meeting, which he ordered the Magistrate to attend. When that official "refused to attend a rebel meeting" General De Wet sent six men to compel him, and to use violence if necessary.

Having thus forcibly secured the attendance of the Magistrate, he proceeded to unbosom himself as follows: "Ladies, gentlemen, and burghers, I have asked you to come together here to explain to you my position."

Then turning to the Magistrate, he said: "Magistrate, I want you to get a shorthand writer to take down every word that I am going to say, because whatever I may do in future I can never commit a greater act of rebellion than I have already committed. I am going through to Maritz, where we will receive arms and ammunition, and from there we are going to Pretoria to pull down the British flag and proclaim a free South African republic. All those who side with me must follow me, and those who side with the Government must go to it. I signed the Vereeniging Treaty and swore to be faithful to the British flag, but we have been so downtrodden by the miserable and pestilential English that we can endure it no longer. His Majesty King Edward VII promised to protect us, but he has failed to do so, and allowed a Magistrate to be placed over us who is an absolute tyrant, and has made it impossible for us to tolerate it any longer. I was charged before him for beating a native boy. I only did it with a small shepherd's whip, and for that I was fined 5s.* (Here the Magistrate interrupted him and asked him whether he did not plead guilty. He admitted that he had pleaded guilty, and ordered the Magistrate to keep quiet, and he would allow him to say as much as he liked when he had finished speaking, and if he would not hold his tongue he would make him hold it.)

— * General Smuts, after this, christened the rising as
  "the Five Shilling Rebellion". —

"But," continued General De Wet, "after the Magistrate had delivered judgment, instead of reprimanding the boy and ordering him in future to be obedient and do his duty, he looked at the Native as if he would like to give him a kiss. The Magistrate is a brother-in-law of a man for whom I have the greatest respect and who is very dear to me (President Steyn), and for that reason I will give him another chance, otherwise I would have taken him prisoner and handed him over to the Germans. The Magistrate's father was one of the staunchest pillars of the church, and if he were alive to-day he would be heart and soul with me in this movement, and condemn the dastardly act of robbery which the Government are going to commit.

"The ungodly policy of Botha has gone on long enough; the South African Dutch are going to stand as one man to crush this unholy scandal. Some of my friends have advised me to wait a little longer until England has received a bigger knock, but it is beneath me and my people to kick a dead dog. England has got her hands full enough. I hate the lies which are continually being spread to the effect that thousands of Australians, Canadians and Indians can be sent to fight us. Where will England get them from? She has enough to fight her own battles.

"I am going through the town to take the following six articles, viz., horses, saddles, bridles, halters, arms and ammunition, and if anybody should refuse to hand to my men these articles, if they should be found in their possession, I will give him a thrashing with a sjambok. I now order the storekeepers to go and open their shops and I will select men to go round and take whatever I require apart from the above articles, and they will give receipts for what they take; and if they do not open their shops willingly I will open them in another way. My advice to you English is to remain quiet in your houses and not interfere with my men, and if you don't, beware when I come back! I have got my eight sons and sons—in—law here with me, and the only people left on my farm are my wife and daughter. Anybody can go and see if they like, and I request the Magistrate to give them any help they may require, if he will do so."

Mr. Wessel Wessels, a famous "Free" State politician, having taken possession of Harrismith in the name of General De Wet, was alleged to have had the audacity to send letters to Chief Ntsane Mopedi, of the Harrismith district, and to the Paramount Chief of Basutoland, informing them that, with the assistance of the Germans, the Boers were going to drive away the English and re—proclaim a Dutch Republic in South Africa; and requesting those chiefs to remain neutral while the annihilation of the English was in progress. Only in case the English should arm the Indians, were they to mobilize their warriors (the Basutos) on the side of the Boer—German combination.

> Dit is ver weg na Tippererie,
> Dit is ver om te gaan;
> Dit is ver weg na Tippererie,
> Om my hart se punt te zien.
> Goen dag, Pikadillie
> Vaarwel, Lester—squeer;
> Dit is ver, ver weg na Tippererie
> Maar my hart le net daar.
> "Tipperary" in Cape Dutch.

The Dutch, like other people, also had a prophet. Many stories were told since the outbreak of the war by the seer, Van Rensburg, and among other visions credited to him he was said to have dreamt of the impending "removal of the British yoke from the necks of Afrikanders", and the forthcoming expulsion from South Africa of the English people and their flag, with the aid of Germany.

Whatever might be said about what the prophet Van Rensburg had foretold in other respects, the prophecies attributed to him in regard to the European War resemble other war prophecies (credited to French, Russian, and German women), in that the wish, it seems, is often father to the thought.

The lower middle—class Boers attach great weight to the guesses of native bonethrowers. It is strange sometimes when a Malay charmer is prosecuted for imposing on the public to find Dutch witnesses giving evidence of the healing powers possessed by the accused and emphasizing the absurdity of prosecuting a man who benefited them and their relatives more than many a certificated medical man.

Moreover, the forecasts credited to Van Rensburg seemed to have found ample corroboration in the cabled newspaper accounts of the rapid advance of the armies of General Von Kluck through Belgium towards Paris, and in the minds of such gullible patriots as the South African Boers this telegraphic war news acted like manure on a fertile field.

==

The Seer Van Rensburg*

— * "U.G. No. 10—'15". —

The seer was Nicolas van Rensburg, of Lichtenburg, a simple and illiterate farmer. He was a prophet not without honour in his own country. On many occasions he had given proof positive of the possession of extraordinary powers of prevision, so men said and believed. It would be out of place here to give examples of the many telepathic forecasts (or happy guesses) with which he was credited. It is certain that he had a great hold on the imagination of thousands of his people. During the Anglo–Boer War some commandos, when Van Rensburg was in their lager, neglected all precautions. If "Oom Niklaas" declared that the English were not in the neighbourhood, it was a waste of energy to post sentries and keep a look out.

His reputation had, strangely enough, not diminished since the war. This was perhaps due to several causes. He had never attempted to exploit his "gift" and impressed most of those who came in contact with him with his apparent sincerity. If he duped others, it seemed he also duped himself. Moreover, and this was perhaps the secret of his continued success, his "visions" were invariably symbolic and mysterious; they possessed an adaptability of character that was truly Delphic. Indeed, his hearers were compelled to put their own interpretation upon his visions. The seer seldom pretended to understand or explain them himself.

General De la Rey took a great interest in the seer, who had belonged to his commandos during the Anglo–Boer War. Van Rensburg again had the greatest admiration for General De la Rey, and had frequently hinted to his circle that great things were in store for the General. One of his visions had been well known to General De la Rey and his friends for some years. The seer had beheld the number 15 on a dark cloud, from which blood issued, and then General De la Rey returning home without his hat. Immediately afterwards came a carriage covered with flowers.* What these things portended, Van Rensburg could not say. He believed that they signified some high honour for the General. . . .

— * General De la Rey was accidentally shot on the night of September 15.
  The last house he stayed in was No. 15, and the funeral train
  that brought his body to Lichtenburg had a carriage full of floral tributes. —

When the war at last broke out, the effect in Lichtenburg was instantaneous. The prophecies of Van Rensburg were eagerly recalled, and it was remembered that he had foretold a day on which the independence of the Transvaal would be restored. One officer actually called up his men to be in readiness on Sunday, August 9, as that would be the day on which the prophecy would be fulfilled. After this, too, certain individuals could be seen daily cleaning their rifles and cartridges in order to be ready for THE DAY. Several men in this district claimed to be in regular communication with German South–West Africa before August, 1914. Within a week of the declaration of war between England and Germany the district was further profoundly stirred by the news (now become generally known) that a great meeting of local burghers was to be held at Treurfontein on August 15, and that certain local officers were commandeering their burghers to come to this meeting armed and fully equipped for active service. . . .

The meeting was to be addressed by General De la Rey, and it was generally believed that the assembled burghers would march on Potchefstroom immediately after the meeting.

The prophecies of Van Rensburg had a great deal to do with the excitement which had been produced locally. The strange vision of the number 15, which had long been common knowledge, was now discussed with intense interest. The 15, it was said, signified August 15, the day of the meeting. That would be THE DAY, which had been so long expected — the day of liberation. Van Rensburg was now the oracle. His prophecies with regard to the great war had been signally fulfilled. Germany was at grips with England, and her triumph was looked upon as inevitable.

The day had arrived to strike a blow for their lost independence. Van Rensburg assured his following that the Union Government was "finished". Not a shot would be fired. The revolution would be complete and bloodless.

Between the 10th and the 15th the plotters in Lichtenburg were actively preparing for the day. There is evidence that German secret agents were working in concert with them. The 15th would mark the beginning of a new era. When doubters asked how they could be so certain that the 15 signified a day of the month — and of the month of August in particular — they were scornfully if illogically told that "in God's time a month sooner or later made no difference."

The Government had been informed by its local supporters of these alarming preparations. It was quite clear that an attempt was to be made on the 15th to start a rebellion. Everything would depend on the meeting which was to be addressed by General De la Rey. General De la Rey's position in the Western Transvaal was unique. He possessed an unrivalled influence and was looked up to as the uncrowned King of the West. His attitude at the meeting would sway the mass of his adherents and decide the question of peace or war.

General Botha summoned General De la Rey to Pretoria some days before the meeting, and was able to persuade him to use his best endeavours to calm the excited feelings which had been aroused and to use his influence to see that no untoward incidents should occur.

On Saturday, the 15th, the great meeting was held. About 800 burghers were present. General De la Rey addressed them and explained the situation in Europe. He exhorted his audience to remain cool and calm and to await events. After the address "a strange and unusual silence" was observed. A resolution was passed unanimously expressing complete confidence in the Government to act in the best interests of South Africa in the present world–crisis. The address seemed to have had a very good effect. The burghers appeared to have taken their leader's advice to heart, as they dispersed quietly to their homes.

All danger of a rebellious movement had apparently been averted, but only for a time.

The Potchefstroom `Herald' tells a story of what it describes as "the inner history of a damnable plot", and of how near Potchefstroom* was to falling into the hands of the rebels through the treachery of Beyers and his accomplices on the night of September 15, which was the date on which the late General De la Rey was killed.

— * The old capital of Transvaal where General De Wet and General Kemp
held the dramatic meeting on October 2, 1914. —

196

It is unquestionable (says the `Herald') that Beyers, who was forced to admit that he was on his way to Potchefstroom when the accident happened, was to have started an attempt to overthrow the Government with the aid of the men, over 2,000 in number, who had just finished their period of three weeks' training in the Active Citizen Camp at Potchefstroom. Both he and Kemp had resigned their positions, and, knowing the treacherous mission upon which he was setting out that night as the emissary of the German enemy, little wonder was it that at Langlaagte Beyers cowered with fear, and lost his nerve entirely, because he thought his own arrest was at hand.

Continuing the account, the paper says: On the morning parade on Tuesday morning the rebel Colonels Bezuidenhout and Kock had each addressed their men in an attempt to imbue them with a spirit of revolt against their own Government. All the Dutch–speaking Afrikanders were advised not to volunteer for German South–West; that was the job of the Englishman. The officers plainly said that they had no intention of doing their duty: they had other fish to fry. And they permitted the few volunteers who stood out in spite of them to be jeered at by the "neutrals". The disgrace of that early morning parade scene must for ever be upon the traitors concerned. It was certain that dastardly influences were at work, but thanks to the sterling loyalty of certain men from among the Dutch population, the plans of the conspirators were more or less known, and arrangements were made to checkmate them. All honour to these true patriots who took a big risk for the safety of the country.

That evening a meeting of Britishers took place in Potchefstroom to discuss the situation (says the `Herald'), and it was agreed that its seriousness was such as to necessitate direct communication with General Smuts, which was duly carried out. For one thing, practically all Britishers were unarmed. How critical was the position, or how near Potchefstroom was to complete disaster, was not then fully realized. On that night, too, there was another and more sinister meeting in the town. It was at a certain house in Berg Street, where a number of residents, male and female, who can be named, expected the arrival of the chief conspirator. Then, too, at the Defence Force headquarters Kemp had stored a quantity of ammunition that was altogether out of proportion to the requirements of his district, and during the week there had been frequent communications with the Lichtenburg "prophet". Beyers had arranged to reach the Defence Force at 3 a.m., where motor–cars waited.

Later he was to have marched upon the town with all the armed men he could bring under his influence, knowing full well, by previous arrangement, that he could rely on the aid of rebels within Potchefstroom itself. So intense was the feeling of danger in camp that night that loyal officers slept with loaded revolvers at hand and all the spare ammunition under the beds. The Union Jack was to be supplanted and the new Republic was to be declared with the Vierkleur flying — or would it have been the German flag? That was the morning of September 16, and as showing the concerted character of the traitorous plans, it should be noted that the proclamation signed by the Governor–General of German South–West Africa, the "scrap of paper" used as a sop for the Boers, was dated for the self–same day.

Plot Providentially Thwarted

But the motor–car tragedy in the dark at Langlaagte was the second blow to this criminal plot (continues the paper), and when Beyers, trembling and unnerved, spoke through the telephone at midnight on September 15, telling of the fatal shot, and that his journey had been cut short, those who had waited in the camp and in the town knew that, for the time being at any rate, the little game was up. Kemp, of course, at once tried to withdraw his resignation, but luckily General Smuts gave the snub direct. Already the names of local men to be terrorized, and even shot, were in the mouths of the irreconcilables — skulking cowards for the most part — of whom more must yet be written in the interests of public morality.

That night Potchefstroom might easily have fallen into the hands of the rebel crew, sharing the fate of the Free State towns or worse, and loyalists, both English and Dutch, must thank an ever-watchful Providence for being saved from a position of ignominy and humiliation.

If all this be true,* and the Government had been informed of it, one cannot understand why General Beyers, with his fingers steeped in treason, was let loose upon the community to poison the loyalty of the Dutch along the country-side and to complicate the task of the Government. It seems that he should have been detained that evening, and thereby, having been turned from the path of suicide, other lives would also have been saved. When one considers the amount of harm that he was able to do subsequently, it is staggering to think what the task of the loyalists would have been had his plans been reinforced by the success of this night plot. It would have given a link of tremendous power to the rebel movement throughout the country if they had captured the stores, munitions, and a ready army that awaited General Beyers's arrival at Potchefstroom. The fact that some Burghers were found organizing rebel commandos in the "Free" State and Transvaal even after the capture of General De Wet and the drowning of General Beyers ought to show the prevailing Backveld spirit up to the early months of 1915.

— * The `Herald's' story has since been confirmed by the Government Blue Book
on the Rebellion. —

When the rebels were tried in Pretoria and elsewhere in January and February, Burghers crowded the law courts and rose to their feet, as if in token of their fellow-feeling with the prisoners, each time a rebel was placed in the dock. At Pretoria, this vaunting demonstration seems only to have been ended by the announcement of the Magistrate that if they did it again he would have to clear the court. It is not stated, however, whether the prisoners duly acknowledged the sympathy thus shown with a bow from the dock. One member of Parliament (not a rebel) is said to have swaggered into the Bloemfontein court and, after shaking hands with the prisoners, conversed with them in an audible tone.

Nothing better illustrates the unsatisfactory nature of the South African military appointments than the Press report that the English artillerymen who served under Maritz were in constant danger of their lives, and that, realizing this fact, they were compelled sometimes to keep their machine guns trained on their comrades. The poor men must have had an awful time, literally "sleeping with one eye wide open".

When Colonel Maritz at length threw off the mask and openly proclaimed his treachery, he put these artillerymen under arrest and handed them over to the Germans as prisoners of war.

Of course, if the Government of the Union was as well administered as was the Cape Government before it, such things would have been impossible, because only tried men with military experience would have been appointed to the command of the Union Forces — men whose loyalty was beyond reproach — that is to say, if high official appointments went by merit and not by favour. A professional lawyer like General Beyers would have been the last person to get a position which should have been given to a trained soldier, of whom there are many in the country. But as his appointment took place at a time when some English officials were politely removed from high positions to make room for influential Dutchmen, and in certain cases useless posts, such as "Inspector of white labour", and inspector of goodness–knows–what (all of them carrying high emoluments), were created for political favourites, General Beyers's appointment caused no surprise, as the "pitchfork" had already become part of our Government machinery. But how such a man as Manie Maritz became a Colonel in the Colonial Defence Force is one of those things which, as Lord Dundreary would say, "no fellah can understand".

The man is not only said to have rebelled during the South African war, but he is also said to have escaped to German South Africa to evade the consequence, and that he only returned to British South Africa when the Boers got their constitution. And when British officers like Colonel Mackenzie and Colonel Lukin apparently acquiesce in an appointment that places them on a level with a man like that, the voteless black taxpayer who has no control over these appointments cannot be blamed for feeling perplexed at the turn events are taking.

Here is an expression of this perplexity: The old chief Tshabadira asked the Government Secretary in 1913, at Thaba Nchu, "How many kings have we? Is there an English King and a Dutch King, each trying to rule in his own way? And since we cannot very well follow both, which one are we to obey?" Dutch and English colonists have ruled the Cape for forty years and no such questions were ever asked.

If General De Wet were to be tried by a court of native chiefs, who followed "the wheels of administration" during the past five years, they would in all probability decide that the British Government, to which he pledged his allegiance, and the semi–Republican Government against which he rebelled are two entirely different bodies. They would possibly reason that he pledged his allegiance to a Greater Britain — or to localize it, to a Greater Cape Colony, not to a Greater Transvaal.

The Cape Colony is often reproached because native taxpayers within its boundaries have votes and help their white neighbours to elect members of Parliament. But strange to say, when a revolutionary mob seized the South African railways in 1914, it was the railway men of the much–abused Cape who, in spite of the native vote, dragged the Government out of a serious situation. Similarly when these high officers of the Defence Force in Transvaal and Orange "Free" State rebelled and joined the Germans with their commandos, the Dutchmen of the Cape (presumably because "they vote side by side with the Kafirs") denounced the treachery in unmistakable terms. The South African party at the Cape beat up its followers to the support of the Government, and the voice of the Cape section of the Dutch Reformed Church rang from pulpit and platform in denunciation of disloyalty and treason. But in the Northern Provinces, where white men are pampered and guarded by the Government against the so–called humiliation of allowing native taxpayers to vote, there the rebellion, having been regarded with seeming approval, gained a marvellous impetus.

And the strangest of all these things is how men with bank balances like the Dutchmen of Transvaal and the Orange "Free" State could fail to appreciate the debt they owe to the British Navy, by which the commercial routes from South Africa to the outer world are kept open to them, when practically the whole world is ablaze.

The banner of revolt having been unfurled, the "Free" State towns of Reitz, Heilbron, and Harrismith being in the hands of "Free" State rebels, martial law was proclaimed, and General Botha, as forecasted in the native letter quoted in a previous chapter, assumed command of the Union Forces and squelched the upheaval. Altogether the rebellion cost South Africa some of the finest of its young men. Dutch, English, coloured and native families suffered the loss of their sons in the flower of their youth, including among many others, prominent South Africans, such as Mr. W. Pickering, the general secretary of the Kimberley mines, and Mr. Justice Hopley of Rhodesia, who each lost a son.

One loss which the Natives, judging by articles in their newspapers, will not easily forget is that of Captain William Allan King, the late Sub-Commissioner of Pretoria. He was shot by a rebel, on November 23, near Hamaanskraal, whilst helping a wounded trooper. In his lifetime his duties brought him in touch with employers of labour in the Pretoria Labour District and with Natives from all over South Africa. A non-believer in the South African policy of least resistance, he was without doubt the ablest native administrator in the Transvaal Civil Service, and as such the vacancy caused by his death will be very hard to fill. He was an expert on Native matters, and no commission ever sat without his being summoned to give evidence before it.

The Natives called him "Khoshi-ke-Nna", which means "I am the Chief". A firm but just Englishman, with a striking military gait, he would have been an ideal leader of the native contingents had the offer of native help been accepted by the Union Government.

The casualty list on both sides exceeded one thousand. Over ten thousand rebels were imprisoned, of whom 293 leaders will be tried, the rest being detained up till the end of the trouble.

After various encounters with the Union forces under General Botha, General De Wet suffered a series of heavy defeats. Many of his followers surrendered, and his son was killed on the battlefield. He tried to escape to German South West Africa, but was overtaken and captured in Bechuanaland, with fifty followers, including his secretary, Mr. Oost, formerly editor of a Pretoria weekly paper.

Considering his initial bounce and bluster, General De Wet's surrender was a particularly tame affair. Said the captive to the captor: "I seem to know you — are you not Jordaan?" "Yes, General," replied the captor. "I saw you at Vereeniging where we made peace." "Very well," rejoined the captive, "I must congratulate you on your achievement. It was very smart. Anyway, I am glad that I am taken by you and not by an Englishman."*

— * Gen. De Wet was tried and sentenced by the Special court
  to six years' imprisonment and a fine of 2,000 Pounds. —

General Kemp succeeded in eluding his pursuers by means of forced marches across the Kalahari desert, and effected a junction with Maritz in German South West Africa; but after only a few weeks' taste of German rule he returned to the Union and surrendered with his commando and all arms, evidently satisfied with British rule. Some of his men were wearing German uniforms. The prophet Rensburg, carrying a big umbrella, also surrendered with him.

General Beyers was the first to succumb. Cornered by the loyal forces, he was driven up against the Vaal River in flood. With his pursuers on the one side and the raging torrent on the other, he was drowned in an ill-starred attempt to escape across that treacherous river. Parties were sent out to drag the river and search for the body, and a reward of 50 Pounds was offered to the finder. Mrs. Beyers left Pretoria in a special train with a coffin on board, to join the search party. She was accompanied by a few relatives and friends, including one doctor of medicine and one minister of religion. They travelled along the Johannesburg–Kimberley line as far as Maquasi, near the river, where they received tidings of the recovery of General Beyers's body. It was found by a Dutch farmer, who promptly claimed the 50 Pound reward.

A telegram to Pretoria brought back a reply from General Smuts stating that it was inadvisable to convey the body to the capital at the time, so he was buried by the parson on the veld to the accompaniment of lightning flashes which blind the eye, and salutes of loud peals of African thunder, which shake the earth in a manner that is known only to persons who have spent a summer in the interior of South Africa.

It is said that the late General insured his life so heavily before the outbreak that representatives of the several insurance companies concerned had to meet after his death and consider the matter of their liability.

The remainder of the story of the "Five Shilling Rebellion" is soon told. After the proclamation of martial law the Premier assumed the supreme command of the Union forces and called out all the citizens — the whites to arms and the blacks as drivers and manual labourers at the front. Some Boers who could not give a satisfactory excuse disobeyed the call, and were sentenced to terms of imprisonment with hard labour under the Defence Act. Thus backed by the overwhelming support of the various peoples of the Union of all creeds and colours, the Prime Minister made a clean sweep of the rising, and in less than two months the Rt. Hon. Louis Botha was once again master of the situation from the shores of the Indian Ocean in the east to the Atlantic coast in the west. And when the rebel leaders were cogitating over the situation in durance vile, the Prime Minister was sending a message from German South West Africa, on February 26, asking Parliament to deal leniently with the rebels.

Keise qusa Tipereri,
Kgam'se gaqu ha;
Keise qusa Tipereri
Artie ti gxawo si mu.
Hamnci gqo Pikadili.
Hamnci Gqo Lester Skuer
Keise qusa, qusa Tipereri
Mar, ti xawo nxeba ha.
             "Tipperary" in Qoranna.*

201

— * This language is also spoken by the Namaquas and some of the tribes in German South West Africa. —

Chapter XXIV Piet Grobler

Lecture delivered by Mr. Sol T. Plaatje before the "Marsh Street Men's Own" Literary Society in the Lecture Room of their Institute, Hoe Street, Walthamstow, on February 26, 1915.

> Keep me in chains? I defy you.
> That is a pow'r I deny you!
> I will sing! I will rise!
> Up! To the lurid skies —
> With the smoke of my soul,
> With my last breath,
> Tar–feathered, I shall cry:
> Ethiopia shall not die!
> And hand in hand with Death,
> Pass on.
>
> I shall not curse you. But singing —
> My singing fatefully ringing
> Till startled and dumb
> You falter, the sum
> Of your crime shall reveal —
> This do I prophesy . . .
> O Heart wrung dry,
> Awake!
> Startle the world with thy cry:
> Ethiopia shall not die!
>   Otto L. Bohanan.*

—

* In the Kalahari language, BOHANAN means: `Be combined'.

—

The gentleman whose name forms the title of my lecture is a lawyer, a grand–nephew of the late President Kruger and, till lately, a member of the Union Parliament. He represented the Dutch constituency of Rustenburg, a district whose Burghers were responsible for a kind of administrative native land arrangement in the Transvaal Republic. This arrangement, the result of a petition from Rustenburg, made it compulsory for native landowners in the Republic to register their farms in the names of white people. In accordance with it, Natives who bought land had to register it in the name of the Minister of Native Affairs. But as such Ministers did not always command the trust of the Natives they resorted to the expedient of registering their farms in the names of some European friends, missionaries or otherwise. Some European gentlemen thus became the registered owners of land belonging to Natives, giving the Natives receipts for the money and documents explaining the nature of the transaction. Other Europeans, including missionaries, were not so scrupulous. They gave the Natives no receipt, so that after their death the properties of these Natives passed into the estates of the deceased. The following case is an example.

The native peasants on a Transvaal farm found themselves in such a dilemma after the death of General Joubert, late Superintendent of Natives of the Transvaal Republic. The black "owners" had no document showing that they were the real owners of the farm and that General Joubert's name was only registered to meet the requirements of the Volksraad. In such circumstances they received notice from his executors to leave the General's farm. They appealed to the law–courts and adduced verbal evidence in support of their purchase and ownership of the farm; the sale had been a public one. Besides, according to their ideas, it needed no documentary evidence, since they were legally in possession. The Court, after listening to the evidence concerning the sums paid by individual Natives of the tribe, of the total sum paid for the farm, and of the legal reason why the title bore a white man's name, held that however unfortunate was the position of those Natives if their story was true, it could only give judgment in terms of the title deeds. Thus Natives who were originally dispossessed of their land by conquest, and who swore to having purchased in hard cash land in their own country from the conquerors, were now for the second time, so they stated, dispossessed and turned off that land all owing to the complicated registration under this "Besluit" from Rustenburg.

After the British occupation in 1900, the Courts held that the "Besluit" and its practices did not have the force of law, and Natives took advantage of the ruling to transfer their properties to their own names; but in 1913, Mr. Piet Grobler, M.L.A., moved and succeeded in getting the Natives' Land Act carried in the Union Parliament, which has placed the Natives of the whole country in a more terrible plight than were the Natives of the Transvaal Republic before the war.

Since he took his seat in the Union Parliament, Mr. Piet Grobler, like Mr. Keyter of Ficksburg, has given the Natives no rest. He first made his power felt in 1911, when General Smuts introduced a Bill to consolidate the marriage laws of the four Provinces. Mr. Grobler then moved a fatal colour clause which had the effect of killing the Bill, for the Ministry, on finding that the Bill could only be carried with the assistance of the Unionists, preferred to drop it rather than divide the Boer majority; and hence, thanks to Mr. Grobler, the chaotic confusion still obtains in the South African marriage laws.

This gentleman, in 1913, led the attack in Parliament on Sir Richard Solomon, the Union's representative in London, for not keeping his mouth shut when he is among British foreigners, and for daring to suggest British emigration to South Africa. As stated above, Mr. Grobler demanded, among other things, that the Government should introduce "during this session" (1913) a law to stop the purchase and lease of land by Natives, and the Natives' Land Act of 1913 was the result of the demand — a measure whose destructive severity forced the Natives to sue for Imperial protection against the South African Parliament.

When the present European War broke out, Mr. Grobler was among the Parliamentary clique of representatives whose Christian principles forbade them to vote for an armed expedition against their friendly neighbours, the Germans. They said that, in Deuteronomy 19:14, God specifically warned the Boers against moving the landmarks of their neighbours. But strange to say, the religious scruples of these pious objectors never revolted against removing the landmarks of their native neighbours and of appropriating, not only their land and their labour, but even the persons of these neighbours. The Natives, according to Mr. Luedorf, a German evangelist among the Bechuana, witnessed the Boer trekkers maltreating conquered Natives and taking their children as slaves. Children who were unable to walk to their serfdom being gathered in a heap and burnt alive. This, says Mr. Luedorf, caused the Natives to exclaim: "Mzilikasi, the Matabele King, was cruel to his enemies, but kind to those he conquered; whilst the Boers are cruel to their enemies and ill–treat and enslave their friends."*

— * "The Boer States" (Keane), pp. 137–138. —

Now, Mzilikasi had no Bible, but the Boer has the Bible and professes to honour it. But his Bible, being of a flexible sort, it did not prevent a certain clique of Boers from taking up arms against the Government of which Mr. Lloyd George (a gentleman who staked his reputation and risked his life in his fearless protests against the annexation of the Boer Republics) was a prominent member; and against the Liberal Government, which, as compensation for the mere change of flags, made them a nice little present in the shape of the two old English Colonies of South Africa and the undisturbed permission to rule all that is therein. Mr. Piet Grobler, the author of most of our miseries, reached the climax of his career when, after voting against the Union expedition to German South West Africa, he not only persuaded British subjects not to volunteer for service in the expedition, but himself joined a force, as alleged by the South African papers to hand by the latest mail, to shoot down the King's loyal subjects. He was taken prisoner by General Botha's forces at the head of a rebel commando, presumably whilst on the way to join the Kaiser's forces in the German Colony. He is thus one of the members of the Union Parliament who forfeited their seats by breaking the Parliamentary oath and participating in the recent rebellion.

Mr. Solicitor Grobler's ideas about the sacredness of an oath are curious and original. Every member of the Union Parliament, before taking his seat, has to subscribe to the following oath of allegiance "before the Governor–General, or some person authorized by him", usually a Judge of the Supreme Court:

I, M. . . . M. . . . do swear that I will be faithful and bear true allegiance to His Majesty King George V, his heirs and successors according to law. So help me God.

Mr. Grobler, it is said, was caught red–handed in the treasonable act of leading a force of fifty armed rebels against the Government, and for his breach of the oath he was taken prisoner. Last week, whilst his trial was still pending, he applied for bail, and in support of his application, he pleaded that he was anxious TO ATTEND TO HIS PARLIAMENTARY DUTIES. Here is a bit of Boer candour for you!

The honourable and learned member is further stated to have pleaded that his district provided the largest proportion of rebels and he was anxious to be in Capetown when Parliament opens this afternoon,* in order to be able to represent their case when the Legislature discusses the rebellion. That is South African logic in a nutshell. The Judge, however, took a rational view of things and dismissed the application.

— * The S. A. Parliament opened on the afternoon of the same day as the Lecture. —

There may be motives other than those stated by the incarcerated member of Parliament actuating his desire to get to Capetown.

Every member of Parliament who absents himself without leave forfeits 2 Pounds a day out of his Parliamentary emoluments, so that Mr. Grobler's continued confinement in prison would entail a serious financial deficit. This was not the only instance in which anxiety of this kind was betrayed by recipients of Government bounties in South Africa. There are a large number of well–to–do Boers who draw annually hundreds of pounds from the Union Treasury, salaries which a paternal Government taxes the poorly paid labourers of South Africa to provide. This is particularly the case in the Transvaal. There, princely salaries are paid for filling such superfluous posts as that of "Inspector of White Labour", "Field Cornet", and kindred offices. The Field Cornet of each sub–district of the Transvaal is a very important gentleman, as is evinced by the intense labour attached to his office. The duties of this "hard–worked" functionary consist of the checking of the Parliamentary voters list of his ward, once every two years, and of acting as chief canvasser and election agent for the Ministerial candidate, who, however, is usually returned unopposed; and for these onerous duties he is rewarded by an ungrateful Government with the "beggarly" salary of 260 Pounds a year.

Besides these, there are sundry little sinecures, equally remunerative, to which well–to–do Dutch farmers, who are the more generally preferred, aspire; and each fills his role with acceptable dignity and a serious sense of responsibility. Consequently, there is more gnashing of teeth on the farm over the loss of one of these appointments than over the failure of a whole year's crop.

Several of these nominal "members" of the Union Civil Service were said to have taken up arms and joined the rebellion. According to the South African papers, the wife of one of them applied to the defence office for the salary of her husband. When it was pointed out to her that her husband was at that time engaged in fighting against the forces of the Defence Department, she coolly told the official that that had nothing to do with his private affairs, i.e., the income from the Government. In regard to the faithfulness of the class of officials just mentioned, I cannot refrain from drawing the attention of my audience to the fact that, as the electoral supporters of the Cabinet, they guided the policy of the Union Government during the past five years, and they are the type of legislators in whose tender care the Imperial Government would fain entrust the liberties of the voteless Natives without even the safeguard of a right of appeal.

Personally I am not revengeful, and would wish Mr. Grobler every success in his defence; the Transvaal native taxpayer, on the other hand, earns an average wage of 20 Pounds per annum: out of this he pays taxation on the same scale as the white labourer who earns 25 Pounds a month; in addition, he pays a native tax of 3 Pounds 4s. per year, presumably as a tax on the colour of his skin, for no white man pays that. This extra tax, apparently, is in order that Transvaal Field Cornets and members of Parliament should more easily draw their pay. In return for all these payments, and as a result of Mr. Grobler's legislative efforts, the Transvaal native taxpayer got the Natives' Land Act of 1913; and I am afraid that HE will not be very sorry to know that some one else enjoys the 400 Pounds per annum hitherto received by Mr. Grobler, together with his free first–class travelling ticket over the South African railways.

British pioneer officials, in Africa and elsewhere, have for generations been left in charge of mixed communities of white Colonials and black Natives and other immigrants. In spite of occasional human lapses, they have ruled these communities successfully throughout the past century, and maintained the high administrative reputation of the English in Africa, Asia and other parts of the globe. The dominant race in South Africa, on the other hand, may be fit to govern themselves, but their dealings with us show them to be wholly unfit to rule the native races. There is no more glaring illustration of this weakness than the conduct of the rebel Boers and the loyal Boers during the present war. According to my latest information from different centres of South Africa, native peasants were horsewhipped into the enemy's service as soon as the standard of rebellion was unfurled. There can be no reason to doubt the veracity of my information when the Press reports have clearly shown that even a white skin has ceased to be a protection against illtreatment. At least one loyal Magistrate and a postmaster were violently assaulted by General De Wet's Burghers, so the official dispatches say. Those shopkeepers who hesitated to open their stores to the rebels were sjambokked as were the ordinary Natives, and the Mayor of a "Free" State town was also flogged.

After the proclamation of martial law General Botha marshalled the loyal Boers throughout the country. These loyal Burghers, taking advantage of the presence of martial law, committed all kinds of excesses against loyal coloured civilians. These atrocities not only took place away in the Backveld, but sometimes in Capetown and Kimberley, the centres of African civilization; there black men were frequently tied to the wagon−wheels and lashed by the loyal Boers, and some of these coloured victims, I am told, have been cruelly done to death.

Of course, if the particular Burgher who dealt the death−blow can be identified he will be prosecuted, but that will not resuscitate the victims. It will only add misery to the innocent family of the offender. But the fact remains that during the South African War, South Africa was a huge military camp, yet the unarmed Natives, many of whom were then in the enemy's service, suffered nothing but kindness at the hands of Imperial troops, and there never was any conflict between the military and native civilians. And it but reveals the unfitness for self−government of the dominant race out there that the Natives, who sympathize with the Government, should be exposed to violence immediately the loyal Burghers are armed. That is the condition of life under true South African ideals.

Having had the ear of the Union Government since the federation of the South African States, Mr. Piet Grobler and other men of his way of thinking have been largely responsible for the repressive native laws that have found their way into the statute book of the Union. If the Natives of the other three Provinces had votes like those of the Cape Province, they would help to return sober−minded members to Parliament who are not inimical to the public welfare, instead of which they have been represented in the South African Parliament by budding subalterns of the German Army in South−West Africa. But since the Imperial Government in its wisdom when granting a Constitution to South Africa saw fit to withhold from the blacks their only weapon of protection against hostile legislation, viz., the power of the ballot, they surely, in common fairness to the Natives and from respect for their own honour, cannot reasonably stand aside as mere onlookers while self−condemned enemies of the Crown ram their violent laws down the throats of the Natives. The Imperial Government by the obligations of its overlordship and its plighted word to the Natives, at the time of the federation, is in duty bound to free the unrepresented Natives from the shackles of these laws, or otherwise, declare its guardianship of the interests of the Natives to have ceased, and counsel these weaker races to apply elsewhere for relief.

* * * * *

Epilogue

Oh, hear us for our native land,
The land we love the most:
Our fathers' sepulchres are here,
And here our kindred dwell;
Our children, too; how should we love
   Another land so well?
         Wreford.

After partaking of hot cross buns at the family table of a dear old English family the day before yesterday (Good Friday), I went to Walthamstow, and there heard a moving discourse delivered by the Rev. James Ellis on the sufferings and death of Christ for the redemption of mankind.

At my abode this morning, after receiving such tokens of friendship as Easter eggs and artistic picture cards, I attended an Easter service at the London University Hall and heard the little choir of four voices rendering mellifluous anthems to the glory of God. At the invitation of the Rev. R. P. Campbell this afternoon I went to Lloyds Park to tell the P.S.A. there about a South African Easter and to deliver at the same time the native message to the British public.

In the evening I went to the City Temple, where I listened to an intellectual Easter sermon, by the Rev. R. J. Campbell, on the triumph of Christianity, and heard the uniformed choir artistically sing doxologies to the risen Christ.

As I recall these services, I am transported in thought to St. Martin's Church in the heart of the "Free" State, 6,000 miles away, where thirty—seven years ago, as an unconscious babe in my godmother's arms, I went through my first religious sacrament, performed by an aged missionary who made the sign of the cross on my forehead and on my breast. I think also of another church on the banks of the Vaal River where, over twenty years ago, another missionary laid his white hands on my curly head and received my vow to forsake the Devil and all his works. I know that in these two places, as well as in all other native churches and chapels throughout South Africa, native congregations have this day been singing in their respective houses of worship and in a variety of tongues about the risen Christ. But thinking also of the lofty spires of the Dutch Reformed churches in the South African towns and dorps, I am forced to remember that coloured worshippers are excluded from them. Still, in these churches as well, Dutch men and Dutch women have this day been singing of the triumphs of the risen Christ. Yet to—morrow some of these white worshippers, in the workshops and in the parks, will be expressing an opposite sentiment to that conveyed in their songs of praise, namely, "Down with the verdoemde schepsels" (damned black creatures) — the Natives — for whom also, these white worshippers say, Christ died.

The Infant Christ, when King Herod sought to murder Him, found an asylum in Africa.

The Messiah, having been scourged, mocked, and forced to bear His cross up to Golgotha, and sinking under its weight, an African, by name Simon of Cyrene, relieved Him of the load.

To–day British troops are suffering untold agony in the trenches in a giant struggle for freedom. In this stupendous task they are assisted by sable Africans from the British, French, and Belgian colonies of the Dark Continent, thus fulfilling the Biblical prophecy, "From Africa (Egypt) I have called my son." But other Africans, again, are debarred by the South African Constitution on account of their colour from doing their share in this war of redemption. This prohibition surely carries the conviction that the native complaint against the South African Constitution is something more than a mere sentimental grievance.

The newspapers are telling us of "a growing spirit of justice in South Africa"; but in the face of what is happening to–day, the Natives are wondering if the word `justice', in this newspaper allegation, is not a misprint for `hatred', for up till as late as 1914 whole congregations have been arrested on leaving some of their farm chapels on "Free" State and Transvaal farms. They had their passes in their pockets, but the police contended that they had no special permits, signed by the landowners on whose farms the chapels are situated, to attend divine service at the particular places of worship on that particular day, and the courts upheld this contention. Up to five years ago no such sacrilegious proceedings interfered with the Sunday attendances of native worshippers in the same country, so that there is no mistake as to the kind of spirit that is "growing in South Africa".

* * * * *

When a man comes to you with stories about a "growing spirit of justice in South Africa", ask him if he knows that in 1884 there was a great debate in the Cape Parliament as to whether Natives should be permitted to exercise the franchise, and that the ayes had it. Ask him, further, if he thinks that such a proposal could ever be entertained to–day by any South African Parliament. If he is honest, he will be bound to say "no". Then ask him, "Where is your growing spirit of justice?"

* * * * *

In 1909, a South African Governor made a great speech in which
  he declaimed against the South African policy of pinpricking the blacks.

In 1911, another South African Governor authorized the publication
  of regulations in which, by prohibiting the employment of coloured artisans
  on the South African mines, the pinpricks were accentuated.

In 1913, a South African Governor signed the Natives' Land Act
  which made the Natives homeless in South Africa. Whereas the Government
  have announced their intention not to disfranchise the South African rebels,
  judging from the present legislative tendency we fear that,
  unless the Imperial Government can be induced to interfere,
  it is not improbable that should the rebels return to power
  after the general election

In 1916, there will be horrible enactments in store for the blacks.

* * * * *

In 1906, His Majesty's Government gave the Transvaal Colony
  self–government under a constitution which included a clause placing
  the voteless native taxpayers under the special protection of the Crown.

In 1907, His Majesty's Government likewise gave the Orange River Colony
  (now Orange "Free" State) self–government under a constitution
  which contained a similar provision. At this time the Governor of Natal,
  as representing the King, was Supreme Chief of the Zulus in that Colony.
  The Natives lived happily under these protecting reservations,
  and the white people had no complaint against the just restraint
  of the Imperial suzerainty.

In 1909, His Majesty's Government passed the Union Constitution, sweeping away
  all these safeguards. In that Act they practically told South Africa to do
  what she liked with the Natives in these three Colonies and South Africa
  is doing it. Where, then, is this "growing spirit"?

* * * * *

During the South African War in 1901, the Imperial Government
  informed the Federal (Dutch) Government that no peace terms
  could be considered which did not extend to the native races
  the same privileges — the rights of the franchise — which are enjoyed
  by the Natives of the Cape Colony.

In 1902, the British Imperial and Dutch representatives signed the Peace terms
  at Vereeniging. In these, the rights of the coloured citizens
  were postponed till after the old Republics had responsible Government.
  Responsible Government has since been granted, and has in turn
  been succeeded by the Union. But when the Imperial Parliament,

In 1909, considered the Act of Union, English and Dutch South Africans
  came over and represented to the Imperial authorities that there would be
  a striking demonstration (or words to that effect) against the federation,
  and even against South Africa's relation to the Mother Country
  if native rights were as much as mentioned in the Constitution;
  and the South African Native Franchise has now receded as far off
  as the Greek calends. So where is that "growing spirit of justice"?

* * * * *

Native Life in South Africa

When you speak of converting Mohammedans, let the question be asked: "What must Mohammedans think of those whose religion having said `In the sweat of thy brow shalt thou eat bread,' they nevertheless uphold the policy of rulers who pass regulations debarring one section of the community from following an honest occupation in their native land? And what impression must be created in the minds of black converts who are subjected to discriminations, including prohibitions that were not in existence five years ago?"

And if in spite of beautiful voices that I have heard this Easter Sunday singing anthems concerning the triumph of the kingdom of love the British flag continues to defend the policy of repression and colour hatred in South Africa, then I fear that the black victims of this policy, many of them converted to Christianity through your efforts, might very well class your Easter anthems and their great teaching with the newspaper canard relative to a "growing spirit of justice in South Africa"; for our bitter experience proves that spirit to be at best but a dwindling one.

Two years ago I was alarmed by the impious utterances of a coloured man whose friendship I valued. He being influential among our people, I gently remonstrated with him lest through his action many of our people become unsettled in their faith. This was his explanation: He was going along an East Rand suburb at eleven o'clock one Sunday morning when the bells were ringing. He saw a number of people entering a Dutch church, and as he was far from home he mingled with them, intending to spend the hour at worship instead of continuing his walk. But no sooner was he inside than the usher jostled him out of the church, hailed a policeman and handed him in charge, so that he spent the next hour in the charge office instead of at chapel. On the Monday morning he was convicted by the East Rand Magistrate and fined 1 Pound for trespassing on a private place, to wit, a church. And that was a Dutch Reformed church, the State Church of South Africa. Others had reproached him before me for such utterances, he said, but he will have "no more of our religious mockery with its theoretical `Come unto Me' and its practical `1 Pound or a month with hard labour'."

John Ruskin, writing on `State Intervention', says:

"When a peasant mother sees one of her careless children fall into a ditch, her first proceeding is to pull him out; her second, to box his ears; her third, ordinarily, to lead him carefully a little way by the hand, or send him home for the rest of the day. The child usually cries, and very often would clearly prefer remaining in the ditch; and if he understood any of the terms of politics, would certainly express resentment at the interference with his individual liberty: but the mother has done her duty."

Ruskin goes further and depicts the calamities of a mother nation which, like a foxhunter, complies with the request of its daughter nations "to be left in muddy independence."*

— * `Political Economy of Art': Addenda (J. E., Section 127). —

Let us appeal to you, in conclusion, to remember that the victorious Christ "has gathered your people into a great nation, and sent them to sow beside all waters and multiply sure dwellings on the earth. . . .

"Let not the crown of your pride be as a fading flower. But be equal to your high trust: reverent in the use of freedom, just in the exercise of power, and generous in the protection of the weak."

* * * * *

This has been the most strenuous winter that the writer has ever experienced: a dark, dreary winter of almost continuous rains, snowflakes, cold, mud and slush. Reading of the severity of English winters at a distance, I never could have realized that the life I have lived in England during the past four months was possible. An existence from which the sun's rays are almost always obliterated by the inclement weather, by snow and by fog. I cannot describe the sensations caused by the dismal gloom of the sunless days — a most depressing life — especially in December, when it would suddenly turn dark, compelling one to work by gaslight when the clocks indicated that it was high noon. Not till then did I realize why some people are said to worship the sun. I find that I have unlearned my acquaintance with the larger planets and heavenly bodies (a knowledge acquired since boyhood) because the winter fog and clouds have continually hidden the moon and stars from view.

* * * * *

But now that the country is throwing off its winter cloak and dressing itself in its green, gorgeous array; now that King Day shines in all his glory through the mist by day, and the moon and stars appear in their brilliancy in the evenings; now that, as if in harmony with the artistic rendering of Easter anthems by your choirs, the thrush and the blackbird twitter forth the disappearance of the foggy winter with its snow, sleet and wet; now that the flocks of fleecy sheep, which for the past four months have been in hiding and conspicuous by their absence, come forward again and spread triumphantly over the green as if in celebration of the dawn of the new spring; now that the violet and the daffodil, the marguerite and the hyacinth, the snowdrop and the bluebell, glorious in appearance, also announce, each in its own way, the advent of sunny spring, we are encouraged to hope that, "when peace again reigns over Europe", when white men cease warring against white men, when the warriors put away the torpedoes and the bayonets and take up less dangerous implements, you will in the interest of your flag, for the safety of your coloured subjects, the glory of your Empire, and the purity of your religion, grapple with this dark blot on the Imperial emblem, the South African anomaly that compromises the justice of British rule and seems almost to belie the beauty, the sublimity and the sincerity of Christianity.

Shall we appeal to you in vain? I HOPE NOT.

[Map was inserted here.]

Report of the Lands Commission

An Analysis

To attempt to place the different people of the country
in water–tight compartments is very attractive in a general way,
but it is bound to fail.

You have got a comparatively small European population
  — a million and a quarter — and something like
  half a million mixed race, and then you have got between
  four and five million of the aboriginal inhabitants of the country.

Any policy that aims at setting off a very small proportion
  of the land of the country for the use and occupation
  of the very vast majority of the inhabitants, and reserving
  for the use and occupation of a very small minority of the inhabitants
  the great majority of the land of the country, is a policy
  that economically must break somewhere. You can start and move
  in that direction to a certain extent, but you will be driven back
  by the exigencies of a law that operates outside the laws of Parliament —
  the law of supply and demand.

This theory of segregation is to some minds attractive,
  but the forgotten point is that you need the Native.
  You cannot segregate him because you need him. If you drive him
  out of his existing life and occupation, you run a great risk
  that you will lose many of your Natives.
        Hon. W. P. Schreiner, K.C., C.M.G.,
          (High Commissioner for the Union of South Africa,
          Ex–Premier of Cape Colony,) before the Lands Commission.

If we are to deal fairly with the Natives of this country,
  then according to population we should give them
  four–fifths of the country, or at least half.
        Hon. C. G. Fichardt, M.L.A.

The best way to segregate the races would be by means of a boundary fence
  along the main line of Railway from Port Elizabeth,
  straight through to Bloemfontein and Pretoria, to Pietersburg,
  putting the blacks on one side and the whites on the other side
  of the Railway line.*
        M. J. M. Nyokong, before the Native Affairs Commission.

—

* This would give about one–third of the Union to the four and a half
  million blacks, the one and a quarter million whites retaining two–thirds.

—

During the past two years while the Empire was involved in one of the mightiest struggles that ever shook the foundations of the earth, South Africa was wasting time and money in a useless and unprecedented attempt at territorial segregation betwixt white and black. Judging by the recently published Report of the Lands Commission, however, she has failed ignominiously in the task.

Whenever, on behalf of the Natives, the hardships disclosed in this book were mentioned, the South African authorities invariably replied that these hardships would cease as soon as the Commission submits its Report. This has now been done. General Botha laid the Report on the table of the house on May 3, 1916, and intimated as he did so that "the Government propose to take no immediate action upon the recommendations, but will give the country twelve months to consider the Report and the evidence." Meanwhile the eviction of Natives from farms continues in all parts of the country, and the Act debars them from settling anywhere, not even in Natal, although Natal witnesses (like the Chairman of the Commission) have definitely claimed the exemption of their Colony from this form of Union tyranny.

It is a Report of many parts. A good deal of it is instructive and much of it is absurd. Most of the Commissioners and many of the witnesses have expressed themselves with a candid disregard for the rights of other people.

Government publications, at least, should be beyond question; thus, old Government archives give correct histories of native tribes for 500 years back, because their compilers invariably sought and obtained reliable evidence from Natives about themselves. But this Commission's Report (to mention but one instance among several inaccuracies) tells us, on page 27 of U.G. 25-'16, of "the original inhabitants of Moroka ward who had lived in Bechuanaland under the Paramount Chief Montsioa (sic). Their original chief was Sebuclare" (!)

No Barolong tribe ever had a chief by this name. The fact is, that Governments of to-day frequently publish unreliable native records, for they are mainly based on information obtained from self-styled experts, who, in South Africa, should always be white.

Again, it is not explained why the Commission publishes, in a permanent record, particulars of encumbrances on native farms such as we find on page 29 of the same volume. Is it to damage the credit of the native farmers? Supposing some of the hypothecations given in the "list of mortgaged native-owned farms in the Thaba Ncho District" were wiped off before the Report was issued, will it be fair to the native owners to read, say in 1999, that their farms are mortgaged for those amounts?

In the published evidence given before other Commissions questions put to the witnesses are usually printed along with the answers. This has not been done in the present instance, and consequently some of these replies are so clumsily put that the reader cannot even guess what the witness was answering. If the questions had also been printed, the whole Report might have been illuminating. It is interesting, for instance, to read what was apparently a lively dispute between the Commissioners and one witness — Mr. J. G. Keyter, M.L.A., the arch-enemy of the blacks and one of the promoters of the whole trouble — as to what is, or is not, the meaning of the Natives' Land Act. Indeed the various definitions and explanations of the Act, given by the Commissioners and some of the witnesses, contradict those previously given by the Union Government and Mr. Harcourt. And while the ruling whites, on the one hand, content themselves with giving contradictory definitions of their cruelty the native sufferers, on the other hand, give no definitions of legislative phrases nor explanations of definitions. All that they give expression to is their bitter suffering under the operation of what their experience has proved to be the most ruthless law that ever disgraced the white man's rule in British South Africa.

The Report and the evidence at any rate bear out the statement set forth in this book, namely, that the main object in view is not segregation, but the reduction of all the black subjects of the King from their former state of semi–independence to one of complete serfdom.

The Commission's Awards

The population of South Africa is very commonly overestimated. As a matter of fact there are in South Africa about one and a quarter million whites and four and a half million blacks. According to the Census of 1911, the exact figure is a million less than the population of London, — viz., 5,973,394 — scattered over an area of 143,000,000 morgen — nearly ten times the size of England. A morgen is about 2 1/9 English acres.

But if we are to understand what is proposed, we would have to consider the position in the sub–continent under different heads: —

I. English or Urban Areas, inhabited by 660,000 whites and 800,000 blacks:
   1 3/4 quarter million morgen; and

II. The remaining 141 1/4 million morgen, which the Commission
   would divide as follows: —

   (a) NATIVE AREAS, for the Bantu and such other coloured races as are
       classed along with them numbering just about 4,000,000 SOULS:
       18 1/4 MILLION MORGEN.

   (b) EUROPEAN AREAS, or nearly the whole of Rural South Africa,
       for the occupation of 660,000 RURAL WHITES (mainly Boers):
       123,000,000 MORGEN.

The English Areas (I) are not affected by the troubles which form the subject of this book. None but the four million blacks will be allowed to buy land in the Native Area (II(a)); while all the blacks who hitherto lived on the Boer Areas (II(b)) must clear out. They would only be allowed to come back to Union territory as servants to the white farming population.

That, in a nutshell, is the Report of the Segregation Commission.

The Chairman Dissents

On the whole these drastic findings are against the weight of evidence. The Report, moreover, shows that the decisions were not carried through without some difference of opinion. It would seem that Sir William Beaumont, the Chairman of the Commission, a retired Judge of the Supreme Court (whose legal training and experience were assuredly entitled to more respect than they received) gave a saner interpretation of the Natives' Land Act. He evidently wished to treat the amount of land awarded to Natives as an instalment to which additions might be made in the future. This, he said, was quite within the power of the Commission to recommend. But his colleagues presumably preferred, not the legal, but their own interpretation, namely, that this sane interpretation was "contrary to the intention of the legislature". The Chairman's well-weighed judicial verdict appears on page 42 of volume one of the Report: —

In my opinion, neither the Natives' Land Act, nor the terms of its reference, require the Commission to delimit the whole extent of the Union into European and Native Areas respectively . . . and I think it is quite competent for this Commission, where this cannot be conveniently done, to leave undefined areas which would be open alike to white and black for the acquisition of land. But this opinion is not shared by my fellow-commissioners, who regard it as contrary to the intentions of the legislature and the terms of the Act.

Sir William Beaumont's rejected opinion is supported by the evidence of Senator T. L. Schreiner, who said: —

When the Bill was before the House, I brought to its notice the fact that there were areas in the country which it was impossible to declare native areas or non-native areas. The late Minister said it was not the intention to divide the whole country of the Union; therefore I thought that the difficulty was covered (p. 224 vol. ii).

But as in Parliament so also in the Commission it would appear that the steam-roller was set in motion; and it operated in each instance in favour of repressing the black races.

These four Commissioners presumably thinking that Imperial attention would be too much engrossed with the war to notice such insignificant affairs as the throttling of the South African Blacks, seem to have decided that now or never was the opportune moment for degrading the aborigines into helots; therefore, the Chairman, finding that he could not persuade his colleagues to adopt his view of things, indited the following minority report respecting his own Province of Natal and Zululand (vol. i. p. 41): —

The conditions in Natal are, and have been, totally different to those in the other Provinces. There has been no demand in Natal for the enforcement of a Squatters Act or for any further segregation of the natives. Indeed, the opinion of Natal, as expressed in the evidence given before the Commission by those best qualified to know, is against the application of the Natives' Land Act to Natal.

In Natal, since it became a British possession, the Natives have always had, and largely exercised, the right to purchase land outside their defined locations, and they regard any infringement of this right as a breach of the terms of the Proclamation issued by Her late Majesty Queen Victoria at the time the country was annexed by Great Britain. (See the petitions presented to the Commission.) The Natives in Natal now privately own about 359,000 acres, on which are residing some 37,000 Natives. These lands are, in certain areas, so intermixed with lands owned by Europeans that any line of demarcation can only be arbitrarily made, and may result in serious hardship or injustice to both European and Native owners.

The area set aside for native occupation (including mission reserves) and preserved for their use by Royal Letters Patent and by the South Africa Act, amount to nearly two and a half million acres, or about 15 per cent. of the whole of Natal. These areas are, according to the native mode of occupation, almost all fully occupied, and do not afford more than a very limited opportunity for the introduction of Natives from outside.

A further point which has to be considered, and it is one on which the Natives lay great stress, is that it seems unjust to debar the native from purchasing land in areas where the Indian, who is alien to the country, is free to do so.

Zululand

As regards Zululand, it is sufficient here to point out that Zululand was delimited into native reserves and Crown lands by the Zululand Delimitation Commission of 1902–1904, the Crown lands being made available for disposal by the Natal Government, to which the country was annexed. It was not, however, intended, nor did the Zulus understand, that they were to be deprived of their right to acquire any portion of the reserved Crown lands by purchase.

The delimitation was made after a very thorough inquiry by persons well acquainted with the Zulus and their country; but, even so, we find that whole tribes or large portions of tribes who had long been in occupation of their lands — some of which were not acquired by conquest but by voluntary surrender — were not provided for, and were left on the reserved Crown lands. There are to-day some 24,328 Zulus and Amatonga occupying these lands, and they are asking to-day for their lands to be restored to them. The delimitation was acquiesced in by the Zulus only because they had no alternative, and the inevitable had to be accepted. Since the delimitation they have remained loyal and peaceful and the bitterness of the losses suffered is past.

The Delimitation Commission in its report expressed the hope that the delimitation would be: "as final a settlement as it is possible to effect, and that no further changes will be initiated in the near future . . ."; but if the question is now re-opened and European and native areas are defined anew, I think endless trouble is likely to ensue. If any alterations may be found necessary in the future, either in the interests of black or white, the machinery exists whereby such alteration can be effected with little or no disturbance of the natives.

Colonel Stanford Reverses His Views

One redeeming feature in a Report which otherwise is melancholy reading is to be found in the consistency of the statesmen of Natal, which is admirable in comparison with the fast degenerating land policy of Cape Statesmen. Ten years ago the Native Affairs Commission reported on the question of Land Tenure in South Africa. Messrs. Marshall Campbell and S. O. Samuelson, Natal representatives on that Commission — ably supported by Colonel Stanford, the Cape representative — expressed themselves unambiguously against this limitation of native progress. History was about to repeat itself in favour of justice in the latest Commission but for the manner in which Colonel Stanford completely reversed his former attitude. He is the only member of this Commission who had a seat on the first Commission, and in 1905 he was reported thus: —

Col. Stanford dissented from the view of the majority on the question of restricting to certain areas only the right of the individual Native to purchase land. He holds that the acquisition by the more advanced Natives of vested individual interests in the land is a powerful incentive to loyalty. In his opinion sufficient cause has not been shown for the curtailment of privileges enjoyed for many years in the British Colonies. . . .

The contention that the safety of European races must be guarded by such restrictions as have been under discussion he does not hold to be sound. The Church, professions, commerce, trade and labour are open to the ambition and energy of the Natives, and with so many avenues open to their advance the danger of their swamping Europeans, if a real one, is not avoided by denying them the right individually to buy land.

He can see no decadence of the vigour, the enterprise and the courage which, since the occupation of the Cape Peninsula by the early Dutch settlers, have resulted in the extension of European control and occupation to the limits now reached. Moreover, artificial restrictions of the occupation of land in the late Dutch Republics resulted in the evasion of the law by various forms of contract whereby native occupation of farms was effected, while at the same time advantage was taken of the opportunities thus afforded of fraudulent practices on the part of Europeans employed as agents or so–called trustees. . . .

If the design be to allow purchase by Natives in localities regarded as unsuitable for Europeans, sight is lost of the fact that usually the Native who desires to become a landed proprietor belongs to the civilized class, and such localities offer to him no attraction.

Europeans are more and more entering into occupation of land regarded as set aside for Natives. Missionaries, traders and others are permitted to establish themselves and carry on the duties of their respective callings. Townships spring up at the various seats of magistracy and Census Returns clearly show that such influx is steadily increasing in volume. It is thus demonstrated that the idea of separate occupation of land by Natives, even in their own Reserves, is not maintained at the present time, nor can it be in the future.*

— * `Colonies and British Possessions — Africa (Session 1905)',
   vol. lv. pp. 102–103. —

But now we must conclude that the gallant Colonel has fallen a victim to the new reactionary spirit, for he has deserted Sir W. Beaumont, the Natal Commissioner, and taken up with the Northerners, a position diametrically opposed to the noble sentiments he then laid down.

The Cape Land Policy

The pronounced inconsistency of the Cape representative on these Commissions is in harmony with the reaction which has set in as regards the Land Policy of the Cape. It is true that the Cape, so far, has been more liberal in the matter of the Franchise. And the very fact that some of the Cape voters' lists included some native names has had a restraining influence on the utterances of certain Cape members of Parliament who would otherwise have given expression to reactionary sentiments. But it is no less true that in later years the same native Franchise has been hypocritically used as a cloak to cover a multitude of political sins, such, for instance, as free trade in liquor among the Natives and the systematic robbery of native lands. To my own personal knowledge, the Cape Government have on several occasions, arbitrarily, on the slightest pretext, or none whatever, confiscated lands that were awarded to native tribes by Imperial representatives, in the name of Queen Victoria, and parcelled them out to Europeans.

A striking instance of such rapacity on the part of successive Cape administrations appears on page 30 of the Minute by Sir William Beaumont, Chairman of the Lands Commission. Sir William shows how loyal black taxpayers in Griqualand West had been systematically robbed of Queen Victoria's gifts and driven from pillar to post. Commission after Commission had been sent out to them at intervals of ten years, systematic spoliation and pillage following the visit of each commission. It has been my sorrow to be among those who witnessed the coming and going of some of these decennial commissions and the truculent attitude of the Cape Government, who, trading on the people's ignorance, treated Queen Victoria's awards like so many scraps of paper, drove these tax-payers from their homes, and invited white men to occupy their territories.

This is what Sir William writes about the Commission of the last decade: —

The case of these Natives calls for special consideration. They were promised that they would never be removed so long as they remained loyal, and in the end they were burnt out. There is a very strong feeling amongst them that there has been a want of faith towards them.

The subject was specially reported on by Mr. P. Dreyer, Civil Commissioner of Kimberley, on August 27, 1909. He made specific recommendations, which appear to be quite sound, but do not appear to have been adopted.

Now, this is only with reference to Griqualand West. But similar acts of violence have marked the land-grabbing propensity of the Cape in Bechuanaland, in Peddie and the Transkei, even during my lifetime.

The So-Called Native Areas

Turning to the evidence, we find that if we omit the depositions of Natal whites, of Missionaries and of Natives, the remaining witnesses — a minority of the whole — emphatically declared that the aborigines were not entitled to a square yard of their ancestral lands and that they should be tolerated only as servants. Those, at any rate, who thought that we were entitled to some breathing space, were willing to concede certain little "reserves" in the centre of groups of white men's farms, into which black men and women could be herded like so many heads of cattle, rearing their offspring as best they could and preparing them for a life of serfdom on the surrounding farm properties. They held it to be the duty of the parent serfs to hand over their children, as soon as they were fit, to the farmers who would work them out; and when age and infirmity had rendered them unfit for further service, they could be hustled back to the reserved pens, there to spend the evening of their lives in raising more young serfs for the rising white generation. The Commission's findings seem to have been influenced largely by the latter type of white witness, for all that they award us, in our ancestral South Africa, might be called human incubators considering the amount of space.

A contemplation of the circumstances attending these selfish recommendations leads one to wonder whether the Commissioners suffered from the lack of a sense of humour or an undue excess of it. In North and South America, for instance, we read that the slave–pens were erected and maintained by the farmers at their own cost. That "the interest of the master demanded that he should direct the general social and moral life of the slave, and should provide especially for his physical well–being;" but the pens proposed by the South African Land Commission, on the other hand, are to be maintained entirely by the slaves, at their own cost, the farmer's only trouble being to come to the gate and whistle for labourers.

It is lawful in certain parts of South Africa for Natives to dispose of or "sell" their daughters to men, the purchase price being sometimes fixed by the Government. It is thus that white magistrates have at times condemned unfortunate black girls to cohabit with men they hated, provided the latter have paid the price; and having regard to the object for which the proposed native pens are to be set aside, the reader can picture to himself the coming commercial traffic in black girls within the enclosures of the said "native areas".

Several of the witnesses have made the statement that Natives are not making economic use of the land. As far as we have read, not one of such witnesses supported his point with figures. But most of those who expressed the contrary view — that native lands are shockingly overcrowded — have backed their statements with figures. Prominent among them, there was Mr. Adamson, the Natal Magistrate. In answer to further questions by Commissioner Wessels — questions which this Report does not disclose — the same witness also said: "I say the Location is crowded because there are too many Natives for the ground, which is very poor and precipitous. It is only down towards the valley where they can do a little cultivation. The population is 12,368."

Other magistrates and farmers gave similar evidence regarding their districts. They included Mr. J. S. Smit, the Klerksdorp Magistrate, who incidentally exploded the stale old falsehood about Natives living on the labour of their wives. The Rev. J. L. Dube said inter alia: "It is a fact that none can deny that the white man has got the best land. In the Free State you can go for miles without seeing anything; but if it had been native land there would have been an outcry, `Look at this beautiful land, and the Kaffirs not cultivating it.' Going to Johannesburg by the mail from here any day one can see waste land belonging to white people."

Mr. E. T. Stubbs, Commissioner of Louis Trichardt, said: "The density of the native population on reserves is 106 to 177 per square mile; on white farms only 28, and on Crown land 3 to the square mile." Yet in the face of these and similar official figures, the Commission reiterates the unsupported allegation of prejudiced witnesses that "Natives are not making economic use of their land." But on turning to the Census figures one sees at once how unfounded is the repeated charge. Take only one of the Provinces — Cape Colony — in which it is said the Natives hold (and therefore "waste") the most land.

Province of the Cape of Good Hope

Cape Colony is about 83 3/4 million morgen in extent. It is usually referred to as: —

(a) THE COLONY PROPER: 78,800,000 MORGEN, feeding 560,000 WHITES
   and 1,090,000 BLACKS, with their 1,603,625 cattle,
   240,000 horses and 20 million sheep and goats; and

(b) THE TRANSKEIAN NATIVE TERRITORIES: 5,000,000 MORGEN,
   feeding 20,000 WHITES and 900,000 BLACKS, with their
   1,111,700 cattle, 90,000 horses, 3 1/2 million sheep and goats,
   and more poultry and pigs than in the Colony Proper.

Surely, no further mathematical demonstration is needed to show on which side of the Kei there is a waste of land, if any. But it is a maxim in South Africa that, except as mechanical contrivances, Natives do not count, and cattle in their possession are not live–stock; thus the districts in which they eke out an existence are so much derelict land. The Commission, therefore, propose the following alterations: —

The 20,000 whites in the Transkei must not be disturbed. A million morgen in the Transkei is set aside for them, and it shall be unlawful for the blacks to live there except as servants. On the other hand the million odd Natives in the Colony Proper must betake themselves to the remainder of the Transkei, with their cattle and other belongings. A million morgen of Kalahari sand–dunes, worthless for farming purposes, and the small tribal communes near Queenstown and King Williamstown, are also set aside as native areas. And then the whole of Cape Colony (supposing the Commission's extraordinary recommendations be enforced) will balance itself as follows: —

(a) EUROPEAN AREAS: 76,392,503 MORGEN, feeding 560,000 WHITES,
   their 1,030,000 CATTLE, 180,300 HORSES AND 15 MILLION
   SHEEP AND GOATS.

(b) NATIVE AREAS: 7,356,590 MORGEN, feeding 1,500,000 BLACKS,
   with their 1,580,000 HEAD OF CATTLE, 154,630 HORSES AND 8 MILLION
   SHEEP AND GOATS.

At first sight it would appear that these awards allotted say 288 acres per white and 7 acres per black person; but, as the bulk of the English (a quarter of a million) live in towns and are not affected by this trouble, we may deduct the Urban districts and their white and black populations. Then the Commission's allotments really work out at about 589.31 acres per Boer (man, woman or child) and only 10.3 acres per Native. And even then, this would be by no means the limit of the disproportion. Appendix VIII (Annexure I) of the same Report recommends future inroads by whites upon these attenuated native reservations, but, to the blacks, there is to be no territorial compensation from the Colony, which an adoption of all these recommendations would practically depopulate.

As things are at present, the black population of these areas is as much as 70 to 90 persons to the square mile. In density of population, some of these "rural" native districts are second only to Capetown, Durban, and Johannesburg — South Africa's most populous centres. Not one of the other South African "cities" can show a population of more than 20 to 30 persons to the square mile. So that every individual inhabitant of a city occupies a larger space than some of these native farmers can have for themselves, their livestock and agricultural pursuits. So says the Census Report (U.G. 32–'12), which is fully borne out by the writer's own observations in a travelling experience of more than ten years.

The average density of the rural population in white areas is about five to eight persons per square mile. In native areas the average is ten times that number, while the black belt along the Indian Ocean contains from 100 to 140 Natives per square mile (see Schedule F. and Tables XIII–XVI, of the Census Report). Yet the Commission would saddle these congested native areas with additional populations from the Colony Proper and raise the density to something over 200 souls per square mile.

The density of cattle to the square mile in Cape Colony is 6.39 in white areas, and 61.15 in native areas (see U.G. 32h. 1912. pp. 1227–1228). Adopt the Commission's Report and you will have in white areas 0.24 and in Native areas 163.26 cattle per square mile.

Is it fair or reasonable that the indigenes of an open country who pay taxation for the benefit of their rulers and not of themselves, should be forced to live the overcrowded lives of the Belgians without Belgium's sanitary arrangements, or the precautionary hygienic measures necessary in other thickly populated areas?

Is it natural that their cattle should be subjected to this starvation process, while the grassy tracts of their God–given territories are mainly untenanted and preserved as breeding grounds for venomous snakes and scorpions?

Has it come to this that the standard of our unfortunate country has sunk so low that dog–in–the–manger stories are now read in Parliamentary publications?

It is clear that under the proposed arrangement native cattle must starve and their owners with them. For it has come out in evidence that even now (while many Europeans hold large tracts of idle land) some of the blacks have not enough grazing for their stock. But that little difficulty the Commission solves by proposing that Natives should be taught to give up cattle breeding, which alone stands between them and the required serfdom!

An African home without its flock and herd is like an English home without its bread–winner.

"Von Franzius considers Africa the home of the house cattle and the Negro the original tamer. . . . Among the great Bantu tribes extending from the Soudan toward the South, cattle are evidence of wealth; one tribe, for instance, having so many oxen that each village had ten or twelve thousand head. Lenz (1884), Bouet–Williaumez (1848), Hecquard (1854), Bosman (1805), and Baker (1868) all bear witness to this, and Schweinfurth (1878) tells us of great cattle parks with two to three thousand head, and of numerous agricultural and cattle–raising tribes . . . while Livingstone describes the busy cattle raising of the Bantu and Kaffirs."*

— * `The Negro' (Du Bois), pp. 108–109. —

But the Commission would force us to give up our agrarian occupation when we are debarred by Acts of Parliament from following other profitable industries in our own country. This is equivalent to saying that Englishmen must be taught to close down their shops, stop their shipping industry and give up their maritime trade.

The Orange "Free" State

The Provincial difficulties I have endeavoured to point out become more serious when we regard the conditions in the so–called "Free" States. There the native position is rendered exceptionally desperate by a number of rigorous class enactments. Formerly these discriminating laws were eased by the action of the State Presidents who were in the habit of issuing exemption certificates to Natives who wished to buy land, either from other Natives or from Europeans; but now, these harsh laws, besides being rigidly enforced against all Natives, were made more acute in 1913, while there is no one in the position once occupied by the President, who might be able or inclined to grant any relief.

Whenever by force of character or sheer doggedness one Native has tried to break through the South African shackles of colour prejudice, the Colour Bar, inserted in the South African Constitution in 1909, instantly hurled him back to the lowest wrung of the ladder and held him there. Let me mention only one such case.

About ten years ago Mr. J. M. Nyokong, of the farm Maseru, in the Thabanchu district, invested about 1,000 Pounds in agricultural machinery and got a white man to instruct his nephews in its use. I have seen his nephews go forth with a steam sheller, after garnering his crops every year, to reap and thresh the grain of the native peasants on the farms in his district. But giving evidence before the Lands Commission two years ago, this industrious black landowner stated that he had received orders from the Government not to use his machinery except under the supervision of a white engineer. This order, he says, completely stopped his work. The machinery is used only at harvesting time; no white man would come and work for him for two months only in the year, and as he cannot afford to pay one for doing nothing in the remaining ten months, his costly machinery is reduced to so much scrap iron. This is the kind of discouragement and attrition to which Natives who seek to better their position are subjected in their own country.

The Native Affairs Department

Perhaps the greatest puzzle in this ocean of native difficulties, to which one can but slightly refer in this chapter, is the attitude of some of the gentlemen in charge of the Native Affairs Department — the only Branch of the South African administration run exclusively on native taxes. It is perhaps as well to cite one instance illustrative of their methods of administering native affairs. The Rev. J. L. Dube, President of the Native Congress, gave evidence before the Lands Commission and produced letters addressed to him by certain Natal firms, from which I extract the following passages: —

If you are prepared to purchase this land my Company would be prepared to do business with you. . . . In view of the fact that you and Cele have already purchased portion of the Company's property adjoining the land now offered for sale, we think there would be no objection on the part of the Governor General in giving his consent to the transfer.*

— * U.G. 22, p. 557. —

Another extract runs: —

"We have a piece of land at the edge of our estate cutting right into land owned by various Natives, and we are willing to dispose of this land to Cele for this reason. We understood that the Department of Native Affairs raised no objection, but we were astonished when everything was "cut and dried" to find them refusing the application."*

— * U.G. 22, p. 557. —

How then can the Native be expected to survive this organized opposition, on the part of the authorities, and also of these official beneficiaries and prospective pensioners of native taxes? Will it be believed that these gentlemen of the Native Affairs Department, whose salaries are actually paid by us, should have sent messengers at our expense to convene a meeting of their colleagues, at which letters were dictated prohibiting the sale of this land to Zulus — the stationery, the typewriter and the typist's labour, to say nothing of the cigarettes smoked by those present, being paid for out of native money?

Is it surprising if we feel that their adverse interference in matters which so vitally affect us has long since become intolerable?

It may be asked what useful purpose is served by the Native Affairs Department as it now stands? This would be my answer: —

The Department is responsible for the gathering in of all native taxes throughout the Union. And after paying the salaries of the staff, it pays over annually a huge surplus to the Union Exchequer for the benefit of "a white South Africa". Further, the Transvaal Natives believe that they would get along much better with the white population, and with officials of other Departments of State, were not "the Native Affairs Department continually stirring them up against us." The justice of this complaint is well exemplified at Johannesburg, where the autocrats of this department are armed with, and liberally exercise, the peculiar and exceptional powers of locking up Natives without warrants, without any charge, and without a trial — powers which even the Judges of the Supreme Court do not possess.

General Hertzog's Scheme

It may interest the reader to know that General Hertzog is the father of the segregation controversy. The writer and other Natives interviewed him before Christmas, 1912, at the Palace of Justice, Pretoria, when he was still in the ministry. We had a two hours' discussion, in the course of which the General gave us a forecast of what he then regarded as possible native areas, and drew rings on a large wall–map of the Union to indicate their locality. Included in these rings were several Magistracies which he said would solve a knotty problem. He told us that white people objected to black men in Government offices and magistrates in those areas would have no difficulty in employing them.

General Hertzog was dismissed shortly after, and it has been said that in order to placate his angry admirers the Ministry passed the Natives' Land Act of which this Report is the outcome. Judging by the vigour with which the Union administration has been weeding Natives out of the public service and replacing them with Boers without waiting for the Commission's Report, it is clear that they did not share General Hertzog's intention as regards these magistracies. I cannot recall all the magistracies which General Hertzog mentioned as likely to fall in native areas; but I distinctly remember that Pietersburg and Thaba Nchu were among them; while Alice and Peddie (and possibly a neighbouring district) were to be included in a southern reserve into which the Natives round East London and Grahamstown would have to move, the land vacated by them to be gradually occupied by the white settlers now scattered over the would-be native block. He went on to forecast a vast dependency of the Union in which the energies and aspirations of black professional men would find their outlet with no danger of competition with Europeans; where a new educational and representative system could be evolved for Natives to live their own lives, and work out their salvation in a separate sphere. But the lands Commission's Report places this plausible scheme beyond the region of possibility, for no native area, recommended by this Commission, includes any of the magistracies mentioned.

General Hertzog's plan at least offered a fair ground for discussion, but the Commission's Report is a travesty of his scheme. It intensifies every native difficulty and goes much further than the wild demands of the "Free" State extremists. Thus even if it be thrown out, as it deserves to be, future exploiters will always cite it as an excuse for measures subversive of native well-being. In fact, that such legislation should be mooted is nothing short of a national calamity.

How They "Doubled" a Native Area

Near the northern boundaries of Transvaal there lies a stretch of malarial country in which nothing can live unless born there. Men and beasts from other parts visit it only in winter and leave it again before the rains begin, when the atmosphere becomes almost too poisonous to inhale. Even the unfailing tax-gatherers of the Native Affairs Department go there only in the winter every year and hurry back again with the money bags before the malarial period sets in. A Boer general describes how when harassed by the Imperial forces during the South African war, he was once compelled to march through it; and how his men and horses — many of them natives of the Transvaal — contracted enough malaria during the march to cause the illness of many and the death of several Burghers and animals. Of the native inhabitants of this delectable area the Dutch General says: "Their diminutive, deformed stature was another proof of the miserable climate obtaining there."*

— * `My Reminiscences of the Anglo-Boer War' (General Ben Viljoen), p. 222. —

When the Land Commissioners contemplated this "salubrious" region, their hearts must have melted with generosity, for whereas in our own healthy part of South Africa they have indicated possible native areas by little dots or microscopical rings (as in Thaba Nchu for instance), here, in this malarial area, they marked off a reserve almost as wide as that described by General Hertzog himself at our Pretoria interview. It is possibly in this way, and in such impossible places, that the Commission is alleged to have "doubled" the native areas. In the rest of the country they ask Parliament to confiscate our birthright to the soil of our ancestry in favour of 600,000 Boers and aliens whose languages can show no synonym for HOME — the English equivalent of our IKAYA and LEGAE!

The Britishers' vocabulary includes that sacred word: and that, perhaps, is the reason why their colonizing schemes have always allowed some tracts of country for native family life, with reasonable opportunities for their future existence and progress, in the vast South African expanses which God in His providence had created for His Children of the Sun. The Englishman, moreover, found us speaking the word `Legae', and taught us how to write it. In 1910, much against our will, the British Government surrendered its immediate sovereignty over our land to Colonials and cosmopolitan aliens who know little about a Home, because their dictionaries contain no such loving term; and the recommendations of this Commission would seem to express their limited conception of the word and its beautiful significance.

Natives Have no Information about the Coming Servitude

All too little (if anything at all) is known of the services rendered to the common weal by the native leaders in South Africa. In every crisis of the past four years — and the one-sided policy of the Union has produced many of these — the native leaders have taken upon themselves the thankless and expensive task of restraining the Natives from resorting to violence. The seeming lack of appreciation with which the Government has met their success in that direction has been the cause of some comment among Natives. On more than one occasion they have asked whether the authorities were disappointed because, by their successful avoidance of bloodshed, the native leaders had forestalled the machine guns. But, be the reason what it may, this apparent ingratitude has not cooled their ardour in the cause of peace.

To-day the Native Affairs Department has handed over 7,000 Pounds from native taxes to defray the cost of the Land Commission, consisting of five white Commissioners, their white clerks and secretaries — the printing alone swallowed up nearly 1,000 Pounds with further payments to white translators for a Dutch edition of the Report. But not a penny could be spared for the enlightenment of the Natives at whose expense the inquiry has been carried through. They have been officially told and had every reason to believe that the Commission was going about to mark out reservations for them to occupy and live emancipated from the prejudicial conditions that would spring from contiguity with the white race. For any information as to the real character of the contents of the Dutch and English Report of this Commission, they would have to depend on what they could gather from the unsalaried efforts of the native leaders, who, owing to the vastness of the sub-continent, the lack of travelling facilities and their own limited resources, can only reach a few localities and groups.

It may be said with some reason that English leaders of thought in South Africa have had a task of like difficulty: that they worked just as hard to get the English colonists to co-operate loyally with a vanquished foe in whose hands the Union constitution has placed the destiny of South Africa. It could also be said with equal justice that the Boer leaders' task has been not less difficult, that it required their greatest tact to get the Boer majority — now in power — to deal justly with the English who had been responsible for the elimination of the two Boer flags from among the emblems of the family of nations. But the difficulties of their task is not comparable to that of the native leaders. English and Dutch Colonial leaders are members of Parliament, each in receipt of 400 Pounds a year, with a free first class ticket over all systems of the South African Railways. They enjoy, besides, the co–operation of an army of well–paid white civil servants, without whom they could scarcely have managed their own people. The native leader on the other hand, in addition to other impediments, has to contend with the difficulty of financing his own tours in a country whose settled policy is to see that Natives do not make any money. His position in his own country approximates to that of an Englishman, grappling single–handed with complicated problems, on foreign soil, without the aid of a British consul.

Bullyragging the Natives

For upwards of three years the Government of the Union of South Africa has harassed and maltreated the rural native taxpayers as no heathen monarch, since the time of the Zulu King Chaka, ever illused a tributary people. For the greater part of our period of suffering the Empire was engaged in a titanic struggle, which, for ghastliness is without precedent. I can think of no people in the Eastern Hemisphere who are absolutely unaffected by it; but the members of the Empire can find consolation in the fact that almost all creation is in sympathy with them. Constant disturbance has brought a realization to the entire universe that nature, like the times, is out of joint. The birds of the air and the fishes, like other denizens of the deep, are frequently drawn into the whirlpool of misery; and a mutual suffering has identified them as it were with some of the vicissitudes of an Empire at war. And they too have in their peculiar way felt impelled to offer their condolence to the dependants of those who have fallen in the combat on land, in the air, on sea, and under the sea. And while all creation stands aghast beside the gaping graves, by rivers of blood, mourning with us the loss of some of the greatest Englishmen that ever lived, South Africa, having constituted herself the only vandal State, possesses sufficient incompassion to celebrate the protection conferred on her by the British Fleet and devote her God–given security to an orgy of tyranny over those hapless coloured subjects of the King, whom the Union constitution has placed in the hollow of her hands.

Is there nobody left on earth who is just enough to call on South Africa to put an end to this cowardly abuse of power?

We appeal to the Colonists of Natal, who have declared themselves against the persecution of their Natives; and would draw their attention to the fact that in spite of their disapproval, expressed to the Lands Commission, the Union Government, at the behest of a prisoner, is still tyrannizing over the Zulus.

We appeal to the Churches. We would remind them that in the past the Christian voice has been our only shield against legislative excesses of the kind now in full swing in the Union. But in the new ascendency of self and pelf over justice and tolerance, that voice will be altogether ignored, unless strongly reinforced by the Christian world at large. We appeal for deliverance from the operation of a cunningly conceived and a most draconian law whose administration has been marked by the closing down of native Churches and Chapels in rural South Africa.

We appeal to the Jews, God's chosen people, who know what suffering means. We would remind them that if after 1913 there was no repetition of a Russian pogrom it was largely because the native leaders (including the author) have spared neither pains nor pence in visiting the scattered tribes and exhorting them to obey all the demands of the South African Government under the Grobler law pending a peaceful intercession from the outside world. But for this self–imposed duty on the part of the native leaders, I am satisfied that numbers of the native peasantry would have been mown down early in 1914, and humanity would have been told that they were justly punished for disobedience to constituted authority.

We appeal to the leaders of the Empire — that Empire for which my own relatives have sacrificed life and property in order to aid its extension along the Cape to Cairo route, entirely out of love for her late Majesty Queen Victoria and with no expectation of material reward. We ask these leaders to honour the plighted word of their noble predecessors who collectively and severally assured us a future of peace and happiness as our membership privilege in the Empire for which we bled. They were among the noblest Englishmen that ever left their native shores to create a prestige for their nation abroad. They included heroes and empire–builders too many to mention, who all told us that they spoke in the name of Queen Victoria and on behalf of her heirs and successors. What has suddenly become of the Briton's word — his bond — that solemn obligations of such Imperialists should cease to count? And if it is decided that the Victorian Englishman and the Twentieth Century Englishman are creatures of different clay (and that with the latter honour is binding only when both parties to the undertaking are white), surely this could hardly be the moment to inaugurate a change the reaction of which cannot fail to desecrate the memories of your just and upright forebears.

We would draw the attention of the British people to the fact that the most painful part of the present ordeal to the loyal black millions, who are now doing all they can, or are allowed to do, to help the Empire to win the war, is that they suffer this consummate oppression at the bidding of a gentleman now serving his term for participating in a rebellion during this war. We feel that it must be a source of intense satisfaction to Mr. Piet Grobler in his cell, that the most loyal section of the King's South African subjects are suffering persecution under his law — a fact which, looked at from whatever standpoint, is equal to an official justification of the ideals for which he rose in rebellion. And if there is to be a return to the contented South Africa of other days, both the Natives' Land Act — his law — and the Report of the Lands Commission — its climax — should be torn up.

Courting Retribution

For three years and more the South African Government have persecuted my kinsmen and kinswomen for no other crime than that they have meekly paid their taxes. I had come to the conclusion, after meeting Colonials from all quarters of the globe and weighing the information obtained from them, that in no Colony are the native inhabitants treated with greater injustice than in South Africa.* Yet in spite of all I had seen and heard, I must say that, until this Report reached me, I never would have believed my white fellow–countrymen capable of conceiving the all but diabolical schemes propounded between the covers of Volume I of the Report of the South African Lands Commission, 1916, and clothing them in such plausible form as to mislead even sincere and well–informed friends of the Natives. There are pages upon pages of columns of figures running into four, five or six noughts. They will dazzle the eye until the reader imagines himself witnessing the redistribution of the whole sub–continent and its transfer to the native tribes. But two things he will never find in that mass of figures; these are (a) the grand total of the land so "awarded" to Natives; and (b) how much is left for other people. To arrive at these he has to do his own additions and subtractions, and call in the aid of statistics such as the Census figures, the annual blue books, etc., before the truth begins to dawn on him. They talk of having "doubled" the native areas. They found us in occupation of 143,000,000 morgen and propose to squeeze us into 18 million. If this means doubling it, then our teachers must have taught us the wrong arithmetic. Is it any wonder that it is becoming increasingly difficult for us to continue to love and respect the great white race as we truly loved it at the beginning of this century?

— * Some white South Africans in recent years have migrated
to the Katanga region in the Belgian Congo. I have read
in the South African daily papers, correspondence from some of them
complaining of their inability to make money. They attributed
this difficulty to the fact that the Belgian officials will not permit them
to exploit the labour of the Congolese as freely as white men are accustomed
to make use of the Natives in British South Africa. —

We would submit a few problems in this Report for the British People and their Parliamentary Representatives to solve: —

First: Who are to become the occupants of the lands from which the Commission recommends the removal of the native proletariat?

Secondly: In view of certain upheavals which we have seen not very long ago, and others which might take place in the future, it is pertinent to ask, concerning the "very small minority of the inhabitants" — the Whites — alluded to by Mr. Schreiner at the head of this chapter, (a) what proportion is in full sympathy with the ideals of the British Empire; (b) what proportion remains indifferent; and (c) what proportion may be termed hostile?

Thirdly: Does the autonomy granted to this "small minority" amount to complete independence, or does it not?

Fourthly: Would it not be advisable also to inquire: Of "the vast majority of the inhabitants" the King's Black subjects, doomed by this Report to forfeit their homes and all they value in their own country, (a) how many of these are loyal, and (b) how many are not?

Finally and solemnly we would put it to all concerned for the honour and perpetuity of British dominion in South Africa, can the Empire afford to tamper with and alienate their affections?

As stated already, this "very vast majority of the inhabitants" of South Africa has been strafed by the "very small minority" for over three years. And when the burden loaded on our bent backs becomes absolutely unbearable we are at times inclined to blame ourselves; for, when some of us fought hard — and often against British diplomacy — to extend the sphere of British influence, it never occurred to us that the spread of British dominion in South Africa would culminate in consigning us to our present intolerable position, namely, a helotage under a Boer oligarchy. But when an official Commission asks Parliament to herd us into concentration camps, with the additional recommendation that besides breeding slaves for our masters, we should be made to pay for the upkeep of the camps: in other words, that we should turn the Colonials into slave raiders and slave-drivers (but save them the expense of buying the slaves), the only thing that stands between us and despair is the thought that Heaven has never yet failed us. We remember how African women have at times shed tears under similar injustices; and how when they have been made to leave their fields with their hoes on their shoulders, their tears on evaporation have drawn fire and brimstone from the skies. But such blind retribution has a way of punishing the innocent alike with the guilty, and it is in the interests of both that we plead for some outside intervention to assist South Africa in recovering her lost senses.

The ready sympathy expressed by those British people among whom I have lived and laboured during the past two years inspires the confidence that a consensus of British opinion will, in the Union's interest, stay the hand of the South African Government, veto this iniquity and avert the Nemesis that would surely follow its perpetration.

Her mind must have been riveted on South Africa when, quite recently, Ida Luckie sang: —

> Alas, My Country! Thou wilt have no need
> Of enemy to bring thee to thy doom. . . .
> For not alone by war a nation falls.
> Though she be fair, serene as radiant morn,
> Though girt by seas, secure in armament,
> Let her but spurn the vision of the Cross;
> Tread with contemptuous feet on its command
> Of mercy, Love and Human Brotherhood,
> And she, some fateful day, shall have no need
> Of enemy to bring her to the dust.

> Some day, though distant it may be — with God
> A thousand years are but as yesterday —
> The germs of hate, injustice, violence,
> Like an insidious canker in the blood,
> Shall eat that nation's vitals. She shall see
> Break forth the blood-red tide of anarchy,
> Sweeping her plains, laying her cities low,
> And bearing on its seething, crimson flood
> The wreck of Government, of home, and all
> The nation's pride, its splendour and its power.
> On with relentless flow, into the seas
> Of God's eternal vengeance wide and deep.
> But, for God's grace! Oh may it hold thee fast,
> My Country, until justice shall prevail
> O'er wrong and o'er oppression's cruel power,
> And all that makes humanity to mourn.

[End of original text.]

Native Life in South Africa

[Original Advertisements.]

Some Opinions of the Press on the First Edition

"It is difficult to believe that such barbarities are possible; but Mr. Plaatje gives chapter and verse for every one of his indictments; the Act itself is quoted in extenso; various debates in the Colonial Parliament are given, and arguments for and against the Act furnished by the different speakers. The whole book is really interesting, and will come as a great surprise to many English people who know little of the South African Native as an educated, thinking human being, and will certainly excite sympathy with his present precarious state under colonial laws, which seem to be little inspired by the principles of justice and liberty which British supremacy formerly guaranteed." — `Yorkshire Observer'.

"Whatever may have been the intention of the home Government, in practice this Act has meant the restriction of Natives to their reservations, or to servitude among the white population. Mr. Plaatje states his case clearly and asserts that this movement is reactionary and a false step on the part of the Government to placate the extreme Dutch party in South Africa." — `Glasgow Herald'.

"The author makes an excellent case for the consideration of the Imperial Government. He convincingly proves that the fortunes of the native races should not have been handed over to the Dutch Republicans without adequate safeguards. He gratefully acknowledges the enthusiastic support given to the Natives by the British settlers and appeals for an inquiry. The interest of the book for the Punjabis consists, not in the similarity of the grievances, for we here have no such grievance against the Government, but in showing the way for inviting attention to the injustice involved in excluding a large class of Hindus from agriculture." — `The Tribune', Lahore.

"It is a serious case, well and ably put, and the evidence embodied in it is very disquieting. Here at any rate is a book which makes the native agitation intelligible and may conceivably have an influence on future events in South Africa — and at home, for by no legal fiction can the Imperial power dissociate itself from responsibility for Native affairs." — `Birmingham Post'.

"The supporters of the Act do not make the principles attractive in explaining them. Mr. J. G. Keyter, Member for Ficksburg, said "they should tell the Native as the Free State told him, that it was white man's country, that he was not going to be allowed to buy land there or hire land there, and that if he wanted to be there he must be in service." — `New Statesman'.

"There is the spice if not the charm of novelty about this book. It is written by a South African native and he holds strong views on some recent public questions. He occasionally expresses himself well and forcibly, and it is all to the good that South African publicists should have the advantage of reading the opinions of a native observer when dealing with legislation affecting his race." — `South Africa'.

"In this well arranged and lucidly written book the author shows from authentic sources how changeable and often unreasonable has been the treatment of the loyal Natives under the South African flag. Mr. Plaatje is no fire-brand; he writes with moderation, and his book should attract sympathetic attention." — `Booksellers' Record'.

"Mr. Plaatje has marshalled his facts with considerable skill. He sets forth the case of his countrymen with energy and moderation. His conclusions seem to be warranted by the information at his disposal, and the facts he adduces seem to bear but one interpretation. And lastly, in the existing circumstances, he is fully justified in appealing to the court of public opinion." — `United Empire'.

Books by the same author

730 Sechuana Proverbs With Literal Translations and their European Equivalents (Diane Tsa Secoana, Le Maele a Sekgooa, Aa Dumalanang Naco). By Solomon T. Plaatje.

An interesting and instructive comparison of African and European Proverbs

A Sechuana Reader (In International Phonetic Orthography, with English Translations) By Daniel Jones, M.A., and Sol. T. Plaatje.

The Texts include native fables and stories of adventure, and form a collection of reading matter suitable either for native Bechuanas or for foreign learners.

Both word–for–word translations and free translations are given throughout.

In the introduction will be found detailed information with regard to the pronunciation of the Sechuana language.

[End Original Advertisements.]

Notes to the text:

The Titles listed in the Table of Contents are not always identical to those in the text. Therefore, the longer versions have been used, or in those cases where they are significantly different, both titles have been given.

Cases of battered type, and even missing letters, where obvious, are too numerous to be commented on in detail. Less obvious cases are noted.

Chapter II:

(p. 42) [delivered by the Governor–General at the opening af the session]
  changed to: [delivered by the Governor–General at the opening of the session]

(p. 44) [H. Mentz and G. A. Louw, teller]
  changed to: [H. Mentz and G. A. Louw, tellers.]

Chapter VI:

(p. 82) [my hushand's and children's peculiar wants, if Anna]
  changed to: [my husband's and children's peculiar wants, if Anna]

Chapter VIII:

(p. 106) [under notice to leave, We informed them]
  changed to: [under notice to leave. We informed them]

(p. 110) [Pieter Dout consented, and joined the exlpedition]
  changed to: [Pieter Dout consented, and joined the expedition]

(p. 112) [to mulct them in more money than the land. is worth. The best legal advice they have received is that they should sell their inheritances to white men]
  changed to: [to mulct them in more money than the land is worth. The best legal advice they have received is that they should sell their inheritances to white men.]

Chapter IX:

(p. 120) [says Dr. Kellog,]
  changed to: [says Dr. Kellogg,]
  (This is the correct spelling of the name of a doctor who was famous
  about the time that Plaatje was writing, and who was undoubtedly
  the source for the quote.)

(p. 132) [Hence, let the leaders direct them into cruel way as they are seemingly]
  changed to: [Hence, let the leaders direct them into cruel ways as they are seemingly]

Chapter X:

(p. 142) [went unarmed to hold with the Matebele chiefs]
  changed to: [went unarmed to hold with the Matabele chiefs]
  (in accordance with other usage, and another edition.)

(p. 144) [the papers and the public chorus with joy hear that the C.S.A.R.]
  changed to: [the papers and the public chorus with joy to hear that the C.S.A.R.]

Chapter XIV:

(p. 178) [and Mid–Illovu,] (end of paragraph)
  changed to: [and Mid–Illovu.]

(p. 179) [July 20, 191.]
  changed to: [July 20, 1913.]

Chapter XVI:

(p. 197) [(Mr Alden) and the hon. Baronet th Member for Hackney (Sir A. Spicer]
  changed to: [(Mr. Alden) and the hon. Baronet the Member for Hackney (Sir A. Spicer)]

(p. 221) Regarding the reference to `The Biglow Papers', the quote is from No. VI, and `The Biglow Papers' was written by J. R. Lowell (see below).

Chapter XVIII:

(p. 225) (subtitle) [Bear ye one another's Burdens"]
  changed to: ["Bear ye one another's Burdens"]

(p. 231) [F. R. Lowell]
  changed to: [J. R. Lowell] James Russell Lowell [1819–1891], the Massachusetts poet, wrote these lines, under the title "Stanzas on Freedom". As the italic forms of "J" and "F" are similar, and frequently confused, this error is not to be wondered at. The 1st, 3rd, and 4th stanzas are quoted in the text. The complete text is presented here:

Stanzas on Freedom

Men! whose boast it is that ye Come of fathers brave and free, If there breathe on earth a slave, Are ye truly free and brave? If ye do not feel the chain, When it works a brother's pain, Are ye not base slaves indeed, Slaves unworthy to be freed?

Women! who shall one day bear Sons to breathe New England air, If ye hear, without a blush, Deeds to make the roused blood rush Like red lava through your veins, For your sisters now in chains, — Answer! are ye fit to be Mothers of the brave and free?

Is true Freedom but to break Fetters for our own dear sake, And, with leathern hearts, forget That we owe mankind a debt? No! true freedom is to share All the chains our brothers wear, And, with heart and hand, to be Earnest to make others free!

They are slaves who fear to speak For the fallen and the weak; They are slaves who will not choose Hatred, scoffing, and abuse, Rather than in silence shrink From the truth they needs must think; They are slaves who dare not be In the right with two or three.

Chapter XIX:

(p. 242) [to those of the Barolongs, who used their own rifles,]
  changed to: [to those of the Barolongs who used their own rifles,]

The Crest of Queen Victoria, mentioned in brackets, is, of course, unavailable in ASCII. The letters V R. are for "Victoria Regina", or, "Queen Victoria".

Chapter XXI:

(p. 276) [both missionaries, also poke offering to associate themselves]
  changed to: [both missionaries, also spoke offering to associate themselves]

(p.278) [the districts of Calvania, Kenhardt, Keimoes, and Upington]
  changed to: [the districts of Calvinia, Kenhardt, Keimoes, and Upington]
  in accordance with other use in the surrounding text.

Chapter XXII:

(p. 291) [her privileges of free citizenship (Cheers.)]
  changed to: [her privileges of free citizenship. (Cheers.)]

(p. 302) [half a million Boers.] [people's gathering.)]
  changed to: [half a million Boers.)] [people's gathering.]
  Closing parenthesis was at end of wrong paragraph.

(p. 303) [the harm that as likely to follow a provocation]
  changed to: [the harm that is likely to follow a provocation]

(p. 308) [in addition to his own rebels commando.]
  changed to: [in addition to his own rebel commando.]

(p. 312) [assaulted a policeman.]
  changed to: [assaulted a policeman.)]
  Clause missing closing parenthesis.

Chapter XXIV:

(p. 336) [a petition from Rustenberg, made it compulsory]
  changed to: [a petition from Rustenburg, made it compulsory]
  in accordance with other use in the surrounding text.

(p. 338) [Deuteronomy xix. 14,]
  updated to: [Deuteronomy 19:14,]

Epilogue:

(p. 348) [signed the Natives' Lant Act]
  changed to: [signed the Natives' Land Act]

(p. 351) [has done her duty.]
  changed to: [has done her duty."]

Report of the Lands Commission:

(p. 357) [Chairman of the Commission a retired Judge]
  changed to: [Chairman of the Commission, a retired Judge]

(p. 358) [and the terms of the Act."]
  changed to: [and the terms of the Act.]
  unmatched quotation mark removed according to surrounding usage.

(p. 364) [the Klerksdorp Magistrate, who incidentalgl exploded the stale old falsehood about Natives liviny on the labour]
  changed to: [the Klerksdorp Magistrate, who incidentally exploded the stale old falsehood about Natives living on the labour]

(p. 376) [the Empire was engaged in a titantic struggle,]
  changed to: [the Empire was engaged in a titanic struggle,]

Terms:

lager/laager: a defensive camp formed by circled wagons.

sjambok: a rhinoceros or hippopotamus−hide whip.

The following lines contained characters that cannot be presented in ASCII:

under the Republican re/gime, no matter how politicians raved
  Ils se sont endormis, le c(oe)ur rempli d'espoirs,
  Dans un re\ve d'amour et de concorde humaine!
  Qui monte des hameaux consume/s par la flamme,
  Ni le ge/missement des vie/illards et des femmes! the inquiries of the Commission, whose report is nai"vely alleged did its best to fill the ro^le of an enemy. but who, after three months' drill and man(oe)uvring, were as expert and that Nakob Su"d was clearly depicted in the old maps (Sued)
  of high−resolve\d men, bent to the spoil,
    Goe^n dag, Pikadillie of these neighbours. The Natives, according to Mr. Lu"dorf, gathered in a heap and burnt alive. This, says Mr. Lu"dorf, (Luedorf) generally preferred, aspire; and each fills his ro^le * `Political Economy of Art': Addenda (J. E., Section 127). (Symbol used for "Section")

Also numerous instances of fractions, here presented, for example, as 1 1/2 for one and a half, and the symbol for the British Pound, so that where the original may have said L100 (where L represents the symbol for Pound) it now says 100 Pounds (Pound or Pounds has always been capitalized as above in such cases).

Printed in the United States
55106LVS00005B/37-42

9 781419 136757